PARENTING

PARENTING

Everything You Will Ever Need
To Know From Conception to
Leaving Home

Annie Ashworth, Meg Sanders, Karen Dolby

ORION

To our children:
George, Freya, Tom, James, Harriet, Louis and Toby

'Having a family is like having a bowling alley installed in your brain.'
Martin Mull

Copyright © Meg Sanders, Annie Ashworth,
Karen Dolby, Maverick TV Ltd 2003

Meg Sanders, Annie Ashworth, Karen Dolby,
Maverick TV Ltd have asserted their moral right
to be identified as the authors and proprietors
of this work.

First published in Great Britain in 2003 by
Orion Media
An imprint of Orion Books Ltd
Orion House, 5 Upper St Martin's Lane,
London WC2H 9EA

A CIP catalogue record for this book
is available from the British Library

ISBN: 0 75285 264 7

Illustrations by Staziker Jones Design Consultants, Cardiff

Index compiled by Indexing Specialists

Printed in Italy by Printers Trento srl

The publisher and authors wish to thank the Department of Health
for the information on immunisation on pages 306–07, taken from
their website www.immigration.org.uk.

CONTENTS

....

FOREWORD

··

For most jobs you need qualifications: a degree, an HND, at the very least a few GCSEs. You need to learn from the experts, practice and study, and sit rigorous tests, before you are allowed to unleash your skills on the unsuspecting.

But there is one job for which there is no training, no exam and little formal back-up in place to support you when you go wrong. It's a full-time job, with no salary, unpaid over-time and no bonuses. It's a job that involves a host of skills – those of nurse, teacher, artist, counsellor, nutritionist, chef, psychologist, taxi driver, driving instructor, policeman (with talents in riot control), diplomat and negotiator at a level that would impress the United Nations. It's called parenthood – and it makes being chief executive of a multi-national company seem like a picnic.

From the minute you know that a baby is on the way, you imagine what sort of parent you will be. You'll be calm and understanding; your child will be easy, clever, witty and beauti-ful. You won't make the mistakes you see other people making. You have it taped. Then you are handed this wriggling, squirming baby in the delivery room, and sent home with a farewell wave to face the music. Buy a car and at least you get a manual explaining every knob and dial. Have a baby and you're lucky if you get five minutes' explanation on how to change a nappy. Within days both you and your partner are run ragged, delirious through lack of sleep and beginning to wonder what on earth has happened to the people you were last week.

And that's just the start. Children grow up. They challenge you. They misbehave. They go to school, make friends and become independent people in their own right. Before you know it, they've spread their wings and they're off. Did you get parenting right? Could you have done it better?

If only we could have a practice run! Perhaps then we wouldn't stumble about in a haze of ignorance, picking things up as we go along. The generation now in their mid-thirties were more often than not the product of stay-at-home mothers. These days, because of the grow-ing number of single-parent families, spiralling house prices and dwindling pension provi-sion, often both partners have to go out to work. It may not even be for financial reasons; some of us actually want to pursue the careers we worked so hard for. Add to this the fact that often any family members who could support us live far away. As a result, parenting today comes with enormous pressures. No wonder we turn to books for advice.

But most books available on childcare are very worthy tomes. They use words like 'rearing' and 'little person', discuss anatomy and physiology, boss us around and make us feel inade-quate. They also finish at around school age. After this you are pretty much on your own.

We've tried in this book to get back to basics. We've talked to everyone involved with chil-dren – from midwives to paediatricians, doctors to health visitors, nannies to employers, teachers to psychologists – for hints and tips they've learned as professionals. But perhaps more importantly, we've also tapped into the expertise of the real cognoscenti, parents and grandparents. People who have been there and learnt by their mistakes. People who know that, when you are awake at 2.00 a.m. because your baby has colic or your teenager still isn't home, most professional 'childcare' books fall far short of the mark. The best teacher is experience.

You'll find information here covering everything you will ever need to know, from pre-conception to applying for a further education grant, and every milestone in between. So whether you are a first- or fourth-time mum or dad, on your own or with a partner, a step-parent, grandparent, adoptive parent or fosterer, you'll find answers to your questions, and strategies that professionals and other parents have found do the trick.

We have tried to make this book as readable and easy-to-use as possible. To avoid saying 'his or her' or 'their', we have described a child as 'him' or 'her' as far as possible alternately; we have referred sometimes to one child, sometimes to children. But the book is of course intended for parents of children of either sex, and for parents who have one child or more than one child. The chapters are divided into age groups, but children are not an exact science and some information may appear in an earlier or later section. We have provided cross references to help, but we advise readers to use the index too when looking for information. The list on page 29 provides addresses and websites of organisations who can provide specialist information and help on particular subjects, including some less common health issues that it has not been appropriate to cover in this book.

To those we have badgered for their pearls of wisdom: we thank you for your patience and generosity. Thanks too to Alex Fraser for a great original idea and to our editor, Laura Meehan, for her patience and support. With seven offspring between us, we thought we knew something about bringing up children. Now we wish we'd researched this book before we started out.

Annie Ashworth, Meg Sanders and Karen Dolby

1 CONCEPTION TO BIRTH

....

'If pregnancy were a book, they would cut the last two chapters.'

Nora Ephron

You're on the brink of the biggest adventure of your life. The fact that the majority of the adult population will, at some time, have their own similar adventure doesn't make it any less thrilling, terrifying, dramatic, fulfilling, frustrating and life-changing. From the moment that blue line appears on the pregnancy test, you've not only joined the (not very exclusive) club known as 'Parents', you've received life-long membership.

If you are a mum-to-be, you will find that the changes during pregnancy and birth are probably the most dramatic you will ever experience, for both your body and the way you view yourself and those closest to you. This should be a time when you are treated with love, tenderness and consideration – by yourself as well as by everyone else. You may not be feeling too great. There are lots of physical drawbacks associated with pregnancy and you'll certainly experience at least some of them. But there are special moments that make up for it all. The first scan, feeling your baby move, holding your baby for the first time. Enjoy every moment you can!

For dads too, this is an amazing time of change. You are moving fast towards a whole new role and a new set of responsibilities. It can feel overwhelming at times, particularly as you are also having to adapt to the way your partner is changing. Despite your essential (we might even say seminal) role at the beginning, you may feel shut out as pregnancy progresses, and this can continue after your baby is born too. Yet you are needed, and in ways you may never have imagined. Back rubs and cups of tea in the morning are only the tip of the iceberg. By the third trimester, your partner probably won't be able to reach her feet, and may need you to put her socks on for her, and as for the birth – well by then you'll be an expert, supplying ice chips, tennis balls and truck loads of moral support. This may all sound a bit daunting before you've even got started on the fun bit, but if you try to stay well informed, keep your mobile phone switched on at all times, and memorise the phone number for the pizza delivery service, you won't go far wrong.

CONCEPTION

Planning Ahead

Start taking folic acid now. You reduce your chances of giving birth to a baby with a neural tube defect (for example, anencephaly or spina bifida) by 50 per cent to 70 per cent if you start taking at least 0.4 mg of folic acid each day two to three months before you start trying to conceive and continue all through your pregnancy.

Consider getting yourself screened for STDs. Chlamydia is a very common cause of pelvic inflammatory disease and infertility, and can be symptomless.

Ask your GP to give you a pre-conception check-up, to include a smear test, rubella immunity test, possibly a test for toxoplasmosis and a chat about your lifestyle. If you are much over- or underweight, your GP will give you advice on reaching a healthy body

National Childbirth Trust (NCT), enquiry line: 0870 4448 707, www.nctpregnancyand babycare.com; Dr Kate Crocker, GP; Caroline Donley, health visitor; Ruth Hargreave; Clare Baines weight. If you are on the Pill, your doctor will advise you on how long to use barrier contraception instead before trying to get pregnant – usually about six months.

See your dentist now. Even though dental treatment is free once you are pregnant, if you need to have X-rays or any major procedures, it is preferable to get them over with before you are pregnant.

Start keeping a menstrual calendar. Note the date when your period starts, the number of days it lasts and anything else your doctor might want to know about. This information could prove helpful if you experience problems in conceiving. It can also prove invaluable in pinpointing the date of conception – and consequently your due date.

If your menstrual cycle is longer or shorter than twenty-eight days, you probably won't ovulate on day fourteen. Ovulation usually occurs fourteen days before the start of the next menstrual cycle – not fourteen days after the end of the last one, which is much trickier to work out.

If you're monitoring your cervical mucus to predict your most fertile days, do your checks before you shower, bathe or swim. These activities can all affect the quantity and quality of your cervical mucus.

Make your vagina a sperm-friendly environment. Don't use vaginal sprays, scented tampons or artificial lubricants.

Don't go on a crash diet. Starvation diets, purging, bingeing, yo-yo dieting and excess exercise affect ovulation and sperm production, and consequently your fertility. Being either obese or underweight could also cause problems.

Think about workplace hazards, such as chemical exposure, for both partners. Certain substances can affect both the quality of sperm and the development of the embryo. Ask for a transfer if you are concerned.

If you take any prescription or over-the-counter drugs, ask your doctor if it's safe for you to continue taking them once you start trying to conceive.

Coffee addict? Time to give it up, or at least switch to decaff! Caffeine may impair fertility and is thought to restrict the growth of a developing baby by constricting blood vessels and reducing blood flow to the uterus. And both partners should give up smoking.

Only got one ovary? Your chances are not halved, because they don't take turns. Ovulation is a random event each month, with both ovaries competing on a first-come, first-served basis. If you have only one ovary, it wins the draw by default.

Men: at the gym, use the treadmill rather than the stationary bike, which can affect sperm production.

Abstaining from sex for more than seven days can decrease sperm quality. Any gain in sperm count from lack of use is more than offset by the fact that older sperm cells have lower fertilization potential.

It takes three months to form mature sperm, so start your healthy lifestyle changes well in advance.

Have sex! Make love every forty-eight hours during your fertile period (the five days leading up to ovulation) to ensure that there's a fresh shipment of sperm waiting in the fallopian tube at any given time.

Don't jump out of bed right after you finish making love. Although sperm are programmed to make their way through the cervix, don't make it harder for them.

Want a boy?

- Have sex the day of ovulation or the day before. Male sperm move faster but die quicker than female ones, so if they can get to the egg first, you're in with a chance.

- Avoid sex three to five days before ovulation. This should raise the sperm count, which increases your chances.

Want a girl?

- Have lots of sex to reduce the sperm count. Avoid sex until a couple of days after ovulation. This will ensure that most of those male sperm have died out.
- Eat foods with lots of magnesium – such as green vegetables and nuts.
- Have sex with a fighter pilot! They seem to father an unusually high proportion of girls.

Don't assume that you're going to hit the jackpot first time. Even if you do everything 'right', you still have only a 25 to 30 per cent chance of conceiving in any given cycle.

Tempted to light up a cigarette or have a drink? Don't until you know for sure that you're not pregnant. One of the most critical periods in embryonic development happens before a woman even knows that she's pregnant. All the more reason for giving up completely in the preconceptual stage, although many women find an occasional drink relaxing once pregnancy is established.

Think You Might Be Pregnant?

Don't panic if you experience a small amount of spotting. Some women experience implantation bleeding about a week after conception – the point in pregnancy when the fertilized egg attaches itself to the uterine wall. If you mistake this light amount of bleeding for your period, it can throw out the calculation of your dates for your entire pregnancy. You can distinguish it from a period because the bleeding is dark and very scanty.

Pregnancy is by far the most common reason for missing a period, but you can miss a period for other reasons: jet lag, severe illness, surgery, shock, bereavement or stress. And just to confuse you totally, some women continue to have menstrual-like bleeding throughout at least part of their pregnancies.

Two weeks after you ovulate, if your period hasn't shown up, you should be able to get a reliable result on a home pregnancy test. (If you test too soon, there won't be enough hCG, the hormone produced in early pregnancy – in your urine to make the test show positive.) If you get a positive test result, you're probably pregnant, because false positives are unusual. When errors occur, they tend to be false negatives.

Planning to use a home pregnancy test tomorrow? Check to make sure that the test hasn't passed its expiry date and read the test instructions so that you'll know what you're doing when it's time to do the test.

The symptoms of early pregnancy – tender breasts, mood swings and spots – are all similar to the symptoms of pre-menstrual syndrome (PMS), so don't rely on them. Take a test.

INFERTILITY

Child, www.child.org.uk; Issue (National Fertility Association), www.issue.co.uk; Jane Bradbury; Andy Gibbs; Danny and Nadia Shepherd

Infertility treatment is not a big priority with most GPs, and if you've only been trying to get pregnant for six months or so, your doctor is likely to send you off to keep trying. Be prepared to push for primary tests to be carried out as quickly as possible, and do everything at the first opportunity. The kind of tests your GP might run include giving you a temperature chart to fill in, running blood tests and offering a sperm test.

Make a policy decision with your partner about who you're going to tell about your treatment and who you're going to discuss it with. Telling both sets of parents may help to curtail those awful hints about grandchildren.

If you have children already, it's easy to assume that you'll be able to have more. And you won't be the only ones to make that assumption. Persuading other people to take secondary infertility seriously can take a major effort, so persist.

Be prepared for the daft comments that many, many people will make, all variations on, 'Well, you've got one already. Can't you be satisfied with that?' Either ignore them or think of something to say in advance. Don't let them grind you down!

Temperature Charts

Asked to keep a temperature chart? Use a digital thermometer rather than mercury. It's easier to read, doesn't need shaking and even beeps to remind you to record your reading if you accidentally go back to sleep.

Don't eat, drink, talk or get out of bed before you take your temperature. Each of these activities can affect the accuracy of your reading.

Sleepless nights? Make a note on your temperature chart. Getting less than three consecutive hours of sleep can make your reading unreliable.

If you're taking your temperature to try to pinpoint your most fertile days, don't wait until it starts shooting upwards before you start trying to conceive. By that time, ovulation will have already occurred and you will have missed your babymaking opportunity.

Sperm Counts

If you need to give a sperm sample, follow carefully the instructions given to you by the doctor or clinic. This really is important.

Specialised infertility clinics are better at doing sperm counts than your local hospital, and may provide more detailed information on motility, so see if you can be referred at an early stage.

Wearing boxer shorts instead of Y-fronts really does help sperm counts, as can taking baths rather than showers, avoiding excess alcohol, not cycling too much, not smoking and (just when you thought it was all bad news) having regular sex.

Try also taking a vitamin supplement that contains vitamin E and zinc.

Infertility Clinics

Get yourself as well informed as you can because a lot of technical terms get bandied about at infertility clinics and it helps if you at least know some of the acronyms.

Some infertility treatments produce a high proportion of multiple births. Before you seek treatment, think realistically about what having twins or triplets would mean to your life.

Any hormone drug treatments are likely to make you feel – well – hormonal. Added to the stress of what you're going through, this can be quite an emotional load, so be good to yourself and make sure that everyone else is too.

As a first line of treatment, you may be given a drug that stimulates ovulation. Provided everything else is in working order, this may work perfectly, but ask to be scanned as you approach your fertile time, as some women produce too many eggs, which results in high-order multiples.

If you go for one of the high-tech options, such as in vitro fertilisation (IVF), make it your main project and don't try to pretend it isn't happening. It's so expensive and time-consuming that you owe it to yourselves to give it your very best shot – and nothing will protect you from the disappointment if it's not successful.

If you can bear to learn how to give yourself injections, you'll save a lot of time and effort going to your GP's surgery to have them administered by a nurse.

After embryo transfer, do yourself and everyone else a favour by taking it really easy. That way, if the treatment cycle is not successful, at least you'll know that you did everything you could.

Don't make any rash pronouncements at the start of treatment about how many times you're prepared to try before giving up. It won't seem so black and white if you've produced good eggs but they haven't implanted, or if you have a miscarriage. It's very difficult to give up if you've been partially successful.

If you or your partner are prepared to donate eggs or sperm, you may be treated favourably by infertility clinics and get treated sooner.

If it comes down to having to use donor eggs or sperm, make sure that you both feel the same about the issue before going ahead, and think through the implications as thoroughly as you can. Counselling may help you work out how you feel about this.

PREGNANCY: FIRST TRIMESTER

Gill James, midwife;
Susan Clark,
www.whatreallyworks.co.uk;
Chris Warren

If you're expecting your first baby, make friends with someone at the same stage as you. Since most antenatal care doesn't start until the second trimester, you'll probably have to ask around your circle of friends.

When you announce that you're pregnant, all sorts of people will tell you all about their experiences. Take these with a large sprinkling of salt. Every pregnancy is different.

Take care when planning holidays. Doctors don't recommend flying before three months and after seven months.

Write a diary of your pregnancy, maybe not every day, but every week – it's a great gift idea for your child later.

You may never have felt so tired before. Go with it as much as you can, and take plenty of naps.

Be optimistic that the second trimester will be better than the first. It almost always is.

Things you'll wish you hadn't said:

- I'm definitely going to have a natural birth and I'm certainly going to breastfeed.
- Having a baby isn't going to change my life.
- I'm not going to talk about my baby all the time.
- I'm going to be just as committed to my career after I have the baby as I am now.
- I'm never going to bribe my child with chocolate.
- I think boys and girls are exactly alike – it's just the way people raise them that makes the difference.
- I think tantrums are a sign of poor parenting.
- I'm not going to fit my social life around my baby's naps.
- I'm going to make sure I don't get stretch marks.

Breasts

Some women have very tender breasts early on in pregnancy, far worse than pre-menstrual discomfort. In fact, it can be one of the earliest signs. Get yourself some well-supporting bras.

Itchy or tingling nipples is another sign. Avoid wearing a bra with seams across the nipples or lacy cups, which can also irritate the skin.

Avoid using soap on your breasts when showering or bathing, and try rubbing in a really gentle moisturiser, such as E45 cream, to soothe itching and tenderness.

Prominent blue veins on the breasts are another giveaway of pregnancy. They look a bit alarming, but they're perfectly normal, and will disappear.

Morning Sickness

It's all down to hormones, they say, and perfectly natural. But that's little consolation. Sometimes even the smell of food can be enough to set you off. In most cases, morning sickness resolves at twelve to fourteen weeks, once the placenta takes over and the hormones calm down. In rare cases, morning sickness can be dangerous. If you can't keep anything down, there's a danger that you'll become dehydrated.

Here are some tips that may help:

- Choose very fresh foods. Don't let fruit get too ripe and steer clear of milk that is close to its expiry date.
- Eat small meals and snacks throughout the day. Don't let your stomach get too full or too empty. Both can make you feel sick.
- Keep plain biscuits by your bed and eat a couple before you get up in the morning.
- Stick to starchy foods. Dry crackers and pretzels can help settle a queasy stomach.
- Keep your body hydrated by sipping fluids, particularly if you've been vomiting.
- Try making ice lollies out of fruit juice. When something is really cold, it doesn't smell as strong.

The homeopathic remedy pulsatilla can often stop morning sickness in its tracks, but only use remedies under the guidance of a qualified homeopath or pharmacist.

Vitamin supplements can trigger nausea in some women. If you suspect that this is the case, talk to your doctor, who can suggest alternatives; try taking them before you go to bed; or take them on an empty stomach.

The same acupressure treatments that ease motion sickness (such as wristbands) can help ease the nausea.

Try some of the following:

- ginger tea made either with tea bags or grated ginger root steeped in hot water, ginger ale or ginger beer, ginger biscuits, crystallised ginger
- peppermint tea or peppermint sweets, or chewing gum
- lemon, hot with honey, lemon aromatherapy oil or a slice of cut lemon to smell, lemonade, lemon sweets
- carbohydrate-rich foods – rice, mashed potato, plain bread, rice cakes, porridge, rice crispies, dry crackers, chips

- protein-rich foods – cheese, ham, peanut butter, etc.
- salty foods – crisps, salty crackers, miso soup
- sweet foods – toffees, jelly cubes, jelly babies
- apples, apple juice, apple cider vinegar with hot water and honey
- cola or carbonated drinks (for a good satisfying burp)
- acupuncture
- following your cravings
- giving up coffee
- wearing loose clothes that don't constrict your waist
- pressing two fingers firmly but gently on your belly button, just for a minute
- sleep – and lots of rest during the day
- eating some protein just before bed, such as a peanut butter sandwich and a glass of milk, or even setting your alarm clock to wake you up in the early hours to eat a snack conveniently placed beside your bed.

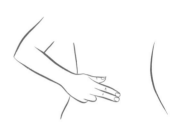

If you are sick, brush your teeth or use a mouthwash and floss afterwards to prevent stomach acid damaging the enamel on your teeth.

Keep some nappy sacks with you, in case you have to throw up when you're out, plus baby wipes and some peppermints to freshen yourself up.

Eat sensibly – three-quarters of mums remain at least 2lb/1kg heavier after the birth. However, you need to increase your intake by 500 calories a day.

Constipation

Constipation is very common in pregnancy. This is apparently due to the body's high level of progesterone, which relaxes the bowel and makes it less efficient. Iron supplements can make constipation worse, so if you are taking them counteract the effect by eating lots of fibre, fruit and vegetables.

Try taking psyllium husks or linseed (available from health food shops), sprinkled on to food or stirred into fruit juice. This is not the most appealing concoction but far better than getting piles. You can also grind them to a powder in a coffee grinder and mix them into smoothies.

Regular gentle exercise helps, particularly walking. This will also help fend off varicose veins, also brought on by hormonal changes.

Drink plenty of water, juice or milk, because your blood volume increases during the early stages of pregnancy and you need more fluid in your body to help produce it. If you don't drink extra, your body will use what you've got and the result could be worse constipation.

Cramp

Cramp in your legs and feet is another unwelcome problem during pregnancy. Try:

- drinking tonic water – the quinine in it can help relieve cramp
- eating bananas and tomatoes – both contain potassium, which can help prevent cramp
- drinking more milk – the calcium should help.

For cramp in the legs or feet, stand on a small step or on a phone directory with your heel hanging over the edge to stretch your calf muscles.

Gentle exercise will also help – swimming, walking or ballet pliés; also walking on your toes for a few minutes, then on your heels.

Raise your feet on a pillow when lying in bed.

Metallic Taste

Many women have an odd taste in their mouths during early pregnancy, usually described as a metallic taste. It can be tempting to keep eating to make it go away. Sweet foods seem particularly attractive at this time, but stick to fruit or sugar-free gum with xylitol, a natural sweetener, which can help protect your teeth. Dried apricots are great if you are constipated.

This odd taste may stop you enjoying the taste of food and drink. Most women find it puts them off coffee, alcohol and cigarette smoke. Eating liquorice root or ginger can help to disguise it.

Bleeding Gums

Hormones are to blame again for gums which bleed, especially when you clean your teeth. This is normal, so don't give up cleaning your teeth.

- Brush teeth gently, especially along the gum-line.
- Use dental floss.
- Avoid sugary foods and drinks.

See your dentist regularly. Let him or her know from the earliest stage that you are pregnant and remember that X-rays are not advisable during pregnancy. In the UK, all visits to the dentist are free while you are pregnant and up to a year following the birth.

Change to a soft-bristled toothbrush, and brush gently from the gums over the teeth.

If your gums recede a bit, causing sensitivity to hot or cold foods around the base of your teeth, use a toothpaste for sensitive teeth and, after brushing with it, squeeze a little dab on to your finger and rub it into the sensitive spots. Don't bother to rinse, and repeat daily. Your teeth should feel better in a couple of weeks.

Stuffy Nose

A stuffy or runny nose without other symptoms of a cold is probably down to hormones again.

- Do not blow your nose too hard.

- Try steam inhalation. Consult your doctor before taking any decongestants.

- Try sprinkling a few drops of eucalyptus oil on your hanky and sniff it during the day.

If you get a nosebleed, it might be heavier than usual. Don't panic. Pinch the sides of your nose gently, just below the bony part, and lean forward slightly.

You may be snoring for the first time. Reassure your partner that it's temporary!

Pelvic Floor Exercises

Do not delay! Get working on your pelvic floor muscles straight away, for lots of reasons (see below). For women, they are the most important muscles after the heart.

- Tighten up around your vagina as though trying to prevent a tampon from dropping out or trying not to wee. Hold for a count of four and release.

- Repeat the exercise in batches of six or eight as often as you can during the day.

- As well as holding for a count of four, try doing some rapid squeeze, release, squeeze, release exercises.

- Breathe normally throughout.

Most women get a far-away look on their faces when doing them, so it's probably better to do them in the privacy of your home or car. It can be helpful to associate them with something you do regularly – for instance, if you're driving, try doing them every time you stop at a red light, or if you always watch a particular programme do them when the theme tune starts.

Test that your muscles are getting stronger by trying to stop your flow of urine briefly when you're on the loo, then letting it go. This will come in handy during antenatal appointments when you have to give urine samples in tiny pots. Only do this once a week, or you may increase the risk of getting urinary infections.

Around 50 per cent of women have stress incontinence after childbirth. This means that when they run, sneeze, cough or laugh they experience slight leakage of urine. Make sure that you are in the happy 50 per cent with no such problems by doing the pelvic floor exercises religiously.

Another reason to strengthen your pelvic floor is that once you have a baby, you'll be so busy that you'll only get to the loo about once a day.

And then there's the sex. When you finally get round to it again, you'll be glad you did them.

Dizziness

Your blood pressure may be low so, if you stand for a long time or get up too quickly, the blood supply to your brain may be temporarily reduced, making you dizzy. If this happens, sit down again straight away, wait a minute or two, then try again – but slowly this time.

Avoid standing for long periods of time. This also helps avoid varicose veins.

Get up slowly from a sitting or lying-down position.

Another cause of dizziness can be low blood-sugar levels. Avoid this by eating small snacks on a regular basis.

If you feel faint, sit down and put your head between your knees, loosen any tight clothing and breathe deeply.

Thrush

Increased vaginal discharge is normal in pregnancy, but thrush is more common too, so if you get vaginal itching along with a thick white discharge, you probably have thrush.

- Use an antifungal cream or pessary. If you buy this over the counter, tell the pharmacist that you're pregnant.
- You may be tempted to use panty-liners if your discharge is heavy, but the plastic lining in them makes them less breathable and more likely to cause irritation. Instead, change your knickers during the day.
- Eat less sugar and more live natural yoghurt.
- Wear cotton knickers and don't wear tights.
- Apply some natural yoghurt to your vaginal area to soothe itching and help restore the acid/alkaline balance of your vagina.

Headaches

The fact that your body makes almost 50 per cent extra blood during pregnancy can cause an increase in pressure in the blood vessels in your head. To relieve headaches:

- Massage your scalp with your fingers.
- Cut out caffeine and drink more water.
- Make time to relax and try some deep breathing.
- Have a nap.
- Take paracetamol in preference to aspirin.

MISCARRIAGE

Gill James, midwife;
Dr Kate Crocker, GP

Most miscarriages occur in the first trimester of pregnancy, although about 5 per cent happen later. And at least one in five pregnancies end in miscarriage. You are not alone.

Spotting around the time your period would have been due is not uncommon, and does not necessarily mean that your pregnancy is threatened.

However, any bleeding, persistent backache or stomach cramp could be a sign of miscarriage.

If you have any of these symptoms:

- Rest in bed immediately until the bleeding or cramps stop.

- Try not to take any painkillers. You need to know whether the cramps are getting better or worse.

- Don't use a tampon and don't take a bath or have sex.

- Always call a doctor if the symptoms get worse, or you feel faint, chilled or feverish.

If you miscarry, you may feel angry with your body for letting you down. But you need to take care of yourself – miscarriage is a trauma for your body and mind.

Don't minimise the trauma or let anyone else do so. Find someone who understands and who you can talk to, and speak to your GP if you want further help, counselling or advice about attempting to become pregnant again.

For support and advice, contact the Miscarriage Association: 01924 200799, www.miscarriageassociation.org.uk.

See also Stillbirth And Neonatal Death, page 24.

PREGNANCY: SECOND TRIMESTER

Monica Shaw;
Glynis Fletcher, NCT

As morning sickness recedes and the placenta is fully formed, you feel less victimised by your hormones. But don't overdo things just because you have a sudden burst of energy.

If you're ever going to 'bloom', it's now or never, so wear your bump with pride.

Take regular photos of your expanding belly, and make sure you date them.

You may not need maternity clothes yet, apart from tracksuit bottoms a size larger than normal and well-supporting bras, but invest in a maternity swimsuit.

You'll only need maternity clothes for about the last ten weeks, so don't buy too much. Select tops, nighties and pyjamas that open easily for breastfeeding.

Keep a chair or stool in your kitchen for tasks that really don't require standing. Do you really need to stand up to chop your veg or to make packed lunches? Sit down on the job and save your energy for better things.

Now that your baby's ears are starting to develop, try playing music or reading to your bump. Research shows that, once babies are born, they recognise sounds played to them in the womb.

Make time to put your feet up during this and the next trimester, to avoid varicose veins and swollen ankles caused by water retention. Avoid sitting cross-legged for the same reason.

Try to get out of the habit of sleeping on your back. As the baby gets bigger, this starts to get uncomfortable, so side sleeping is best, probably with a pillow to tuck under the bump.

For better sleep and greater comfort, get one of those V-shaped pointy pillows shaped like a boomerang, with a couple of spare covers. You'll use it increasingly as you get bigger, and it'll be perfect for breastfeeding.

Make sure that you drink plenty of milk or eat calcium-rich food, because the baby will take exactly what it needs from your body, whether you can spare it or not.

Walk for exercise, preferably somewhere calming and beautiful. Antenatal yoga classes are excellent, and aquanatal classes, held at many leisure centres, are fantastic and a great opportunity to meet a circle of pregnant women.

Antenatal Appointments

Join the National Childbirth Trust (NCT) for antenatal classes, social events, advice, counselling, equipment for rent and some excellent second-hand sales. For contact details, see page 298.

This is the stage where your pregnancy is taken seriously by the medical profession, and you'll start antenatal check-ups and classes.

This is a great opportunity to meet other women at a similar stage, and you could make some friends for life.

If you're working, you are entitled to reasonable time off to attend antenatal appointments, at your full rate of pay, regardless of how long you have been in your job.

Your first antenatal appointment, some time between eleven and thirteen weeks, is the longest one, because the midwife will take your history and need to ask lots of questions.

If you have other children, try to leave them with someone else when you go for antenatal appointments, particularly ones at hospital clinics. You frequently have to wait ages, and having a toddler around will certainly increase your blood pressure and put all the questions you wanted to ask out of your mind.

Peeing in a pot is an art you'll have to master. What's wanted is a mid-stream sample, so start weeing, apply your pelvic floor muscles to arrest the flow, get the pot in place, release the brakes and fill the pot. There is no known way to do this without weeing on your fingers and all over the label on the pot.

Take a notebook with you to antenatal appointments with any questions you want to ask, and make a note of anything your caregiver tells you.

At your first hospital antenatal appointment, you'll have your first scan, a very exciting event. You'll need the radiographer to interpret what she sees on the screen, because it probably won't look anything like a baby to you. Be prepared for the radiographer not to say anything as she looks at the monitor. This doesn't necessarily mean that there is something wrong: she will be measuring the baby and checking that everything is in the right place.

You need a very full bladder to get the best scan image. Getting it full enough without needing to pee is a fine art, particularly if you are kept waiting. The waiting room will usually be full of pained-looking women, either crossing their legs or swilling water.

If you ask to be told the gender of your baby, don't invest too much money, in terms of buying blue or pink, on the basis of what you are told. Radiographers can be wrong sometimes. This is especially true if you are having more than one baby, when there are extra limbs waving around in unexpected places.

Indigestion

Once the sickness is out of the way, you have indigestion to look forward to, as your belly gets bigger and leaves less room for your stomach. This sometimes takes the form of oesophageal reflux, which causes a horrible burning sensation right at the back of your throat. Try any of the following:

- Eat small regular meals.
- Drink peppermint tea.

- Drink pineapple juice before and after meals.

- Sip soda water or tonic water. This can sometimes result in a large and satisfying burp, so is best done at home.

- If you are suffering from heartburn, a glass of milk will help to neutralise stomach acid.

- If it is really bad, see your GP or pharmacist, who will recommend an antacid.

Piles

The final indignity, piles (engorged blood vessels around the anus) are very common during pregnancy, although they may not occur until the second or third trimester. Take steps to avoid them early – they are caused by a combination of constipation and hormones. Follow the tips on page 7 for avoiding constipation.

Painful though it may be, don't put off going to the loo – this will only make them worse.

Strong chemical laxatives should be avoided during pregnancy, as they may induce miscarriage. Your pharmacist can recommend a cream or suppository that can be safely used in pregnancy.

Ease the discomfort of piles during pregnancy by applying a flannel soaked in witch hazel or an ice pack covered with a soft cloth to the area.

Use flushable wipes rather than loo paper when you go to the loo.

Pregnancy Itchies

Feeling itchy? About 20 per cent of pregnant women feel the same way. Probably caused by hormones (again) and the fact that your skin is having to stretch to accommodate your growing belly. And 60 per cent will develop red and itchy palms and soles. This usually clears up straight away after the baby is born.

In the meantime, rub in some moisturiser or try a warm oatmeal bath (porridge oats tied up in a sock and dangled in the water) to soothe your skin. Add half a cup of bicarbonate of soda to your bath to soothe itching.

In hot weather, itching can be even worse. Wear loose cotton clothing and have a cool shower if you get too hot.

Stretch Marks

Most people get stretch marks, some (lucky few) don't. Whether you do or not is largely down to genetics, but you can tilt the odds in your favour by making sure that your vitamin and mineral intake is adequate – lack of zinc is thought to make the skin more susceptible.

Massage in plenty of cream – E45 is perfect, and cheap.

Neat olive oil massaged into the bump, hips, sides and bosom works for some women, but coconut oil smells better.

Stop using soap on your boobs and belly. It strips the skin of its natural oils, and you need it all (and more) to keep your skin supple.

Try to avoid putting on too much extra weight – for this and lots of other reasons.

PREGNANCY: THIRD TRIMESTER

Su Down, Derby
General Hospital;
Association of Radical
Midwives; Midwife
Information and
Resource Service;
Independent Midwives
Association

Eat frequent small meals, because you simply can't fit any more into your tum.

Keep fresh fruit around the house to pick at. It's healthier than biscuits and helps with constipation.

Get used to being regarded as public property. Complete strangers will bombard you with questions and many won't be able to resist stroking your tummy. Enjoy being the centre of attention. It doesn't last!

When supermarket shopping, use the shallow trolleys, not the deep ones. The last thing you need is to put your back out. Ask for help with packing and carrying to the car.

As you get larger (and larger) odd things get difficult, like putting your knickers on, cutting your toenails, and getting in and out of the bath. Get used to asking for help.

Backache is common in pregnancy. When washing up, rest the bowl on another inverted bowl to make it higher – it will be much more comfortable for your back.

Go out with your partner or even go away for a holiday. It'll be the last for a while.

Maternity jeans are excellent, particularly the ones with an elasticated panel at the front, although you have to wear a long shirt over them. Overalls and dungarees are fine until you need to go to the loo in a hurry. If you buy any clothes, try to buy ones that you can wear after the baby is born.

To accommodate your bump without splashing out on lots of special clothes, wear trackie pants or elasticated waist trousers back to front.

If you're going to be breastfeeding, buy yourself a few all-stretch sports bras and take one to the hospital with you. They come in all sizes, even plus sizes, they give excellent support and they're much more comfortable to sleep in than nursing bras.

If you haven't already bought them, buy your nursing bras, whenever your pre-pregnancy bras start to feel uncomfortable.

Nursing bras with zip-up cups may sound like a good idea, but if you try to do one up one-handed, and catch your boob in the zip, you'll feel quite differently about them.

Bras that do up with hooks and eyes, poppers or Velcro, or where you can just pull down one cup at a time, are better options. Try on loads, but don't buy too many of a particular style until you've road tested it to make sure that it is easy to use.

You will often have to open your bra with one hand, so look at all the fastening options before you buy.

Follow the washing instructions carefully. Nursing bras are expensive and you don't want to buy more than you strictly need just because you shrunk one.

Make sure that you have room to fit breast pads inside the cups.

Get plenty of breast pads. Washable ones are more comfortable than disposables, but get a net washing bag for delicates to put them in before machine-washing them because they are small enough to disappear into the mechanism and never reappear again.

Sleeping

Having to get up in the night to wee can be regarded as excellent practice for getting up for your baby. Leave a light on to show you the way. It's easy to stumble when you're sleepy.

Babies who thrash around when you're trying to sleep lose their charm after the first few times. Try avoiding coffee, which can make babies frisky.

Sleep on your left side so that the weight of the baby doesn't bear down on large arteries. This often helps you sleep better too.

If you find sleeping difficult:

- Avoid drinking coffee, and try chamomile tea.

- Warm milk with a teaspoon of molasses may sound revolting, but it's soothing and provides calcium and iron.

PREGNANCY WITH MULTIPLES

Linda Jones, Tamba, the Twins and Multiple Births Association (www.tamba.org.uk); the Multiple Births Foundation; Jennifer Davis; Adele Degremont; Jack and Evelyn Patterson; Clare Porter

Whether you're delighted at the news that you're expecting more than one child or horrified, you have to cope with it. The idea of twins doesn't take too long to sink in, but the more babies there are, the more intimidating the whole thing becomes – during pregnancy, delivery and afterwards. Fortunately, this is a well-trodden path and there is plenty of information and support out there to help you and your family.

More babies means more symptoms. The more hormones you have racing around your body, the more tired, sick, constipated and emotional you are likely to be. This is why you need to be at least twice as good to yourself, and follow all the suggestions in this chapter on making pregnancy easier and healthier.

You will also get bigger sooner than women enjoying singleton pregnancy. This means that you are likely to need maternity clothes at an earlier stage, you're likely to get more stretch marks and the discomforts of late pregnancy will start earlier for you.

It is worth buying some decent maternity clothes, because you'll get more wear out of them than singleton mothers.

Don't worry if your bump looks a funny shape compared with those of singleton mums. Your babies have to fit somewhere, and it may end up being round your sides.

In single pregnancies, kicking babies take a break sometimes, but your dynamic duo (or more) can take it in turns – or at least that's what it feels like sometimes.

Getting comfy in bed can be much more of a challenge. A V-shaped pillow – or even two – is a must to help support and cushion your rapidly growing bump.

Because you have more than one baby on the way, your pregnancy will be regarded as higher risk, with more antenatal checks, longer scans, more monitoring.

From your scans, the radiographer will not necessarily be able to tell you if your twins are identical or not. You will have to wait until delivery for a definite answer.

Ask for a scan picture early on, when you can still see the two (or more) babies. Later on, all you can see is a mass of limbs.

Around twenty weeks, you will have a very detailed scan, as any pregnant woman would, but there is the added frisson that this will be the last opportunity the radiographer will get to check that there is no other baby – one more than everyone thinks – playing hide and seek in there. Such a discovery has been known to happen.

Everyone will advise you to rest, which is sensible in a singleton pregnancy but absolutely essential with multiples. Do it!

When people ask you about your pregnancy, and you tell them it's triplets, or whatever, be prepared for some pretty dodgy responses. 'Oh no! You poor things!' is not unheard of, as well as 'How on earth are you going to manage?' Rise above it. But generally, avoid people who give you negative messages of that sort – and explain why you're doing so.

Full term for a single child is generally accepted as 40 weeks. Twins generally go to 37 weeks, triplets to 34 weeks, quads to 33 weeks. Be prepared for the fact that your babies might spend some time in Special Care.

Be practical and don't be proud. When getting equipped (see below), borrow as much equipment as possible and if you can't find anyone to borrow from, buy second-hand. Buy clothes in sales or second-hand well in advance of when they will be worn.

GETTING EQUIPPED & PREPARED

Alison Wallis;
Anna Knight; Jane
Alexander, writer,
www.janealexander.org

You may feel superstitious about buying too much, but be realistic: there are basic items you must have and you won't be in any condition to go shopping with a newborn. It's possible to buy a lot of what you need second-hand, or to borrow from friends, but it's still fun to go round the shops.

Baby equipment and clothes are much cheaper in French supermarkets – so forget the booze cruise, stock up on supplies for your baby.

Don't rule out second-hand equipment and clothes. Most people buy too much and many things are hardly used. Accept everything and pass on what you don't want once you've had a chance to look through.

You may be intent on breastfeeding, but if your baby has other ideas you'll need at least a couple of bottles, some way of sterilising them and some formula milk. Set some by as an insurance policy.

Don't waste money on a special changing station. A mat on a chest of drawers at the right height will work just as well – simply tack in some wood around the edges so that the mat doesn't slip. You can remove it when you no longer need the station. If you're up to it, changing on the floor is ideal – all you need is a change mat.

Even if you're not expecting to use cloth nappies (see page 48), buy a few packs and some muslins, too. They're pricey but they go on for ever and have a million uses.

You'll certainly need a rear-facing car seat to bring your baby home. Don't buy a used one unless you know for certain that it hasn't been in a car accident. Make sure that you know how to fit it in your car, and practise a few times.

Moses baskets are brilliant for small babies. They're easily portable, and small enough for newborns to feel secure. (They look good too.)

Sheepskin fleeces are fabulous for babies. You can buy specially cleansed ones and they are incredibly comforting. Use them to provide continuity when you travel.

Before you have your baby, take a chosen 'special toy', a teddy, rabbit or whatever, to bed with you and hug it close for several weeks or longer. Your scent will become infused in the toy and will provide instant comfort for the baby.

Baby clothes in tiny sizes often come as gifts, so don't buy any fancy ones yourself – just buy plain ones with poppers up the front, not the back. You can't use all-in-ones that are too small, because they cramp the baby's toes, but you can use ones that are a little bit big, so go for 0–3 months rather than newborn size.

Second-hand baby clothes, from friends or sales, are a godsend. And you'll find out when you start handing them on that it's a great pleasure to give them too.

Your baby won't spend long in a pram, so get a convertible type with a really decent pushchair instead.

When looking at prams for your baby, pay most attention to the pushchair. How easy is it to manoeuvre and collapse? Does it have somewhere to store bags and essentials? You will be using this far longer than the pram.

Accost women in the street and ask them about their buggies. Most are only too happy to tell you about the pros and cons of each type.

If possible, try pushing a buggy with a six-month-old baby, a changing bag and some shopping in it to give you an idea of how it will feel when it's loaded up.

Second-hand buggies are well worth considering. Another advantage is that the previous owner can show you exactly how to fold and unfold – often rather a puzzle.

Your choice of pram/buggy will also depend on what time of year your baby is due. For autumn and winter babies, you'll need more protection than for a spring or summer baby. If the baby isn't sufficiently protected from cold winds, you won't feel like taking it out. Will you be driving a lot? If so, the buggy has to be easy to put up and down.

For further advice on clothes and equipment that you'll need, see page 58.

Getting Equipped For More Than One Baby

You are going to need so much, and all at once. If friends and family ask what kind of presents you would like for your newborns, suggest gift vouchers from stores. Then you'll be able to get just what you need when you need it. Borrow from friends, or buy second-hand for things that you won't be using for long. You'll find people are only too glad to help out in this way.

If you have mixed-gender babies, they don't need gender specific toys in the early stages. Plenty of time for that complication later!

Multiples attract a great deal of attention when you're out. A big old-fashioned pram with a hood, if you can borrow one, protects your little ones from prying eyes and foolish comments.

Moses baskets and carrycots won't last long but can be very useful for putting your babies in separately. Borrow, if you can.

You can put all your babies to sleep in a single cot for the first couple of months, either side by side or head to toe. It looks very comical.

Car seats can present problems, because there are very few cars that have enough diagonal seat belts to allow for more than four rear-facing car seats. The car will have to be a people mover (or two), for sure.

Ask friends for advice on the varying merits of buggies. Side-by-side buggies are wide but easier to manoeuvre up kerbs than tandem buggies. And although the babies can pull each other's hair and pinch each other's noses (and they will) in a tandem, they can't see one another at all, and one gets a better view than the other.

Baby's Room

Don't spend ages getting a nursery ready. For the first few weeks at least, the baby will probably sleep in your room.

In the early days, the decorations in your baby's room are more for your benefit than his. Try to choose furniture and wallpaper that will appeal as he gets older.

To begin with, all your baby needs is a safe warm place to sleep where she feels happy and secure.

As your baby grows, she will begin to recognise her special toys, pictures and mobiles.

A chest of drawers to store baby's clothes which can also double as a changing station is a good idea.

A rocking chair or somewhere comfy for you to sit while feeding or cuddling your baby is essential.

A radio, CD or tape player can be useful – for your benefit as well as baby's.

Advance Planning

Prioritise making life easy when you get home. Make sure that your freezer is stocked up with meals that will just need warming up, like lasagne, casseroles and pasta sauces. That way when you get home from hospital with your new baby, you will have lots of nutritious things to eat without the hassle of getting them ready.

If any kind friends ask what they can do for you, ask for some contributions to your freezer so that you won't have to spend time cooking and shopping.

Enlist huge amounts of support – particularly for the first month. If you can possibly swing it, get someone (or a whole team) to organise your house, shopping, other kids – so that you can spend time just being, healing and bonding with your baby. You also need someone to take your baby from you so you can rest totally. Don't feel guilty about appearing selfish – selfish is good for new mums. If you don't rest, you run the risk of poor milk production, post-natal depression and a lowered immune system.

If you're hoping to breastfeed, find someone who can advise you at home. If feeding isn't going to plan, you really need a calm, experienced helper.

Invest in an answerphone.

Make sure that your partner is happy to be with you during labour. Some men can be heroic when actually they would rather not see you suffering. Give him the option of opting out, or leaving after the first stage, and letting you have a birthing partner – a very good friend – instead. One that's given birth herself is best.

Write your birth plan with care and attention. Make sure that your birthing partner knows your wishes and is prepared (see page 21). There may come a moment when he or she has to fight your corner for you when you can't do it for yourself.

Don't listen to horror stories about other people's labour. For some reason, women love to share all the gory details – but your labour is yours, not theirs.

Ask your mother what sort of labour she had – long or short labours can sometimes run in families.

Packing For Hospital

Have your bag ready and by the door from about week 37. You never know!

Pack for labour:

- short nightie or long T-shirt
- socks – your feet can get cold
- reading material or a crossword – it could take a long time
- tapes or CDs
- V-shaped pillow with an extra cover
- pain relief (TENS machine, paracetamol)
- tissues

- face cloths
- usual toiletries
- food/snacks and drinks for your partner and you (afterwards) (see page 23)
- water spray to keep your face cool in the delivery room
- chips of ice in a thermos flask to suck on
- a tennis ball to squeeze when labour pains increase, unless your partner or birthing partner is very brave and will let you squeeze on his or her hand
- homeopathic first-aid kit for birth – whatever kind of birth you have, this will help you heal quicker; available from Helios Homeopathic Pharmacy with clear instructions
- a camera to take early pictures of the baby
- anything that you think might soothe you during labour – see page 23.

Pack for your baby:
- clothes (vests, sleepsuits, hats)
- blankets, but label them so that they don't disappear
- nappies in newborn size
- nappy sacks
- petroleum jelly for getting meconium off tiny bottoms
- wipes
- cotton wool
- muslin squares.

Pack for afterwards:
- soft loo paper
- paper knickers or, for a more comfortable option, cheap cotton ones you don't mind throwing away
- plenty of sanitary towels – night-time-quality ones
- toothbrush and toothpaste
- shampoo
- cheap, front-opening nighties or pyjamas that you can chuck if they get stained
- nursing bras and breast pads
- slippers
- dressing gown that preserves your modesty in front of visitors
- your address book, pen, stationery, stamps
- notebook and/or post-it notes so that you can write down notes and questions for the midwives and doctors and stick them on your chart, who sends you what or lists of things you need from home
- change for phones, or a mobile, although you won't be allowed to turn it on in all areas of the hospital
- personal stereo and some calming music
- a good book – newborn babies sleep a lot and it may be the last chance you have to read
- mascara, some lippy and your favourite bath smells/soap

- food – hospital food never comes when you are hungry – that won't give your baby tummy ache if you're breastfeeding (steer clear of oranges and grapes); biscuits and high-fibre snacks; chocolate for late-night, high-cal snacking
- a typed list of names and phone numbers for someone to call after the baby arrives
- an outfit for you to come home in that won't press on any sore bits. Don't expect to be able to get into your size 10 jeans. If you've had a Caesarean, your feet will be puffy with water retention, so choose loose shoes
- baby's car seat
- outfit for the baby, bearing in mind that hospitals are always overheated and the contrast with the real world will be a shock.

BIRTH

Jane Alexander,
www.janealexander.org;
Gill James, midwife;
Glynis Fletcher, NCT

Starting Labour

If you have given birth prematurely in the past, eating oil-rich fish, such as mackerel and sardines, will help reduce the risk of pre-term birth.

To get your baby into a good position for delivery, particularly if your baby is breech, try cleaning the skirting boards – being on all fours with your bum in the air will shift things about.

If you've gone past your due date, you'll be desperate for the baby to come. To avoid a hospital induction, try nipple stimulation to help the uterus to contract.

Sex also helps to bring on contractions. Try to find a position you can stay in for some time afterwards to keep the semen in contact with your cervix. That's what does the trick.

Kick-start a late baby by eating certain foods. Curry, chilli and other strong foods are believed to trigger things off.

Bring on labour by rubbing a little jasmine oil on to your abdomen or adding a couple of drops of clary sage oil to your bath.

You can usually recognise the start of labour by one of these three signs:

- the start of regular, strong contractions
- waters breaking
- the 'show', a small plug of pinky mucus from the neck of the cervix.

Once any of these three happens, it's time to start thinking about calling your birth partner, the hospital, your midwife and whoever is going to look after your other kids.

First-time mums often arrive at hospital far too early. To avoid boredom and nerves, take lots of coins with you so that you can phone friends and have a good natter.

Avoid being in hospital too early. Once contractions begin, try setting yourself a little task to finish before you leave. Tidying a drawer or writing a letter not only kills time but will also help to distract you from the discomfort of early labour.

Timing contractions? Go in to hospital when they are five minutes apart.

To help you relax and prepare you for labour, try running a warm bath. You'll enjoy it far more at home than in a hospital bathroom.

Labour has been compared to running a marathon. Prepare yourself for the big event by eating lots of carbohydrates – potatoes, pasta, bread and vegetables.

Don't forget your poor partner – he will be hungry, especially during a long labour and hospitals are not always very good at catering for his needs. Pack him a picnic.

Partners/Birthing Partners

Partners or birthing partners have a very important role. Make sure that you have discussed the birth with the mother so that you know what she really hopes for during the birth.

Labour is not the time to be hunting through a pregnancy and birth manual, so do all your reading beforehand. You'll feel more useful, too, if you have some idea of what to expect.

Bring a few things for yourself. You'll probably be spending the night at the hospital too. A clean T-shirt and comfortable shoes are essential.

If the mother opts for a birthing pool, bring your swimwear so that you can get in there with her.

Although there won't be any shortage of highly qualified people around, you will be your partner's most important support. Focus entirely on her needs and do whatever it takes to keep her comfortable. Whether it's getting sweets from the vending machine, letting her squeeze your hand till it goes white or being yelled at, just do it!

The middle of a contraction is not a good time for the mother to be making any decisions. Stick with what you've agreed previously and don't let the professionals swamp her. When the contraction has passed, you can discuss what she wants with her relatively calmly.

Doctors and midwives don't always explain what they're doing, or why, so keep asking questions.

Be emotionally supportive and offer encouragement. It is easier to do this if you keep talking to each other and maintain eye contact. That way you can reassure her about how well she's doing and how far she has come.

When you can see the baby's head, make sure that your partner can too. Hold a mirror so that she can see the head and the body emerging.

Labour

Be prepared for everything to go differently to how you plan it. Try not to have too many hard-and-fast ideas. Be flexible.

There is no medal for suffering during childbirth, and you aren't doing your baby any favours by being a martyr – now or ever. Nothing is as important as your health and that of your baby. There may come a point when you really want to have some pain relief – go for it, and if that baby needs to come out fast, then do whatever it takes, whatever you have in your birthplan. Ask yourself if you really care if your mother had a natural birth, epidural or Caesarean when she had you.

Labour is a huge, overwhelming, extraordinary experience. Your body will do things you never realised it was capable of, show power that you can't control and release hormones like you've never felt. Just do your best!

Labour can be disappointingly slow, especially the first time. Be prepared for events not to happen as quickly as you had hoped.

When you are in labour, try to walk around, or at least stay in an upright position for as long as possible, as this can really speed up the process.

Discuss how you would like the labour to go with your midwife whilst your contractions are still coming slowly. But be guided by her expertise. She will know when you are tiring, and if she suggests pain relief (epidural, for example) it may be for a good reason.

Make a noise when the contractions set in. Moaning, groaning and good old-fashioned yelling can be very therapeutic.

Keep your mouth relaxed and your vagina will follow.

To avoid an episiotomy, your midwife can apply warm oil compresses or warm water compresses to your perineum and around your baby's head as it begins to show.

A natural tear easily heals on its own. A surgical incision will often take twice as long to heal, but if your doctor or midwife recommends an episiotomy it may be for the best reasons.

Back pain can be a real problem in labour. Try the following:

- Make a simple back rub by filling a sock with some uncooked rice mixed in with a little massage oil, and knotting the open end. When you need it, ask the midwife to pop the sock in the microwave (most hospitals have them) and then get your partner or anyone else who's with you to rub it over the painful part of your back.

- Take the weight off your spine – kneel on all fours with your bottom in the air and your head on a pillow.

- Pop two tennis balls in an old sock and tie the top to keep them together. Lean against a wall with the gadget against your lower back and you can move around and press against it so that it soothes any discomfort in your lower back.

Many women can't face eating or drinking during labour. Your mouth gets very dry, so take a damp sponge to suck on for when you get dry.

For reassurance and comfort, take a hot-water bottle with you into hospital, to put on your back or front during labour and afterwards on your tummy for afterpains.

Women in labour often get very hot. Delivery rooms are always kept warm because babies can't regulate their body temperature. Ask your partner or someone else with you to have to hand a plant spray or travel-size spray dispenser filled with cool water, and mist your face with it at sweaty moments.

If you have long hair, take a hair band. There's nothing worse when you're hot and sticky than having your hair flop all over your face.

Take a pair of thick woolly socks with you – it's amazing how cold your feet get when the blood supply is busy round the uterus.

Women often feel a burning sensation around the vagina in labour. Try holding a hot or cold pad against the skin to ease the pain.

Ventouse/forceps – there is no failure on your part if your baby needs help to be delivered. Your doctor may 'prep' you for a Caesarean and ask you to sign a consent form before using forceps or ventouse, because if it fails he may need to perform an emergency Caesarean. Make sure that you ask to have everything explained to you – midwives/obstericians are usually very good at keeping you informed, but they may need reminding that this is your baby.

During second stage or transition, you may well feel very sick and actually be sick. Don't panic. You may also experience an overwhelming irritability and an urge to get off the delivery table and go home. Don't!

Let the midwife know if you want the baby delivered on to your stomach.

Home Birth

Make up a fresh bed. Then put a plastic sheet over the top – bought from a DIY shop or garden centre. Put old towels or sheets over the top of that. This protects the bed and once baby arrives the midwife can whip off the plastic sheet while you relax in a warm bath and – hey presto! – there will be a fresh bed.

Have plenty of easily digested snacks to hand: yoghurts, flapjack, dextrose tablets, bananas, honey, crisps, etc.

With bendy straws you can sip sugary drinks without changing your position.

Put a notice on your front door to dissuade unwanted visitors, and turn on the answering machine.

Peroxide takes out amniotic fluid stains, should your waters break on the furniture or carpet.

Have someone on hand (and on call) to take care of other children.

Pack a hospital bag – just in case.

For advice on labour, see page 21.

Water Birth

Birth pools, even used for just part of labour, can be very helpful because they allow ease of movement and a feeling of weightlessness that is very welcome for a woman at full term.

The water should be kept at a fairly constant 36.5–37.5°C, about normal body heat. If it is hotter than this, it is exhausting and may cause the baby's heart to beat too fast; if cooler, it will not give you the benefits of the warmth.

The water should be deep enough for you to be able to move to any position you find comfortable.

You can be monitored in the water, but you may need to raise your bump for the midwife to listen to the heartbeat, unless she has a special waterproof gadget.

Don't get into the water until you are in established labour. If you enter the pool too soon, it can slow things down.

To check for meconium or blood in the water, drop a torch in the pool.

It is better not to wear anything in the pool, because as the water starts to evaporate off a wet T-shirt, you can get very cold.

For a home water birth:

- Put the pool up before labour starts.

- Get a large tarpaulin to go under and all around the pool, in case of splashing.

- You will probably want a cooler temperature during the first stage of labour, and warmer – nearer blood temperature perhaps – for the second stage. The warmer water then acts like a heat pack or compress on your back and tummy, and particularly on your perineum, where it does the same job as the traditional midwife's hot compresses.

- Plan how you will warm the water if necessary. Even if the pool comes with a heater, this will not normally work as quickly as simply tipping in a few buckets of hot water.

- Make sure that your water heater can keep up with the demand for more hot water.

- When it comes to the crunch, you just may not feel like using the pool at all, or you may use it but not find it helpful. Just because you rented it, you don't have to use it.

Multiple Birth

Linda Jones, Tamba, the Twins and Multiple Births Association (www.tamba.org.uk); the Multiple Births Foundation; Jennifer Davis; Adele Degremont; Jack and Evelyn Patterson; Clare Porter

A multiple birth is unlikely to be an intimate, quiet affair. In fact, there may be so many people and so much equipment in the delivery room that you will wonder if there is any room for you. This is even more the case if you have a Caesarean.

Your babies may spend some time in the Special Care Baby Unit (SCBU). Twins have a higher chance than singletons of spending time in this unit. Triplets and other multiples are more than likely to go to the SCBU. If you've had a Caesarean, you'll be glad of the break this gives you.

It is perfectly normal for multiples to be smaller and lighter than singletons. Newborn- and even most early-arrival-sized clothing will swamp your babies, and that's rather upsetting. SCBUs usually keep some tiny clothes in stock, and if your babies are really tiny, you can always buy dolls' clothes. Specialist suppliers are your best bet for clothes that really fit. And you'll find that kind friends will knit tiny items for your babies.

Try to take an active role in caring for your babies in SCBU and don't leave it up to the nurses. Getting the practice at this stage will make you feel more confident when you go home.

Going to the SCBU for feeds and nappy changes may be a long haul but you will feel the benefits of having spent those first few days very close to your babies. In addition, walking is very good exercise to help reduce swelling, and to speed recovery after a Caesarean, although you may want to get all the tubes removed first!

The ratio of nurses to mums is far higher in SCBU, and provided the other babies there are stable, the staff will have time to help you. You are likely to get far more help with breastfeeding in SCBU than on the maternity ward.

STILLBIRTH & NEONATAL DEATH

SANDS (Stillbirth and Neonatal Death Society); Clare Porter

If you've had a previous stillbirth, you may still be asked to keep a kick chart, like any other pregnant woman. This can make you feel very nervy, particularly if it let you down before. Kick charts are not infallible, but they are the best we have. Keep yours religiously and if there is any change in pattern in your baby's movements, get yourself into hospital as soon as possible to be monitored.

If you've had a previous stillbirth, you'll probably be asked to come into the hospital regularly during the final weeks of your pregnancy to have your baby's heart monitored. This is more reassuring than kick charts and means that you will be in regular contact with your carers.

If your baby dies inside you, the hospital will want you to deliver it as soon as possible. This may be the last thing you want, but there are medical reasons for hurrying you.

If your baby has died inside you, when you get ready to go into hospital to deliver it, just phone one reliable person and get them to tell everyone else. It's just too hard to say it over and over again.

You probably won't be able to bear looking at anything you take in with you again – books, nighties – so don't pack your treasures.

If you can stand it, take one last photo of yourself with a big belly. And take the camera with you to the hospital, just as you'd planned if things had gone as you wanted. You'll need those photos later.

You'll probably be tucked away in some quiet part of the hospital – and if you are not, ask to be. And they'll send you home as soon as they can, too.

If your baby lives but is very poorly, you'll spend time in the special care baby unit (SCBU). It's always hot there, so wear a T-shirt under your outdoor clothes. The SCBU is not a restful or relaxing place, although everyone tries very hard. Be prepared for it to be too bright, too noisy (because of machines), as well as hot.

Do as much for your baby as you can. These memories have to last you a lifetime.

If your baby dies or is stillborn, hold him and say goodbye. The nurses won't take him or her away until you're ready.

Ask a midwife to cut a lock of the baby's hair for you to keep. There's so little else to take home.

You can take tablets to prevent your milk coming in. Ask for them before you leave the hospital.

Once you start going out again, there will be people who knew you were pregnant but don't know what happened. Prepare in advance what you're going to say when they ask the inevitable, well-meaning questions. Try something like, 'We had a little girl, but she didn't live.' If you're caught unprepared, it's terribly hard to say anything at all. Don't be ashamed if you break down. People will feel for you and be very sympathetic.

… But some people just won't know what to say, so they'll avoid you for a while. It's their problem, not yours, so just worry about yourself and don't take it personally.

Make sure that you have someone to talk to, who really listens and doesn't tell you how you should be feeling.

Collect all the souvenirs you have of your baby's short life – ultrasound images, hospital tags, sympathy cards, photos, even the death certificate – and keep them somewhere very special.

Give yourself time to recover. You have been pregnant and have had to deliver your baby, so you need time to get over that physically. Both you and your partner will need tremendous emotional support too. It is not something that you suddenly recover from, but a process that you must honour for yourselves and your baby. Let yourselves grieve.

Your partner may react differently from the way you expected him to. His grief will be no less devastating but may manifest itself in a different way. He needs time and support too.

For help and support from people who really know what you are going through, contact SANDS (Stillbirth and Neonatal Death Society): helpline 020 7436 5881, www.uk-sands.org.

AFTER THE BIRTH

Alex Fraser;
Lis Martin;
Jane Alexander,
www.janealexander.org

You are likely to be starving. Be prepared and have some high-energy food ready, such as a chocolate bar or a banana. You'll also be desperate for a cup of tea, so make sure that your partner has plenty of change if you're in hospital.

Try to start breastfeeding as soon as possible after the birth. Most midwives will encourage you with this and be happy to offer help and advice.

Make sure that you eat plenty – it takes on average an extra 500 calories per day to feed a baby. Make sure that you have a supply of high-energy food to tuck into after night feeds. Ask all your visitors to bring something yummy.

After a home birth, take your first bath with your new baby and try breastfeeding him there.

Contrary to popular current myth, not all women can breastfeed and not all babies will do it. Yes, of course, it's worth trying (and trying hard) but you should not feel a failure if you and your baby just can't do it. Too many women beat themselves up and feel guilty when they can't breastfeed.

When your milk starts to come in (about day three), after the colustrum, your boobs are likely to feel rock hard, very tender and enormous. This is scary, because you think they are going to stay that way all the time you are feeding. They certainly don't, but they are subject to fluctuations.

For more on breastfeeding, see page 34.

Think about your child's first day at school when you pick his or her name. On the whole children love to conform and can get teased mercilessly with a weird or unusual name. If you're wedded to the idea of Wayflower or something with too many vowels, keep it as a second name, or get a cat and use it for that.

Ask someone to buy a copy of the local newspaper and a couple of nationals on the day of the baby's birth as an intriguing souvenir.

For introducing your baby to an older sibling, see page 93.

If you've had an episiotomy or tear, you will have some stitches to look after. Here are some ideas for feeling a bit more comfortable:

- Change your maternity pads often.

- Going to the loo can be very painful. Try peeing in a bath of warm water or in the shower. If you need a pooh, press a maternity pad firmly against your stitches as you bear down – and remember to eat more fibre. Use disposable wipes instead of ordinary toilet paper.

- Keep your perineum clean. Have a shower after going to the loo, or use a small jug to trickle warm water between your legs as you sit on the toilet. Pat dry with a soft cloth.

- Have a bath whenever you can. You can add some salt or antiseptic to the bath or, even better, some good-quality lavender oil (you can buy this from most chemists), but plain water is just as good.

- Drying stitches after bathing or washing can be excruciating. A hair dryer on a cool setting is the answer.

- Try holding a bag of finely crushed ice, or a bag of frozen peas or sweetcorn, covered with a soft or lint-free cloth against the painful area.

- Having stitches makes it painful to sit down. Sit down and get up slowly, and sit on something soft. Try sitting on a child's rubber ring – you may feel a little silly but it's a great way to reduce painful pressure on the sore area. Cushion rings can help, although they may also pull on tender stitches. A soft, square, Continental pillow is often more comfortable.

- Try to 'get the air' to the stitches as often as possible – it will help them to heal. Lie in bed without knickers but make sure you do so at a time when you're not expecting visitors!

- Get out of bed and walk around as soon as you feel able. This may be the last thing you feel like doing, but it helps your circulation and reduces swelling.

- Pelvic floor exercises (see page 9) may be too painful at first, but after a while they can help with healing.

- Homeopaths recommend Arnica 30 tablets to reduce bruising and swelling, and for exhaustion. Taking it before you give birth as well as after is said to be even better. Hypericum is ideal for cuts and wounds.

- A pad soaked with witch hazel tucked inside your knickers can be very soothing.

If you've had a Caesarean:

- Try to stand up as soon as possible afterwards, sitting down again immediately. But always listen to your doctor's advice.

- You can wear pyjamas (dark) while you're in hospital because no one is going to want to look lower than your scar.

- After a Caesarean, it's very common to retain water in your feet, lower legs and hands. This looks and feels awful, but after a few days you'll start weeing like nobody's business and you'll return to normal. It might make it difficult to get shoes on when you leave hospital, though.

- You'll be advised not to lift anything heavier than your baby. Follow this advice to the letter, and ask for help with anything that feels uncomfortable.

- See also page 29.

Soon after you've had your baby, a nice doctor will come round and talk to you about contraception. Since sex will be the very last thing on your mind, you'll be tempted not to pay any attention, but unless you want to be listening to him saying the same thing in a year's time, listen up!

2 BIRTH TO SIX MONTHS

'The joys of parents are secret, and so are their griefs and fears.'

Francis Bacon

You're finally at home with your new baby. This is the moment you've been waiting for throughout the past nine months and suddenly you realise that all you've learned at the antenatal classes and most of what you have been told doesn't apply after the birth. So what now?

For many people, this is the instant when they feel grown up. It's hard to imagine life without this small dependant bundle, impossible to comprehend just how much you love him and scary how totally responsible you feel.

Don't panic. Every phase passes, even the most tricky. What worries you now will be a distant memory in six weeks' time. Remember, you're not alone – most new parents will have exactly the same concerns as you. This is a time to get to know your new baby and enjoy the close intimacy of your new family.

NEW MOTHERS

Adèle Degremont; Alison Wallis, dancer and exercise teacher; Amanda Stevens; Anna Knight; Caroline Donley; Clare Porter; Diana Starte; Glynis Fletcher, NCT; Jack and Evelyn Patterson; Jennifer Davis; Kevin Sweeney, hairdresser; Linda Jones, Tamba, the Twins and Multiple Births Association (www.tamba.org.uk); Dr Ruth Marchant; the Multiple Births Foundation

Sleep when you can. If you've been awake half the night and your baby is now sleeping quietly, forget about everything else and rest yourself.

When the baby is asleep or someone is looking after him for you, try to do something that you enjoy – read a magazine, have a warm soak, listen to some music.

Don't go on a strict diet because you will be tired and need all the energy you can get. There isn't a prize for getting back into your jeans within a fortnight.

Everyone will want to come and visit. Be tough about restricting your visits – they are very tiring – and ask your partner or the person caring for you to man the phone/front door and put people off.

Take time out for yourself whenever you have the chance. Don't feel guilty.

It's normal to feel tired and as if you can't cope. Do tell other people, especially your partner, how you feel. Remember that the feelings won't go on for ever.

You don't have to be superwoman. No one can do everything. Relax, work out what's most important to you and concentrate on getting that done.

If you possibly can, get some help in the house, at least for the first few months. Having someone to do your ironing and/or cleaning makes less for you to do, and if you have a cleaner it is wonderful to have your messy house, clean, tidy and organised. Anyone can do the dusting but there's only one Mummy.

If you have no help, relegate housework to the bottom of your priorities. Keep chores to a minimum and don't feel bad about that. Life is too short to iron.

Don't be afraid to ask for help if you need it.

Accept offers of help. New mothers need looking after. In traditional Chinese families, it is customary for the grandmother to stay for six weeks, just to look after the mother.

Don't feel as though you are taking advantage of people offering to help – they wouldn't have offered if they weren't willing. Even someone pushing the baby around in the buggy for half an hour will give you a break – and helping gives immense pleasure to the person who's offered.

Make things as easy for yourself as possible. Many essentials can be delivered – make the most of Internet supermarket shopping, organic vegetable deliveries, the milkman and other local shops and services.

This is a time when you need to eat well. Casseroles cooked in advance and stored in the freezer make easy meals.

Don't answer the phone. Use your answerphone to screen calls and ring back when convenient. If you want to make calls, do so during the baby's naps. Recognise what your answerphone is for and keep it switched on at all times when you really don't want to be interrupted – including during a well-earned rest.

Grab a moment for a shower by taking your baby into the bathroom with you and sitting her in a car seat or bouncy chair. Get clear shower curtains so that she can see you, and you will have a captive audience for your early morning singing sessions.

Order newspapers to be delivered, or if you don't think you have time to read a daily paper, order one of the news round-up magazines, such as *The Week*, to retain the gist of what's going on in the world.

You & Your Body

Unfortunately it is totally normal to feel as if you had just fought several rounds in a boxing ring. Rest as much as you can and keep your feet up.

Stitches are very painful. For ideas to help you feel more comfortable, see page 26.

If You've Had A Caesarean

Don't attempt to lift anything heavier than your baby, and don't forget that you've had a major operation.

It's tempting to hunch over a bit to protect your tender tummy, but try to stand up straight and walk around to speed recovery.

Arnica can help speed healing. Ask an expert on which strength to buy and the dosage.

Bending over can remain tiring for a long time. Ask someone else to bath your baby and help with anything you find tricky.

Wear big pants to avoid them rubbing on your scar.

Don't be tempted to start driving again for six weeks after the Caesarean. There are insurance issues here, as well as health ones. If you drive after major surgery, and before you've been given the all-clear by your doctor, you may not be covered by your insurance.

Once your periods start again you might feel slight cramping and heaviness around the site of the incision.

When you're finally out and about, use a shallow trolley at the supermarket to avoid lifting and bending, and ask for help with packing and loading. Don't fill your bags too full, because you'll have to lift them out of the boot of your car when you get home.

Post-Natal Exercise

Do the exercises suggested by your midwife regularly. They will help you to regain muscle control. But don't be obsessive or overdo them.

Many local authorities or fitness centres run classes specifically for new mothers where you can take baby with you and even include them in the exercises.

There is a wider variety of exercise classes available than ever before. Try different types to see what suits you. Pilates, yoga and swimming are particularly good after giving birth.

Crèches at leisure centres can work, especially if you get your baby used to them when he is still little. You can then get fit and meet other mothers at the same time.

If you do nothing else, remember your pelvic floor exercises (see page 9).

You shouldn't even think about vigorous exercise for at least six weeks after your baby is born and preferably not before your post-natal check-up.

Even if you ran regularly before pregnancy and birth, restart very gently. Ligaments and joints remain soft for some while and it is very easy to injure yourself.

Join together with other new mothers to organise a personal trainer to come to one of your houses. This often works out cheaper than classes at a gym and is more relaxed if you have to break off because your baby needs you.

Take it in turns with friends to look after each other's babies while you exercise.

Pelvic Floor Exercises

Get started on your pelvic floor exercises (see page 9) as soon as you can bear to. You know it makes sense!

- Whatever kind of delivery you've had – even a Caesarean – these exercises are essential.
- If you've had stitches you will be sore, but the exercises will improve your circulation and help your perineum heal.

If pelvic floor exercises don't seem to be making any difference, no matter how hard you try, you can buy pelvic floor toners from good pharmacists. These are basically cone-shaped weights which you insert into the vagina for up to fifteen minutes. The advantage of using them is that it's completely obvious if your pelvic muscles aren't all they should be and any improvement in tone will be equally apparent. Aqua Flex is one recommended brand, but your doctor or nurse will be able to give you advice.

Hair

Hair can change in the weeks immediately after giving birth. Sudden hair loss after birth can seem worrying, but it is quite normal. There can be other changes – new fluffy hair may begin to grow around the hairline, curly hair can straighten and straight hair can begin to wave; blondes often notice that their hair is darker. Luckily, most changes are temporary. A healthy diet helps. Try eating lots of oily fish and fresh vegetables – seaweed is particularly good.

It is not a good idea to have hair permed in the first months after birth. Results are very unpredictable.

If you are worried about the chemicals in hair dyes affecting your breastmilk but desperate to do something about the colour of your hair, find a colourist who uses vegetable dyes or stick to highlights, as the colouring solution shouldn't come into contact with your scalp.

Babies and hair salons don't really mix. You might be lucky and find that your baby sleeps through your appointment but you won't really relax. Team up with a friend and mind each other's babies while you each have your hair cut.

Some stylists will visit you at home. There's no harm in asking and you could make a home visit more worthwhile by gathering together a group of friends who also want hair cuts and making a day of it.

You & Your Partner

Especially with a first baby, partners can feel left out. The arrival of a baby is a big change to your life together. Try to find time for each other.

Share your feelings. Your partner won't automatically know how you are. New fathers can feel very isolated and excluded from the mother–baby relationship.

Share the day-to-day care of your new baby. New dads often feel less competent than mothers when it comes to tasks like nappy changing and bathing baby, which can make them feel less useful and involved. Encourage your partner to help out.

Try to be practical. If your partner is working during the week, let him sleep at night, even if this means using a spare bed during the week. It's pointless having both of you exhausted and if you're breastfeeding there's little he can do to really help. He could get up while you rest on Friday and Saturday nights.

When you first come home, sore and with stitches, the last thing you will feel like is making love, but it's important to reaffirm your own special relationship alongside your new role as parents. Don't ignore each other's physical and emotional needs, and find other ways of showing affection.

It's a good idea to try making love before your six-week post-natal check-up – but only if you feel comfortable enough. Talk to your doctor or midwife.

How partners can help:
- Prop up and rearrange pillows.
- Fetch you drinks and food.
- Talk to you.
- Listen when you're feeling weepy.
- Make sure you have a radio, TV and remote control, and telephone to hand.
- Bring you books and magazines.
- Change nappies.
- Hold the baby while you are getting dressed or bathing.
- Empty waste bins.
- Take away dead flowers and bring you fresh ones.
- Massage aching shoulders and neck.

When You Have More Than One Baby

Get as much rest as you can. Following the advice on page 28 on making life easier for yourself is all the more important when you have more than one baby.

Contact colleges that offer family placements for students on childcare courses. Having multiples will make you of great interest to the trainees.

The only way to make sense of the chaos is to get frighteningly organised. Try to settle on a routine quickly and stick to it. Keep a big board on the wall in the kitchen to keep track of everybody's schedule – food, sleep, dirty nappies.

Try to keep a supply of nappies, wipes and cotton wool upstairs, downstairs and in the car.

Each of your children will be different, so respect this. Make allowances for different temperaments and abilities from the start. If twins are fraternal, there is no reason why they should be any more similar than siblings of different ages.

Recognise that caring for twins or more takes up a lot of energy. If one parent is at home and the other goes out to earn a living, remember that you are both 'working'. Neither parent should be expected to deal with the nights alone.

Save yourself the hassle of getting to the clinic and ask the health visitor to come to you.

Find out about local twins clubs. Check out what Tamba, the Twins and Multiple Births Association can offer. For details, see page 297.

Post-natal Depression

Quite apart from the hormonal turmoil your body is in, you've just undergone an extraordinary, possibly traumatic, certainly life-changing event – and then, to top it all, you're sleep-deprived. Really, it would be strange if you weren't depressed. So accept it as a quite normal response, and don't pretend to be superwoman.

Mostly the 'baby blues' go by the time your baby is about six weeks old. If they haven't and you feel low, down, anxious, tearful, sad, unable to cope or depressed, do seek help. Post-natal depression (PND) is a hugely underestimated problem which affects a vast number of women.

You won't necessarily need medication – some research shows that psychotherapy can be as effective as meds in treating PND. For some people a short course of antidepressants or therapy will turn the world back into a nice place. Others find homeopathy, herbalism or acupuncture helpful.

Many areas have 'meet-a-mum' groups where you can get together with other women in a similar position.

NEWBORNS' HEALTH

Alison Wallis; Alison Tweedale, nanny; Amanda Stevens; Cry-sis; Anna Knight; Clare Porter; Diana Starte; Deborah Woodbridge; Glynis Fletcher, NCT; Liz Chowienczyk; Margaret Cave; Dr Ruth Marchant

If you're worried about your baby, talk to someone – your doctor, midwife, health visitor. That's what the experts are there for. However silly you think you're being, don't worry in silence.

If you think that your baby might be unwell, there are a few basic questions to ask yourself. Is she alert? Does she respond to noise or other stimuli? Is she feeding? Are her reflexes as normal? If you have any doubts, don't delay: go to your GP, baby clinic or hospital at once.

For birthmarks, see page 230.

Always watch out for signs of dehydration:

- It doesn't matter how often a baby wees, but nappies should not stay dry for more than 4–6 hours in the early weeks.

- The fontanelle appearing sunken is also a sign of dehydration. (The fontanelle is the soft area of the skull where the bones haven't yet joined. You may be alarmed to see the pulse beating beneath the skin of the fontanelle, but don't be: that is normal.)

Newborn babies can display various symptoms that, although quite normal, can be worrying for you. These include:

- Vaginal bleeding or discharge, just like a light period. This is quite normal in newborn girls during the first week of life and is caused by oestrogen from the mother passing into the bloodstream just before birth. It will stop quite quickly.

- Swollen breasts, maybe even with a little milk, in boys as well as girls. Again, this is caused by maternal hormones, is quite common and will settle down within a few days of birth.

- Reddish wee. Newborns' urine often contains something called urates, which makes it appear red on the nappy. It looks very like blood and if you have any doubts, always show the nappy to your midwife.

- Babies' first pooh is a greenish/black tar-like substance called meconium. Always tell your midwife if none has passed by the second day.

- Odd-shaped head. This is literally due to the pressure of birth and will correct itself over a period of months.

- Eyes appearing to squint. This often happens with newborns and is probably due to the folds of skin at the edges of the eyes. If you suspect that your baby's eyes really do wander, point this out to your doctor.

- Sticky eye. A yellowish crust and discharge is a common problem, caused by a mild infection. Doctors will prescribe drops or an eyewash solution. You could also try bathing with breast milk as the antibodies contained in it may help.

- Peeling skin. Babies' skin often peels in the first few days, particularly on their hands and feet. This is completely normal and will clear up of its own accord.

- Spots. These are very common in newborn babies as the pores of their skin aren't yet very efficient. Usually these need no treatment and will clear by themselves, even the red ones with yellow centres, which look infected but aren't

---

You will be obsessed by the current problem – and there will usually seem to be at least one. Don't worry. This will pass. Ask for medical advice when you need it and take comfort in the fact that you're not alone.

Keep a list of emergency numbers, including your doctor's out-of-hours service, by the phone.

If there is a night service centre, make sure that you know how to access it.

For general medical information, or to find out more about a condition, www.nhsdirect.nhs.uk is a useful website.

Umbilical Cords

Bathe around the cord stump with cooled, boiled water and dry the area thoroughly with clean cotton wool.

Your midwife will check that it's healing cleanly, but always tell her if it becomes red or there is any discharge.

If you suspect that the stump is becoming infected, see your doctor. She will take a swab and prescribe antibiotics if necessary.

Try to tuck nappies below the cord stump. This helps to make sure that they don't get damp, which encourages infection.

The clips sometimes fall off by themselves. Otherwise leave for your midwife to remove.

An umbilical hernia is a small swelling close to the cord, which becomes more prominent when a baby cries. This is not uncommon and is caused by a weakness in the muscle wall. Most will heal by themselves before the baby is one year old and very few need an operation. It is nothing to worry about, but always check it regularly with your doctor.

BREASTFEEDING

Amanda Stevens; Anna Knight; www.breastfeeding.com; Clare Porter; Deborah Woodbridge; Diana Starte; Glynis Fletcher, NCT; Linda Jones, Tamba, the Twins and Multiple Births Association (www.tamba.org.uk); Liz Chowienczyk; Dr Ruth Marchant; Sydney Morrel Whittle; the Multiple Births Foundation

Nothing is better for your baby than your milk, and nothing else brings you quite as physically close as breastfeeding.

Breastfed babies are less at risk from infections and allergies. Mother's milk supplies everything that young babies need.

There are health benefits for mothers too. Recent research suggests that breastfeeding reduces the risk of breast cancer significantly.

Breastfeeding reinforces the close bond between mother and baby. It's a special time for both of you – relax and enjoy it.

Newborn babies don't need much food to begin with, but the colostrum you produce in the first few days after birth gives your baby vital antibodies to help build up her immune system as well as the right amounts of protein, minerals, sugar and water.

You will begin to produce proper breast milk rather than colostrum after about three or four days and it's very common to feel tearful or down around this time. This is what's meant by the terms 'baby blues' or 'fourth-day blues' and you might also feel slightly feverish as your milk comes in. It's hormonal, completely normal and will pass quickly.

Breastfeed as often as possible in the first few days. This way you know your baby is getting the colostrum that is so important to her and also getting used to feeding while your breasts are still soft, before they fill with milk and become larger and harder.

Are you sitting comfortably? It doesn't matter if you sit or lie to feed but it's important not to lean down over your baby or lift her up to you; if you do, you'll end up with a bad back. Always make sure that you are well supported by pillows and if necessary, lie your baby on top of a pillow on your lap or next to you if you are lying down.

Always bring baby's head up to your breast. This saves breast and nipple damage and helps your posture and back.

Make sure that your baby's head is at a higher level than his tummy while he is feeding. This way there's less chance of air being trapped while he feeds and makes burping easier.

Cradle your baby towards you so that her head is well supported in the crook of your arm.

Some babies are born knowing how to suck. They quickly latch on to your breast and learn to associate sucking with comfort and food. Other babies have to be encouraged to learn.

Make sure that your baby takes the areola as well as the nipple completely into his mouth. If he only takes the nipple, he will close the openings: he will get no milk and you will probably get sore nipples.

If your baby is slow to start feeding, gently stroke her cheek on the side next to your breast. She should turn her head towards your touch and pucker her lips, ready to latch on to your nipple. She has a natural sucking reflex but don't stroke both cheeks or touch her lips first as you will confuse the signals.

Your baby will not be able to suck properly if your breast blocks her nostrils. Try changing position, or gently press the breast down just above your areola to give her breathing space.

It's better to completely empty one side in a feed. It used to be standard practice to feed for a fixed number of minutes on each side. Nowadays, it's generally thought that it's only necessary to offer the other breast if your baby still seems hungry.

There may be health benefits to emptying the breast. The first part of mature milk, foremilk, and the second part, hindmilk, have different nutritional compositions and by emptying one breast completely you are making sure that your baby drinks both. Foremilk is more watery, has a blueish tint and helps to quench your baby's thirst. Hindmilk, is richer with a creamy yellow appearance and satisfies his appetite.

As a reminder of which side you need to begin feeding with next time, tie a ribbon on to your bra strap.

Different babies take different amounts of time to feed. One baby might drain a breast in ten minutes, while another takes twice as long. You will get to know what's right for your baby.

To break your baby's suction and take him off the breast, gently slip your little finger between your areola and his lips. Never try to pull him away – it will hurt your nipple.

Breastfeeding on demand allows your baby to regulate his food intake to match his needs. His sucking also stimulates your breasts to produce milk and the more milk he takes, the more you will make. Supply and demand should be balanced.

It's normal for newborn babies to lose weight immediately after birth. It's not a sign that you're producing insufficient milk. Babies generally regain their birth weight by the time they're ten days old.

Especially in the early days, it can seem as though you are permanently breastfeeding. Make sure that you have everything you might need near by. This could include: something for you to drink and eat, a book, newspaper or magazine, fruit or another snack, the TV remote control, a radio and the telephone.

You can suddenly feel overwhelmingly thirsty while breastfeeding. Make sure that you have a cold drink close at hand before you start.

Try to keep feeds comfortable and quiet. Make sure that your baby can see your face and focus on you. Encourage him by talking gently to him.

Babies like the sound of their mother's voices. If you are alone together, try reading your book or newspaper aloud while you're breastfeeding.

Babies love holding on to your hand or stroking your breast as part of breastfeeding.

If your baby gets distracted and won't feed properly because there is too much going on, breastfeed in a quiet room. You may find that it helps to draw the curtains and dim the lights.

Don't try to force your baby to feed when he is very sleepy. He will wake up when he needs more.

Calm a crying baby first before you try to feed her. She won't be able to suck properly if she is upset.

Try to breastfeed before your baby gets too hungry and upset. Watch out for early hunger signs like finger sucking, yawning and touching his mouth.

It's not only your baby's sucking which prompts your breasts to produce milk. Your body has its own 'let-down' reflex which responds to your baby's sucking, crying or even just the fact that she's there. The hormone oxytocin is released into your bloodstream, triggering the muscles around the milk glands to contract and force milk into the milk ducts. The let-down reflex can make breasts leak when they are full and while your baby is feeding from one breast the other side will often drip milk.

Oxytocin also makes the muscles in your womb contract and in the early days after birth, you may notice the contractions, like mild period pain, while you are breastfeeding.

If you're worried that the let-down reflex is working too well and milk is flowing too fast and choking your baby, regulate the flow by pressing gently on each side of your areola with your middle and forefinger.

To encourage milk flow, gently massage your breast with the flat surface of your fingers.

If you're worried that you're not producing enough milk, try using a breast pump or hand expressing between feeds to stimulate milk flow.

Your ability to produce milk is nothing to do with the size of your breasts. The milk-producing glands are not in the surface tissue.

When breastfeeding a heavy baby, pile up three or four pillows at your side and lay your baby on top to feed.

When a normally settled baby becomes fretful or starts to graze rather than feeding properly, it may be a sign that she is teething (see page 68).

Another cause of fretful feeding is yeast infection – this can affect both your baby's mouth and your nipple. If you suspect this, see your doctor, as you will both need treating.

If your baby has a stomach upset, the best thing you can do for him is to carry on breastfeeding.

Older siblings often want to try breastfeeding again when they see you feeding a new baby. If you can, let them. They won't remember how to suck properly and won't actually get any milk. Don't make a big deal out of it but give them lots of extra cuddles and point out all the yummy food they can eat which the new baby can't have.

If you have problems breastfeeding, even when you've tried everything, don't worry alone. Speak to your doctor or health visitor, or contact an experienced breastfeeding counsellor for one-to-one support. The National Childbirth Trust and La Leche League (for details, see page 292) offer excellent advice and will put you in touch with someone who can help.

Burping & Winding

After feeding, lean your baby gently forward on your lap so that he is sitting upright with his head and chest supported by your hand. This should allow any trapped air to escape naturally without extra patting or help from you.

Rest your baby over your shoulder so that she is upright with her tummy resting against your chest. It's a good idea to spread a muslin over your shoulder first, just in case …

If your baby hasn't burped after a few minutes, she probably doesn't need to.

Most babies bring up some milk when they burp. As it's mixed with saliva, it can look like quite a lot.

Sicky babies may bring up milk more than once after every feed. If your baby's nappies are wet without extra drinks of water and he is gaining weight steadily, don't worry –

he's not losing more milk than he can spare. But always check with your doctor or health visitor if you're in any doubt.

Always see your doctor if your baby projectile vomits. This is very different from hiccuping up a little milk with air, as the milk is ejected with some force.

Mastitis & Engorged Breasts

Mastitis is a common problem and can happen very suddenly. Your breasts feel sore or tender, engorged and lumpy. You may find you have a temperature. If your symptoms are extreme, or you have any doubts at all, always see your doctor or health visitor.

For less severe cases of mastitis and for engorged breasts, you might find some of these suggestions helpful:

- **Cabbage leaves!** Yes, they do work, but make sure it's a white cabbage. Try tucking them inside your bra (see page 38) or better still, lie down with them on your breasts.

- **Combing the lumps gently downwards** with a wide-toothed hair comb while you stand in a hot shower can be very soothing.

- **Try lying on your tummy in a hot bath.** Gravity and the warm water can ease the soreness and you can help by gently pushing downwards on your swollen breasts.

- **Lay warm flannels** over your breasts.

- **Alternately if you find cold more soothing,** place wrapped ice cubes on to your breasts to reduce swelling.

After bathing with warm water, you may find that your breasts leak some of the excess milk naturally. If not, express small amounts of milk to relieve the engorged feeling – but not too much or your breasts will take this as a signal to produce even more milk. To do this, stroke downwards towards the areola evenly all round, then, supporting your breast, press in and up with your thumb on the edge of your areola. Milk should begin to squirt out.

Sore Nipples

To avoid sore nipples:

- Don't use soap. Your nipples produce a natural lubricant and soap washes this away.

- Wash nipples frequently with warm water.

- Air dry nipples after feeds and avoid rubbing dry.

- Waterproof breast pads are effective, but try not to use them all the time as they keep out air and can leave nipples damp and chapped. Use ordinary breast pads or make your own from one-way disposable nappies (or try cabbage leaves – see below).

- Don't let your baby suck directly on the nipple.

- Change your position at the first hint of soreness to relieve pressure on a particular area.

Some nipple creams contain peanut oil, usually listed as arachis oil, potentially harmful for your baby (see page 39), so ask a pharmacist to recommend a cream that is peanut free.

Nipple cream is great for other sore places, too. You can use it on chapped skin or lips because it's so mild.

If your nipples crack they will be extremely painful – you will feel a sharp pain particularly when your baby latches on. See your doctor for treatment at once and ask your midwife for advice.

Sometimes you may be advised to rest the cracked nipple and only feed from the other breast, in which case you will need to express milk from the painful side. It may be possible to carry on feeding, providing you take extra care.

Enzymes in cabbage leaves help heal cracked and sore nipples (and work on stitches, too). Tuck them inside your nursing bra, where they will work as efficient breast pads. You need a really hard white cabbage. Cut down the stem so that the leaf forms the right shape and if you keep the cabbage in the fridge, it is soothingly cool. The leaves will also act as a reminder that a feed is due because they begin to gently steam after about two to three hours.

Other Breastfeeding Problems

Occasionally, one of the milk ducts gets blocked and causes a small, painful lump to develop. Try bathing the breast in hot water and gently massaging it. Breastfeeding may also help. Sometimes the blockage will clear itself; if not, see your doctor. A lump could also be a sign that an abscess is forming.

You'll know if you've developed a breast abscess if you have a painful, throbbing, red area on your breast. Abscesses usually develop because of infection through an untreated crack in a nipple. You can feel feverish and unwell and should always seek immediate treatment.

Sometimes the let-down reflex works too well and your breasts will leak milk whenever they are full or you see another baby who reminds you of your own. This usually settles down, but in the meantime keep a ready supply of breast pads. Avoid waterproof ones, which can make your nipples damp and sore.

Looking After Yourself While Breastfeeding

Breastfeeding can leave you dehydrated and unable to produce enough milk. Aim to drink around 500ml/1pt of water before and during the feed.

What you eat affects your milk. Alcohol should be limited as much as while you were pregnant.

The food you eat flavours your milk. This is especially true of strongly flavoured foods, so if you eat lots of onions, for instance, you'll have onion-flavoured milk. Some research suggests that this helps babies get used to a variety of foods.

Take the time to eat properly. This will boost your milk supply and help you to feel less tired and more able to cope generally.

A sensible balanced diet is obviously healthiest for both of you. There is usually no reason why you can't eat what you like (but see below). You don't have to avoid garlic, spice, chocolate or any of the other things that make eating fun.

If something you regularly eat disagrees with your baby, it is usually obvious. He may be less keen than normal to feed, or have an upset tummy, or eczema may flare up. If you suspect an allergic reaction, talk to your GP.

Spicy food can sometimes make babies very hiccuppy. Try a small amount first and watch for side effects.

Avoid eating oranges or too many citrus fruits, as they can make breast milk acidic. Grapes and raisins can also have a bad effect on babies' tummies.

Eating strawberries can also give your baby a sore tummy.

Don't eat nuts. Scientific research shows that eating nuts while breastfeeding (and during pregnancy) may increase your baby's chances of developing a severe nut allergy later.

What you eat at lunchtime provides the milk for the evening feeds – so eat! Plenty of protein, calcium, carbohydrates, fruit and vegetables – and lots and lots to drink.

To keep up your milk supply, try to rest in the afternoon. That way you should still be producing plenty of milk for the evening feeds, and so have more chance of ensuring a settled night's sleep.

Express any milk left over after breastfeeds early in the day when you tend to have more milk.

For discreet breastfeeding in public, don't wear dresses and avoid wearing anything that opens from the top downwards. Go for tops that you can tuck your baby underneath or shirts that you can unbutton sufficiently for easy access but not so much that everything is on view. Pashminas, scarves and shawls make very useful cover-alls.

Breastfeeding Multiples

It is possible to breastfeed multiples, but it makes tremendous demands on your body. If you are going to try, resolve to eat very well and to get plenty of rest – you'll need it.

Many mothers go for a partial solution, breastfeeding some of the time and topping up with bottles.

Whether you manage to breastfeed multiples is very much up to the babies, and how quickly they feed. If they are snappy and efficient feeders, you can feed and still have a life. Some babies take so long with their feeds that you just couldn't manage, no matter how organised you are.

Midwives are very keen on mothers feeding twins simultaneously. It takes practice to find the right chair and arrangement of pillows for you all to be comfortable.

To have the best chance of feeding two babies successfully (and comfortably) at once, put a V-shaped pillow around your front, lay the babies on the pillow with their heads pointing forwards and their legs tucked under your arms, like a pair of little rugby balls.

If you feed twins separately, you have the opportunity to concentrate entirely on one baby at a time – something you rarely get to do.

For a mother of higher order multiples – good luck! It can be done. The combinations are many and varied. You could feed two at once, and then the third afterwards, but make sure that you change breasts halfway through with your third baby to maintain a balanced milk flow – basically providing one and a half feeds with each breast. Another option is to let someone else feed some of the babies with a bottle, using formula or expressed milk, while you feed the others yourself.

Keep a record of the times, duration and types of feed, and from which side. You're bound to forget otherwise; it's a most confusing business and almost demands a spreadsheet to keep track. You really need to do this to ensure that all the babies are thriving on the regime you have chosen.

Don't imagine that bottle-feeding multiples is an easier option – and don't let anyone imply that. All the mixing, cleaning and sterilising is a monumental amount of work and whilst you can never forget to take your boobs when you go out the same cannot be said for bottles.

Whatever solution you choose, don't imagine that it's all up to you. The babies will have their say and demonstrate their preferences.

With more than one small baby to care for you'll be running around so much that feeding yourself will probably be the last thing on your mind. Be sure to following the advice on eating properly on page 38.

Introducing Bottles To Breastfed Babies

It's useful to get breastfed babies used to taking a bottle so that you are not their only source of food. Fathers can be a big help with this, as babies often reject bottles from their mothers, associating them too closely with breastfeeding.

There is no reason why you can't carry on breastfeeding successfully in the morning and at bedtime even after returning to work. Your milk flow will adjust to your baby's demand.

If you know that you are returning to work before your baby is ready to take solid food, plan ahead and make sure that she is happy to accept a bottle – if not from you then at least from your partner, friend or relation.

Assuming that your baby is well established on the breast, first introduce a bottle at about four weeks, preferably filled with expressed milk. If you leave it any later, it can be tricky and babies are more likely to refuse to take a bottle.

It is best if you are nowhere near by when a bottle is first offered – certainly not in the same room and possibly not even in the house. Babies seem to have an instinct where you're concerned and are unlikely to accept a bottle if they think that breast is on offer.

Avoid making bottle feeding a power struggle. If your baby is very reluctant, leave it for a while, then try again in half an hour.

Don't offer a bottle for the first time when your baby is already very hungry or getting fretful.

Look for early hunger signs – finger sucking, yawning, coughing and hand-to-mouth movements.

Keep rubbing your baby's lip with the bottle. Aim to have the teat at the roof of his mouth and make sure that you have the bottle in far enough.

Try warming or cooling the bottle teat to make it more appealing.

Experiment with different types of teats and bottles. Check the flow from the teat – there should be several drops per second.

You may find that the flow from a bottle is too slow for your baby. Try using a teat with three holes if you think this is a problem.

If bottles don't work for you, try a feeder cup. You can find ones with soft spouts which are ideal for four- or five-month-olds. At least later on when other people are struggling to switch to cups you won't have to.

Expressing Milk

Try expressing at different times of the day. Your supply might be better at one time than another.

Supply often falls towards evening, especially if you've had a busy day or your baby has been particularly hungry.

While your baby is feeding from one side, express from the other. That way, the let-down reflex happens naturally and there is the added advantage that you don't end up feeling lop-sided.

Try expressing after a warm shower. The warmth of the water can help stimulate milk production.

If you are expressing in the early days to establish your milk supply, you really need a big electric pump. These are available to rent from most hospitals, or through the NCT. Hand pumps aren't effective enough for this.

Don't be afraid to ask for special treatment if you need to express milk at work. Ask for a room that can be locked and don't be fobbed off with the ladies' loo – you wouldn't eat your lunch in there, would you?

If you're expressing at work, try sniffing one of your baby's worn vests or something else that has been next to her skin. The smell can help the let-down reflex.

Get extra sets of expressing equipment so that you don't have to spend time washing them at work.

Keep two plastic bags with you for the pump parts – one for the clean parts and one for holding the milk-covered parts before you rinse them.

Try doing something else at the same time as expressing, such as checking your e-mails. You won't feel guilty about the time it's taking, so you'll be more relaxed.

Cutting Down The Number Of Feeds

You need a strong will to cut down on night feeds. When your baby cries in the night, offer reassurance, cuddle him and comfort him but don't offer the breast.

For some people, it works to offer a cup of milk, but others find that this just prolongs night-time feeding because the baby is still waking up expecting a milky drink.

It's up to you to decide what you are happy with and what gives you the best chance of a good night's sleep.

You'll probably find that as babies become more active during the day the number of night-time breastfeeds will go down of their own accord. Your baby should also begin to sleep for longer.

BOTTLE–FEEDING

Alison Wallis;
Sally Walker;
Diana Starte;
Sarah Griffiths

Formula milks are now highly developed to provide your baby with everything she needs. There is no need to feel that by bottle-feeding instead of breastfeeding you are supplying an inferior product.

A bottle-feeding mum can share the task with Dad, allowing him to take a greater part in looking after the baby.

Some bottle-fed babies sleep through the night earlier than their breastfed contemporaries. This may be because many women's supply of breast milk is reduced in the evening, often because of tiredness. Even if you are breastfeeding, topping up with a bottle can be a way to encourage your baby to sleep a bit longer.

All formulas taste different, so experiment to find out which your baby likes best. So don't buy a huge tin until you establish that your baby will drink it.

Use the formula that is right for the age of your baby and discuss the choices with your midwife or health visitor.

Cow's milk is not suitable for babies under twelve months. It has too little sugar, too many minerals and contains the wrong types of protein and fat for human babies.

Newborn babies are very susceptible to germs. Always be scrupulous about washing your hands before making up a bottle and always thoroughly sterilise bottles, teats and any other equipment you use.

Buy a steam steriliser. If you're planning to bottle-feed long term, it's a worthwhile investment that will save you time and effort.

Always use cooled, boiled water and measure ingredients exactly. Never guess at quantities.

Put bottles of formula in the fridge to keep cold as soon as you've made them up. Only warm them when you are about to offer them. For heating in a microwave, see page 43.

Always throw away any milk that's left over from a feed.

Feeding with a bottle is a special time for both of you. At least in the early days, try to follow the same pattern of demand feeding that breastfeeding mothers use. As your baby grows, she will probably settle into a regular pattern of feeds.

It is possible to overfeed a bottle-fed baby. You can tell if he is getting overweight, because his length and weight will no longer match on his growth chart. If you have any doubts, talk to your health visitor.

As with breastfeeding, when bottle-feeding twins or multiples, keep a record of the times and length of feeds for each baby, as otherwise it will be easy to forget.

Make up a day's feeds in one go, especially if you have more than one baby. If you haven't enough bottles, fill those you have and leave the rest of the formula in a jug ready for later. All can be stored in a fridge.

A small fridge upstairs with a bottle warmer makes the night shift far easier.

INTRODUCING SOLIDS

Adèle Degremont;
Alison Wallis; Alison
Tweedale, nanny;
Amanda Stevens;
Anna Knight;
Catherine Wilson,
nanny; Clare Porter;
Diana Starte; Jack and
Evelyn Patterson;
Jennifer Davis;
Linda Elderkin, nanny;
Linda Jones, Tamba,
the Twins and
Multiple Births
Association,
www.tamba.org.uk;
Liz Chowienczyk;
Margaret Cave;
Marianne Bell, nanny;
Sandra Wroe; the
Multiple Births
Foundation

Babies don't need solid food before four months, unless there are specific medical reasons.

Always offer first tastes of solid food on a spoon. Specially designed plastic ones with a wide, shallow bowl are widely available.

Let your baby get used to a spoon before you start on solids. Give her one to chew on and hold, but stay in control of the one loaded with food yourself, unless you enjoy washing baby rice out of her (and your) hair.

Don't be tempted to add solids to a bottle. The idea is to gradually encourage your baby to try different tastes and textures and for him to realise that food doesn't only come from a breast or a bottle.

Baby rice mixed with expressed milk is a good starting point.

Never try to force solids on your baby and start with very small amounts, keeping the quantity of milk high.

Once your baby is getting used to the idea of a spoon, offer a variety of foods and flavours. She may have strong ideas about what she likes and dislikes and it's best to work with these for a while.

If babies are still breastfeeding a great deal, they may be too full to eat other food. Try to watch for your baby's early hunger signs (hand-to-mouth movements, sucking fingers, yawning) and offer a taste of solid food before you breastfeed.

You may need to ask a partner or other carer to offer your baby his first tastes of solid food.

Introduce one new food at a time, just in case your baby reacts badly to it. If so, you'll know what the culprit is and be able to withdraw it straight away.

When your baby is ready to eat, he will. Just give him tiny amounts at first. You don't have to start with rice. Taste it, and you'll see why so many babies spit it out. Try mixing it with puréed pear or apple, or serving the fruit alone.

To reduce the chance of allergies later, avoid dairy- (cow's milk) and wheat-based products for the first year of a child's life.

Avocados, natural sheep or goat's milk yoghurt, and bananas are all excellent weaning foods.

Stewed or puréed fruits are excellent first foods too. Babies can find the taste quite surprising but often really like them. You can make the flavour less strong by mixing with expressed milk.

Most fruit is ideal but avoid strawberries as they can cause allergic reactions. Pippy fruits such as raspberries are also best left until your baby's older.

Parsley contains lots of vitamin C, iron and calcium, and you can hide it in almost any savoury food.

Try introducing a variety of foods and flavours to encourage your baby's tastes to develop. Offer him small spoonfuls of your food, without seasoning.

If your baby loves, say, pear but doesn't like carrot, try mixing the two together; then if she'll eat that, alter the proportions until it's just carrot. Let her try everything and build up a store of what she will eat.

You can't force a baby to eat, so you might as well go with his appetite. The more stressed you get at mealtimes, the more uptight your baby will feel. Babies sometimes have periods of eating very little for no apparent reason. It's not that they hate your cooking, so don't take it personally.

Don't lavish huge amounts of time and effort on making baby meals. It's so demoralising when most of it ends up on the floor. Keep it simple for you and your baby.

Cooking tiny amounts is a waste of time, and if you invest too much effort in preparing your baby's food, you can feel very hurt if he chucks it all on the floor. So buy fresh (preferably organic) food and cook up batches of fruit and veg (vegetables like carrots, potatoes, sweet potatoes and broccoli are good), then whizz in a blender and freeze in ice-cube trays to give you a ready store of varied baby food. Put each batch in a freezer bag labelled with the date and contents and then defrost one or two lumps for a feed.

As your baby's appetite increases, freeze meals in recycled yoghurt pots to keep up with the demand.

Hand-held blenders are a really good investment at this stage. They're easy to use and will purée small amounts of food, quickly.

Start with single foods and combine the cubes to find out what your baby likes best. Then you can blend and freeze them together.

Get a couple of blocks out in the morning for lunch and allow them to thaw naturally, but if you forget, a quick blast in the microwave does the trick.

Avoid using a microwave to warm food. It can leave very hot areas that may burn your baby's mouth. Pour boiling water into a few of the cups in a muffin tin and stand the jars of baby food or bottles into the cups. They should be warm after about five minutes.

However, although all the books tell you not to use a microwave for baby foods, the fact is that everyone does. The trick is to do it in ten- or twenty-second increments, testing the temperature after stirring the food thoroughly. If it's too cool, add another ten seconds; too hot, let it sit or add an ice cube and stir until it's cool enough, then remove the cube. For formula, take the top off the bottle (teat, ring, etc) and use the same general idea as for solids, testing after so many seconds. After a while, you'll know how long to do a full bottle versus a 'short' one. Put the top back on, shake it well, and test it on the inside of your wrist for temperature. If there are any hot spots, shaking the bottle or stirring the food will get rid of them.

If you thaw and reheat frozen baby food in the microwave, add a little cooled, boiled water to stop the food drying out.

Use gravy or stock (unsalted) to mix up with baby food and vegetable purées.

Keep a constant supply of cooled boiled water – you never know when you will need it – to make up drinks, or to mix with food to make it less solid. As soon as the kettle is empty, refill and reboil.

Mix vegetable purées with fromage frais for reluctant eaters, or if you prefer to avoid dairy products, use sheep or goats' milk yoghurts instead.

When you are going out, take puréed baby food with you in a jar. You can ask a restaurant to warm it for you by standing the jar in hot water – most places are happy to oblige.

Or take a food flask with you. Then instead of having to go to a restaurant and feed them you have warm food ready on hand and can feed them anywhere.

Although bananas are a fantastic weaning food they stain light colours surprisingly badly and are best kept away from delicate upholstery.

Once babies start on solids, it's time to stop dressing them in white! As well as banana, carrot and chocolate make stains that are very difficult to wash out!

Puréed carrot stains plastic as well as clothes. Avoid serving it in white bowls or to a baby dressed in white.

White chocolate buttons don't make anywhere near as much mess as milk chocolate.

Avoid bananas if your baby is constipated. They make the problem worse.

Some babies prefer to try feeding themselves from an early age. Let your baby play with her own spoon and once she has worked out what it's for but hasn't quite mastered getting a spoonful of food into her mouth, swap her empty spoon for your full one. For more on children feeding themselves, see page 75.

Now that your baby is eating all kinds of solids, you can get some truly spectacular nappies. You'll need scented nappy bags as never before!

See also Eating Solids, page 75.

High Chairs & Bibs

There will be mess. There's nothing you can do to stop it, but you can 'manage' it so that it is easily cleared afterwards. Spread newspaper – which can be bundled up and thrown away – below your baby's high chair and use a bib to catch spills.

Cloth bibs with Velcro closures are great for keeping clothes clean, but they don't catch fallen food and they soil easily. Plastic pelican bibs with a tray catch fallen food and are easy to clean, but they don't fit well around the neck to catch dribbled milk down a chin. So use one of each type, the cloth one underneath and the pelican on top. Or use a pelican bib worn over a waterproof painting apron with sleeves.

A splat mat on the floor under the high chair makes clearing up much easier.

Choose a high chair that 'comes apart' for easy cleaning. It must have a removable tray, so that you can chuck leftovers straight into the bin and easily wash it in the sink with running water – particularly useful for the remains of finger food, or when you are not using a bowl. It should also have a removable seat or seat cover and easy access to the frame, especially between the seat and frame – it's amazing how much food can collect there. Once in a while, take the whole thing outside and turn the hose on it.

High chairs that can easily be folded and stacked away are a good idea too, because they can take up an awful lot of room in the kitchen and they are useful if you often visit friends and relations. Some convert to a low chair and table later, while the tray on others can be detached to leave you with a 'high' chair for children to sit at a normal height dining table.

If you buy a good booster seat, you can do without a high chair, and go straight from bouncy chair to booster.

Baby slips down in her high chair? Fix non-slip bath stickers to the back and seat.

Make sure that the high chair has a crotch strap to prevent your baby slipping right through, but be careful with shoulder straps. If your baby chokes, it can be hard to get him out quickly.

Feeding More Than One Baby

Very small babies have trouble sitting up in high chairs and tend to loll over to one side. With multiples, you can't hold just one on your knee for first tastes the way you would with a singleton. Bouncy chairs to the rescue.

Line the babies up, or for greater entertainment value sit them facing each other and let them try solid food one at a time. Be prepared for a lot of tears (including yours).

Don't expect the babies to all eat the same amount. They certainly won't.

If you want to avoid a total mess, keep control of the food yourself. Give the babies spoons to wave around, by all means, even bread sticks to chomp, but keep all the food in one bowl and use one spoon to feed the babies in turn.

Don't be too fussy about sharing a spoon between the babies. If one of them has a bug, the others are bound to catch it anyway even if you use separate spoons for each.

Finger foods are great for multiples but keep an eye on them all in case of choking. Cooked pasta shapes, cubes of potato, avocado, banana – all these and more can be placed on their high-chair trays for them to help themselves. Don't bother with plates – a single slip and one baby's food is all over the floor in one go.

Your babies are quite likely to develop different tastes but just dish up the same to all of them – they'll get used to it. And whatever you're serving is bound to be the favourite of one of them some of the time.

WASHING & GENERAL CARE

Alison Wallis;
Alison Tweedale,
nanny; Amanda
Stevens; Anna Knight;
Catherine Wilson,
nanny; Clare Porter;
Deborah Woodbridge;
Diana Starte; Glynis
Fletcher, NCT; Linda
Elderkin, nanny; Liz
Chowienczyk; Margaret
Cave; Marianne Bell,
nanny; Sarah Brown,
nursery school teacher;
Tracy Martin

Always use cooled, boiled water to wash your newborn's face and eyes. Use a fresh cotton wool pad for each eye and wipe from the inner corner outwards. This helps to avoid infection.

Cotton wool – pure cotton or viscose mix? Viscose is cheaper but it sometimes contains little sharp pieces and can leave behind strands that stick to the baby's skin.

Stockpile nappies and cotton wool. Look out for offers and go for them. In the earliest weeks you can get through fifty nappies per week, per baby.

Buy a large pack of muslins. They may seem expensive but you can use them as bibs, for babies to lie on, to mop up spills and to protect your own clothes.

Even when it's cold, choose several light layers of clothes and cover your baby with a shawl and light cotton blankets.

The best way to check whether your baby is too hot or cold is by feeling the back of his neck.

Babies aren't very good at conserving their heat and while research has linked over-heating with cot death, it's not good for them to get too cold either.

Tiny babies get cold easily. They need hats when you go out – for warmth when it's cold and to protect them from the sun when it's hot.

Choose light, loose clothes when it's hot to allow sweat to evaporate and cool your baby.

Calm babies with gentle music and soothing talk.

Babies love being massaged. Gently stroke tiny fingers and toes, arms and legs – you can use pure gentle oils like almond oil if you wish. Encourage fathers to take part. Massage reinforces bonding and helps babies' own body awareness. Choose somewhere quiet. An ideal time is after a bath or before a nap, never straight after a meal.

The use of gentle aromatherapy oils can be helpful, such as camomile and lavender in a baby's room. Never use oils directly on skin or more than two or three drops at a time mixed with a bland oil such as almond.

Cranial osteopathy or a general check-up with an osteopath or chiropractor specialising in babies is a good idea, especially if your baby is unsettled or whinges for no apparent reason. Birth is physically demanding for babies too and sometimes an expert massage is just what's needed.

It is not uncommon for babies to hate having their fingernails cut. If this is a problem, simply do it while your baby's asleep.

Many babies have very little hair for months but others need a haircut fairly early on. It's easiest to do this yourself, using a sharp pair of scissors, preferably while baby is sleeping and not likely to move his head.

Choose washing powder especially formulated for sensitive baby skin.

Be careful about using fabric softeners. They may irritate delicate, newborn skin.

Bathing

In the early days, it's often easiest to bath babies in a wash basin or sink. It's much less strain on your back, too.

Pack a bath bag with all the things you'll need for the baby and for yourself, including your mobile phone, so that you never have to leave the room.

Always put cold water in the bath first, then top up with hot until you reach the right temperature.

Remember that the hot tap stays hot even after the water is turned off. Cool it down by holding a flannel dipped in cold water over it before you put your baby in the water.

A floating bath thermometer is far more reliable than your elbow.

Use very gentle baby bath when bathing your baby if you prefer, but plain water is usually quite sufficient.

Most baby bath and skin products are packed with strong chemicals – even the ones labelled 'dermatologically tested' and 'paediatrician approved'. Babies don't really need tons of cream and stuff – and certainly no talcum powder. If they get sore, calendula cream works wonders. Otherwise, keep them the way nature intended. What smells nicer than a clean baby?

Terrified of washing a wriggly, slippery baby? Get in there with her. She will feel so safe if she can cuddle up to you in the water. This is fun for baby and means that you have a chance to relax and wallow, too. Add a few drops of tangerine oil to the water and enjoy.

Drape a towel over a bouncy seat or car seat and place it on the floor next to the bath and after bathing, you can lay your baby on the towel then bundle him up in it. That way you can stay in the bath, wash and shampoo your hair while he is safe, warm and happy next to you.

Cradle cap a problem? See page 79.

A bath makes a great winding-down routine before bed. For some reason, babies always seem more tired after a bath.

If your baby hates being bathed, don't force the issue. It will unsettle him and upset you. Topping and tailing is quite sufficient until he is happy in the water.

NAPPIES

Alison Wallis; Anna Knight; Clare Porter; Diana Starte; Margaret Cave; National Association of Nappy Services (NANS); www.changeanappy.co.uk; the Real Nappy Association, www.realnappy.com

Changing nappies will be part of your everyday life for a long while. Make sure that you have a well-stocked, convenient changing station at the right height for you.

Set up a permanent changing area equipped with everything you need – waterproof changing mat, cotton wool, wipes and cream, nappies, nappy sacks if you use them and a flip-top bin. You might want to keep a changing bag with wipes, nappies and a roll-out mat to hand, but it's useful to have a particular place to go. Your baby will also get used to this routine.

Some people like to set up this area in their baby's bedroom but a bathroom is often more useful since you automatically have running water and everything you need to wash and change your baby to hand.

Wait until after feeding to change nappies. Babies invariably fill clean ones during their feed.

Boys often wee as soon as you take their nappies off to change them. Be prepared! It might help to have a plastic pot close at hand to catch it in, or a cloth to mop up afterwards.

Changing boys' nappies? Remember to point willies down or you'll find the wee just goes straight over the top of the clean nappy.

In the middle of the night, when your baby is sleepily content after her feed, assess just how necessary a nappy change really is. Otherwise, you may just end up with a clean but wide-awake baby who has no intention of going quietly back to sleep.

As your baby grows and becomes more mobile, it's useful to have a toy or something to distract her to hand while you concentrate on nappy changing. Positioning the changing mat in front of a mirror can work well – she'll enjoy watching herself and what's going on.

Using terries? Keep a cake of soap next to your changing table to use as a nappy-pin cushion. The soap acts as a lubricant and allows the nappy pins to slide easily through layers of cloth.

Sweeten your nappy pail by squeezing a few drops of essential oil on to a cotton wool ball and taping it under the lid.

When you get a container of wipes, cut them in half so that they last longer.

Other uses for baby wipes include: to clean nubuck shoes, toys, laminated books, telephones and car dashboards; to remove washable crayon marks from walls; to remove the smell of diesel or oil from your hands after checking car levels.

If you are out of nappy cream, try nipple cream. It works just as well – sometimes even better.

If you suddenly run out of nappy sacks, use any small bag and sprinkle talc or aromatherapy oil inside.

Use your scented nappy bags in the car for holding smelly trainers and picnic leftovers.

Which To Choose – Disposables Or Cloth?

There is now a greater choice than ever before in both disposable and cloth nappies. You may already have very definite ideas about which type you want to use. If not, here are some facts to help you. It's a good idea to find a system that works for you. There's nothing to stop you trying out several different types.

Disposable nappies:

- These are divided into age groups and designed specifically for boys and girls to ensure an optimum fit.

- Unisex newborn nappies are also available – though don't buy too many of this first size as new babies can grow fast.

- Try out different brands, including supermarket own-brand, to see which fit and suit your baby best.

- Most now have adjustable waists and elasticated legs. They fasten with tapes and there is no messing about with pins or other fastenings.

- You do not need waterproof pants as well as disposable nappies – most will have a one-way lining on the surface to keep your baby's bottom dry, although the nappy is wet.

- Disposable nappies can be quite thin, as a layer of granules absorbs any moisture.

- Disposable means just that – throwaway. You don't have to soak, store or clean them, though it's a good idea to put soiled ones in a nappy sack or plastic bag before putting them out with the rubbish.

- When you've found a brand that suits your baby, look out for bulk delivery schemes to your door – disposable nappy packs are awkward to carry home.

Cloth nappies:

- Cloth nappies are better for the environment – disposable nappies account for 4 per cent of household waste.

- You don't necessarily have to use pins or even fold nappies any more. Modern cotton nappies come in several different shapes and sizes as well as the traditional terry towel. There are shaped, fitted nappies with elasticated waists and legs, and Velcro or popper fastenings to ensure a good fit. All-in-ones also have a built-in waterproof barrier, while flat nappies include wraparound shapes in knitted cotton with ties. Pre-folds have rectangles of several layers of fabric.

- Traditional terry nappies can be folded and pinned, or folded into a pad held in place by a waterproof wrap or pants. Biodegradable, flushable paper liners make washing dirty nappies easier.

- When washing cloth nappies, always check with the supplier for specific instructions as some sterilising powders are not suitable for Velcro fastenings, for instance. It's worth buying specialist nappy products as soiled nappies need thorough cleaning and disinfecting.

- Avoid using fabric softeners for cloth nappies as they reduce absorbency.

- You will need to use waterproof pants with some cloth nappies. They are now made from breathable fabric or wool and may be pulled on, popped, Velcroed or tied.

- Choosing cloth nappies does not have to commit you to hours of soaking and washing piles of dirty nappies. Contact a local nappy service that will deliver freshly laundered nappies to your door and take away the soiled ones, which you store in specially designed bins.

- There are masses of companies offering this service. Check out the National Association of Nappy Services (NANS), tel. 0121 693 4949, www.changeanappy.co.uk, or the Real Nappy Association, www.realnappy.com, for more information and details of firms in your area.

- You don't have to commit to a particular service straight away. Trial packs are usually available.

If you have twins or multiples, think carefully before you opt for cloth nappies. You may have intended to use a nappy service, but do you really want to store upwards of 100 soiled cloth nappies a week waiting for the nappy service to come and collect? Never mind saving the earth, save yourself!

Some parents find disposable nappies more convenient during the day but use cloth nappies at night. These can be more efficient with a booster pad or liner as babies grow and produce more wee.

Nappy Rash

Nappy rash is a very common problem. Damp skin gets sore or chapped and the effects of nappies rubbing and lack of air make everything worse. In its mildest form, nappy rash can mean slightly red skin, but if there are sores or yellow spots you should always see your doctor. Here are some suggestions that have worked for other parents:

- Change nappies as soon as they become damp or soiled.

- Leave nappies off for as long as possible between changes. If it's a warm day, let your baby kick her legs outside, lying on a soft towel. She will enjoy the freedom.

- If you are inside and worried about spills, lie your baby on a clean, unfastened nappy. Again he will like the airy sensation and freedom to move.

- Place a clean terry nappy on the change mat so that your baby won't feel the cold plastic cover, and to mop up any unexpected showers.

- Make sure that cloth nappies are really well rinsed so that no trace of detergent remains to irritate sensitive skin.

- If skin tends to become sore, don't irritate it by using wipes or any type of soap. Stick to cotton wool and water.

- When even water stings, try using a gentle oil-based cleanser especially formulated for babies.

- Gently pat skin dry before putting on another nappy.

- Every time you change a nappy, smooth on a liberal layer of barrier cream – silicone-based ones work well, as do Vaseline, zinc and castor oil and Metanium. Try different types to work out which works best for your baby.

- Barrier creams are most effective as a preventative measure. If nappy rash has developed and skin is already sore, cream can sometimes make the problem worse by not allowing air to the skin.

- Another good nappy rash treatment is Hypercal homeopathic cream. It's gentle and non-invasive, and safe on newborns. It is also healing and soothing – a combination of hypericum and calendula without all the other additives.

- Some babies suffer skin irritation from baby wipes. If your baby has recurring nappy rash, try using plain water with a flannel, kitchen roll or tissues instead.

CRYING

Anna Knight;
Cry-sis; John Knight;
Diana Starte; Dr Ruth
Marchant; Sarah
Brown, nursery teacher;
Kate Crocker, GP;
Caroline Donley, health
visitor; Glynis Fletcher,
NCT counsellor; Jane
Alexander, writer,
www.smudging.com

Babies cry. They just do, and sometimes there is nothing at all you can do about it!

Check for the obvious first. Crying is a baby's way of communicating and there is usually a specific reason why he's crying. Here is a checklist of the most common causes to work through when your baby is crying and you are trying to find something to do to help:

- He is crying because he's hungry.
- He may be uncomfortable or have a tummy ache.
- He needs changing.
- He is too hot or too cold.
- He needs the physical comfort of being picked up and cuddled.
- It's all suddenly too much – too many people, too much play, too noisy, too light …
- Babies often cry from shock rather than pain if their bath water is too cold or hot, or when they bump themselves.
- Sudden bangs can set them off.
- Though the hoover delights some babies, others are frightened by the sound.
- With older babies, check for teething, clothes pinching or rubbing, or favourite toy out of reach.

Try rocking and swaying with your baby. The motion often calms even the most distressed child. You need to aim at around sixty rocks per minute, which is surprisingly fast.

Hold your baby close against your shoulder, then dance, rock, walk up and down stairs. If he doesn't stop yelling, at least you'll get fit.

Walking with your baby automatically rocks him at the optimum rate for soothing.

Rhythmical sounds help. The noise of a washing machine or car engine can work like magic.

Recordings of a mother's heartbeat or whale sounds can calm a crying baby as well as lulling him to sleep.

Sucking can help. If your baby's well fed, try helping her to find her fingers or thumb. Or try letting your baby suck on your little finger. Nice short nail, please, and fingernail underneath so that it doesn't scratch the roof of her mouth. If she sucks hard, she might be hungry or thirsty. If she bites, it may be teething problems.

Try swaddling her. Some babies cry because they want physical comfort. If you've held and rocked her for what seems like hours, wrap her securely in a soft shawl or cellular blanket.

Lay your baby face down across your lap and rhythmically pat his back.

If being undressed makes your baby cry, try laying a towel or muslin over her tummy.

Going for a drive is a sure way to calm many crying babies – but only use it as a last resort. If your baby gets used to it, and won't settle for anything simpler (see below), your mileage could go up considerably.

White noise works for some babies, so leave the radio on but tuned so that all you hear is static.

For distraction purposes, try turning on the hoover. Or to avoid having to run the hoover constantly, make a tape recording of the hoover and play that instead.

If you have one of those big rubber exercise balls, lay a towel on it and then lay the baby tummy down on the towel and, holding the ball and baby securely, rock it back and forward. This can work particularly well for babies with sore tummies.

Sing a familiar song, quite loudly at first, and gradually decrease the volume. With any luck, baby will quieten down too so that she can hear you.

Some babies get anxious and grumpy at around 6.00 p.m., just when you're running out of steam. In good weather, get him into his jim-jams and take him for a walk in his buggy. He may be distracted out of his bad temper and may even fall asleep.

Watching the washing machine go round and round from the comfort of a car seat or bouncy chair can calm some babies down.

Try classical music, but you're probably safer with a pre-recorded tape of soothing pieces rather than the radio. Imagine the 1812 Overture!

Read to your baby. It doesn't matter what – even the financial pages of the newspaper. What matters is your tone of voice – soft and calm.

The more tense you are, the less relaxed and easy to comfort your baby will become.

If you have someone else with you, take it in turns to try to pacify the baby while the other one gets away for half an hour. Taking a warm shower is incredibly soothing, and the sound of the water blocks out the yelling.

Parents, especially mothers, are programmed to feel upset by the sound of their baby's crying and to want to respond to it.

With twins or more it can seem as if there is no break. Don't let the crying get to you: take time out if you need to. When you go back to the babies after a few moments, they may have stopped or cried themselves to sleep. If things get really bad, contact Tamba's Twinline on 01732 868000.

Colic

Just when you think your month-old baby is settling and crying less generally, he begins to cry more distressingly in the late afternoon and evening for anything between half an hour and three or four hours. He pulls his legs up when he cries, is hard to comfort and does this practically every day. Sadly, there is no magic cure for colic. Some of the following tips might help:

- Rock the baby in a pram, inside or outside the house. The old-fashioned prams with bouncy suspension work particularly well.

- Lay your baby tummy down, across your lap and gently jiggle your knees up and down.

- Hold your baby face downwards across your arm with the heel of your hand gently pressing into his tummy. Fathers are good at this because their hands are generally bigger.

Ask your children's health visitor or doctor for advice and talk to other mothers. It's helpful to know that you're not alone.

Colic isn't your fault. No one knows exactly what causes it, but you are certainly not to blame.

Remember that however awful it seems (and colic is bad at the time) it doesn't harm your baby and it won't last for ever – after three months at the longest your baby will have grown out of it.

Dummies & Thumbs

Some babies are soothed by sucking and find it hard to distinguish their need to suck for comfort from their need to feed. You can try to encourage your baby to suck her thumb, although small babies have difficulty finding their own hands. Some people find that if they've tried everything but their baby is still unhappy, a dummy makes a huge difference.

Some advantages to offering your baby a dummy are:

- If your baby accepts a dummy it can act as an instant comforter if she is miserable or upset.

- A dummy will help soothe a wakeful baby to sleep and help her to go back to sleep if she is disturbed.

Disadvantages of dummies include:

- It can be hard to encourage children to give up their dummy once they are used to it.

- Losing her dummy in the middle of the night may wake your baby and if she can't find it she will cry.

- It can be hard to keep dummies really clean.

- Parents can come to rely on the dummy as a pacifier and may not find out what is really troubling their babies.

- When babies are constantly sucking a dummy, it can stop them exploring other toys and their own hands with their mouths, which may hinder coordination and development.

- When older children carry on sucking a dummy during the day, it can make talking and mixing with others harder.

If a dummy seems to be the only option, try limiting it to evenings or bedtime rather than offering it during the day.

You could also try it for a few months until your baby seems more settled.

There's no doubt that complete strangers seem to feel they that have a right to comment or criticise the fact that your child is sucking a dummy. Be prepared for this reaction, but don't feel that you have to justify or excuse yourself. If it works for you and your baby that's good enough.

If your baby can't function without a dummy, attach it to the car seat with a length of webbing. That way, you can just reach round in the car without having to turn round, and pop it back into his mouth, and it never falls on the floor and gets dirty.

Once you decide to stop your baby using a dummy, remove it and never let her see it again. She may be distressed at first but will soon get used to the absence.

SLEEPING

Adèle Degremont;
Amanda Stevens;
Anna Knight; Clare
Porter; Cry–sis; Glynis
Fletcher, NCT; Jennifer
Davis; Linda Jones,
Tamba, the Twins and
Multiple Births
Association,
www.tamba.org.uk; Dr
Ruth Marchant; the
Multiple Births
Foundation

Playing tapes of womb noises and whale sounds can be very soothing for newborn babies and may help them to sleep.

Babies love motion. Try rocking a restless baby in his pram or crib.

If you are desperate, a pram ride, the bumpier the better, sometimes works and even a short car journey can act like magic.

Musical mobiles hung near a baby's cot can be a useful part of the bedtime routine. Your baby may soon associate the tune with going to sleep.

Gently stroke the bridge of your baby's nose between his eyebrows and eyes. Some babies find this very soothing.

Talk or sing softly to your baby when she's snuggled in her cot. Keep the palm of your hand gently resting on her tummy so that she can feel that you're near.

When you think your baby's sleepy, lay him in his pram or cot. It will help him associate sleep with these places and should help get him to sleep at night.

To reduce the risk of cot death, always lay your baby on his back to sleep. Following extensive research, doctors and government medical advisers strongly recommend this practice. Once babies can turn over by themselves, you obviously can't ensure that they stay this way all night, but it's still a good idea to at least start them off lying on their back.

If your baby wakes frequently in the early evening, try singing or talking gently without picking him up out of the cot. He may settle where he is, and this avoids the problem of putting him back on to a cold sheet.

Some babies take time to get used to a cot. If your baby sleeps well in her car seat, try putting that inside the cot to begin with. Once she sleeps soundly there you can try removing the car seat.

If your baby can touch both ends of his Moses basket, it's definitely time to move him into a cot. You can try placing the Moses basket inside the cot at first, just until he is used to his new bed.

After you put the light out and lay your baby down in her cot, don't leave the room immediately. Spend a little time quietly folding clothes or tidying up, but without speaking, to make the transition easier.

White noise, such as the sound of a fan or vacuum cleaner, works wonders for sending babies off to sleep. Instead of running the appliances themselves, make a cassette and play it at bedtime.

If your baby needs a dummy to get off to sleep, make sure that he has several in his cot. If he wakes up and can easily find one, he may – just may – get himself back off to sleep. Make sure that you have a box of clean ones at the ready so that you can just grab a new one, rather than have to rummage through the cot covers to find the one that dropped out.

Don't try to take your baby straight from having a stimulating time in a brightly lit room with lots of people to her cot.

Don't be too interesting at night. Late night and early hours nappy changes and feeds should be quiet, with low lighting and minimal conversation.

Instead of tossing out your old lava lamp, try recycling it into your baby's room to serve as a night light. The gentle movement of the oil is very soothing, but make sure it is safely out of reach.

Try changing the nappy before you feed, so that you won't have to disturb your drowsy baby afterwards.

Don't tiptoe around because your baby's asleep. However desperate you are that she shouldn't be disturbed, it's much easier for everyone if she gets used to sleeping through normal household noise.

Sleepless nights when your baby is poorly or teething are inevitable, and you have to make allowances.

Pick up your baby as soon as he wakes and begins to cry. If he knows that he can have your attention when he needs it, he will be happier to be left in his cot to sleep.

If you lift your baby to comfort her or feed her, she may not like being put back on to a cold sheet. If she sleeps with a muslin nappy under her head, you can tuck it up your jumper at the back while you feed her so it stays warm, then replace it in the cot before you lay her back down.

Babies can take a long time to distinguish between night and day. To encourage your baby to sleep most soundly at night:

- Try to make a distinction between going to bed for the night and daytime naps.
- Bath or 'top and tail' her before bed.
- Change her clothes into night clothes.
- Make the evening feed extra calm and relaxed – it might help to give the final feed in a softly lit bedroom.
- Make extra sure that she is comfy. Some babies like to be wrapped securely.
- Make sure that the room is warm enough and she is properly covered, though not too hot.
- Draw the curtains so that the room is darker.
- Keep any night-time feeds as quiet and brief as possible. Try to manage without turning on the main light.
- Only change nappies at night when absolutely necessary.
- Generally avoid anything that will wake her fully or make her think it's fun time.

Sleeping – Multiples

Put your babies to sleep at the same time, during the day as well as at night. And keep a daytime nap going for as long as you can. You need that break during the day.

Put your babies to bed drowsy but not asleep. Help them to learn to fall asleep on their own by letting them drift off once they're in bed, rather than just before you put them down to sleep. (Either that or learn to juggle!)

Let your babies sleep in the same cot so that they can gain comfort from each other's presence. You will need to separate them before they start teething, or else they might bite their sibling, but when you split them up, make sure that they can still see and hear one other.

Attend to your calm baby first. This may go against your instinct, and you'll have to put up with the other's wailing, but if you don't do this, the quiet one will miss out on your attention, possibly falling asleep before she has even had her cuddle.

Most twins and multiples don't seem to be bothered by their sibling's crying, even when they're in the same crib.

Your babies may not sleep through the night as early as their singleton contemporaries but sleeping through often seems to relate to birthweight rather than age.

Cut down on the number of times you are woken at night for feeds by waking the other babies up to feed as soon as you have dealt with the first to wake.

Sleeping Yourself

Alongside helping your baby to sleep, you also need to ensure that you have sufficient sleep and rest. There is no simple answer to sleep problems and what works for one person doesn't work for another. The trick is to find out what's best for you. Here are some suggestions:

- Let your baby sleep in your bed. The comfort of having you nearby may mean that he wakes fewer times in the night. Sleeping with your baby also means that when he wakes wanting to feed it will disturb you far less. The drawback is that at some point you will want him to stay in his own bed and he may be reluctant to do so. But for a few months it can make a huge improvement to the amount of rest you get, and all habits can be broken.

- Alternatively, go to your baby as soon as he cries, feed him as briefly as possible and settle him down again.

- If his night-time snufflings disturb your sleep, move him out of your room into his own as soon as possible.

- If you're bottle-feeding, make sure that the bottles are ready made in the fridge with a thermos of hot water to warm them.

- Try to sleep as soon as your baby is asleep.

- Wake your baby to feed him when you're about to go to bed rather than waiting for him to wake you.

- Catnap when you can during the day. If your baby's kept you awake for most of the night, sleep when he does the next day.

DEVELOPMENT

Alison Wallis;
Judy Cooper,
nursery teacher;
Margaret Cave;

There are masses of books written on babies' development outlining what they are likely to do and when. Remember that these are only guides and don't be too concerned that your friend's baby is already on the next stage. It's not a sign of intelligence. Always talk to your health visitor or doctor if you're worried.

Sarah Brown,
nursery teacher;
www.signtome.com

Don't assume that because your baby can't roll over one day he won't be able to do so the next.

It's amazing how much ground babies who can't yet roll over or crawl can cover. Don't take chances leaving them unsupervised on a sofa, bed or anywhere they could fall off.

At about four or five months your baby will enjoy trying to sit up. Help her by holding her hands and letting her pull herself forward using your support.

When your baby is beginning to sit up by himself, make sure that you have plenty of cushions around him as a soft landing place. You can also buy special ring cushions to help him.

Encourage your baby's body awareness and coordination by gently bringing her right arm to meet her left leg across her body and the same with the other side.

Stick names on everything while your children are still babies. This can encourage early word recognition.

Play games with your baby. Playing peepo with you hiding behind a blanket or covering your face with your hands usually raises a chuckle and try body rhymes which involve you naming and touching his features or parts of his body. When he's older he'll happily join in.

Sign up for baby swimming lessons as soon as your baby is old enough. (Midwives and doctors usually suggest waiting until after the first set of vaccinations are complete.) The earlier babies become used to the water the better and as you will be in the pool with your baby, it's good for you too. It's also another way to meet mothers with babies at the same stage as yours.

Signing With Your Baby

An easy form of sign language can be an excellent way to communicate with your baby.

Keep it simple. You don't need to learn many signs – start with signs for specific things like drink, cup, bottle, bed, tired, pain and the people in your immediate circle.

You don't have to follow any particular method, but there is a baby sign system, which is based on sign language, though not as sophisticated. This was developed by Joseph Garcia in the US and there are several books on the subject. You can find out more on www.signtome.com.

Signing helps to bridge the communication barrier and is a useful tool for parents to communicate. It also gives children an outlet to express their feelings, wants and desires.

Babies who use signs are usually less frustrated and have fewer tantrums. They can tell you what they need and be understood before they have developed verbal speech.

Far from limiting language development baby sign has been shown to help the development of spoken language.

Baby sign can help to avoid tantrums as it allows babies to communicate their needs before they are capable of verbally forming words.

All babies begin to learn through movement, touch and experience and baby sign builds on this.

Many babies who have grown up with baby sign continue to use signs as well as words initially.

If you start early enough, parents can have proper conversations with children as young as ten months. Children begin by using signs for single words but they can string thoughts together and tell you things like: 'I'm tired. I need a bottle.'

Keep a sheet showing the signs used for members of the family and for different things. That way the whole family, including older siblings, can join in.

TOYS

Alison Wallis;
Amanda Stevens;
Liz Chowienczyk;
Sarah Brown,
nursery teacher,
Just Twos nursery

Avoid offering only plastic toys and try to find ones with different surfaces and textures, including wood and material.

Look out for soft animals or toys that squeak, crunch and rattle.

Put soft toys in the freezer once a month, for at least six hours, to kill dust mites, which cause allergies. Once you take a toy out of the freezer, vacuum it to remove mite faeces.

Activity quilts are a good choice. They often have squares of different-textured material, mirrors, bells and shakers. As your baby grows, he will discover new areas and uses for it.

Activity quilts or blankets are also useful when you're staying away from home. Bundle little rattles, shakers and teethers in the quilt and spread it out ready for play when you arrive.

Even a young baby responds to activity frames. As he begins to move more, he will enjoy trying to touch the toys, and you can customise and ring the changes by adding your own toys or mobiles.

Mobiles, especially musical ones, hold even a young baby's gaze. Attach to the cot or fasten to a shelf out of reach but in her line of vision.

Choose toys that can be easily held and manipulated by tiny hands.

Babies love putting things in their mouths – they're not fussy what. Keep older children's toys, especially those with small parts, well out of reach.

Have a variety of teethers, including ones you can cool in the fridge. Remember to sterilise them occasionally.

Babies find the sight of their own face fascinating. Position your baby's bouncy chair or car seat in front of a mirror to keep him amused.

CLOTHES & EQUIPMENT

Avoid Babygros that button at the back. Always go for ease of access – poppers around the legs make nappy changing much easier.

Vests with envelope necks are far easier to pull on than ones with round necks, which can be a real struggle to tug over baby's head.

Bodysuit vests with popper fastenings stay put and are far more comfy than ones that finish at the waist.

Hand knits look lovely, but check inside for loops of wool that your baby could catch her fingers in when you dress her.

When putting tops or trousers on your baby, always put your hand up through the sleeve or trouser leg from the open end, wrap your fingers around his hand or foot and guide it through the opening.

Cut the feet off Babygros that are getting too short to get a few weeks' extra wear from them.

When asked what clothes you need for your new baby, always ask for the next size up. When your baby is newborn, ask for three–six-month size. Babies grow so quickly that first-size clothes are soon too small.

When you buy tops and sweaters, make sure that the neck stretches enough to make them comfortable to put on and take off. If it's too tight your baby will hate it – and so will you. Jumpers with buttons or poppers on the shoulder seam are the best for tinies.

Try to buy unisex clothes as far as possible, and stick to neutral colours like green, yellow and orange so you can hand them on to younger brothers or sisters, or friends' children.

If you are buying cheaper brands, buy a size larger than you would normally go for. Your baby will still grow out of them before she wears them out.

When you go up a size in all-in-ones, your baby might feel uncomfortable because the legs are probably a bit too long and she can get tangled up. Position her feet in the feet of the outfit, and slip a pair of socks on top to stop her feet slipping out.

Save the hangers you get when buying new underwear for yourself. They're an ideal size for baby and toddler clothes.

Dress babies in any colour but white once they are weaned or on solids, unless you don't mind food stains or want to keep on changing them.

For twins or multiple mixed-gender babies, don't bother trying to dress them in pink and blue appropriately – you're bound to get the clothes mixed up. Go for neutral white, yellow, green or red – and buy multi-packs.

Carry a soft blanket or lamb's fleece snuggly with you. You can use it to line your pram or pushchair to make it extra cosy and also lay it on the ground as somewhere safe and familiar for your baby to lie.

Once your baby has outgrown his Moses basket, travel cots are essential if you often stay away from home. They fold flat to make them easy to pack and mean that wherever you are, you know your baby has somewhere safe and familiar to sleep.

Travel cots are also useful once your baby is more mobile, as a safe place to play when you're travelling.

Save money by using a bread bin, ice-cream container or any other large plastic container or bucket with lid for a sterilising unit.

OUT & ABOUT

Alison Wallis; Anna Knight; Amanda Stevens; Clare Porter; Deborah Woodbridge; Diana Starte; Helen Richardson, Child Accident Prevention Trust; Jack and Evelyn Patterson; Jennifer Davis; Linda Jones, Tamba, the Twins and Multiple Births Association (www.tamba.org.uk); Liz Chowienczyk; Margaret Cave; Sandra Wroe; Sarah Brown, nursery teacher, Just Twos nursery; the Multiple Births Association

Keep a ready-packed bag for going out. This doesn't have to be a proper changing bag, but it's useful to include a waterproof roll-up mat or towel for your baby to lie on.

Pack the following:

- nappies – two more than you think you'll use
- barrier cream
- wet wipes and tissues
- nappy sacks
- one or two muslins
- a simple change of clothes
- a rattle, shaker or teething ring
- for bottle-fed babies, bottles with formula (stored in a coolbag) ready to heat when needed
- for breastfed babies, drinks and snacks for you
- a sun shade and baby sun protection cream for summer days
- rain covers for winter days.

When going out for the day with your baby, make sure that you have a clip for hanging your handbag on the pushchair.

Always keep disposable nappies stashed in a seat pocket in the car. Not only for all those emergency nappy changes when you forgot the change bag – they are also terrific for drink spills in the car. They suck up the liquid in no time.

Carry spare baby blankets or towels with you so that you can provide an instant, clean, soft surface on the floor wherever you are, for nappy changing or a kicking session. Wash them straight after use so that they are ready for your next outing.

Out And About With More Than One

Shopping presents new challenges. You'll rapidly get to know which checkouts in which shops you can get a double buggy through and you may have to resort to internet banking if your branch is not very accessible.

Although multiples attract a lot of attention in the early years it dies down once they are three or four. Any shopping trip will be interrupted by comments and questions from total strangers. Bask in the celebrity while it lasts!

Baby slings work for some people, but don't be tempted to wear two and carry twins around at the same time. It can hurt your back.

Slings can be useful if you need to take three babies out on your own. Two can go in a double buggy and the third in the sling.

As your babies get heavier, you'll be tempted to hang more and more shopping bags on the handles of the buggy. Don't overdo this, though, as it could tip the buggy (and babies) over backwards.

Just accept that there will be some days when, by the time you're ready to go out, it'll be time to come home again.

Getting out to toddler groups won't be as necessary for your babies as for singletons, but although your babies won't need the company, you might. Beware, though: you might find that mothers of singletons resent you a little, although their way of showing it might be to go on about how marvellous you are. The problem is that any complaints or problems they have, you can top – not that you would, but they know you can.

Twin clubs are great places to meet women with similar experiences to yours and no hidden agenda. Check out what Tamba and the Twins and Multiple Births Association can offer. You can also find details of local clubs from the NCT, your community midwife or health visitor, or at baby clinic. For contact details, see page 297.

Trips out get easier as the babies get bigger but to give yourselves maximum time out, aim to leave straight after breakfast or lunch.

Get the babies ready first, then yourself. But be prepared for a couple of last-minute nappy changes, which usually announce themselves just after everyone is strapped into the car!

TRAVELLING

Amanda Stevens;
Anna Knight;
Clare Porter;
Liz Chowienczyk;
Margaret Cave;
Sandra Wroe

It's relatively easy to travel with a breastfed baby – all she needs is you! Once she is taking solids or formula, it's still possible: you just need to take more kit.

Remember to get your baby her own passport.

Taking passport photos of newborns can be tricky. You could try improvising in a photo booth holding your baby up to the correct height but many photographers offer a reasonably priced passport photo service which may be cheaper and less hassle in the long run.

Check whether you and your children need any vaccinations at your health centre.

If you're going somewhere hot, think about buying a UV-protective tent for your baby. Many children's equipment catalogues stock them.

Make sure that you are well stocked with sunblock – the highest protection factor possible and preferably one that is specially formulated for babies' delicate skin.

Take sun hats and a sun shade for the buggy. Be ready to give plenty of extra drinks.

Babies don't normally like sand. It gets everywhere and is very uncomfortable.

Baby wipes in a plastic sachet with a resealable opening flap are useless on the beach. Sand sticks to the flap, and then it won't stick down any more. Put the sachet in a resealable plastic bag.

Disposable nappies are available virtually everywhere now, but they are sometimes very expensive, so try to remember to take plenty with you.

Take handwash solution in a pump bottle to sterilise your hands even when no water is available.

Whatever your destination, pack a medical kit, for dealing quickly with minor injuries without having to brave a pharmacy where they don't speak your language. It's not easy to get hold of paracetamol in the middle of the night in the back of beyond. Not only is a medical kit essential in an emergency, but medical costs can be high in foreign countries, even for minor complaints. Include plasters and bandages, sterilising tablets, sunscreen, insect repellent, bite-soothing cream, formula for dehydration and infant paracetamol.

Be scrupulous about good travel insurance.

Don't be surprised if you have two or three unsettled nights when you first arrive. Children take time to get used to a different bed and climate, but they will in the end.

Car Journeys

Try to ensure that your journey coincides with your baby's usual sleep time. Most babies will be lulled to sleep by the soothing motion of the car and may sleep for an hour or two if they're not hungry or uncomfortable.

Check that the sunlight isn't shining in your baby's eyes, or making him hot. A sunshade on the car window can help. The type that clips over the top of the window and can be pulled down like a blind is better than the small ones that fit on with a suction pad.

Use motorways wherever you can. They are faster and what's more most motorway service stations have baby rooms.

Make your baby's car seat more comfortable by placing a folded blanket under his knees so that they are slightly bent.

A bottle and food warmer that plugs into a cigarette lighter is ideal for meals on the move.

Make frequent stops to break the journey into manageable chunks.

Look out for car seats that can be fitted with a tray for toys.

Avoid toys that could distract the driver – nothing hard that could be thrown and no loud noises.

Singing and an adult dedicated to amusing her during the journey makes car travel easier with a baby.

Air Travel

Fly before your children are two years old. They usually travel for free.

Charter flights may be generally cheaper and for some destinations may even be more convenient. The problem is that the later in the day you fly, the more likely you are to be delayed. Scheduled flights are more expensive for a reason. They always retain their precedence in the take-off order.

Be prepared with spare clothes as well as extra nappies to take on to the plane with you in case of unexpected delays.

Take more ready-made bottles or solid food than you think you'll need for the journey. You may have to spend longer waiting than you expect.

Take a small bag of favourite toys. Avoid anything with little parts that can be dropped between the seats.

Check in advance if your car seat will fit an airplane seat. You may be able to use it if there happen to be any spare seats.

Book in advance for a sky cot if you need one on a longer flight. You need to sit in certain seats for the cot to fit and the airline will need warning. The sooner you book one the better, but do check the size: they are often only suitable for very young babies.

Ask whether you can keep your pushchair with you until you board the plane. It makes life much easier if you can keep your buggy with you while you are waiting at the airport. It could save you having to carry your baby along miles of corridor between check-in and boarding. Some airlines will allow you to take the pushchair to the boarding gate, and then take it from you to put in the hold on the plane.

Remember to take your car seat with you if you are planning to hire a car. Or find out whether you can hire a suitable seat at the same time.

Most airlines will check in buggies and car seats, but it's a good idea to check first.

Happy landings (and take-offs): children under two haven't got a fully developed middle ear, so they find take-off and landing much more painful for their ears than older children. Breastfeed or bottle-feed your baby while the plane takes off and lands as they cannot understand the need to swallow otherwise. Sucking will help with the pressure changes and keep ears clear.

When you're flying, bear in mind that even with just one piece of hand luggage most of your things will need to be stored in an overhead locker that's hard to get at. Keep the paraphernalia that you know you are going to need in one small accessible bag that fits just under your seat.

Airline staff will normally warm up bottles and baby foods on request.

When your baby is sitting on your lap during the flight, ask an air stewardess to show you how to fit the extra seat belt to go round you and your baby.

Draw a smiley face on the flight sick bag to make an instant hand puppet.

Travel With Twins Or More

If you have two or more babies to be held on adult passengers' laps, try to get your seats assigned in advance. Some airlines limit the number of lap babies in a single row.

For some reason, perfect strangers like to make annoying comments like, 'Double Trouble'. Counter with your own version, 'Double Fun' or 'Dynamic Duo'. It'll make you feel better.

Make sure that you tell the airline or travel agent that you will be travelling with several infants or toddlers. Even if there is not advance seating generally on offer, the airline might assign yours so that there is no trouble on the day of the flight.

You can just about manage three babies per person, with two in a buggy and one on your back.

On holiday, it is worth sticking to your usual home routine. Each child will react differently to disruption, and you could end up with one awake or eating at any given time.

Having multiples with you in another country is a great way to break down cultural and language barriers. You'll attract friendly interest from locals who would not even have noticed you without the babies.

SAFETY

Anna Knight;
Clare Porter;
Helen Richardson,
Child Accident
Prevention Trust;
Liz Chowienczyk

If you regularly stay with parents or another relative, it's worth thinking about child-proofing at least one room in their house where you know your baby will be safe.

Never assume that your baby can't do something because she's never done it before. There's a first time for everything and babies often take you by surprise.

Avoid hanging a mobile directly above a cot in case it falls in. It should be fixed well out of baby's reach.

Wear only stud earrings; they're harder for little fingers to rip out. Make sure that your rings aren't sharp, give chains and dangly necklaces a miss, and wear a waterproof watch that you don't have to take off to give baths or to wash the dishes.

Make a trail of plug-in night lights from your bedroom to your baby's bedroom. It's a path you'll be following many, many times, and you don't want to stumble when you're half (or three-quarters) asleep.

Always remember to empty out the bath straight away once bathtime is over.

Don't leave your child unattended in a bath even for a moment. Let the phone ring.

You'll need to make your house safe when your baby starts crawling. Adopt the safety measures described on page 66 before you really need to.

IMMUNISATION

Dr Kate Crocker;
Dr Ruth Marchant;
Serena Griffiths,
paediatric nurse

For an explanation of immunisation and what vaccines your baby needs, see Appendix, page 305.

Don't be afraid to talk to your doctor or health visitor to find out as much as you can.

Voice any doubts or concerns you have. Try to assess both the positive benefits of the vaccination and the dangers posed by the diseases they protect against as well as any direct risks from the vaccination itself.

The doctor or nurse giving the injection will give you advice on how to hold your baby.

For inoculations, sit your baby on your lap, facing you with her legs hanging down over your hips, and hold her close so that she can't see or jerk away when she is jabbed in the thigh. Give her a dose of infant paracetamol straight afterwards.

It sometimes helps to breastfeed while your baby is being vaccinated or at least be ready to calm her by feeding immediately afterwards.

Injections can make babies fretful or feverish. Stock up on infant paracetomol to bring temperatures down quickly.

For extra information on immunisation, check the NHS website: www.prodigy.nhs.uk.

3 SIX MONTHS TO TWO YEARS

'People who say they sleep like a baby usually don't have one.'

Leo J. Burke

This is a time of tremendous change for your baby, from passive little bundle to walking, talking toddler. It's also a time when you can start introducing routine into your child's life – which will be of tremendous benefit to you and the rest of your family. Sleeping and eating are the obvious areas where order can emerge, but there are hundreds of little rituals you can develop in every aspect of your baby's life, which can also make his life fun and reassuring. Nappy changing, going out, getting dressed – virtually everything at this stage offers the opportunity for you and your baby to bond and share special moments. Babies of this age are really good fun, giggling appreciatively at your funny faces and interested in everything – you'll be making up daft songs every day. Your child probably won't have reached the stroppy, tantrum phase, so enjoy this period to the full.

All this, however, depends on you feeling up to it – and that depends on how well you are sleeping. If you've been leaping out of bed at every whimper, every night since birth, you've almost certainly run out of steam by now, and are probably running on pure adrenaline. Do yourself (and everyone else) a favour: get some rest! Even if your baby is still not sleeping right through the night, he is old enough to be entrusted to someone else for a while during the day so that you can catch up on what you need most – your precious sleep. Sweet dreams!

LOOKING AFTER YOURSELF

Diana Cockerton;
Debby Davies;
Caroline Donley,
health visitor;
Amanda Stevens;
Jo Caseby

Take naps when your baby does. You will enjoy your baby more if you are rested than exhausted from trying to do jobs while she's asleep.

If you're feeling deprived of 'me' time, use your baby's nap to catch up on e-mail, watch a video you've taped or read a magazine. You may be able to clean up when the baby is awake, but you won't be able to make time for yourself.

Even if you don't work to a routine, create one for your baby and try to stick to it. Regular naps and feed times make life easier for everyone.

Baby socialising can be great fun but exhausting. There's no need to go to toddler group every day just because it's there.

Try to get out for a walk with the buggy every day. You look at things quite differently when you have a tiny companion. Doggies, tractors and buses take on a whole new meaning. Also, if you have a baby who starts yelling at 6.00 a.m. every day, it can be a very good way to preserve your sanity.

Your baby may be getting too heavy for a sling. A good backpack can open up a new world for you both.

If you feel up to resuming your social life, look around for a reliable babysitter (see page 84), then make a regular booking, say every month, and arrange to go out with your partner. You often won't feel like it, in which case the only thing that will get you out is knowing that your babysitter is turning up in half an hour. But going out, even for a walk in the park and a drink, will make you feel like a new person.

Being away from the house for an evening means that you actually talk to one another in a way you don't at home. It seems to work however tired you are. It's good to be a couple again even if only for a few hours.

Ask a responsible teenager to help you out sometimes, to come shopping and to play with your baby while you get on with something else. When you feel confident in her and know that your baby is happy, she will be able to babysit.

Once you're a parent, you don't have much time to get to the gym. But congratulations on your new hand weights! Once your baby's neck can support the weight of her head, you can use her to practise your bicep curls and bench presses, by gently lifting her up, and she'll love the sensation. Carrying your growing baby round is a workout itself, so focus on your posture as you go – you don't want to put a strain on your back.

Babies and toddlers love to 'exercise' with their parents. Jogging strollers and bikes with seats are great for outdoor excursions. On rainy days, put your baby in a sling and use a stationary bike.

Your baby is now old enough to cope for a night without you. Arrange for her to stay overnight with a grandparent, relative or reliable friend and treat yourselves to a night away. Don't stay at home, no matter how tired you feel. The silence will be deafening.

Twins & Supertwins

Try your hardest not to compare your babies to each other or to the children of other mothers you know. And don't compare your ability to cope with other mums – they have no idea

Don't feel guilty if it all gets too much for you sometimes. Having one baby is overwhelming but they haven't invented the word yet that describes what having more than one is like.

Although the early days are probably a blur, in many ways having twins is easier than having two children close together in age. At least yours are eating the same thing and at the same time, you don't have to sort their clothes out, they can go to the same swimming lessons and you won't have to be rushing from school to play group several times a day. Also you have fewer worries about sibling rivalry. Both twins have always been there, so there is no question of one having supplanted the other. But don't tell anyone this – go for the sympathy vote every time!

GROWTH & DEVELOPMENT

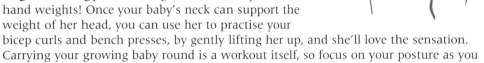

Monica Shaw; Marie-Laure Legroux; Caroline Donley, health visitor; Andrew Williams, paediatrician; Rachel Burn; Mary Cheeseborough

If your baby can just about sit up, try sitting her in a plastic laundry basket, complete with a pile of toys and a couple of cushions, to save her falling.

If you have twins, your babies will be interacting a lot now. Make sure that they can see each other when they are in the house by turning their car seats, high chairs or bouncy chairs to face each other and they will keep each other amused, at least for a while.

With twins, once they are both in cots, make sure that they can see but not touch each other, because they can and will pull each other's hair and tweak noses. Don't leave hard toys in the cots, or they might throw them at each other.

Remember how fast your baby is growing, and check all-in-ones for length regularly. When they get too small, they can cramp his toes.

Take a picture of your toddler with the same toy on the same day every month or two. It's a lovely way of charting growth and development.

Once your baby can stand, you can start marking her height against a chart or wall. But unless you're planning to stay in your house for ever, use a piece of wood that you can stand against the wall. It's heartbreaking to have to leave behind the record of your children's growth when you move house.

Not all babies crawl, but they all find a way of getting around, rolling or shuffling along on their backs or bums, and they'll do it before you expect.

Encourage your baby to crawl by placing his favourite toys just beyond reach.

For a very early walker move furniture close together so your child can fling himself from one padded object to the next without hitting the deck in between.

Remember, the toddler who walks at ten months will not be a better walker long term than the one who takes their first steps at fifteen months.

Recent research suggests that fine motor skills generally develop faster in girls. But don't fret about your boy – it all evens up in the end.

SAFETY

Anna Knight;
Clare Porter;
Helen Richardson,
Child Accident
Prevention Trust;
Liz Chowienczyk

Get down on the floor and look at your house from a child's perspective. Look for hidden hazards. Get rid of heavy objects that can be pulled down, and tie cords dangling from blinds or curtains well out of reach.

Don't attempt to child-proof the entire house initially. Pick a few interconnected rooms and concentrate on those, then block exits with stair gates.

When child-proofing your house for twins, imagine how much more trouble two babies can get into than one (think Phil and Lil from *Rugrats*), and try to double-proof. They'll work together to get through all your defences.

Crawling babies are very inquisitive so plug socket covers are essential.

Cover electric outlets with the plainest, least interesting safety covers you can. Don't attract your baby to them by picking ones that look like ladybirds or cartoon characters.

Make sure that plug sockets are securely fixed to the wall and use plastic covers on any that aren't being used.

Keep all flexes and wires well out of reach of small hands. Be especially careful with anything hot like irons and kettles. Babies can tug quite hard and you don't want them to pull anything down on top of themselves.

Reorganise your kitchen and bathroom so that anything harmful is well out of reach. Look at things like bleach and cleaning agents as well as sharp objects such as knives.

Make sure that your cleaning products are locked away in the kitchen cabinets, and go a step further by changing to natural cleaners. Keep any medicines in a high, locked cupboard.

Simplify your cleaning products. White vinegar can be used to clean soap scum off tiles, baths and hand basins, and bicarbonate of soda gets rid of lime scale. Safer if your toddler gets hold of them and much cheaper too.

Turn saucepan handles in and use the back rings on hobs whenever possible. Try to position cookers so that children can't stand at the sides of them and make sure that they are away from doorways.

Make sure that your rubbish bin is secure. The kinds of things you throw away could be very dangerous to a baby – particularly things like empty tin cans.

Empty your bathroom bin every morning to get rid of used razors and empty bottles.

Get a loo lid lock and make sure that everyone uses it. Put a post-it on the inside of the lid to remind all users.

Cover sharp corners on tables or other pieces of furniture that are at children's head height. You can buy special plastic corner covers from the children's departments in most big stores, or improvise and make your own – from cork, felt, bubble wrap or even a ping-pong ball with a hole cut to fit.

Foam pipe insulation tubes, which you can get at any DIY store, can be used to cover edges around the house. Just cut to length, open the tube along the cut side and you can slip it on to the sides of doors, desks or wherever your baby could hurt herself.

Make windows safe for children. Instead of child bars, fix garden trellis across the bottom of the window. Fasten with safety locks any that are at a low level or that children could open. The type that only allows you to open windows a fixed amount is ideal. (Make sure that you keep the keys handy in case of emergency.)

Low-level panes of glass should be strengthened safety glass. Mark big panes of glass with tape or stickers to remind children that they are there and stop them running straight into them.

Fit cupboard locks before you really need to. Most DIY shops stock locks for kitchen and bathroom cupboards as well as fridges and freezers.

Stop children from getting into cupboards and drawers. Elastic bands make ideal safety catches. Just stretch them across adjacent door-knobs and the doors can only open a short distance.

For emergency cupboard and door locks, put fabric hair scrunchies over the knobs. They come off easily for adult access, but toddlers can't turn the handle because they just slip round. Use them wrapped around two handles on two doors close together in the kitchen too. Neither can then be opened.

Leave one cupboard door without a lock and fill it with things your baby can safely play with – wooden spoons, plastic tubs and sieves. This may encourage him to leave the others alone.

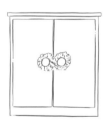

To stop little fingers getting trapped in a slamming door, glue a small cork to the doorframe so that the door cannot slam shut.

Before storing carrier bags, tie them in a knot. It will then be much more difficult for a child to put one over his head without thinking.

Keep a distraction box in the bathroom so that when you are getting ready to go out, you can bring your baby in with you, secure the cupboard and loo, and let him play while you do your thing.

Any pictures or mirrors hanging close to your child's bed should be secured with mirror plates. Ideally they shouldn't be directly above the bed or within a child's grasp.

A large stuffed toy can be used to keep a baby away from hazardous areas of a room until you find a more permanent solution.

Don't give babies heavy toys. They're liable to drop them on themselves when they're lying down or whack you hard.

To test the safety of folding toys, insert a pencil in any nooks or crannies where little fingers could go and see if you can snap the pencil. If you can, don't let your child play with the toy.

When your baby starts learning to climb upstairs, fit a stair gate about three steps up and lay a thick quilt on the floor so that she can practise safely.

Fit stair gates at the top and bottom of stairs, especially if your child tends to wander about at night. You can often pick these up very cheaply second-hand.

Teach your child to go downstairs as well as upstairs safely. Most babies try to go down head first. Turn him around and encourage him to come down backwards. He'll soon realise that it's easiest (and safest) that way.

Don't forget your garden. Ponds should have a secure weight-bearing wire mesh fitted across the surface, and look out for poisonous plants. Many shrubs produce very appealing berries that are poisonous. Apart from prickly or poisonous plants, look out for parts of garden games like croquet hoops or cricket stumps, and make sure that they are tidied away. Do a regular dog pooh check.

Get used to not opening or closing doors without first checking that your darling baby isn't behind or in front of them.

If you're using a bucket of water – for cleaning the car or floor – remember how heavy it is. If a baby fell in head first, his weight wouldn't be enough to tip it over.

If you have drinks with ice cubes, don't leave the empty glasses around. Babies can choke on them.

Use your noticeboard to display safety information for babysitters. Include a list of all of your child's medications or allergies, a list of safety rules or tips to remember, where to find first-aid supplies and emergency phone numbers.

When shopping, strap babies and toddlers into shopping trolleys, and don't accept a trolley without a functional strap. It's a long way to the hard floor.

For car safety, see page 87.

See also page 63.

TEETH & TEETHING

Clare Baines, dentist; Rachel Burn; Mary Cheeseborough

Research suggests that breastfeeding babies helps to delay the appearance of the first teeth, which may make them stronger and healthier when they do come through.

If your baby seems out of sorts, grizzly and a bit miserable, suspect teething. It can cause all sorts of misery, from spots and rashes to a runny nose, poor appetite and yucky nappies.

Teething babies will chomp on anything, including you, so be ready for a kiss to turn into something a bit more painful. You can open a baby's jaws by putting the knuckle of your little finger between them, and twisting it gently until they let go.

A bagel is great for teething. It is naturally chewy, slightly sweet and easy to hold.

Try also peeled carrot that has been in the fridge or freezer. It helps to cool the gums. But don't leave your child unattended, just in case he bites a piece off.

Dried apple rings from the health food shop are a great alternative to rusks for a baby over six months old.

Keeping teething rings and toys in the fridge helps to soothe sore gums.

Teething toddlers enjoy ice lollies made of puréed fruit, frozen in lolly moulds. Very messy, but tasty!

If you have cubes of frozen baby food, choose your baby's favourite flavour and wrap a single cube in a clean muslin cloth. Tie it securely, then give it to your baby to suck on to soothe the discomfort of teething.

For a baby who loves her bottle, take a small (4oz/100ml) bottle and put a little water in it, and freeze it upside-down, so that the teet is full of ice. Your baby may take to it better than an unfamiliar teething ring and it will be very soothing.

If your baby will accept a dummy but not your finger with teething gel on it, squeeze the gel on to the dummy, then, when he opens his mouth rub it on his gums. He might look a bit outraged at your trick, but at least his gums won't hurt so much.

Try squeezing teething gel on to a baby toothbrush and give it to your baby to chomp on.

Homeopathic teething granules work brilliantly for some teethers, and even if you don't buy into it, they can provide a helpful distraction from the discomfort. Your baby has to concentrate enough to open her mouth and let you tip the granules on to her tongue, and it can distract her enough to make her forget that she was crying. The main ingredient is chamomilla.

For young teethers who can't manage to get a teething ring to their mouths, try a dummy – but choose a strong one.

If your baby doesn't take to teething rings, take a clean lint-free cloth (a muslin square is ideal), dampen it with water or teething gel, put it in a freezer bag and leave it in the freezer. Give it to your baby to chew on to cool and soothe those gums. If your baby takes to this idea, freeze a batch so that you always have one ready.

For dribbly babies with sore necks, rub some petroleum jelly on the neck and chest as a barrier, but don't let it get near their mouths.

For world-class dribblers with wet tops and sore necks, tuck a little bandanna into their vest or jumper, John Wayne style, to soak it up.

If you are breastfeeding a teething baby, keep your little finger ready to lever her jaws apart. A teething baby can draw blood! Some teething babies never bite when breastfeeding, however, so don't panic.

Check teeth regularly and make sure that you choose an orthodontically approved shape dummy.

Dentists & Tooth Brushing

Take your child along to your dentist somewhere between one and two years. Dental check-ups will soon seem routine and familiar. Let her sit on your lap while you open your mouth and the dentist has a look inside. When its her turn, she'll know just what to expect.

Play dentists at home. Use a teaspoon to touch lightly inside her mouth while your baby lies back and opens wide. That way, she won't freak out at the feel of the dentist's tools.

When you take your child to the dentist, say that the dentist wants to count her teeth. This ensures that your baby will open her mouth – particularly if you've practised at home.

You need to start brushing teeth as soon as your baby has any. Rubbing the teeth gently with a clean flannel with just a dab of toothpaste on is a good way to start.

Make sure that your child always brushes her teeth before bed. This is especially important, as there is less saliva in your mouth at night to counteract bacteria.

Let your baby have a go with his toothbrush himself, than take over and do the real work.

For successful tooth brushing without tears, sit your child across your lap, facing to the side. Put your arm around her shoulders and brush her teeth with the brush held in that hand.

Small children need only a tiny amount of toothpaste – less than pea-sized.

Be careful about using fruit-flavoured toothpaste. Once kids get used to the taste, the transition to stronger mint flavours around the age of six when they need higher fluoride levels can be a nightmare. Try using a very mild mint one from the start.

Baking-soda toothpastes and herbal varieties are often milder in flavour and may suit younger tastebuds. There are so many to choose from now that it's easy to find brands that also contain fluoride.

If your baby runs off when you try to brush her teeth, do it in the bath. She can't escape, and any mess can be rinsed away.

Invent a little tooth-cleaning song. Go on – no one else is listening! Three or four verses should ensure that you brush for long enough to do some good.

It's easier to brush your baby's teeth when you're standing behind her and you're both looking in the mirror. That way, she learns what to do herself by watching you.

For a better chance of healthy teeth:

- Avoid giving children drinks in bed, especially fruit juices.
- Only milk should be drunk from a bottle.
- Always give children juice in a feeder cup or to suck through a straw.
- Chocolate is less bad for teeth than sweets.
- It's better to eat sweets in one go rather than spreading them over a few hours.

Never give fluoride drops to children without first checking with your dentist. Tap water in your area may already contain added fluoride.

TOYS, BOOKS & OTHER FUN

Rosie Clementi,
teacher;
Simon Holden,
toymaker

For cot toys, and toys for babies who like to play lying on their backs, select only soft light items. If a baby drops a heavy toy and it lands on his face – ouch!

Improvise with a metal mixing bowl, plastic measuring spoons, toy key rings and a tea towel to cover them all up. Most babies will spend ages with a combination like this.

Don't give your baby plastic cutlery from planes or fast-food outlets to play with. They are not nearly strong enough and can be bitten or broken in half.

Fill a tall opaque container with lots of little objects and let your baby fish around in there. It seems to be particularly fascinating that they can't see everything in there at once, rather like a bran tub, and the container can keep a baby occupied for ages.

Make lovely noisy toys out of see-through plastic containers with tight-fitting snap-on lids filled with colourful beads and cotton reels. Lovely to shake and to look at. Old film canisters are ideal.

Give your baby his own set of kitchen implements to play with while you're cooking. He'll love to join in with his plastic bowls and wooden spoons, and he could be a Jamie Oliver in the making!

For babies who are starting to pull themselves up, put a set of toys, plastic rings, wooden bricks and plastic containers on top of a low table, as a great incentive to stand there and throw everything on to the floor. Then you pick it all up again – and so on.

Curling ribbon from bouquets or presents is fascinating to little ones. They love to straighten it out and watch it curl up again, but don't leave them unattended with it.

Fill a plastic mesh bag (the sort that oranges come in) with bits of coloured cellophane and shiny crinkly paper, tie the top securely and hang it up just where your baby can grab it. Sight, sound and touch stimulated in one go.

Don't chuck out big cardboard boxes. They make absolutely the best toys for crawlers and toddlers, with a few peepholes cut in the sides (but nothing big enough to get their heads stuck in).

You can help your baby develop hand–eye coordination as soon as she can sit up, by playing throwing and rolling games. Choose a very lightweight ball about the size of a grapefruit, and remember to put cushions behind her, because she's almost bound to topple over backwards.

Don't indulge in baby talk! If you want children with excellent language skills, talk to them using normal language and throw in some interesting terminology.

Dads are very interesting things. They have quite different textures to mums, so let your baby explore your rough face, but beware of sudden sharp tugs on your chest hair.

All day music provides wonderful stimulation for your baby, but make sure that you vary the style and fit the mood to the time of day. Start your day with energising music, and end it with soothing music, and play classical, jazz, world, rock, folk – everything you can lay your hands on.

Babies need to learn that life is sometimes quiet. Choose a regular time of day to put some toys on your baby's blanket, in the playpen or crib, and leave your baby alone for a few minutes. Do something quiet near by.

Many babies hate their playpen, particularly if it's been introduced once they've tasted freedom. Try to make a playpen more appealing by making it really fun in there. If you also use it to store cuddly toys, you can create a 'ball-pool' effect by plonking your baby in the middle of them, but be prepared for most of them to be chucked out.

If you let your child watch TV, stay with him to help interpret what's going on.

When the weather gets hot, take the high chair outside but not in the direct sun, strap the baby in the seat, then pour water in the tray. Let him splash to his heart's content.

Rotate your child's toys. Keep a box or two hidden every month, then swap them round with the ones she's been playing with.

Buy a cheap photo album with clear lift-up page covers, and make your baby his own album with pictures of himself, neighbours, friends, relatives, pets and the places you go to regularly. Looking at it together and talking about it can really bring on early language skills.

Turn clean-up time into a game. Play your child's favourite song on her tape recorder, and by the time she hears the final notes of 'Five little men in a flying saucer' (or whatever) all toys should be put away.

Use shower curtain rings to clip toys to buggies and car seats. If you can find brightly coloured ones, even better. Just make sure that they can't pinch your baby's fingers.

Toys that attach to high chairs with suction may seem a great idea, but if your baby pulls hard, they can come off very suddenly and whack him in the face.

Keep a list of the names, manufacturers and batch numbers of your children's toys, in case of product recalls.

Take your baby to play barns, swimming pools and other facilities during the day when the big kids are at school and playgroup. No point in taking them after school and glowering at all the older kids every time they come near your baby. You have a choice about when to go – they don't.

Trips to the park are a way for mothers to regain their sanity. Off-peak times are less stressful in lots of ways. Again, try to avoid the after-school rush when bigger kids will be letting off steam. In summer, it's great fun to meet friends there early for a breakfast picnic, and you won't have to chase your children round with sunblock.

Let toddlers get filthy, mucky and totally dirty. If there's mud, make mud pies. If there's water, splash. If you're gardening, let them get their hands in the earth (no gloves!). If they're painting, encourage using fingers, hands, feet. Obviously make sure they are well washed afterwards but getting mucky is vital for earthing children – and so often we try to keep them in pristine cling-wrapped worlds.

When you introduce a child to dogs, let the dog smell some clothing first so that it gets used to the smell. That way, the dog should be calmer when they meet.

You may also find some of the information on page 108 helpful for a child in this age group.

FOOD & DRINK

Anna Knight;
Alison Wallis;
Serena Griffiths,
paediatric nurse

Breastfeeding

If you're still breastfeeding your toddler by the time she can talk, be prepared for her to demand a feed, at the top of her voice, in the most embarrassing terms and in the most crowded place imaginable. This can be a major incentive for weaning.

Breastfeed your baby in the bath. Nice and relaxing for everyone.

A baby who bites often while breastfeeding may be trying to tell you that she doesn't need it any more. Try just cuddling her instead and see how she reacts.

For more on breastfeeding and cutting down the number of feeds see below.

Weaning

There is no set age at which to wean. You can continue breastfeeding for as long as you both enjoy it and it feels right to you.

Babies need to breastfeed until they can take all their milk from a cup or bottle and longer if you choose.

Some children are ready to wean earlier than others – and the same applies to mothers. You can make your own rules!

Gradually reduce the number of feeds. Don't just suddenly stop, or you will confuse your baby and make him think that you're withdrawing from him. You need to take it slowly to give your breasts a chance to adjust, too.

Wean your baby from the daytime feeds first, then start to drop the night-time feeds. Replace the daytime feeds with milk in a cup or bottle and solid food until you are only breastfeeding first thing in the morning and at bedtime. The last feed either of you will want to drop is the bedtime feed. Many toddlers keep this up for a long time for comfort.

To limit the number of breastfeeds during the day, try to distract with other food, games and play.

When starting a child on milk, start by putting a quarter ordinary milk to three quarters breast. It's easier on the tummy.

Wean your toddler with stealth. Start by introducing a new cup or beaker with some juice or milk instead of feeding at lunchtime (or some other time). With the bedtime feed, you can start off with a cuddle, wearing clothes that make access difficult. Gradually make the cuddle the main event and drop the feed altogether.

If weaning from the night feeds is difficult, try sleeping in a separate room from your baby and leave your partner to deal with the night feeds and changes.

You don't have to wean on to a bottle. Many babies go quite happily on to a beaker. Choose one for the right age group and with a soft mouthpiece.

To help your baby grip a bottle or cup, wrap some elastic bands round it.

For an older toddler, you can make weaning a rite of passage by taking him to pick his own special cup and letting him select the times he substitutes it for a breastfeed.

Avoid familiar nursing positions and places so that your baby doesn't associate them with breastfeeding.

As your baby gets older, it may help to only breastfeed in one place. This means your child would need to break off from whatever he's doing to nurse, and it will help him to cut down naturally, and at his own rate.

As you stop feeding, you can start to develop a new bedtime routine, with reading, a special song and a good long cuddle. With any luck, your baby will feel she's gaining from the new arrangement. Make sure that she knows what a big girl she is now.

See also Introducing Bottles To Breastfed Babies, page 40.

Goodbye To Bottles

It's very demoralising for a toddler to keep tipping his juice. Put only a tiny amount in the bottom of the cup and keep refilling it.

Choose cups at least partly on how low the centre of gravity is. Another vital consideration is how easy it is to clean.

Cups with lids often claim to be leak-proof but they seldom are, and once you've washed them in the dishwasher (against the instructions), they certainly won't be.

Novelty straws are terrific fun – for about five minutes, but a complete pain when it comes to washing them out. Pipe cleaners are invaluable for cleaning round curves. Better still, throw them away!

A toddler who is drinking several bottles of milk will not have much of an appetite for solids. Gradually replace the bottles one at a time over several weeks with cups of juice or water, and watch his intake of solids go up. Once he is used to the new regime, you can give him milk in a cup.

As with breastfed babies, when starting a bottle-fed child on milk, start by putting a quarter ordinary milk to three quarters formula. It's easier on the tummy.

A toddler who shows a marked aversion to cow's milk may know better than you that he has a dairy intolerance. If he also has persistent diarrhoea or eczema, ask your health visitor for advice.

Persuade a reluctant toddler that Santa will bring her presents when he comes to take away her bottles.

If you live near a livestock farm, see if the farmer will allow you to visit for your toddler to 'give' his bottles to one of the baby animals.

To make a simple transition away from bottles, cut an X in the top of the teat, and stick a straw through into the bottle. The bottle will be virtually spill-proof, and your baby knows how to hold it already. It will be easier to encourage the child to use a straw in a beaker later on.

To induce your baby to change from a bottle to a cup, serve her favourite drink in a cup, never in a bottle.

Don't change everything at once. Serve the drink of choice in the new cup, and serve plain old water in the bottle.

Give in to market trends and buy a beaker with a favourite cartoon character – just this once!

Never put your baby to bed with a bottle of juice. The sugars stay in the mouth and can start tooth decay early.

Don't give toddlers 'sugar-free' drinks – they are packed with artificial sweeteners. Try to get them drinking water when possible (if you start early, they will get a taste for it – and many love fizzy water). If they do drink juice, stick to real fruit juice or 'normal' (not sugar-free or 'tooth-kind') squash and limit it to mealtimes.

Eating Solids

Don't give your baby too much to drink before a meal, as it might fill her up too much. Let her have a small drink if she needs it, then a bigger drink after the meal.

Juice, even diluted with water, is very sugary, and can blunt your baby's appetite.

If you have been feeding your baby on follow-up milk, you may find that his appetite for solids improves when you introduce cow's milk at about twelve months. Follow-on milk is very filling.

Put fruit and yoghurt into ice-lolly moulds and freeze them. The child gets calcium and thinks he is eating a lolly.

This is the time to get your baby to experiment with food. There is no more broad-minded age than this, so give your baby celeriac and spinach purée, and the like. But don't get smug about it – by the age of three, she'll probably only eat chicken nuggets and chips.

Introduce a wide range of foods from early on – babies and toddlers have surprisingly enterprising tastes. Pesto, pitted olives and salami are just some of the unexpected things that one-year-olds have tried (sometimes accidentally) and loved.

Babies vary widely in their tolerance for lumps. But they all get there in the end, so don't force the issue. If your baby gags or chokes, it's scary for everyone.

Toddlers love meals made up of lots of little treats. Try serving a few raisins, little cubes of cheese, sliced banana, chopped avocado and so on – real finger food – in a variety of little plastic pots.

Babies can get very impatient in their high chairs when they are waiting for a meal. Bread sticks are good for brandishing and eating.

Tempt your baby to eat by getting her a lunchbox for her to unpack in her high chair. So grown up!

Once you move past purées, use a potato ricer to mash vegetables with just a little more texture.

Keep cereal and biscuits fresh by dividing into baby-size servings and packing them into clear, sealable plastic bags. Store them together so that your baby can make his selection at snack time.

When you start trying your baby on sandwiches, make them really tiny – little more than postage-stamp size – so he can pop them in all in one.

Try starting with open sandwiches. It's messier, but babies like to know what they are getting.

Allow your toddler to feed himself as soon as he is interested. If you're worried about the mess, see page 44.

It can be tricky for a baby to feed himself at first. Cut food into slivers, about the size of fat chips, so that he can pick them up in his whole hand. He can bite off one end, drop the rest back on to his tray, then try to pick up the other piece. This works well with bread, bread sticks, cooked carrot and broccoli, but could be tricky with slippery foods like bananas and avocados.

Children cannot chew very effectively until they are around four years of age. Because of this, foods that are hard or tough to chew, small and round or sticky are the ones most often choked on. These include: frankfurters, crunchy or hard-boiled sweets, raw carrots, nuts, sweetcorn, grapes, peas, popcorn, chunks of meat, raisins, and peanut butter spread too thickly.

To prevent choking, cut grapes into quarters and carrots and beans into small pieces. Cook and mash vegetables such as peas and sweetcorn.

Cut meat into small pieces. It's easier to eat and less likely to choke young children.

Peel, core and seed, and slice fruit for young children. It's easier for little hands to hold, more fun and less messy to eat.

Apples are favourites with lots of babies, but in chunks or slices they present a choking hazard. Instead of handing your baby slices, peel an apple and give it to him whole.

That way he'll only nibble off tiny pieces at a time. Even so, don't give one to a baby in a rear car seat. You need to be able to reach him fast if he chokes.

Finger foods give babies the chance to develop hand–eye coordination and practise motor skills.

If a baby or toddler turns down a particular kind of food, don't make a big deal out of it or insist she eats it. Don't give up on it. Apparently toddlers are genetically wired to be suspicious of unknown foodstuffs (to save them from poisoning themselves). Just keep putting the offending item on the plate (without any comment and alongside other things) and eventually (the theory goes) she will get used to it and start chomping. Or leave that particular food for a while and then try it again at a later date, maybe cut up differently or served with something else.

Personifying food really does seem to help – wiggly worms for spaghetti, little trees for broccoli, cannon balls for peas.

Babies and toddlers will usually fall for the 'Here comes a plane/train/Thunderbirds 2' routine as you shovel in food. It's quite an art! The laden spoon loops the loop or hides behind Mummy's or Daddy's back and then dives into the tunnel or whatever.

Try telling savvy toddlers that a particular food is a character's favourite – for instance, Thomas the Tank Engine adores fish fingers, James always eats muesli for breakfast. Doesn't always work but worth a go.

Don't fill the plate too full. It can be overwhelming for a toddler to be faced with too much food. She can always have more.

Don't panic if your toddler seems incredibly fussy with food. Few starve.

If your baby is determined to feed himself, damage limitation techniques come into play. Give him a small amount of food on the high-chair tray and his own spoon. You keep hold of the bowl and spoon and feed in between him wiping it all over his hair. Alternatively, just give him another spoon – he may be satisfied with that while you feed him.

Bowls with suction pads on the bottom work until your baby is strong enough to push them off the high-chair tray; then they fly off at high speed and splatter the kitchen with food. And once she's done it, she'll keep on doing it.

Let your baby join you at the table and, when he is sitting on your lap, let him try some food from your plate. He may try all kinds of exciting food if he sees you eating it first. You can let him try suitable food from your plate to extend his tastes, but the down-side is that he'll probably offer you some of his.

At family mealtimes, sit the baby in the high chair with the tray off and slide him up to the table with everyone else. It makes it a much more sociable affair, and he can try eating from a dish on the table like everyone else.

Give your baby a warm, damp flannel once you've cleared her food away. She'll wash her hands, face, high-chair tray and anything else she can reach.

If you go out, you can put frozen cubes in small plastic food containers and heat them up at your destination.

If you're braving a restaurant with a toddler, try to get him a seat facing a window. He can watch the world go by and it will keep him amused for longer than you can.

Keep your baby amused (and bemused) in a restaurant by placing an ice cube on his high-chair tray. He can push it around and watch it melt while you eat. It will probably be too slippery for him to pick up, but make sure he doesn't get it into his mouth. Babies can choke on ice.

HEALTH

Virginia Warrender;
Sue Lees;
Marie Rendall;
Susan Clark,
www.whatreallyworks.co.uk

If your baby has a rotten cold, lift the cot at the head end, using books for example. Works well because the mucus runs away instead of blocking baby's nose.

Stuffed-up noses are even worse when the air is dry, as it is in most centrally heated houses. Put a small bowl of water or wet flannel, with baby decongestant oil added if you like, on top of the radiator, making sure that your baby can't reach it. Slow cookers set on low all night with the lid off and enough water work well too, creating a steamy atmosphere in the room.

Put a few drops of baby decongestant oil on to a handkerchief and tie it near (but out of reach) to where your baby is sleeping – to a bedpost or near the pillow. It should never come into direct contact with skin. Karvol capsules are particularly good for young children.

Babies with colds don't feed well. Doctors sometimes prescribe saline drops to put in their noses. They hate this, but loads of goo usually comes shooting out soon afterwards. If you can feed the baby straight away, he may find it easier to breathe and feed at the same time.

Never run out of paracetamol syrup. If you're going abroad, take some with you. The easiest way to give it is using an oral syringe, which allows you to measure the dose accurately at the same time. For small babies, you squirt it into their cheek – not straight down their throats, which will make them choke. Older babies can hold it in their mouths themselves while you gently press the plunger. It makes them feel more in control.

Giving eye ointment is a nightmare. Lay your baby on her back and rest the tube of ointment across the bridge of her nose, with the nozzle above the corner of her eye. Squeeze the tube gently and let the ointment drop on to the corner of her eye, then persuade her to stay still until it softens and goes in. This method avoids any worries about poking her in the eye if she turns her head sharply. Make it fun by turning the whole thing into a game of peepo!

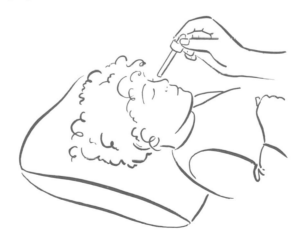

Some toddlers take eye drops more readily than ointment, once they can follow simple instructions. Lay yours in your lap and tell her to close her eyes. Drop the recommended dose on to the corner of her eye; then tell her to blink. The drops go in as she flutters her eyelashes.

To get hold of a baby and administer medicine, you need at least eight arms. Try sitting on the floor with your legs just apart but out straight, with her on her back with her head on the floor in your crotch. Tuck her arms under your legs (her legs too, if you need to) and squeeze your thighs together, just tight enough so that she can't move her head. Now she is immobile and both your hands are free. Use one to open her mouth and the other to stick the dropper in her mouth.

Choose the sugary versions of medicines, if your child is reluctant to take the sugar-free version. You can always clean his teeth afterwards.

Always have a cup of strong-flavoured juice to hand to sip as soon as the medicine has been swallowed. It will help disguise the taste.

With a younger baby, give medicine and vitamin drops by laying him flat on the changing table or floor. Get the medicine ready, then hold a squeaker toy above his head and slowly move it back so that he has to look back at the toy and opens his mouth at the same time. Aim the medicine dropper in the mouth towards the back of his cheek, and squirt a little of the medicine in. Once he swallows, repeat until the dosage is given.

Can't get your toddler to take vitamin drops? Freeze them into a home-made lolly made of puréed fruit and yoghurt.

If children have asthma or eczema, it's really worth trying them on dairy-free diets, or using goat's or sheep's milk, which is often better tolerated. If your baby is still on formula milk, there is a goat's milk formula and even a totally non-allergenic one which can be ordered through your doctor's surgery. Few doctors and health visitors are up to speed on this, so it's worth informing them, and you should speak to a health professional before embarking on any major diet changes. For more on allergies, see page 282.

Average burn times for exposure to the sun apply to adult skin, not to babies'. A baby's skin can be twenty times more sensitive than yours, so always apply sunblock and keep a sun hat in your changing bag.

It's much easier to apply sunblock in stick form to your child's face than to use a runny cream. If it gets in her eyes, she'll never trust you to put on sunblock again.

Put suncream on to your hands first to warm it then rub it on to your child's skin, rather than pouring cold cream straight on to her.

At the beach, put the block on before your baby gets covered in sand. You wouldn't like to be rubbed with what feels like sandpaper, would you?

On sunny days, a toddler spends a lot of time grubbing around on the ground, so always apply plenty of block to the back of your baby's neck, and get him a legionnaire's cap with a flap at the back.

Remember to protect the tops of your baby's feet, her shoulders and forearms when you are pushing her round in a buggy in the sunshine.

There are three types of UV radiation:

- UVC is the most dangerous type, but it is stopped by the atmosphere, so it is only seen in large amounts at very high altitudes.

- UVB is the second most dangerous type. It is largely stopped by the ozone layer but at extreme northern and moderate southern latitudes it can be found in high concentrations.

- UVA is the most common type, which causes us to tan. It is dangerous in large quantities or at high intensity, but is easily stopped by sunglasses, sunblock lotions and sunblock clothes.

According to one cancer research centre, UV light is 50 per cent more intense at 9500ft/3000m than at sea level.

For more advice and travel tips, see pages 60 and 86.

WASHING

Rachel Burn, teacher;
Jane Alexander, writer,
www.janealexander.org

Hair

Cradle cap – crusty, yellowing hard flakes of skin on your baby's head – is very common. Don't pick at it or try to comb it off. Rub olive oil (or almond, baby, coconut or sunflower oil) gently into the scalp. Leave it overnight or as long as possible, then gently comb through with a fine comb and shampoo. Make sure that you apply shampoo to dry hair – otherwise washing out the oil is impossible. This can be very helpful, but you'll probably have to repeat the process several times.

For stubborn cases of cradle cap, massage the scalp gently with a flannel or a baby hairbrush before you shampoo the oil off.

Always use non-sting mild shampoo, especially for babies and children. Use conditioner in the same range to make combing tangles easier.

Try shampooing hair in the bath, when your child can lie back in the water and is less likely to get bubbles in her eyes. If suds are still a problem, let her hold a wet flannel over her eyes.

Wearing a plastic visor for hairwashing is another good way of keeping stingy shampoos out of eyes (sun shields work well).

You can also try drawing a line across your child's forehead with petroleum jelly to stop shampoo running down into his eyes.

If you want to trim your baby's hair, do it while she's watching telly. She's more likely to stay still if she's distracted.

Try saying 'trim' instead of haircut. Your child may think it's going to hurt.

Play at hairdressers with your baby. Give him a pair of plastic scissors to 'cut' your hair with, then take your turn to cut his with real scissors.

Your baby doesn't really need to have her hair washed at the hairdresser's. A quick spray should be enough, and you can practise that at home.

Choose a child-friendly stylist at a hairdressers' where they don't play loud music.

Take your baby's top off before the haircut starts. You can easily brush the cut ends off her skin and it avoids that awful itchy feeling afterwards.

Let your child see you have your hair cut so that she realises it isn't torture.

For more on visiting the hairdresser, see page 98.

Baths

See also Bathing, page 46.

Never leave small children alone in the bath. They can drown in only one or two inches of water.

Once your baby can sit up, put a plastic laundry basket in the bath of water and sit him in there while you wash him. The water can flow through the holes in the side and he can hold on to the sides to make him feel safe.

If your baby still slips in the basket, adhesive non-slip bath stickers work a treat.

A rubber bath mat is invaluable to stop babies slipping in the bath. Always remember to take one with you when you go on holiday.

Keep bath toys and sponge letters clean and fungus-free by rinsing them in clean water after bathtime. Store them in a mesh drawstring or zip-top bag hung over the showerhead or bath taps to allow toys to drip-dry.

Occasionally wash them in the washing machine on a cool cycle. Follow with fifteen minutes in the dryer – it even makes the squeaky toys squeakier!

When you're drying your baby's hair with a towel, get under there with him and make it a game.

Creases and folds can get sore, particularly under the chin, with regular application of dribble – and worse. Try placing your baby on his tummy for a moment and, when he lifts his head you can clean and dry his neck then apply some nappy cream or petroleum jelly from the tip of your finger.

CRYING

See page 50.

SLEEPING

Jackie Wheatley;
Crispin Bearman;
Jane Alexander,
www.janealexander.org;
Andrea Schmidt,
psychologist

See also Sleeeping, page 53.

If you want your baby to sleep through the night at six months, you'll probably have to get tough, so get him used to not being picked up every time he cries when you first lay him down. Put him in his cot after his cuddle, then leave the room. If he starts to cry, check on him after a few minutes but never pick him up. Return every few minutes, but make the interval between visits longer each time. The first night expect him to cry for ages. It will be hell for you but it gradually gets better.

Once your toddler doesn't need the baby monitor, use it in reverse so that she can hear your voices and go to sleep knowing that she isn't alone.

About one in five babies still wakes at least once during the night between six months and one year. And some go on and on and on and on. So don't think you're the only parents in the world with this problem. It will get better, even if you don't do anything about it, but the controlled crying method (see above) will help in most cases.

It is quite normal for a breastfeeding toddler to wake any number of times to nurse each night. Children who haven't been breastfed or are weaned earlier may have soothers, blankets or toys to comfort them, instead of your breasts.

Once your baby is on solids, she really doesn't need a feed during the night, but she might still need it for comfort. Try giving water in a bottle or beaker, and she might decide it's not worth waking up for.

You'll reach a point where your baby needs less sleep during the day, and one sign of this will be that she sleeps less at night. Better to keep her up in the daytime than have to get up yourself at night.

Restless babies kick off their blankets and may wake up because they are cold. Baby sleeping bags with shoulder straps are a good solution.

For bedtime routines that may be helpful to older children in this age group, see page 100.

For nightmares and terrors, see page 101.

Cot To Bed

Once your baby climbs (or falls) out of his cot, it's about time for a big bed.

Don't put your child into a 'proper' bed until he is regularly climbing out or is pushing against the edges of the cot. Confined to a cot is always best – for as long as you can swing it.

If you have space in your baby's bedroom, set up the bed before you make the transition, so that she gets used to seeing it and practising lying on it. Leaving the cot in place makes her feel her options are still open, although few toddlers would choose to go back into a cot when they can sleep in a big bed.

Try using the big bed for daytime naps first of all. The chances are that your baby will then want to sleep there at night too.

If you are worried about your baby falling out of bed, start by laying the mattress on the floor. Or lay some pillows beside the bed, in case your baby falls out.

Try to stay calm when your child falls out of bed. Sometimes they don't even wake up, and other times they go straight back to sleep. Don't fuss unless it's necessary.

Let your child have some say in choosing her bed linen, whether or not it matches the décor. Anything to keep her in bed!

Once your baby is out of a cot and into a bed, she can find her way to your bed – and probably will. Make sure that all stair gates are closed, and leave a night light so she can find her way round.

Remember to baby-proof the room – for safety measures, see page 66. But leave plenty of board books close at hand.

CLOTHES

Denise Fuchs; Melanie Byrom; Marjorie Evans

See also Clothes & Equipment, page 58.

Your baby is growing fast, so cut down on clutter and overflowing drawers by keeping two plastic shopping bags hanging up in the wardrobe for clothes he outgrows: one for clothes you intend to hand on to family and friends, and one for the clothes you could sell on to a second-hand shop. When the bags are full, get rid of them at once and start again.

Convert old or stained T-shirts into over-the-head bibs. Cut up the sides to the sleeve holes to make a bib that covers the whole front, and dye them funky colours if you're feeling creative.

Buy all the same colour socks and padders so that you don't go crazy trying to match pairs. When your child has grown out of old socks, throw them all out once you've bought the new ones, or else they'll get hopelessly mixed up.

Keep padders safely attached to your baby's feet by securing each one at the back to her trousers with a nappy pin.

Buy in the seasonal sales for next year. So for your one-year-old, look for winter clothes in the January sales in two-year-old sizes. It just takes some forward planning. Keep a note of what you've bought, or you might find you've doubled up at full price the following winter.

Have a 'freshen up your kids' wardrobe' party, and invite friends and family with children of similar ages to bring old clothes their children no longer wear. Toss everything into the middle of the room and do a big trade. Everyone usually goes home with something new and it's absolutely free.

CHILDREN'S ROOMS

See page 106.

POTTY-TRAINING

Lizzi Stackhouse,
aromatherapist;
Anna Knight;
Jacqui Ciotkowski

Always go to the toilet in front of babies and toddlers. It makes it much easier when it comes to potty-training. In particular the same-sex parent should do this.

Don't be tempted to start potty-training too soon. It really is easiest to wait until the child really wants to do it for himself – usually somewhere between two and four. Then the child is usually clean within a day or so and doesn't regress.

For potty-training, see page 98.

DUMMIES & THUMBS

Lucy Strauss

A sneaky way of getting rid of a baby's dummy is to cut a little hole in it with nail scissors and tell your baby that it gets worn out when you are too big. Cut away a little more each day, until they're not worth sucking any more. Keep one intact, just in case.

Is your child waking because the dummy has fallen out? Time to get rid of it. Cold turkey is the best way to do it. Remove it and never let one near him again.

If a child remains very attached to his dummy, don't try to force him to give it up. Throwing it away can simply make matters worse. Instead, try not to make a big deal of the issue but encourage him positively to give it up of his own accord – by emphasising what a lovely smile he has, the fact he is older now, all the things he can do.

Don't worry: your child will give up his dummy eventually.

If your child likes having something to suck, give her a clean muslin nappy. You can wash it at 90°C when it gets dirty, and you can buy them in packs of twelve, so she need never be without one. Much better than some ratty old blanket that can't be washed or replaced!

Encourage your child to have a security or transitional object and don't worry about him using it. A scrap of material or blanket can give him just the sense of reassurance he needs to try something on his own, for example, going into a new toddler group, or being left at a friend's house.

Some children are thumb suckers, others aren't. Don't resort to putting something yucky-tasting on the thumb as aversion therapy. Think how awful it must be just when you feel in need of a bit of comfort.

Sucking a thumb is less likely to cause tooth trouble than sucking the middle finger, which exerts far more pressure on the back of the front teeth because of the angle at which it enters the mouth, so divert a finger sucker to her thumb for preference.

Most children will stop sucking their thumbs when they get teased about it at school, but some ten-year-olds have been known to have a quick, sustaining suck in the car on the way to school, to set them up for the day.

Don't fret about thumb sucking. Your child will drop it of her own accord when she's ready.

BEHAVIOUR

Alex Gardner,
psychologist;
Glynis Fletcher,
counsellor;
Gioia Marzullo;
Kurt Klotzle,
paediatrician

When your child is just starting to crawl/walk, leave some old ornaments lying around and when she touches, tell her no. Then when you go to other people's houses she won't be interested in fiddling with ornaments.

If you're losing your temper with your toddler, walk away and let someone else take over, even the video recorder. Take a few minutes to release the negative energy away from your child. Blowing up will only teach your child a bad way to handle anger.

Whether it's choosing what she'll wear or what she'll eat, give your child some options (but not too many) and let her decide. The freedom to make choices instils a sense of independence and confidence.

Planning ahead is so important with behaviour. If you can identify and pre-empt the flashpoints that cause trouble in your day-to-day routine, you'll avoid many pointless fights.

Supermarket shopping can be a real test of tempers – both yours and your baby's. The ideal solution is to go without your kids, but in the real world you may have to. To make life easier:

- Take a list – and tell your children you can't buy anything that isn't on the list.

- Make sure they are fed and watered and have gone to the loo before you start shopping.

- Try to keep toddlers in the trolley seat as long as you can. Don't even offer getting out as an option. This is one place where early independence is not helpful.

- Make it interesting for them to stay in the seat by chatting, having a laugh, playing peepo, singing songs together. You may look daft, but at least everyone is having a good time.

- Agree before you start that they may have a treat – once shopping is over, and if their behaviour has been good.

- If you give them snacks on the way round, avoid sweet or salty things that hype them up or make them thirsty. The end of a baguette or a pitta bread is a good choice.

Most toddlers get cranky in the afternoon. It's just a fact of life, so don't take it personally. Saying, 'I think you're feeling a bit tired and cross,' can help them put a name to their own puzzling feelings. A quiet sit down and cuddle, some juice and a story makes life more bearable for everyone.

Making phone calls with toddlers around is so difficult. Try these ideas to calm things down:

- Have a little bag of toys that you only give your child when you are on the phone. Don't include any rattles or whistles!

- Schedule your calls for when their favourite programme is on.

- See the problem from their point of view, and try to keep daytime calls as short as possible. Save long chats until they have gone to bed.

Biting, Pinching & Hair Pulling

These behaviours are very common and, embarrassing and unpleasant though they are, remember that this is just a phase, so don't get too wound up about them.

The only thing you can do is be consistent – put the baby down and say no, firmly.

Ignore advice to 'Bite her back, then she'll know what it feels like'. Do you really want to hurt your baby?

If your child bites (or pinches or whatever) other children at toddler groups, be prepared to be treated as a social pariah. Stay close enough to move in fast if you need to. Say 'No!' sharply and remove them from the scene of the crime. Stand him on his own. Withdraw attention from him and give attention to the child who was hurt instead.

Get the offender to say sorry after a spell of exclusion, then say something like, 'We never bite our friends, we tell them if something is bothering us.' Try to encourage your child to verbalise rather than acting out.

Tantrums

You are about to enter the tantrum zone. Your previously smiley, cheerful baby will turn into a red-faced, screeching, spiteful, unreasonable little monster! This is when you'll wish you'd never tutted at those women struggling round supermarkets with the baby from hell. See page 91.

CHILDCARE

Jane Larard;
Lucy Strauss;
Anna Knight;
Jo Davies;
Liz Chowienczyk;
Margaret Cave;
Yvette Cumming

For advice on Au Pairs, see page 170.

Nannies, Childminders & Babysitters

If you're looking for a nanny, check adverts in local newsagents. The NCT magazine is another good source and don't forget word of mouth. Talk to other mothers, nannies and childminders you meet at baby gym or mother and baby groups.

Magazines such as *The Lady* carry lists of adverts often arranged by geographical area – for both nannies and families.

You may be able to set up a nanny share, either by joining an established partnership or looking for someone new with another family.

There are nanny agencies that will help find you a suitable nanny for a fee. Again, always make your own checks on references.

Local councils carry lists of registered childminders in your area.

Colleges with courses in education and childcare often have students looking for work placements. Contact them and ask for details on how to go about hiring a student.

An ideal arrangement for families with kids of similar ages is to swap childcare duties, with the kids at one house one day and at the other another. This is great for day-time care, and gives one mum time off while the kids all play together.

The very best way to find a babysitter or childminder is through word-of-mouth recommendation.

Ask friends to recommend babysitters, and pool information and telephone numbers. Go by personal recommendation or teenagers you know. You could book other people's au pairs and nannies if they are free.

For very young children, try to stick to someone who has had children themselves – a granny or friend with older children is ideal until you and your baby feel confident about being apart.

When planning to book a babysitter, remember that most teenagers have a far better social life than you do, and are likely to be out most Friday and Saturday nights, so book well in advance.

Vet any potential childminder or nanny very carefully. Always ask for and carefully check references. If necessary, run a police check. Never accept excuses for a lack of referees. This is the one time when politeness shouldn't hold you back from asking awkward questions.

Have a list of questions for a potential childminder. How do you discipline? Do you have a first-aid qualification? How much TV do you let the children watch, if any? Please show me a copy of a typical week's lunch/snack menu? How many days/weeks during the past year were you unavailable for childcare (not including holidays)? If you go out, where do you take the children?

Get two or three references for a new babysitter, speak to her parents if you can and find out where she lives. Always check references or ask who she has babysat for in the past. Make sure that she meets your baby, and explain any important house rules before you leave her.

Before you leave anyone alone with your child, let them spend some time together while you are there. Ask your potential babysitter to come in as a mother's help first of all, and try to leave her with the baby while you do other things, so that you can see how they are with each other.

Try to set up a regular arrangement. Babies and toddlers don't like a lot of changes.

With nannies and childminders, make sure that the employment terms are clear. Discuss the days you need help, the number of hours, holidays and pay.

It's a good idea to find out the going rate and pay that if you want to keep your carer and make sure that she doesn't feel put upon.

Set out the ground rules from the outset. Make it clear if there is anything you feel strongly about.

Day Nurseries

If you are considering a day nursery, visit several, then go back to spend a few hours in your favourites. Watch what goes on. How do the staff relate to the children? Are they quick to spot any upsets? Do they react to prevent things going wrong?

Talk to other parents with children at the nursery. Ask for their honest opinions and try to find out what they don't like.

Leaving Your Child

Be positive when you first leave your child. Try not to feel guilty. Your child needs to feel that you are completely happy about leaving her with your carer. She will look to you for her lead and she should feel that this is a happy, normal day. If you look anxious she will feel insecure.

Even quite young children can 'punish' their parents for apparently abandoning them for the day. Your child may ignore you or run to someone else for cuddles. Don't worry: he hasn't stopped loving you and will get used to the new routine.

Attach a card to your child's clothing, somewhere where she can't pull it off, with your mobile phone number on it. If she gets lost or hurt, you can be contacted immediately.

Write your name and phone numbers (including all the important contacts like doctor, dentist, next of kin, hospital, etc.) on a piece of card, laminate it, then punch a hole in one corner of the card, and attach it to the changing bag with string. Make sure that this goes everywhere with your baby – day care, nursery and whenever the babysitter comes.

Use your noticeboard to display safety information for carers. Include a list of all of your child's medications or allergies, a list of safety rules or tips to remember, where to find first-aid supplies and emergency phone numbers.

Being Confident Of Your Childcare

Don't assume that someone else will deal with situations in the same way as you.

Make a friend of your nanny or childminder. This helps your working relationship and also means that you are more likely to hear about the fun things that have happened during the day.

Watch how your child relates to the nanny or childminder. Does he seem happy to see her?

The best child carers are not always those who get along easily with parents. Watch closely how they respond to your children.

If you have any doubts, ask friends and neighbours who see your child and minder out together how they seem, whether your child laughs and how attentive your minder is.

It's worth dropping in unannounced at your child's day care or nursery, just to check that all is as it should be, particularly when parents aren't expected.

Listen carefully to what your child says (if he is old enough) about his care arrangements. You may pick up on clues about things going on that you wouldn't accept. Don't ask leading questions – just ask open ones, but try to read between the lines of what he says.

Be alert. Children often behave badly when they feel insecure.

Don't make unfair demands on your nanny or childminder. If you have said that you will be home at 6.00 p.m., make sure that you are back by then.

If you are held up by cancelled trains or a late-running meeting, telephone your carer and explain the situation. Always apologise and try to make the time up to her another evening.

TRAVELLING

Jeanette Davey, Young Explorers: mail order catalogue 01789 414791, www.youngexplorers.co.uk; Ed Barnes; Tony Boyd

See also page 60.

In The Car

Most under-twos can't follow story tapes, but they'll enjoy song tapes, especially if you sing along too.

A clip-on play tray (which attaches to the car seat) is useful for toddlers. They can use it for feeding and playing.

Get a map and study it before you go. Write out simple directions and keep them close to hand so you can see them at a glance. You don't want to prolong the journey or have to stop for directions when you have children with you.

Remember that motorways are faster and less likely to cause travel sickness, and the constant movement will keep your child drowsy. Most motorway service stations have a range of kid-friendly facilities including baby rooms and a play area.

Make your baby's car seat more comfortable by placing a folded blanket under his knees so that they are slightly bent.

Use webbing toy ties to keep favourite toys attached to the car seat itself.

For toddlers on a long journey, pack a back pack full of interesting, even new, toys and something to eat, and offer it halfway through or when the going gets rough just as they start to get bored.

Stock the car with rugs and pillows for long journeys. It's often a good idea to set off when children would normally be sleeping.

Homeopaths recommend Nux.Vom. as a remedy for travel sickness. Ginger can also help. (Always ask for advice from a trained homeopath on dosage for children.)

Pack a cool bag of goodies to eat and drink on the journey. Avoid anything too heavy or messy and make sure that the bag is easily accessible.

Instead of offering drinks and risking the spills, give your kids seedless grapes.

Raw vegetables, fruits, cheese, crackers and tubs of yoghurt are all easily eaten in a car and store well. Remember to take plenty of bottles of water.

Car Safety

When you buy a new car seat, make sure that it is properly fitted and displays the BSS (British Safety Standards) kitemark.

A small mirror, fixed to the passenger visor and aimed straight at the little occupant in the back, is a cheap godsend. You can check that your baby is safe and well, and make faces at him, and later on your toddler passenger will really believe it when you say that you have eyes in the back of your head.

In hot weather, the metal clips on car seats can be burning hot. Make sure that T-shirts are well pulled down over tummies before you do them up.

Always have child locks on, even if you think your baby can't reach or open the door. It's in the nature of kids to be at least five steps ahead of you!

To get kids buckled in quickly and safely, and avoid fingers getting trapped, make it a game that they put their hands on their heads or in the air when they get into their car seats. Once they are strapped in and the doors are shut, the hands can come down – but not a moment before.

Give your kids only soft toys in the car, and put all your shopping in a covered boot. In accidents, loose objects can cause a lot of damage.

It's very dangerous to lean around to hand food/drinks to children.

For the law on seat belts, see page 141.

In The Plane

Ask your tour operator or airline what facilities the airline offers for babies. Some airlines, for example, will allocate aisle-side seats and supply play activities for toddlers.

Ask for bulkhead seating when possible. Some airlines have skycots for very young babies that you can reserve and attach to the bulkhead wall. And toddlers won't be tempted to kick the seats in front of them, and drive the occupants mad, if they can get down on the floor and play.

Check whether airlines provide children's meals and order them in advance.

However, don't rely on airline food. Kids love the little trays, but few will eat what is in them. Bring stuff you know they'll eat. Pack a little snack they can eat with their fingers in plastic tubs with snap-on lids – grapes, cheese chunks, chocolate chip cookies, juice boxes, crackers and cherry tomatoes are all easy to handle. This kind of food also works well for car journeys.

Especially on a long flight, it's a good idea to take along sandwiches, fruit, cheese, crackers and raw vegetables, which can be kept for a short period without refrigeration. You may also want to take a thermos of milk or juice.

When flying, collect up the flight sick bags – they're very handy for car-sick kids.

Spread your children's possessions around the family's luggage. If a case goes missing, you'll still have some of the things they need.

If your flight is long-haul, consider homeopathic remedies to keep children calm and combat jet lag.

If you're worried about your children getting jet lag, make sure that they drink fruit juice or water, and try to book a flight that arrives at your destination in the early evening. Then they can start adjusting to 'sleep' time immediately.

A late afternoon flight also works well because it allows time to be excited, to eat and then to settle down to sleep at roughly the normal hour.

Take a small towel to mop up any spills. You can't rely on attracting an air hostess's attention when you need it urgently. A damp cloth and spare clothes are a good idea, too.

Travel With Twins Or More

Get yourself a good big bag with plenty of pockets, and a jacket or waistcoat with zip pockets, so that you can keep a combination of wipes, dummies, drinks, biscuits, passports, keys, mobile phone and change – and still be able to retrieve any item at a moment's notice.

Pack complete outfits for each child, right down to socks and vests, and store each one in a clear plastic bag with a zip opening. You can put the dirties back into the bag after they have been worn. This saves an awful lot of time on holiday rummaging round in suitcases, wondering what has been worn and what hasn't.

As soon as you arrive, inquire about swimming pools and soft play areas so that your babies can let off some steam after their journey.

At Your Destination

Protect your child with plenty of high-factor suncream for children as well as covering up with sun hats and light clothing when the sun's hot.

If holidaying at altitude, don't ascend to great heights at speed with babies and toddlers to over 8000 feet, for example in a cable car. This affects the supply of oxygen to the baby's brain. They are sixteen times more likely to get altitude sickness than adults. If your child falls asleep, you may be lulled into thinking she is fine, whereas she is in fact shutting down her body to cope with lack of oxygen. Get down that mountain fast.

Don't ski with a baby in a backpack. Firstly, if you had a fall, your baby could be badly hurt; secondly, since she can't move around she is going to get very chilled. There have even been cases of babies dying of hypothermia while their parents thought they were fine.

Mountain tops in the European Alps at the top of cable car runs often have a tremendous range of facilities for babies and children, including heated toilet blocks, nappy-changing tables, playgrounds, cafés and indoor picnic areas.

Let your child follow your routine on holiday – later to bed so that with any luck you all get a lie in.

4 TWO TO FOUR YEARS

'Parentage is a very important profession; but no test of fitness for it is ever imposed in the interest of children.'

George Bernard Shaw

At the age of two your toddler has a distinct personality, though she is still very dependent upon you. She is often frustrated by what she can't do or say and her moods can swing from laughter to despair in a moment.

By four your child is growing fast with her own very definite opinions and ideas, likes and dislikes. She is probably already at nursery school and will soon start at big school, where she will have her own life away from home. She will share snippets of this new life with you but it will be the start of independence.

BEHAVIOUR

Alison Wallis; Amanda Stevens; Diana Starte; Judy and Mike Cooper; Margaret Cave; Sarah Brown, nursery teacher, Just Twos nursery

Two-to-four-year-olds need to know what's expected of them. An established routine for mealtime behaviour, bathtime and bedtime can help them feel safe and secure.

Reading to your child while he sits on your lap or snuggles next to you is a good way of feeling close physically as well as sharing a story.

Look at your child from time to time while you're reading, emphasising something funny, sad or peculiar that has just happened in the story. This helps his understanding of what's going on and makes it more fun.

Praise is very important in building self-confidence. When asking children questions, always praise the answer they give you, even if it wasn't the one you were looking for.

Praise children every day – not just for what they've done but for being them.

Children need eye contact. Crouch down to their level to talk instead of towering above them.

Tell children you love them, especially when they have been upset, after a tantrum or when they have been told off.

Positive discipline works well. Use star charts with an easily achievable number of stars and a small reward at the end.

When your toddler is dead set on something that you really don't want her to do, practise your acting ability and powers of distraction: nothing works better than dropping on to all fours and pretending to be a dog. Be a little careful about where you do this!

Fit children in with your routine and lifestyle. Children are amazingly adaptable and no one will be happy if you impose a regime that doesn't suit you just because you think it's what children need.

As a reward for good behaviour, take your child to a children's book shop to choose a book together. Most now have somewhere for kids to sit and study the books on offer.

When faced with a barrage of questions, try to be patient and answer as simply as possible. Two-to-four-year-olds are naturally curious and you can't ask them to save up their questions for later when you're less busy.

Small children are very demanding of your time and often leave you exhausted at the end of the day. The advice on page 64 holds good for this age group: don't forget that you need time, too.

Negotiations & Rows

Try to always use positive language, even when reprimanding your child.

Avoid negative language and labels. Criticise the behaviour, not the child.

Tell children off for bad or silly behaviour, criticising the action – never tell a child that she is naughty.

Try to set clear boundaries for behaviour.

Admit when you're in the wrong.

Think about your body language. If you are towering over your child, you are already demonstrating your dominance.

It's helpful to remember that your child doesn't want a perfect adult as a parent. You won't always deal with every situation perfectly, but try to make sure that your child knows you love and care for her – even when you're cross.

When disciplining, keep the message short and simple. Most young children can't take in endless reasoning and will only hear the last few comments.

It's important for children to understand that 'No' or 'Stop' must sometimes simply be obeyed. There are occasions when there are reasons why – usually to do with your child's safety – but there either isn't time for an explanation or the reasons are too complex for a small child to grasp.

When your child has done something silly, don't ask 'Why?' There often won't be a reason and being asked to explain his behaviour will force him into a corner where he may well just deny it.

It sometimes helps to remember that small children learn and develop through curiosity, sometimes with unexpected and unfortunate results.

TERRIBLE TWOS – TEMPER TANTRUMS

Anna Knight; Clare Porter; Judy Cooper, nursery teacher; Sandra Wroe; Sarah Brown, nursery teacher, Just Twos nursery; Alex Gardner, psychologist; Glynis Fletcher, NCT counsellor; Gioia Marzullo; Kurt Klotzle, paediatrician

All children of this age have tantrums. They are testing the boundaries. Try distraction or offer a way out for them that doesn't simply mean you give in.

Don't treat your child with kid gloves to avoid tantrums and try not to be embarrassed if he is screaming at the supermarket. Most other parents at least will sympathise.

Heading tantrums off at the pass. First try distraction: 'Hey, Look! What's that over there?' If this fails, try the choice factor: 'Which way shall we go home – via the park, or the shops?' or 'Shall I buy apples or pears for Daddy?'

Whisking your child away from the park just as they are getting involved in a good game is a tantrum waiting to happen – think how frustrating it must be for her. When it is nearly time to go, try to explain in a way your child will understand. Instead of, 'We're going in five minutes,' try something like, 'Three more goes down the slide, then we have to go.' Don't even think about going to the park if you're in a rush.

To avoid a tantrum, always have something else interesting to look forward to. 'We have to leave now so that we have time to feed the ducks/read a story/do some painting.'

When your toddler is gearing up for a real temper tantrum, open and close a window quickly or slam a door. Whether this works by surprise or distraction, you may well find that it stops your toddler in his tracks.

You're in a hurry and suddenly you have a truculent toddler on your hands who absolutely refuses to cooperate and sit in her buggy or car seat. Try distraction – 'Look at that big dog/lorry/fast car/stripy cat …' It doesn't matter what, as long as it interests her enough to allow you to strap her safely into her seat.

A pile of papers to tear up and deposit in the rubbish bin is a useful distraction.

Try to look at what lies behind the tantrum. And remember that it is important for your child to save face.

It is not a question of winning but of managing the situation.

Your child won't be spoilt if you don't always dominate. Children need to feel they have some power and control over their lives.

Try to remember how you felt when you were little – the sense of powerlessness and also the conviction that you are right when no one else seems able to see that.

For as long as a tantrum lasts, a child will not be able to see reason, so there is no point trying to argue or shouting back.

Don't give in to your child's demands in order to stop a tantrum. If you've already said no, stick to that, gently but firmly.

Aim to get the message across that screaming or throwing a tantrum achieves nothing. It doesn't make you cross but neither does it get him what he is asking for.

The very best way to deal with a tantrum is simply not to deal with it. If you possibly can, say firmly to your toddler something like, 'I can't give you any attention when you yell like that. Come and talk to me when you've finished.' Then leave her to it in a safe place. It's not worth having a tantrum if there is no audience.

Don't get drawn into the argument if it's about something specific. Once you start all that 'Well, would you like it in this cup instead?' stuff, you've really lost the plot.

There really is no point giving in over whatever the issue is that has sparked off the tantrum. Sometimes a child just needs to have a tantrum, to get it out of her system. If you give in over this issue, she will just choose something else. Far better to get it over with, and make friends again afterwards.

In a public place where the disturbance is too much, say, 'I'm going to take you out now unless you stop that yelling.' Then just pick him up, put him over your shoulder and take him out.

Don't get hung up about what other people are thinking. If they have children of their own, they know what it's like. If they don't, their opinion isn't valid.

Try to remain cool, or at least to appear so. You're supposed to be modelling the kind of behaviour you'd like your child to exhibit, after all.

Different treatment sometimes works with boys and girls. As long as small boys are safe, have space around them and can't hurt themselves, it's often better to leave them to work out their own tantrum. Girls often prefer to be picked up and comforted. You will get to know what works for your own child.

Toddlers can get themselves into a situation where they no longer know why they are upset. Try to distract or give them a way out.

As soon as the tantrum is over, give plenty of cuddles and kisses and praise your child for regaining control – even if you feel really annoyed and embarrassed.

Once the tantrum is over, behave as usual. Try to treat the episode as unpleasant but irrelevant.

As your child gets more mature, and gets a better command of language, the tantrums will get fewer and fewer. They will still occur, though, particularly if he is tired, hungry, embarrassed or frustrated.

TODDLERS & NEW SIBLINGS

Anna Knight;
Sarah Griffiths;
Margaret Cave

Toddlers will have their noses put out of joint by the arrival of a sibling. What is this thing that has suddenly taken up all Mum's attention? Even though you have been waddling around pregnant for a while, a small child will not understand that you have a baby in your tummy – though letting them feel it kick will help. Explain as much as you can about how you will go into hospital but that you are not ill, and that she can come and visit with Daddy or a grandparent – but don't be surprised if she is distressed by the situation when it happens.

When your older child comes to see you and his new baby sister for the first time, make sure that you aren't holding the baby and can give him your full attention and a big cuddle.

Make sure that the baby has brought your older child a present. It starts the siblings off on the right footing.

Hold your older child's hand when talking to him, especially when you are holding or feeding the baby.

Make physical contact with your toddler so that she doesn't feel excluded when you are feeding the baby.

Chat with your older child when you are feeding the baby. The little one is getting plenty of attention already.

Avoid holding your baby between you and your older child.

Let your older child touch the baby, but it is quite likely that he will be fairly disinterested.

Don't expect a toddler to automatically like his baby brother. Don't push him to 'love' the new baby.

First few days back home with a second child? Once you have fed the baby – if you are breastfeeding – try to hand it over to someone else to wind and/or change the nappy, so as to free you up to concentrate on your toddler's needs. Having your attention will help to ease his acceptance of the new baby.

A toddler will enjoy helping you bath/dress the new baby, but would much prefer just being with you.

Having your third or fourth child? The eldest child will feel threatened, though often more willing to help with and enjoy the new baby. She has had your undivided attention even if she was too young to really remember and it's an easy mistake to make to expect her to suddenly be grown up when younger siblings appear. The second child may well react negatively. Their little world has been rocked by the new arrival. The same strategy of finding one-to-one time with each child still applies, although it can be a juggling act. Get help with the baby, not help with the older children. They will feel shut out from you if they are permanently being taken out of your hair.

For more on sibling relationships, see page 277.

INDEPENDENCE

Amanda Stevens;
Judy and Mike
Cooper;
Margaret Cave

Encourage toddlers to feed themselves, including using knives, forks and spoons. They enjoy the sense of independence and this is also good preparation for school and school meals.

If your child has a security blanket or other comforter, when appropriate, suggest that your child leaves it behind, but don't push the issue if he looks distressed.

For dummies and thumb-sucking, see page 82.

Encourage your child's speech. Expand on what he says and try to add new words for him to learn. For instance, if he points out a truck tell him what colour it is and describe it.

Compromise, distract, keep cool – and give lots of praise when he manages something by himself.

Reverse psychology can work when you're trying to encourage your child to get dressed by herself. Suggest that you help her pull on her tights as she's much too little. She's bound to want to prove you wrong.

To encourage a child to play by herself, spend some time with her setting up a den or a play scenario, then suggest she continues by herself, for as long as a particular piece of music lasts. You will often find that she becomes so involved that she happily carries on.

When your toddler has crept into your bed *again* the previous night, at bedtime try stressing the lovely things you'll do the following day, provided everyone has lots of sleep, and mention how grown up you know he is … well able to stay in his own bed. (It sometimes works!) See also page 100.

On the whole, girls are better at doing things by themselves and generally more willing to try – but remember, they still need the reassurance of being babied some of the time.

Don't force independence on a reluctant child. They all get there eventually and are likely to be happier and more secure if you don't push them.

HEALTH

Clare Baines; British
Dental Association;
Dr Kate Crocker;
Liz Chowienczyk;
Margaret Cave;
Dr Ruth Marchant;
Sian Annous,
dental surgeon

Lots of young children find visiting the doctor and dentist quite scary. Help prepare them by reading stories about children or animals seeing a nurse, being examined by a doctor or having their teeth checked. There are lots to choose from including stories about hospital stays and operations.

If your child has to have an injection, warn him that he is going to have an injection before you go along. Avoid saying, 'It won't hurt.' This just adds fear and introduces the idea that it probably will hurt.

For more on immunisation, see page 63 and Appendix, page 305.

First-aid courses can be very useful, not only for your own accident-prone youngsters. Try contacting St John Ambulance for details of their one-day or basic courses.

Keep a stock of fun, funky plasters. Kids love different colours and characters and they can prove a great distraction even when they're not strictly needed.

Make sure that you know where your nearest Accident and Emergency department is and how to get there.

Accidents

Keep calm! If you panic, so will your child.

However worried or uncertain you are, don't show it. Your child may well be frightened and needs reassurance.

If you have any doubts about the seriousness of an injury, go to your nearest Accident and Emergency department and get it checked.

For cuts, grazes and splinters, see page 136.

Asthma

If your child has a persistent cough that wakes him in the early hours of the morning, and is wheezing, and you suspect he has asthma, take him to see your GP, who will measure his lung capacity and breathing. Don't attempt to diagnose asthma yourself.

Once your child has been diagnosed as asthmatic, she will probably be given an inhaler. Always make sure that she has an inhaler with her, and keep spares. You need one at home and also one permanently at school or nursery.

Small children can find it difficult to use inhalers. To encourage them to breathe correctly ask them to recite or chant a nursery rhyme. Baa baa black sheep works well.

As your child gets older, she will quickly learn to use the inhaler by herself.

Many GPs now have a specialist asthma nurse and you can find out more information from the National Asthma Campaign's website www.asthma.org.uk, which has an excellent Kids Zone.

GPs often have nebulisers at the surgery. If your child needs one, it is often quicker and less traumatic to go there rather than to hospital.

Go for non-biological washing powders, non-perfumed hypoallergenic fabric conditioner and soaps.

Try to avoid anything that you know triggers an asthma attack. The most common triggers are: pets – especially cats, dogs and horses, smoky atmospheres, coughs and colds, exercise, pollen and dust.

Keep children's bedrooms as clean as possible. Dust mites aggravate the condition. To cut down on dust mites:

- Store toys in plastic boxes with sealable lids.
- Boil sheets and pillow cases every week.
- No soft toys (or chuck them in the freezer every week overnight to kill off the dust mites).
- Take up the carpet if possible.
- Get new pillows and quilts every six months.

- Don't assume that feather pillows and quilts always cause problems – for some children, the synthetics are worse.

Some sufferers find a cup of tea soothing.

Steam can also help. If you're worried about a small child with a bowl of steaming water, try to make his bedroom steamy. Shut the doors and windows and boil a kettle a couple of times.

When your child is having an attack, try to get her to relax as this will help her breathing.

Chickenpox

Keep skin as cool as possible. Research shows that spots are far worse where the skin gets hot.

Suggest your child pats on her own calamine lotion with cotton wool whenever she needs to.

Be creative. Use a paintbrush to apply the calamine and let her join the dots.

Warm baths with a cup of bicarbonate of soda dissolved in the water may help with the itching.

Make sure that your child's fingernails are short and clean and when the itching is bad, try to distract him with his favourite story or video.

A pair of light cotton gloves worn at bedtime can also help prevent scratching – if you can get your child to keep them on.

Coughs & Colds

When the weather is chilly and runny noses seem to be a constant problem, give a daily dose of children's chewable vitamin C. If nothing else, it will make you feel better.

Encourage children to eat more fruit. Choose things you know they particularly like – seedless grapes are often a favourite and available all year round, and kiwi fruits halved and scooped out with a spoon are a fantastic natural source of vitamin C.

Offer lots of drinks. Children quickly become dehydrated.

As eggs – boiled, scrambled or poached – have a high zinc content, they're the ideal food to help clear up a cold.

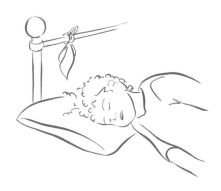

Aromatic oil and drops are helpful at night to keep noses clear. Karvol capsules are particularly good for young children. Drip the oil onto a handkerchief and tie to a bedpost.

Inhaling steam, particularly with some aromatic oil added, helps clear noses and calm tickly coughs. With young children, be especially careful with hot water and always supervise.

Eczema

If your child has itchy, flaking, weepy skin, consult your doctor. Don't diagnose eczema yourself.

Apply moisturiser as often as possible – at least four times a day. This really reduces the amount of steroid cream children need, and is better for their skin in the long term.

Use oil in the bath. There are several brands that are especially suitable for children's skin.

Make sure that the water is lukewarm, never hot, and never use soap.

After washing, dab the skin dry with a very soft towel. Avoid rubbing, as this will make the itching worse.

Keep fabrics natural and as soft as possible. Wool and man-made fibres next to the skin can make the problem worse. Several light layers are better than one thick one.

Use non-biological washing powders and avoid fabric conditioners.

Keep a record of when the eczema flares up or is particularly bad. Try to find the cause.

Some foods can be a trigger. If the eczema began around the time your child was weaned, cow's milk could be to blame.

Always see your doctor before restricting a child's diet or eliminating certain foods.

Rashes

Following the controversy over the measles, mumps and rubella vaccination, and the subsequent lower take-up and reduction in 'herd' immunity, there has been an increase in outbreaks of the diseases. Check suspicious rashes with your GP if you think your child could be at risk.

Nosebleeds

Stay calm and be very reassuring. Your child may well be shocked at the sight of so much of his own blood.

Sit your child on your lap and gently but firmly pinch his nostrils at the centre of his nose. Spread an old towel across you both to catch the drips.

Don't lay down a child with a nosebleed. She will swallow blood and may throw up.

Ice cubes wrapped in muslin or a cloth and held against the nose can help to slow the blood flow. Ask your child to hold them himself.

Teeth

Dental studies in Sweden show that children really need their teeth brushing for them until the age of twelve. In practice, few children will let you help anywhere near that long. Try to encourage good brushing habits and make sure that your children know the correct way to brush their teeth. Dentists are normally more than happy to help.

Little electric toothbrushes work well for small mouths. Choose plug-in not battery versions so that you can recharge them.

Make brushing fun by letting children choose their own toothbrushes.

Set a kitchen timer for two minutes in the bathroom to show children just how long they should be brushing their teeth for.

Tooth decay in milk teeth appears as creamy yellow patches and the teeth themselves may begin to flake. Watch out for early signs.

Get your children into a regular routine of visiting the dentist. They will find the dentist less alarming if they become familiar with the surgery.

If you're out and worried about the amount of sweets your child has just consumed, give him a piece of cheese to eat.

When you're eating out, you could wipe your child's teeth with a clean, damp cloth to clean away any bits of food.

For more on dentists and toothbrushing, see page 69.

Hospitals

See page 137.

Medicines

See page 77.

BATHTIME & GENERAL CARE

Anna Knight;
Clare Porter;
Margaret Cave

It is natural for children to be interested in their bodies at this age. They are also becoming aware of the physical differences between boys and girls.

For more on bathtime, see page 79.

Hair

A few children love having their hair cut. Some have even been known to fall asleep during the process. If yours isn't one of these laid-back individuals, choose a salon especially for children. They will be used to distracting kids and may have tropical fish tanks or videos for them to watch. The chairs will also be the right height and size for comfort. It's worth taking time to look around to avoid the tantrums.

Adult hair salons are not very safe places for toddlers. Try to avoid taking them with you for your own hair appointments. Book your slot for a time when your partner can mind the children or do a swap with a friend.

Is a haircut really essential? If your child is screaming and hates the whole idea, don't force her to stay. It isn't worth it. She won't sit still enough for the hairdresser to cut her hair properly and will remember the episode the next time you try to take her.

If haircuts are a real problem, try trimming at home. Bribery can also help.

For hairwashing, see page 79.

POTTY-TRAINING & LOOS

Anna Knight;
Jacqui Ciotkowski,
midwife;
Lizzi Stackhouse,
aromatherapist

Leave any attempt at potty-training until your child is ready. Don't force the issue.

If a child is really keen to start using a potty instead of nappies, let her take the lead.

If possible, leave potty-training until summer, when children need fewer clothes and the washing dries faster.

Buy lots and lots of pairs of pants. Take your toddler with you to choose them. It's a big deal to wear big kids' pants!

You won't get much warning when your child needs a wee, so use clothes that can be whipped off quick. Dungarees are a big no-no, and even the most inveterate little tomboy is best in a dress at this time. Put girls in dresses or skirts and boys in shorts with elasticated waists. These make for easy access, and fewer clothes to wash after the inevitable accidents. Go one step further and leave off knickers and pants altogether at home. (Theirs not yours.)

For quick access, have potties both downstairs and upstairs.

If you have multiples, you may feel it would be easier to train one first; then the others can follow their lead. Be guided by the toddlers.

If children are scared of going to the toilet, try turning it into a game. Have the 'pooh party' – poohs don't want to stay inside you, they want to get out and join their friends at the pooh party. Disgusting? Maybe, but it's better than having a child who ends up constipated. Get over your own issues so that your child won't inherit them.

Fear of failure can worry some children. Be very reassuring that it's not a big deal.

Star charts can work well as positive encouragement.

If friends come round, don't hide the potty. Children learn by copying their peers.

Carry a travel potty with you when you are out. It's not always possible to find convenient public loos.

The occasional reminder about needing to wee is a good idea in the early stages of training, especially when your toddler is busy playing. Try to keep reminders to a minimum, as it's important that he recognises the need to use a potty by himself.

You're aiming towards independence, so encourage your toddler to go to his potty by himself and to manage his own clothes. He will enjoy feeling he is in control.

If a child has held on for too long and seems unable to wee, turn a tap full on. The sound of running water should help.

Stay calm. There will be accidents and things will go wrong.

Remember that potty-training is not a competition – either between your child and other children, or between twins, triplets or more. Life will be easier if you're not constantly comparing.

Girls are often quicker to learn than boys.

Don't lose heart or patience. It can take a while to get it right. If you are more relaxed about it, the kids will be too.

Loos

To encourage your child to begin using the lavatory rather than a potty, at first position the potty next to the loo.

It's a good idea to place a child-sized loo seat on top of the normal one with a step to allow your child to climb on and off the lavatory by himself. It must feel very wobbly to a toddler to be perched up there, and some of them really are scared that they'll fall in and be flushed away.

Little boys normally start by weeing sitting down. It's only later that they begin to copy their dads or older brothers and stand up.

To help prevent spills and encourage an accurate aim, drop a cork into the toilet bowl and suggest your son tries to hit it.

Dryness At Night

Make sure that your child empties his bladder completely before bed. When he thinks he's finished, tell him to try again, and then once more.

Wake your child to go to the loo before you go to sleep (a few hours after he's gone to bed) and, if necessary, get up during the night to try again.

Dryness at night can come later and sometimes, especially for boys, much later.

Try to be relaxed about dryness at night. It will come, but if you try to force the issue you will end up with wet beds and an anxious child.

A plastic sheet under the cotton one will protect mattresses from accidents.

Before leaving nappies off at night, wait until your child wakes up dry after a whole night and can go for three or four hours without urinating during the day.

If your child has been dry at night and then begins to have accidents, try lifting her at night to sit her on her potty. When you're about to go to bed is a good time.

If wet beds continue to be a problem, cut down on bedtime drinks.

When bedwetting suddenly starts again in a child who has been dry for a long time, it may be a response to some sort of emotional upset. Try to find out what's wrong if a cause isn't immediately obvious.

Minimise the distress of a bed-wetting child by having clean pyjamas ready if he needs them, and minimise yours by making up the bed with a plastic sheet, then a cotton sheet, then another plastic sheet and another cotton one. If the top two layers are wet just whip them off, and the bed will be ready again.

If you use trainer pants in bed, your child may think it's OK to wee in them, and not bother getting up to go to the loo. So try leaving the pull-ups off – and see what happens.

Boys tend to be later with being dry at night, and even during the day. This is so much a fact of life that it is not even considered a special problem by health professionals any more.

Don't let your child drink large amounts before bed and avoid orange or lemon juice, excessive amounts of water and caffeinated drinks, such as cola.

BEDTIME & SLEEPING

Anna Knight;
Judy and Mike
Cooper; Margaret
Cave; Sarah Griffiths;
Sarah Brown, nursery
teacher, Just Twos
nursery; Sandra Wroe

A familiar bedtime routine can help children fall happily asleep at night. You set the agenda according to what you and your children enjoy, but it helps to establish a pattern, say a warm bath, milky drink and bedtime story.

Start bedtime routines really really early – both in age and time. Six or seven o'clock bath, books and bed sets up a good pattern – which works well for young children and is a boon for adults too. You need your rest and 'grown-up' time alone.

Read bedtime stories in bed. Make this a cosy, special time for you both, so that when you get up, your child is warm and comfy and can – you hope – drop easily to sleep.

If your child gets too excited by stories or always wants just a little bit more, try finishing the bedtime goodnights with poems. The rhythms can be very soothing, especially if you choose a familiar favourite. Try reciting some of the Pooh poems from *The House at Pooh Corner* or *Now We are Six*.

Singing a particular song or lullaby just before you leave your child's bedroom can work well as a sign that it's now time to settle down to sleep.

Create a safe, cosy sleeping place where your toddler feels happy to stay. Tuck in special toys or cuddlies, and consider hanging up a mobile or even sticking glow-in-the-dark stars or planets to the ceiling.

If your child has trouble falling asleep, listening to story tapes can be a good way to help her relax as well as making bedtime fun.

Just like adults, not all children need the same number of hours' sleep. Don't worry if your child doesn't seem to need as much sleep as his friends.

Relax about children coming into your bed at night. Everyone always thinks this will last for ever, but it won't.

If you think that your child really is too big to be sleeping with you each night and everyone's sleep is being disturbed, try offering a simple reward if she spends the whole night in her own bed. A star chart or the promise of baking some biscuits together or another shared treat can all work.

When the familiar, small figure appears at the side of your bed in the middle of the night, cuddle him but quietly return him to his own bed. Make sure that he is comfortably tucked in, but keep any chat to a minimum.

Make sure that the route from your child's room to your own is clear of obstacles. When your child comes looking for you at night, you don't want her tripping over things in the dark.

Early Rising

Blackout blinds are excellent for blocking out early morning light and can help children to sleep on later. They also help when the clocks go forward and it's suddenly much lighter than usual at bedtime.

Set an alarm clock to cure an early riser. It may sound strange but children love gimmicks and your child will start to wait for the buzzer to go off, often falling asleep again before it does. Eventually, his body clock will change, and he will have learnt to sleep until your chosen time of waking.

Help an early waker to amuse himself by setting out books and toys, even a drink and snack – things that will encourage him to play quietly until a more reasonable hour.

Early morning children's TV, even when your child is tucked up watching it from your bed, can be great when you're desperate for an extra half hour's rest.

Some children are naturally early risers, and may find it hard to be the only one awake. Pets can be good company, and try leaving a tape machine with a story-tape lined up for him to turn on.

Nightmares & Terrors

When your child has woken from a bad dream, make a point of turning the pillow over to turn the nightmare way.

Leave a night light or soft light on in the bedroom if your child finds it reassuring.

Nearly all children have nightmares from time to time. They are nothing to worry about, unless your child shows signs of being upset during the day too.

If your child is going through a phase of nightmares, try to get to her as soon as she cries, before she has time to get really upset. Settle her back to sleep as swiftly and calmly as possible.

Instead of saying, 'But it's only a dream, so it's OK', which dismisses the child's very real feeling of fear, try saying something like, 'Oh, that does sound horrible. Thank goodness you've woken up and the dream has gone.'

Make a spell for your child to say. 'Bad dream, bad dream go away, you're not real anyway!'

Night terrors are different from nightmares and can be disturbing for you. Your child will appear to be awake with her eyes wide open and may be sitting up or trying to get out of bed. She will appear terrified and may not recognise you – in fact she may think that you are part of the terror.

Night terrors are dramatic, with a child waking up sobbing fearfully, sometimes thrashing around and not sure for a while where he is or who you are. He may not even know why he is crying and scared, and not even seem to be fully awake. Reassure him, but it may take some time for him to calm down. This is something children grow out of, so don't make a big deal out of it, and don't even mention it during the day.

Night terrors are more likely if your child is worried about something in particular or if she is unwell, especially with a raised temperature.

To deal with a night terror:

- Stay calm.

- Don't try to reason or argue with your child – remember that she's not awake.

- If you can, cuddle and rock her and make soothing sounds.

- It sometimes helps to switch on a light.

- Don't try to wake your child. She will probably drift back to normal sleep.

- If she wakes suddenly, she's likely to be disorientated, particularly if she's wandered into another room. Be very reassuring and make light of the incident. Tell her she's had a bad dream and now it's time to go back to bed.

- If necessary, stay with her until she is calmly sleeping again.

- Don't leave her with an inexperienced babysitter if anything makes you think that she is likely to have a night terror that evening.

Fears

Fears or worries often surface at bedtime, especially when a child is beginning to relax and drift towards sleep. Talk through any worries with your child and try to be as gentle, positive and reassuring as possible.

It would be very unusual for a child never to be anxious about something. If your child is anxious, try to find out exactly what is worrying her and talk to her about it. Children want reassurance.

Try to rationalise your child's fears. Make sure that he feels safe, and be as reassuring as you possibly can.

Remember that you can't protect children from everything and fear can sometimes be useful. Encourage your child to discuss her fears and let her know that you are there to keep her safe.

Most children enjoy the thrill of a scary story, but don't push your child to listen or watch something that is upsetting him.

Children often have fears of going upstairs on their own, or of monsters, bad strangers or ghosts, so keep them close to you for the thirty minutes before bedtime so that they feel safe.

Don't dismiss a child's fears, or tell him they are silly. If necessary, look under the bed while explaining that you yourself know there isn't a monster there and that this is for her benefit.

Encourage children from an early age to befriend monsters. Tell them that monsters can show you wonderful things (monster comes from the latin *monstrare* – to show) if you make them your allies. You can also suggest that children can be kind to ghosts (they're usually lonely) and to remember that most witches are exceedingly nice people who stir a darn fine stew. Needless to say, you should never ever threaten children with 'bogeymen' of any description.

If your child is afraid of ghosts or monsters hiding in his room at night, tell him that ghosts or monsters are actually afraid of little children. Try getting the video of *Monsters Inc.* out of the library to prove it.

You can say with great authority that monsters never visit Warwickshire/Cheshire/Balham or wherever you live, because they are very frightened of the children who live there.

Fill a spray bottle with water, maybe with a dash of lavender oil, and label it 'anti-monster spray'. Use it around the room before bedtime to keep monsters away.

FOOD

Alison Tweedale, nanny; Catherine Wilson, nanny; Clare Porter; John Knight; Linda Elderkin, nanny; Marianne Bell, nanny; Dr Lisa Watts; Paula Goody; William Crawford

Don't be surprised if your toddler continues to play with her food or is tricky about tasting something new. Try to be patient. Even if she seems to be eating very little, you would be surprised at how much is actually going in.

Variety! Continue to offer lots of different tastes, textures and colours.

Children can take a long time to accept lumpy food. If your child still won't eat lumps, don't worry – he will eat them eventually. For the time being, serve 'bit-free' yoghurts and soups.

Some breastfed babies never really get used to the taste of cow's milk. If this is the case with your child, make sure that he gets enough calcium by offering plenty of alternative calcium-rich foods. Tinned tuna and oily fish, eggs, fromage frais, yoghurts, cheese and other dairy-based foods are all good sources.

You can also 'hide' milk in soups, on cereals and in cocoa or custard.

Try not to offer flavoured milk too often. It is better for children to get used to plain milk, which doesn't have the added sugar and flavourings.

Avoid making mealtimes a battle. You don't have to win and the more laid back you are about what your child eats, the more likely he is to try different things.

Fussy eaters don't usually stay that way, especially if you don't make an issue of what your child chooses to eat.

Some children get stuck on one particular food and want to eat it at every meal. This is called a 'food jag' and if you go along with it, your child will probably quickly get bored. As long as the food is nutritious and the jag doesn't last too long, there's nothing to worry about.

Encourage children to taste at least one mouthful of a new food. If they reject it after one bite, try again at a later date.

Young children often don't need to eat that much and rarely starve themselves. You would quickly know if your child wasn't eating enough because he wouldn't be growing properly and would lack energy.

You may notice your child's appetite dropping around the age of two when her growth rate falls.

Children should always be sitting upright whenever they eat, not lying down or running around. Always supervise at snack and mealtimes because a child who is choking cannot make a noise to attract your attention. Coughing is a sign that the child is removing the obstacle naturally. Before intervening, give the child the chance to cough out the food.

Encourage children to sit at a table for their meals and to use cutlery.

It's a good idea to buy special children's cutlery. The spoon should have a wide rounded mouth and the fork should have blunt prongs. At first a young child will use only the spoon but he will gradually learn to use the fork.

Sometimes children behave better and enjoy mealtimes more when they sit down to a meal with the family at a properly set table. Allowing older children to have candles makes a meal into a special occasion and little ones can help to blow them out when everyone's eaten.

Try to make sure that children have a quiet time immediately before mealtimes. It's hard to get an excited child to calm down enough to eat properly.

Encourage children to learn about personal hygiene and get into the habit of washing their hands before eating or handling food.

It's never too soon to start learning good manners and mealtimes are a good place to practise. Make sure that you say 'please' and 'thank you' as well. You want to set a good example.

Allow children to eat at friends' homes. This is an excellent opportunity for them to try new foods.

Children love little things. Arrange small helpings of lots of different food on their plates.

Arrange food in different patterns, or spell out your child's name and encourage her to eat a letter at a time.

Let children help choose fruit and vegetables. They are likely to choose something they have never tried before and they are more likely to eat it if they have chosen it themselves.

Even young children can help with cooking and preparing food. Look out for children's cookery sets with rolling pins, plastic cutters and plastic knives and forks, and encourage your children to work alongside you. You will be surprised at how keen they are to help and to taste something they have had a hand in making.

Three- and four-year-olds like to feel challenged. Let them break eggs into a bowl, measure and mix ingredients, knead and shape dough and toss salads.

Children love having jobs to do. Ask them to help by washing vegetables, wiping the table, tearing up salad leaves and clearing their own place settings.

Children enjoy tipping their own cereal into a bowl and can pour over the milk if you first decant it into a small jug.

Make food fun. Cut out bread and sandwiches with pastry cutters. Most cookery departments stock metal ones in a variety of shapes from animals and dinosaurs to stars and flowers. You can usually find themed ones to match the seasons at different times of the year.

Don't let preparing food become a burden. If you spend hours on a meal, only to have it rejected, you're bound to feel cross. Salads, raw vegetables, fruits and ready-to-serve meat, fish and cheese are nutritious and easy to prepare.

Snacks can be healthy. As children only have small stomachs, three big meals a day isn't always the best way for them to eat. Nutritious snacks of fruit, vegetables, dried fruit, cheese, yoghurt and breadsticks help boost vitamin and mineral intake.

Children's blood-sugar level can run low quite quickly. If your child suddenly seems grouchy for no apparent reason, try giving him a small piece of fruit or cheese.

Don't ban sweets. By sometimes including them as part of your child's normal diet, you avoid making them a big deal.

Never offer sweets as a bribe or take them away as a punishment.

Avoid always using sweets as a treat. Offer colourful small fruits like grapes or strawberries and cut-up mixes of vegetables, cheese and raisins instead. Children enjoy differently shaped and coloured finger food.

Children love ice lollies, but can never eat them quickly enough before they begin to melt. Slide a disc of card onto the stick to catch the drips; failing that, a tissue wrapped around the stick also helps.

CLOTHES

Alison Wallis;
Amanda Stevens;
Anna Knight;
Clare Porter;
Judy Cooper;
Sandra Wroe;
Sarah Brown,
nursery teacher,
Just Twos Nursery

Children need to feel comfortable and free to move about. They should be able to play and have fun.

When you know that children are going somewhere where they are likely to get grubby, don't dress them in special outfits. They need the freedom to get dirty sometimes.

Especially when your child starts nursery school, make sure that he can manage his clothes himself.

Easy-access clothes are particularly important when your child is first out of nappies.

Outdoor clothes as well as indoor ones should be comfortable and not too bulky. If it is impossible to play in a coat, your child just won't wear it.

Remember that children get very warm when they are running around outside and don't need masses of layers.

Fleeces are ideal for active children. They keep them warm but are not heavy and don't restrict their movements.

Encourage your child to dress independently. Lay out his clothes so that he can see the whole outfit.

Children feel a real sense of achievement when they begin to be able to dress themselves. Try not to comment if they have done buttons up the wrong way or have a T-shirt on inside out.

Try to allow your child to choose her own clothes sometimes. If her odd combination of colours really bothers you, make an initial selection of a few items for her to choose from.

Whilst it's good to give children a free choice of clothes some of the time, it's also important they realise that there are occasions when it's appropriate to dress a certain way – visits to aged relatives or weddings, for instance. If they learn to accept this when they're little, it can make battles over clothes easier when they're older.

If your small daughter wants to go out dressed like a fairy, let her. She won't be able to (or want to) when she's older. Dressing up is an important part of make believe and allowing her imagination a free reign.

Dressing up can be great therapy for shyness and can be used to persuade or to overcome fears. Superman wouldn't be scared of the dentist, and whoever heard of a fairy without clean teeth and hair?

Small boys like pretending to be animals as well as superheroes. They can be wildly attached to a particular pair of green trousers and T-shirt which in their own minds make them look like a dinosaur.

Help children recognise their left and right by putting stickers on their wellies or write R and L on the inside soles of their shoes with nail varnish.

Iron on patches inside the knees of toddlers' trousers in case of tumbles and to prevent them from wearing through quickly.

To keep laces in shoes, thread them through the first two holes, then tie knots on each side so that they can't be pulled out.

On special occasions when your kids need to stay as clean as possible, spray knees, cuffs and collars with a fabric protector.

If you have a choice of trousers or shorts for your son, choose shorts while he is little. He'll grow out of trousers within months, if not weeks, but not before he's holed the knees!

Some children hate having polo necks pulled over their heads. It's not worth forcing the issue.

CHILDREN'S ROOMS

Alison Wallis;
Amanda Stevens;
Anna Knight;
Karen Mae Birch;
William Crawford

Choose furniture and finished surfaces that can be wiped clean and go for furniture with rounded edges.

Remember to make the room safe – see page 66.

It's easier to repaint a room rather than repaper it. Children's tastes develop and this way you can easily ring the changes. Also, children can't resist tearing off unglued wallpaper. Select wipe-clean brands of paint.

Choose fabrics that won't look too babyish as your child grows. Stripes and checks are always fresh-looking.

For making curtains and curtain poles, see page 167.

You can never have too many shelves or enough storage.

If storage is a problem, double up the rails in the wardrobe. Children's clothes aren't long enough to need the extra hanging space.

Try to leave maximum floor space for play by putting as many things as possible on the wall – either on shelves or hanging from pegs.

Narrow shelves are a great way to display children's toys. Position some out of reach for more special things which your child can ask for when he wants to play with them.

A row of painted Shaker pegs around the wall looks attractive and makes great storage if you hang drawstring gingham bags on each peg for different toys and equipment. Make sure that they are not too high for children to reach.

Make your own storage boxes by cutting down sturdy cardboard boxes to fit beneath a bed. Decorate the boxes by painting them or covering them with pictures or wrapping paper, and protect with sticky-back plastic. Finally, attach a strong string handle to make them easy to pull out. Children will have fun decorating their own.

To keep track of stray children's toys deposited about the house, make personalised toy boxes. For each child, use a strong cardboard box and help her to paint and decorate her own box, marking her name with big colourful letters and finishing with a protective layer of sticky-back plastic. When you find odd toys or socks, drop them into the child's box, ready for her to return to her room.

Decorate drawers or cupboards with pictures of the contents – pictures of socks, for instance, on a sock drawer. That way everyone knows what's supposed to be inside and where to find what they want.

To brighten up a child's room, make a cheap fun border. Get long strips of paper and let children help to decorate them.

Painting a mural isn't as hard as it sounds. Choose a simple drawing from a children's book, and draw a grid over the picture using tracing paper. With a soft pencil mark out a larger grid on to the wall, with the same number of squares, and transfer the design to the wall square by square. The number of grid squares will depend on how complicated your chosen design is.

If your child's bedroom doubles up as a playroom, leave one area of it uncarpeted with wipe-clean vinyl tiles for messy play.

KEEPING YOUR CHILD ENTERTAINED

Alison Wallis; Amanda Stevens; Anna Knight; Clare Porter; Judy Cooper, nursery teacher; Liz Chowienczyk; Marianne Bell, nanny; Margaret Cave; Paula Goody, playgroup leader; Ruth Williams, nanny; Sarah Brown, nursery teacher, Just Twos nursery

Blowing bubbles is such easy fun. When the bottle is empty, refill with baby shampoo (the no-tears formula). It's cheap and blows great bubbles, particularly if you add a drop of water, and it won't sting if it goes in a child's eyes.

Take broken wax crayons, remove the paper and melt slowly in a bun tin in the oven. When they cool, you've got lovely chunky crayons for little hands. If you mix colours, you get rippled, rainbow effects, but don't stir or you'll end up with a murky mess.

A big cardboard box can be a child's dream. Draw on some windows and flowers, even a cat. Cut a door flap and let his imagination run riot.

Spread sheets of newspaper over the kitchen floor before setting out paints and paper and letting your toddler loose.

Use sponges and root vegetables as stamps. Cut out a simple design for your child and leave her to make patterns on paper by dipping the stamps in paint.

When your children have created thickly daubed finger paintings, a quick blast of hairspray will stop the paint flaking off once it's dried (but don't let the children spray it themselves). A drop of washing-up liquid in the water when you mix up powder paints will make them crack less.

Children love magic and surprises. Make special paper by writing messages in white crayon on white paper. When they colour over the paper, they will reveal your message.

Give your little darling a dry duster (the type that are advertised as attracting dust are ideal). It won't harm his hands and he will quite happily while away a few minutes with it. Who knows, you may end up with a shiny TV or table.

Allow children time and space to be noisy and physical. Where possible, create areas for them to be boisterous and run about.

On a warm day, children love water play. This doesn't have to be anything elaborate – a washing-up bowl with floating corks set outside in the garden will provide plenty of fun.

Old baby baths make great sandpits for small bodies. Sterile sand, a plastic beaker, spoons and maybe some shells and water are all that's needed.

When you are baking, set up a chair next to you at the worktop. Your child will enjoy watching, especially if you let him help mix and tip in the ingredients. As a final treat, let him lick out the bowl.

Play doh has been a firm favourite with children for generations. It can be squeezed, moulded, shaped and cut. There are machines for squeezing it and special cutters for making play-doh pictures. You can buy it in tubs, ready coloured, but it is very easy to make yourself and keeps for weeks wrapped in cling film in the fridge. You will need:

2 teaspoons cream of tartar

1 cup plain flour

1/2 cup salt

1 tablespoon vegetable oil

1 cup water

food colouring

Place all the ingredients in a small saucepan and mix together until smooth. Place the pan over a low heat until the mixture begins to come away from the sides and form a ball. Tip out and knead for a few minutes. Soak the pan immediately.

Even chores can be fun for young children. Changing beds means a huge soft pile of pillows and duvets, perfect for burrowing. When your child's finished doing that, she can help you inside the duvet cover by tucking the quilt into the corners.

Keep your old clothes, shoes and scarves for a well-stocked dressing-up box. You can add to it cheaply from charity shops.

Play music and dance. Before long, your toddler will be planning her own shows.

Sing – rhymes, nursery songs or your old favourites, especially songs with actions.

Toddler Groups

Especially for first children, learning how to share toys and even people can be tricky. Mother and toddler groups are an excellent way of helping a child's social skills. They're fun for toddlers and for mums and a way for you both to meet new friends.

Toddler groups are often held in church halls. Phone up your local churches or look on their noticeboards to find out if there is a group near you.

Talk to other mums or carers with older children. They often have useful tips for dealing with problems.

Don't be put off if there aren't any toddler groups in your area. Invite other mothers and children to a coffee morning at your house.

If you're worried about space at home, organise a teddy bears' picnic in the park. Invite mothers you know and ask them to bring along a friend, a simple snack and, of course, a teddy or other cuddly.

Try to find other willing helpers to organise your own toddler group. Church halls are often very cheap to hire. Ask for contributions towards the cost or draw up a rota for tea, coffee and juice. Look out for cheap bumper packs of crayons, paints and paper; search school fairs for toys or set up a toy donation basket.

Many people, when asked, have a skill they can share – it should be easy to find someone to lead singing, read a story, or make potato prints, masks or Christmas decorations. Before you know it, you will have an activity planned for every session.

Do you enjoy running the toddler group? Think about retraining as a playgroup teacher. The hours fit in with your own children. Nursery nurses for 2–3 ½-year-olds can study part-time and there are usually childcare schemes on site at colleges.

Children of this age often love music and rhyme and enjoy singing, chanting and clapping in music groups with other adults and children. Look out for established groups in your area.

Never assume that your children will automatically tell you what goes on or anything that troubles them during the day.

Toys

Children will always play and find things to play with. You don't have to give them specific toys – a wooden spoon and old saucepan can be just as much fun.

There is a huge difference between playing aggressive fantasy games with play weapons and actually hitting or hurting other children.

What a child sees in a toy and what appeals to him will not necessarily be what you see.

Children develop powers of discrimination, detail and imagination through toys they can relate to.

Watch your child to see the types of toys he prefers.

Toy cookers can be great fun, but also encourage children to work alongside you at the real thing, too.

Borrowing toys – from friends or a toy library – is a great way to ring the changes.

For an easy and cheap child's treasure chest, stock a box or wicker basket with things like a wooden spoon, old saucepan, empty cocoa carton and lid, small home-made plastic bottle shaker and pieces of material with different textures. Leave it in a corner on the floor and let your child find it. She will enjoy exploring the contents, especially if you regularly change them.

Rearrange and set up toys such as garages and dolls' houses to make them look inviting and interesting.

Everyone gets bored with the same toys and games. Squirrel away some toys and produce them when your child is at a low point or too tired to let herself fall asleep. If she hasn't seen a particular puzzle for a while she is more likely to be enthralled and you are more willing to help.

Making Friends

Two-to-four-year-olds tend to play solo alongside other children. It is really only from the age of four that they begin to make real friends.

Teach children to respect other children and animals. It takes small children some time to realise that other children feel the same way as they do and that they too can be hurt.

Small children don't automatically think about other children's feelings – but they're never too young to be reminded.

Biting can be a way of expressing anger. Don't be more upset about this than a child hitting another child. See also page 84.

Young children often prefer the company of older children to that of their contemporaries.

Don't worry if your child appears to be unfriendly or unwilling to share. Try to encourage him by reminding him that when he goes to friends' houses he plays with their toys.

If sharing continues to be a problem, try meeting up with friends on neutral territory – in the park, at toddler gym or mother and toddler groups.

Children aren't always very interested in other children, but it is a good idea to meet up regularly with other parents and children of a similar age. It's fun for you and useful social education for your child, getting her used to mixing.

TV & Videos

Television and film open up whole new worlds and experiences for children and can be a useful learning tool. They're also fun.

TV shouldn't always be used as a babysitter but it can be extremely useful to give you some space or to allow you to get on with a particular task.

Monitor TV programmes and try to watch some programmes with your child. If a programme is something new or educational he may have questions and if it's just fun he'll enjoying sharing it with you.

Stick to videos or the BBC to avoid those pesky adverts! No need to turn your toddler into a consumer just yet.

PARTIES

Alison Wallis; Amanda
Stevens; Anna Knight;
Ruth Williams, nanny

Send invitations out early and remind people to reply so that you know final numbers.

If there's a theme to the party, link the invitations to it. Either make your own or customise bought ones.

For an original idea for birthday invitations, write the invitation on inflated balloons, with someone holding the neck closed for you. Deflate them and put in envelopes. The child you invite will have to blow up the balloon to read it.

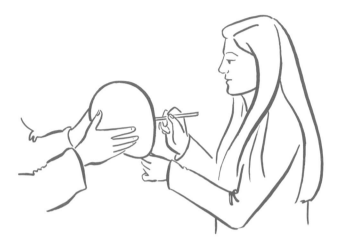

Never just assume that people won't turn up because you haven't heard a definite yes.

Be prepared for extra siblings and parents staying. Have a few extra prizes and party bags to hand.

Make it a rule that you don't unwrap presents at the party. Do it quietly afterwards, making a note of what came from whom, so that your child can write thank-you letters.

Organise an activity for children to do as soon as they arrive – the simpler the better.

At kids' birthday parties, take polaroids of your child with each of the guests and put them in the party bags at the end, as souvenirs.

If you're having a fancy dress party, take a photo of each child as he or she arrives, then get someone to dash the film to be developed in an hour, and present the photos as a good-bye present.

Colouring in is a good idea for two-to-fours. Have a big box of wax crayons or coloured pencils ready (no pens if you want to preserve your home and sanity) and a stack of simple line drawings. Use photocopies of your own drawing, or you can legally print from a children's website – the BBC is a good one to search.

Attach a strip of plain wallpaper or lining paper to a wall with masking tape (it should peel away easily later without leaving any marks). Small guests will love drawing and sticking on this to make a unique party wall frieze.

Spread out a plain paper tablecloth for guests to decorate. Separate areas with brightly coloured sticky tape to make individual spaces.

Throwaway drinking cups can be decorated to match with stickers and glitter glue.

You can also customise straws with slide-on animal shapes, stars, flowers, rockets – anything you fancy and can easily draw and cut out in advance.

Don't buy pretty name labels for guests. Instead buy cheap white computer labels, the bigger the better. Write names in colours and give out stickers as prizes, which each guest can collect on her label throughout the party. They're much more fun and the bigger labels stay stuck.

Make a 'Happy Birthday' banner from lining paper. Everyone can add their own decorations and drawings; then at the end of the party take a photo of the birthday girl, her friends and the banner. It makes a perfect thank-you card.

Children don't have to be organised the whole time to enjoy themselves. A little chaos can be fun – it is a party, after all.

If you are holding the party at home, put away toys you don't want played with and set out ones you do.

Make sure that toys aren't on show during an organised activity or entertainer's slot. Only have them out when you're ready for children to play with them.

Tie up balloons out of reach until you're happy for children to play with them. They will quickly be popped and little children are often scared of the loud bangs.

When you have a crowd of children to control, don't try to shout over them to be heard. Get them all quiet first before you talk to them. Start doing a hand jive (if you go back that far), and once they all join in, you've got them!

When party guests are too unruly, bring them back for something calming like Pass the Parcel. This also works well after food.

Be firm if children are getting too wild. Don't be afraid to sit them all down and remind them that they have been invited and are there for the birthday child. Call order when you have to.

When playing Pass the Parcel, have two parcels if there are lots of children.

Pop the Balloon or Jump on the Bubble Wrap (to music if you prefer) are fun, easy games to arrange.

There is nearly always at least one reluctant child who doesn't really want to join in. This isn't a failure on your part, and it's important not to force him to play. Instead, allow him to watch and ask him to help you by holding the sticker prizes or helping you pick the winner in a game.

Be prepared – two-to-four-year-olds will all finish their tea at different times and there will be a certain amount of chaos. If you don't want guests running about, make sure that you have an activity ready.

If you are holding a party in a hall, save the most raucous games for the end when parents are arriving. You'll be sending children home on a high and parents like seeing their children having a good time.

For fun finales, try old favourites like: 'What's the time, Mr Wolf?' and Sticky Toffee – a tag game where kids caught have to stand in a star shape until they are freed by someone running through their legs.

For great game ideas, check out your local library, especially for books of traditional games, which you can adapt to fit your party or theme.

Make a store of extra little prizes to cheer up someone who is upset. These can be stickers or a lucky dip of sweets or other small prizes. Bribery always works and you don't have time for psychology in the middle of a party.

Keep a shallow box near to the door where you can have everything guests are taking home ready. If there are party bags as well as other prizes and drawings, it's often best to give the bulk of the booty to parents.

Blown-up balloons as going-home presents tend to get lost or pop, upsetting children. Instead, give them an unblown-up one.

EARLY LEARNING

Anna Knight;
Clare Porter;
Helen Platts; Judy and
Mike Cooper;
Liz Chowienczyk;
Margaret Cave; Sarah
Brown, nursery
teacher, Just Twos
nursery

Parents often worry whether their child is developing as quickly as others. All children develop skills at different rates.

Ability in one area often outstrips a child's skills in another. All will equal out eventually. Don't worry! And remember, reading ability rarely equals intelligence.

Make sure that children have easy access to books, pens, paper and sticky shapes. If you can, set aside a child's-height table for drawing and sticking, and have pencils and shapes ready in tubs. Having paper to hand will encourage kids to use this rather than walls.

When you shop for crayons, markers, clays, chalk, pastes, paints, etc., make sure that they are non-toxic and washable.

Stick glue is a lot easier for a child to handle than runny glue.

Keep kids' art supplies in a toolbox with a handle, which will hold a lot of crayons, markers, coloured pencils, rubbers, stampers, glue and sharpeners, and is easy to take in the car, or on holiday.

Keep a box of odds and ends that you can use for drawing, sticking things together or modelling. Old toothbrushes, old office stationery, large buttons, yoghurt pots, cereal packets and that old stand-by, the empty washing-up bottle. Keep everything in shoeboxes for a rainy day.

Yes, your child can scribble on walls! If there is space, a section of wall painted as a blackboard with a box of chalks is a good outlet for creative hands.

Buy a roll of plain white wall lining paper from a DIY store. It's much cheaper than drawing paper and means that you can make huge pictures and murals.

Allow your child to take the lead in learning. Make sure that the materials are available and she will use them when she is ready.

For painting, be prepared for a mess or set aside one day especially for messy play. Cover the kitchen floor with newspaper. Take off shoes, socks and trousers and anything else that you don't want covered with paint. Squeeze about 1/2 in/1cm of different coloured paints into plastic containers big enough for small feet and hands. Children love the feel of the paint between their toes and will have fun making footprint and hand trails across clean sheets of wallpaper lining paper.

When teaching small children colours, associate each colour with something they understand – green with grass, for instance.

Make counting mean something by attaching numbers to something your child can see. For instance, count out a chair for Daddy, one for Mummy, one for baby and one for him. Eventually you can follow this with 'How many chairs does that make?'

Wrap new wax crayons with masking tape to help prevent them from breaking.

Jigsaw puzzles and simple board games can really help children recognise numbers and even days of the week. School fairs are a good source of second-hand games. Always check to make sure that the pieces are all there before you buy.

When your small child first starts holding a pencil, let her hold it as she wants to, at first. She will correct herself with a little encouragement as she gets older.

Look out for triangular pencils. They are easier for tiny hands to hold properly.

PLAYGROUPS & SCHOOL

Carolyn Webb, teacher; Henrietta Sheehey; Julie Cooper, nursery teacher; Margaret Cave; Sandra Richards; Sarah Brown, nursery teacher, Just Twos nursery

Playgroup Or Nursery

When choosing a playgroup or nursery school, concentrate on the amount of playtime and the general atmosphere.

You're ideally looking for somewhere where the emphasis is on learning through play, with a happy, caring, positive ethos.

Ask to spend a morning there. Watch the other children – how happy do they seem?

Look at how structured the sessions are and how many activities are going on. Can you imagine your toddler there? Do you think he would enjoy what's on offer?

How welcome are parents? Are they encouraged to contribute to the nursery?

Check whether parents are encouraged to stay with their children at first. You don't want to be the only one remaining until your child settles. Many nursery and playgroups suggest parents or carers stay with their child until the child is happy to be left. Speak to staff about their policy. They are usually happy to work with parents to make sure children feel secure and confident.

Dress children in sensible clothes for nursery school. It is important for children to be able to manage their own clothes and to feel free to play in them. They also need to have easy access to avoid accidents.

If you want to speak to your child's nursery school teacher, make an appointment. Drop-off and collection times are always too busy to hold in-depth discussions.

Children respond to your emotional panic. When you first leave your child at nursery, don't say goodbye a million times. Your child needs to see you treating the situation as safe and normal.

Do collect children on time. Don't be late, especially while your child is still settling in.

Try not to quiz children about what they have done. They will usually tell you in their own time.

Don't always ask if your child has a painting or drawing to show you. They may have played productively that morning or completed a jigsaw.

Choosing A School

Talk to other parents and listen to their opinions but always make up your own mind about a school. It's usually easy to arrange to visit through the school secretary. Sometimes you'll be invited to join a group of prospective parents.

Look at the classrooms. Are they stimulating and colourful, with plenty of children's work on the walls as well as themed displays?

A certain amount of classroom noise is positive, but watch the pupils during a lesson. Does the teacher have their attention? Are they interested? Do they seem bored?

Find out what sports and extra-curricula activities are on offer. Look especially at areas like art, music, dance and drama.

Ask to see SATs results and find out which schools leavers go on to. The school office should have most of this information to hand. Ofsted reports are also available to anyone, either through individual schools or at your local library.

School reports are also available on the internet. Check www.ofsted.gov.uk/reports/index.htm for state schools and www.isinspect.org.uk for independent schools.

Find out about selection procedures and any particular criteria that must be fulfilled for your child to be offered a place.

If you're looking at private schools, check not only the fees but also how much they are likely to rise by. Find out whether there are any payment schemes and if you can pay by direct debit. For more on paying school fees, see page 155.

Think about the distance the school is from your home. There are years of school runs ahead of you, and there's a lot to be said for being able to walk to school, at least during the primary years.

See also Educating At Home, page 157.

Starting Big School

See page 127.

LEARNING TO SWIM

Louisa Laughlan, swimming teacher

When your child has had a bath, let out most of the water and let her lie on her tummy and kick her legs. Tell her she's swimming, so that she gets used to the idea.

When introducing a child to a swimming pool for the first time or after a long gap, let him sit on the side for the first few visits if he's not keen. After watching the other children for a while, he'll soon want to have a go himself.

When a small child first goes swimming, let her take a favourite bath toy into the water with her.

To boost your child's confidence as he learns to swim, gradually reduce the amount of air in their arm bands.

Teach a child to breathe correctly in the water by getting him to put his mouth slightly underwater and blow bubbles.

Encourage arm movements when your child is in the water. Hold him under the armpits and put a ball just out of reach; then let him try to grab it.

Get your child used to going underwater by playing 'Ring a ring o' roses' in the shallow end of the pool. On 'We all fall down' everyone has to bob under the water.

When teaching front crawl, ask the children to make sure that their eyebrows are in the water. If you say eyes, they freak out.

Children quickly get cold once they've come out of the water, so take a towelling bath robe to the pool edge to pop on as soon as they leave the pool.

To stop little ones catching cold, dry their hair under the hand-dryers in the changing rooms.

Children are often extremely hungry after swimming. Try to have a snack ready, or take them for a hot drink and something to eat in the pool café.

TRAVELLING

Amanda Stevens; Diana Starte; Helen Platts; Jane Breeden, Virgin Atlantic Airways; Fiona Seton,

To keep kids amused on journeys, pack pencils, not felt pens, for drawing – otherwise they lose the lids and drop the pens, messing up the car and their clothes. Also, pencils can't be used to draw on one another when they get really bored or start squabbling.

Spiral-bound notebooks are easier to manage than loose sheets of paper and can be used to draw, write and play games.

Imaginative Travel;
Margaret Cave;
Sandra Wroe

Story tapes are a great way to keep young travellers amused. You don't have to stick to children's books – comic tapes often go down well and are fun for grown-ups, too. A personal tape player and new tape can keep youngsters quiet for miles and they will love the freedom of choosing exactly what they want to listen to.

If your child ever unbuckles his belt, stop the car and tell him that you can't go on until he does it up and keeps it done up.

Just tell your child that the car doesn't work until the seat belts are done up. This is particularly useful for toddlers who refuse to bend in the middle.

Give each child a small rucksack that they can carry themselves. Stock it with a few of their favourite cuddly toys and games to keep them amused. Travel editions of games like Connect Four are a good investment.

Travel light, particularly if there is only you to handle all the luggage. Even if the kids have their own backpacks, they have a habit of dumping everything on you.

Even big kids sometimes have to go to the loo in a hurry. Avoid nerve-racking searches in unfamiliar towns for loos by taking along a portable travel potty. Your kids may think it's appalling, but they'll be glad of it at least once on most journeys!

When flying, to help overcome ears popping on take-off and landing, tell children to pretend to be a crocodile or hippo. This encourages them to open their mouths really wide so that pressure rebalances.

When you are staying in a hotel, take along a night light and a non-slip bath mat. Just be sure to put a note on your door so that you don't forget it when you leave.

A semi-catering venue is a good choice. Eating out for three meals a day with fractious little ones can be very wearing, but it's good to get a break from cooking sometimes.

To help overcome jet lag, try to ensure that your first-night destination has dark curtains to cut out daylight. Make sure that your child has enough food in his tummy to see him through the night, according to the new clock; otherwise hunger may wake him up.

Attach a balloon to your deckchair or buggy to help your children find you on the beach.

Relax! Travelling with children can be fun as they absorb new experiences, but if you are tense they will sense it and become tense or naughty.

See also the travel advice on pages 60, 86 and 140.

CHILD SAFETY

Clare Porter;
Helen Richardson,
Child Accident
Prevention Trust;
Judy Cooper,
nursery teacher;
Liz Chowienczyk;
Sarah Brown, nursery
teacher, Just Twos
nursery

Two-to-four-year-olds need constant watching – young children are unpredictable – but they shouldn't always be aware that they are being supervised. Be watchful, but remember that children do need time to themselves.

Don't leave anything out that is dangerous.

For safety measures at home, see page 66.

Accidents can happen very quickly. Never turn your back on a toddler in any situation where he could injure himself.

Never leave small children unsupervised near water. They can drown in the smallest amount of water.

Mostly, children will only attempt what they can do. Encourage their physical development, but never push.

Play a game of red light, green light with your toddler when you are walking along the street. When you call 'Green light' he can walk but if you call 'Red light' he must stop immediately. You can build on this to make it a fun, routine game you play, so that the reactions become automatic. This can be very useful in an emergency, say when a car is suddenly pulling out and you need your child to stop at once.

When you're going out somewhere busy, like a crowded park or fun fair, tie a brightly coloured balloon to the buggy. If your small child gets lost, he'll be able to find you again more easily.

5 FOUR TO SEVEN YEARS

'Grown-ups never understand anything for themselves, and it is tiresome for children to be always and forever explaining things to them.'

Antoine de Saint Exupery

Once your kids start school, things change for good. You are no longer their sole reference for information about the world, and no longer their sole source of interpretation about the things that happen to them. They begin to look to their teachers, classmates and the big kids in school for role models – and not everything they emulate will be to your taste. Along with the reading books and head lice, they may bring home some attitudes and vocabulary that will make your hair stand on end.

Never mind! You knew it would come, and there are consolations. Your child is soaking up skills and information from all sources like a sponge. He brings home amazing facts and can't wait to share his enthusiasms with you. He has learnt to read, and is very proud to read to you. He can ride a bike and you can go out together exploring your neighbourhood. He writes in his school newsbook, and draws pictures of you doing things you'd rather the teacher never found out about. In short, you have a child who is his own person, and is now sometimes also a friend. The balance is changing. You find he needs you to do less for him, and he brings an awful lot to your relationship. This is a process that will go on for years. Enjoy this early stage.

BEHAVIOUR

Glynis Fletcher, counsellor; Marilyn Bunce, teacher; Rachel Barber, nursery assistant; Julie Weiner, special needs worker; Julie Farrer, educational psychologist; Clare Porter

As your children grow up, in many ways they become more reasonable and easier to be with, but at the same time you become aware of the people they already are. It can be immensely frustrating to see all the things they decide to do that you disagree with, but guess what – this is only the start of it. If you keep in mind that in parenting all things are temporary, you might be able to keep your sanity long enough to see your grandchildren frustrate their parents.

OK – here's a fact: everyone falls short. If you get it right even 50 per cent of the time, you can award yourself a pink rosette and a large gin and tonic. You're a good-enough parent! Congratulations – that's all anyone should hope for.

Really listen to your child when she's speaking to you. Put down the paper, stop texting, get down to her level and listen with both ears. Never minimise or make fun of her problems or her fears. Involve her in problem solving, and speak rather than yell.

When you need to speak to your child about something important, make eye contact and get down to his level. Turn off the television and look directly in his eyes. Do this sometimes for nice things, such as thanking him for helping, not just for telling off.

Join in with what your child is doing, follow his lead and laugh at his childish jokes and silly behaviour, to show how much you enjoy being in his company.

Tickle and wrestle with your child from time to time without overwhelming her, and smile at her as often as you can. This teaches your child to smile in return, and gives her the non-verbal message that you approve of her just the way she is. Hug or pat your child on the back to reinforce the message.

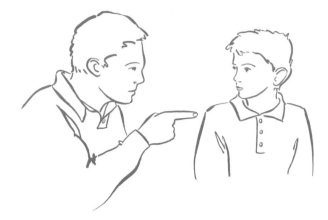

Set aside about ten uninterrupted minutes per child per day to give full attention to her as you talk, play a game or take a walk together. Do it early in the day, and the good vibe it creates can take you right through.

Accept the kind of person your child is and work with his characteristics to smooth his corners, rather than trying to change him – which gives him the message that you don't really like him the way he is.

Provide a regular routine so that your children know what is expected of them at any time. If you keep changing the rules, they don't know where they are.

The family is not a democracy: it should be a state of benevolent despotism, with you at the helm. Encourage your children to question and discuss, and to demand reasons and explanations – but show that in the final analysis, you are the boss.

Tell your child exactly what you expect of her before you go out. General comments like 'Behave' are abstract to a child. Instead, be as specific as you can, explaining, for instance, that she must stay with you at all times in the supermarket and should not pick things up and put them in the trolley without consulting you first. Give your child credit if she tries to comply with what may seem to her like complicated and ever-changing rules, and let her know how far she is succeeding.

Don't underestimate the many calls upon your child's attention. Write notes (or draw pictures) to remind him of the things he has to do. To encourage your child to take his PE bags to school, stick a picture of a gym shoe to the front door, asking, 'Have you packed me?' This is much easier than having to nag, and it works for grown-ups too!

Stick to your word. If you say you are going to take the kids somewhere, do it. If you tell them they are grounded, don't relent. Sticking to your word shows the children later just how much you really love them.

If there is really no choice, don't offer one. Don't say, 'Would you like to clean your teeth,' say, 'It's time to clean your teeth now.'

No 'ifs' about it – stick to 'when'. With certain issues it is best not to introduce an element of choice. Instead of 'You can watch TV if you pick up your toys', say, 'When you pick up your toys, you can watch TV.'

Speed up decisions by giving your child just two choices with the understanding that if he doesn't make his mind up within, say, five minutes, you will decide for him. This works particularly well with what to wear or what breakfast cereal to have.

You can introduce the idea of natural consequences so that your child has a sense of fairness in what happens in your home. This can be as simple as, 'When you help in the supermarket, I'll get you a comic on the way out to read in the car, but if you run off or mess around, I can't get you a treat.' This puts the choice of how to behave into your child's hands, and that's fine as long as they accept the consequences of misbehaviour.

When you're a bit tired and stressed and find yourself saying no to everything, try a bit of negotiation. 'OK, if I let you do that will you let me do this?' will lighten the atmosphere and give you the chance to do what you need to do, and shows respect for your child.

Before you go into your child's room, check your expression. Are you looking bad-tempered, anxious or impatient? Take a deep breath, relax and smile – show your child how glad you are to see him.

Shopping trips can turn into a nightmare with the constant pleas of your children begging you to buy them something. Instead of negotiating every time, set up a reward system, complete with some type of scorekeeping; make it as complicated as you like. Whenever your children do something really good, that you've defined as worthy of a point (or a star), record it on a chart and, once they reach a predetermined number of points, allow them to go shopping to buy whatever it is they want, within a price range set by you. Next time your children are begging you to buy them something, you can tell them to go home and earn it and that then you'll come back and buy it. This system stops the fighting and the whining. And best of all it teaches your children about earning what they want.

Make it an absolute rule that no one makes a noise in the background when you are speaking on the phone. Demonstrate to them how important it is by letting them call their friends, granny, etc., so that they can understand that you need to listen hard with just one ear and there is no room left in your head for noise coming in through the other ear.

Explain to your child that if someone hits him at school, that person will get into trouble (you hope), but if your child retaliates he will get into trouble for hitting the person who started it all. Not fair!

Try not to assume that your child has an understanding of time on a level with yours. To four- and five-year-olds, time is a completely abstract concept; minutes, hours, days, years – they're all the same. 'I'll be five minutes' means nothing to them (which is perhaps not surprising, because it can mean almost anything when adults say it). Explain in terms that he will understand – for instance that something will happen in 'five sleeps' or 'It will take as long as your swimming lesson.'

Whenever you need to tell your children that playtime is over, because for instance you are going out or it's time to leave for school, give a five- or ten-minute warning before doing so and suggest they wind up their game. Then wait approximately that amount of time before pulling them away. As well as cutting down on sulks and tantrums this method will give them time to stop what they are doing and help them to start to have a sense of time.

Show your child you understand how he feels. So instead of saying, 'Don't be such a baby. You know we have to leave the park now,' try something like, 'You really enjoyed being at the park and you're disappointed we can't stay later.' This helps him to rationalise his sometimes confusing feelings.

Naughtiness & Arguments

Choose a code word, prearranged with your child, for high-pressure situations when she's about to flip her lid or is acting over the top. Any time you say the word, she has to stop talking and moving for sixty seconds. During this minute, both of you should try to breathe deeply and think peaceful thoughts. Try a calm sounding word like 'peaceful', 'clouds' or 'ocean'.

Don't be on your child's case all the time. Instead, choose a few rules that are important to you to enforce and ignore the rest.

Try to explain the reason for your rules, in a short common-sense version – although there cannot be a parent alive who hasn't sometimes resorted to 'Because I say so!'

In a confrontation, calmly offer only two options: what you want him to do, and a less appealing option, such as going to his room. Be prepared for him to choose the option you don't want sometimes, so don't make it an impossible threat.

When telling your child off, gradually lower your voice. She has to listen more carefully – and so has to lower her voice.

If your child is football mad, or even if he's not, instigate a system of yellow and red cards. You don't need real cards: the cards can be just verbal warnings to give your child a sense of the seriousness of what he's done. Invent punishments of loss of privilege to go with the system.

Let your child know that she has overstepped the mark by explaining how what she has said makes you feel, but always give her the chance to put things right. For example, you could say, 'That hurt my feelings. Can you try saying it a different way?'

Instead of cutting your child off in mid-sentence, with the usual, 'I don't want to hear it, go to bed *now*!', bite your tongue and let her have her say. It's important to let her know that her ideas matter.

Let your child have her say in an argument, but always in a polite and respectful tone. You have to follow the same rule too. This is an excellent way to teach your kids how to speak assertively with adults.

Ask a question. The next time your child kicks her brother or picks a fight at school, ask, 'What do you think you should do now?' or 'What can you do differently if this happens again?' Encourage her to think of her options.

Avoid labelling your child; label the action instead. So rather than saying, 'You are naughty to throw sand,' say, 'Throwing sand is a naughty thing to do.'

If you're constantly telling off your child for leaving her clothes on the floor, make sure that she has access to low hooks and easy-to-open drawers; if school notes and homework disappear, designate a special table where they must be put; if the guinea pig doesn't get cleaned out, make a chart to show whose turn it is.

Your best defence is a sense of humour. Try to giggle your child out of being grumpy and forget the bad stuff as soon as possible. In the middle of an argument with your child, if you decide it's time to lighten up, reply to her complaint with some ridiculous comment, like, 'That's all very well, but the thing you're forgetting, Annabel, is that you've got a nose like a parsnip!' This usually ends the argument and leads to a tickling session instead.

Be consistent and don't make empty threats.

Sometimes your children genuinely don't know that what they are doing is wrong. Why shouldn't you use spit to make your hair stick up like Beckham's? Instead of freaking out, treat your child as a distinguished guest from a distant country and explain your customs to him politely.

All children who spend time together will fight at some point. Don't intervene unless one of them is getting much the worst of it, and don't assume that the big one started it. It's seldom clear who started it, so if you're going to punish, punish them both.

Ban the word 'hate'. It's far too strong a word for most situations, and it's negative. Make sure grown-ups around the house follow this as well.

Tell your children that to earn respect from others they have to show it themselves. If your son takes things from his sister's room without asking, he can't complain when his sister takes his comic to read.

Use an egg timer (or a kitchen timer) to settle disputes of all kinds. It works as a kind of impartial arbitrator and gets you out of the firing line. Try it for toy-sharing arguments, getting homework done before watching a favourite TV programme, ending a game before you have to go out, brushing teeth for long enough. You'll be amazed at how well it works.

Try to stay out of arguments between children, and you'll find that they will resolve themselves much faster. Kids need to learn how to sort out their disputes without adult logic being imposed on them.

Trouble with sharing sweets? Don't buy sweets unless your children can agree on what to get. In the case of bars, let the one who divides get the last choice of which bit to have. Make sure you do this in strict rotation, so everyone gets a chance.

There are some children who appear to be very naughty, but who just need more love and more praise than would ever seem possible. Give it to them and watch them blossom.

Kids need love the most (hugs, pats, encouraging words and focused attention) when they are at their most unlovable.

If your child has been very rude to one of you, the other parent can step in and try to explain what was so hurtful in what he said or did, and suggest ways of making up. Needless to say, when he comes to apologise you must make up at once.

Boys can show male chauvinist tendencies from an alarmingly young age. As a dad you need to show them that being patronising to a woman is simply not acceptable. If your son is rude to his mother, picking him up on it will show him that women are as important as men.

If you don't want your child to swear, don't do it yourself. But you must accept that at school she'll use language you don't allow at home. It's a good lesson for her to understand that different ways of speaking are appropriate in different places. See also page 147.

You can make a deal with your child that she can use the same language you do. Of course, this means that you will have to keep a check on your own language.

Bear in mind that a dramatic change in behaviour can be a sign of being bullied.

Whining

Pretend you're a broken record if your child whines whenever you ask him to do something. Just pick a phrase and stick to it and you'll wear him down. No need to get angry – just keep saying your phrase, like 'Time to come to the table.' It's even more annoying than whining, so you'll have the pleasure of driving him mad in return.

If you give in to whining, you've had it. Once it's worked, your child will keep trying. Make a feature of resisting by saying something like, 'I can't let you listen to your tape when you ask me in a whiny voice.'

'I'm afraid I can't understand what you're saying when you speak in that babyish way' is the best way to respond to whining requests. As soon as your child speaks properly, respond and give her a big smile, even if you don't do what they are asking – in which case, try to find some acceptable substitute so that they feel there is an advantage to not whining.

When your child whines, respond in the same tone of voice. This drives children mad – but it works.

Lying

If your child lies about a wrongdoing ('I didn't do it'), make lying into a worse crime than what they're lying about. Encourage your child to admit to anything she's done wrong by praising her for owning up, while lying to cover up earns 'double-trouble'.

Try to explain to your child what he loses by not telling the truth. If you can't trust him, you can't give him the freedom and responsibility he craves.

Adopt a sign to use when you think your child isn't telling the truth. A Pinocchio nose sign, with your finger on the end of your nose, then moving slowly away, often does the trick and encourages her to come clean. This works well for kids who are prone to exaggerate rather than lie for malicious reasons.

Lying is too strong a word in many instances. For exaggerations or something like claiming to have seen the latest film when you won't be seeing it until the weekend, 'fibbing' is a more appropriate description.

Although it always pays to encourage your child to tell the truth, if your child feels he needs to keep his end up at school by telling stories at school, don't tell his friends that he's making it all up. Back him up in the playground, but have a chat with him afterwards at home and try to find out why he feels the need to talk himself up.

Look at the root cause of the fibbing. Does your child feel inferior in some way and feel he has to compensate? Remind him often that he is lovely and fine just the way he is.

Telling Tales

Encourage your child to tell a grown-up if anyone is hurting them, of course; but there comes a point when you want to discourage informing against others.

Check out the motives. Ask your child, 'Are you trying to get her into trouble because you don't like what she's doing or are you trying to tell me that she's doing something that may hurt someone?'

Try not to act on information given by a child telling tales, unless it's a genuine emergency, such as when someone is about to get hit on the head with a big stick. Otherwise, just say calmly, 'Oh really? Thanks for telling me,' and carry on with what you are doing.

In response to, 'Well, he started it,' try saying, 'I'm not interested in who started it, I'm interested in who finishes it.'

If the person doing the tale-telling gets half the punishment of the person they told against, it makes for near equality of misery and reduces tale-telling to a minimum. Make sure, however, that your children know that they won't be punished at all if a safety issue is involved.

Presenting A United Front

Never turn a discipline session into an argument between you and your partner. This is very confusing to your child and will ultimately undermine the authority of both parents.

If you strongly disagree with a punishment or sanction your partner is giving, wait until after it has been arranged, and then speak privately about it. If there is an adjustment to be made, the person who delivered the punishment should speak to the child. It's much better to say, 'Look, I've been thinking this over, and perhaps I've been too harsh' (or too lenient, as the case may be) than to make it look as if one of you is good parent and the other is nasty parent.

Invent a secret code to indicate to your partner that you'd like to talk an issue over. This is a cue to send your child to his room while you try to come to an agreement about what to do. Just make sure that your child can't hear your discussion!

When one parent is with the child far more than the other, there may be issues that should influence the decision to discipline that the absent parent doesn't know about. So although you may have a policy on, say, whining, one parent may know of mitigating circumstances that, if you are to be fair, need to be taken into account. When this happens, make sure that you explain to your partner later.

Punishment

Smacking is a very difficult issue for parents. Parents who have smacked feel guilty afterwards, and find it doesn't resolve the problem that provoked it. In an ideal world, you would never smack your children, but when you're tired and fed up it can happen, so try not to be too hard on yourself.

If you have lost it and smacked your child, try to analyse why things got out of control and develop a strategy to head things off next time.

Make the punishment fit the crime. Kicking a football inside means that the ball is taken away for the whole day; write on the wall with crayons and you'll have to wash it off.

Time outs should be a minute for every year of your child's age. But make sure that you send him to a dull place with no distractions. Sitting on the stairs is the usual favourite. Explain what he did wrong and what you expect of him, and be ready to praise any sign of the correct behaviour, rather than rewarding him with an exasperated, 'About time too!'

Never apply punishment retrospectively. So if you decide, say, that from now on your child won't get a comic if he doesn't do his homework on a Friday night, don't take away the comic you bought him on Thursday. It wouldn't stand up in court!

Encouraging Good Behaviour

Try a hefty dose of praise, recognition and positive attention for good behaviour. Frequent comments (when deserved) like 'I'm so proud of you,' or 'I knew you could do it!' will make your child want to do her best to earn more.

Look for anything positive in your child's behaviour and reward it. Even if – and especially if – it's something you would normally take for granted (or feel you should be able to take for granted). For example, if your child is playing nicely alone or with another child, compliment him. If your child is being good in a restaurant, reward him in some tiny way.

Even if your child is being awful, find one tiny thing, like the fact that she is sitting nicely, and make a point of mentioning it. Such a compliment can turn round a miserable occasion in an instant.

Always remark on good behaviour; only mention the bad when it is really posing a problem. Otherwise, ignoring bad behaviour generally makes it go away.

Although modelling the behaviour you want to see in your children works well, once they go to school, a lot of their behaviour will be based on what they see their peers doing. Try to encourage your children to think for themselves, by asking them to comment on things that happen at school or when you are together – say, at the park. Ask them what they think of the behaviour they see in other children, both good and bad; ask them why they think a child is acting in a particular way, and what they think would be a better way to act.

If you're talking to someone and don't want to break off to comment on your child's good behaviour, you can ruffle his hair or scratch him gently on his neck to show your approval.

Remember to try not to give negative commands. So rather than saying, 'Don't run!' try saying, 'We walk sensibly in the supermarket.'

Adopt some memorable phrases so that your children will know eactly what you mean without you having to explain in detail. 'Keep your big voices for outside' is a better way of saying, 'For God's sake don't shout in here.' 'Ears up!' is a pleasing way to get your children to listen to what you are about to say.

Help children keep track of how they're doing, or tackle specific problems using a star chart with stickers and small incentives along the way.

When choosing incentives for good behaviour, try not to make them necessarily toys or material treats. Instead, suggest a favourite activity, like going out for a bike ride or doing Lego together after your child's finished tidying his room. Make the incentive fit the deed – for a small good deed, like staying quiet while you are on the phone, give him a piggy back, for example.

Getting ready for bed is a nightmare in many households. Make it clear that a delay in getting your pyjamas on means less time for a story, whereas getting ready quickly and without complaint means that you have time for another whole chapter.

To encourage slow dressers, make getting dressed into a game, with rewards for doing it quickly. For older children who persist in dallying, set a time limit and give a reward if they get dressed within the limit.

For near siblings, award a morning prize for the one dressed and organised first. For example, let her sit in the front seat of the car and choose what tape you listen to on the way to school.

Minding Ps & Qs

Model the kind of behaviour you want from your child. So always remember your pleases and thank yous and be quick to apologise if you've been ratty or unfair.

If your child forgets to say please, just ignore the request. Hold up your thumb and forefinger to indicate that the 'little' word is missing.

With younger children, you may not only have to demonstrate the tone of voice they should use but also the best way to make a request. 'Speak in a polite voice, please, like this: "May I have another yogurt, please?" Then you can have it.'

Teach children a few polite formulas such as 'Please may I get down, and thank you for my meal' or 'Thank you for inviting me to your party. I had a lovely time.' These sound rather formulaic, and in the case of the latter may come over as 'Mummy says I had a lovely time', but they get something polite said and it becomes a good habit, and the children can think of something a bit more spontaneous when they get older.

Don't insist on your child kissing relatives and friends, but do explain that it's important to be polite to these people.

Invent an innocent-sounding phrase that means 'We'll talk about it later', and explain to your child that sometimes she must just stop asking about something or doing whatever she is doing, because she could hurt someone's feelings. Always discuss it afterwards and explain the intricacies of the situation, to help her develop her social antennae.

DEVELOPMENT

Mildred Hatch, headteacher; Joy Lovett, classroom assistant; Charlie Blackwood; Richard Cameron, art teacher

Children are usually fascinated by the idea of death and can be introduced to it via animals, pets or books. Don't try to hide death from children or pretend it doesn't happen. For bereavement, see page 267.

Where do I come from? This is the age when they start to ask. When telling your kids about the facts of life, ask them what they have heard so far. You may not have to tell them as much as you think, or you can straighten out anything that needs it. You don't need to tell them everything in one go, and once they stop asking and seem satisfied with your explanation, you can stop right there.

Toys, Games & Pastimes

Television or computer games can dominate your child's life. They're fine in small doses but, if left on for too long, can make your child 'vague out' and become ungrounded. Talk to small children about what they're watching, so as to encourage them to think while they're watching. Don't let them sit too close either – and switch televisions and computers off from the plug when they're not on.

If computer games, hand-held games or TV are taking over your life, set strict time limits or agree to watch a specific programme – and that's all. Any infraction should mean less time to play next time, or a brief confiscation.

For more on TV and computers, see page 165.

Board games can be unexpectedly fun with children involved. Try junior versions of Monopoly, Scrabble, Cluedo and Trivial Pursuit, as well as daft games like Twister. These games help with taking turns, paying attention, learning not to cheat and coping with being the loser (and the winner).

Make a junk modelling box. Save things like loo rolls and cereal boxes in it. Open out the cereal boxes, then fold them up inside out, securing them with masking tape so that you can paint on the surface. Shoeboxes and large delivery boxes are fantastic, as are individual foil cake tins (robot eyes!).

Store Lego pieces – sorted out however your child prefers – in a selection of small plastic containers with snap-on lids.

Ask your children to sort through their toys so that you can take them to a local charity shop. This helps to focus their minds on what they really like to play with, but if in doubt, don't throw it out!

It's easy to get into the habit of saying no to ideas your kids come up with. But think about it – is the washing up really more important than listening to what your child suggests making for tea, or going on a bike ride?

Let your children try things – sport, playing musical instruments, joining a club – just to see if they like it. Don't insist they stick with it, or make a big deal over the money you've spent on kit. It is important to foster in your child the courage to try something new.

For music lessons, see page 162.

For more on exercise and sport, see page 163.

Children lacking in confidence and self-esteem, or those who suffer from bullying, should try learning a martial art. There are classes for children, usually from around five or six years old. A martial art is a wonderful way for children to learn confidence, self-control and respect for each other.

Learning to ride a bicycle without stabilisers

- Take the stabilisers off, and lower the seat until your child can put her feet flat on the ground while she's seated.

- The ideal training ground is a grassy slope, not too steep or long, that ends up on the flat or with a slight uphill gradient at the end.

- Get your child to sit on her bike at the top of the slope (wearing a helmet, of course) and show her that she can stop or get her balance simply by putting her feet down on the ground. Then tell her to lift both feet off the ground and freewheel down the hill, with no pedals involved. Let her do this as often as she likes.

- Once she is comfortable with this, let her freewheel down, but with her feet on the pedals this time. Again, repeat as often as she wants to.

- Next time she goes down, tell her to pedal and to keep on going.

- She has now ridden her bike! This is a good moment to take a photo. She can carry on, starting from slightly further down the hill as she gets more confident, until she can start from on the flat.

For activities for older children in this age group, see page 160.

INDEPENDENCE

Gerry Silverman,
psychiatrist; Anna
Paige; David Martin,
head teacher;
Clare Porter

Parents get so used to doing so many little things for their children that it's easy to forget that they can do more and more for themselves each day. So the next time you are emptying the dishwasher or changing the towels, ask yourself if it's a job your child could be taking over. Not only will it boost his self-esteem to be doing a grown-up job, but it helps to teach responsibility and helps you along the way.

Cut out pictures of shirts, shorts, dresses, undies and socks and tape them on the front of the drawers of your child's dresser. That way little ones can put away their own laundry and find what they need for school.

Give your child one chore to do that is hers from an early age. For example, your daughter might collect up the old newspapers and comics and put them in the recycling bin.

Make clearing up toys fun for children by attaching a rope to the handle of a plastic laundry basket. The kids can pull the basket around the house picking up toys and taking them back to where they belong.

Use a small coat rack for your children to hang their coats, sweaters and school backpacks. In the morning, it will be easy for them to get themselves ready.

Attach a towel rack or hook on the back of each child's door and buy coloured towels to match each room. That way, if you find a wet towel in the bathroom, you know who the culprit is.

Whenever possible, let your child have an input into family decisions. It lets him know he's a valued member of the family and part of the team.

Help your child learn to tell the time by putting an analogue clock on her wall and giving her a digital watch to wear. Make sure that the two are synchronised, and she'll gradually get used to comparing the two.

Football boots don't come with Velcro tabs, so tying laces is a skill that all aspiring players must acquire. Putting the lace around twice when making the initial knot helps to keep the laces from slipping as your child makes the loop.

Washing

Give your child a plastic watering can to play with in the bathtub and then use it to rinse her hair.

If your children hate to have shampoo in their eyes, let them wear their swimming goggles in the bath.

Hang a mirror at your child's eye level. Good grooming habits should begin early. This way he can see if he has chocolate round his mouth.

Draw round your child on a big piece of paper, then help her fill in the things she should do – wash her face, brush clean her nails and teeth, comb her hair, tuck in her shirt. Stick it to the bathroom door to remind her of everything she needs to do to get ready in the morning.

Don't let children clean their teeth unsupervised until over the age of eight, and always check their molars to make sure that they have cleaned them properly.

Cleaning a child's face with spit (yours) and a hanky is particularly unpleasant for the child. Keep some wet wipes in the car for quick clean-ups, and let her do it herself in the passenger mirror.

Even up until the age of seven, children will not naturally wash themselves in the bath, so use a gentle bubble bath, and supervise them as they wash themselves, prompting them about which bits are likely to need most attention (they can usually guess).

SCHOOL

Preparing For School

Susan Clark, writer, www.whatreallyworks.co.uk; Ann Harrison; Ben Clarke; Deri Robins

Before your child starts school, help her to get used to the idea by reading story books on the subject. Many children's authors and publishers have written on the topic – good ones to look out for are by Janet and Alan Ahlberg, Shirley Hughes and publishers such as Usborne, Dorling Kindersley and Walker Books.

Videos about starting school such as the Topsy and Tim ones really appeal to children and help make the prospect of big school less daunting.

If your child doesn't know any children in his new class, get a class list and arrange a play date or two before the first day of school.

During the summer holidays, establish a routine with a consistent bedtime as well as wake-up time, and try to get your child used to managing without an afternoon nap.

Help your child to recognize her own name, so that she can identify her things.

What you call your child can become very important. The baby versions of their names are a definite no-no. And calling your son sweet pea in front of his mates is something he may never forgive. Ask him what he would like to be called – and try to stick with it.

Practice taking turns and cooperating by playing more structured games than your child would play at playgroup. Try getting together with other children who will be starting school at the same time as your child, so that they can play together.

Practice cleaning up after play – something that always endears a child to a reception class teacher.

Try playing games such as Simon Says to give your child practice in following instructions.

Take every opportunity to go into the school before term starts. Go to the school fête and any open days the school has so that your child feels comfortable there.

Wash the uniform through at least once, so that it doesn't feel stiff and scratchy.

Let your child have a go at putting on her socks, shoes and PE gear, and anything else she is likely to need to do.

Sending twins or higher-order multiples to school is daunting for everyone – you, them and the teacher. Get them used to being apart by letting each have a regular day at playgroup on their own.

If your children are identical, create some difference in the way they look, so that the teachers don't keep getting them mixed up. One could wear a sweatshirt and the other a jumper or cardigan, one could wear a tie and the other not; girls could wear different colour ribbons.

Some schools always make a practice of separating twins. Talk it through with the teacher and see what they usually do. If they don't have a policy, they will probably agree to what you would prefer. If there is only one class, they could be put on different tables if you want them to spend some time apart.

Toilet-training & Starting School

Your child will probably be toilet-trained by the time she goes to school and certainly you should try to achieve this. However, accidents may still happen, and your child may not always be dry at night. For more on toilet-training, see page 98.

Children who are normally dry sometimes wet their beds if they are very tired or a bit under the weather, so if a child does, consider that it may be a symptom of something else.

Ironically, drinking too little during the day can cause night-time wetting. Encourage your child to drink plenty of water throughout the day, and suggest to the school that they install a water cooler for pupils to use.

School loos are tiny, particularly for the reception class. If your daughter finds her wee goes over the front of the loo, tell her to lean forward and put her weight on her toes. This directs the wee further back.

A clean pair of pants and a plastic bag for the wet pair can be tucked away at the bottom of the school backpack.

Bottom wiping is an important skill for your child. If she loosely wraps loo paper right round her fingers several times, she is unlikely to get pooh on them. Remind her to stick her bottom out when she wipes to make sure she gets it all clean. And make flushing and hand washing a regular part of the regime.

Discreetly check your child's pants when he gets home, and give him clean pants, trousers, a shower, or a wipe with cotton wool and baby lotion, as appropriate. If his bottom stays even a little bit dirty, it can get very sore.

Some kids delay doing a pooh – with predictable results. Signs that your child might need some urging include bad breath, squirming, bad temper and tummy ache.

Clothes

You'll need far fewer clothes once your child starts school (if there is a dress code or uniform), so slow down on your rate of clothes-buying, or else you'll end up with wardrobes full of virtually unworn clothes.

Look out for school clothes in sales, and buy ahead. Even if your child has to wear a specific blazer or sweatshirt, you can save money on trousers, shorts, skirts, shirts and socks – lots of socks!

When your child grows out of first-size school clothes, offer some of the scruffier ones (that you wouldn't hand on to friends) to the reception teacher for the box of spares they keep handy for next year's intake, in case anyone wees, chucks juice down themselves, forgets their gym or swimming kit or neglects to put on knickers – yes it happens!

Keep checking that pumps and trainers still fit. If your kids only wear them at school, you may not realise that they are too tight – and your kids will be uncomfortable.

Sewing in name labels is one of the most boring tasks known to man (or usually woman). In socks you can get away with looping the name label round and sewing both ends in together.

Helping children to change after PE lessons in infants is a nightmare as lots of clothes are unnamed. Mark all your child's school clothes very clearly and show your children where to look for the name so that they can check.

Non-uniform days at school are always a great favourite with kids, and an excellent way to raise money for charity. But it's highly unlikely that the clothes they wear will have names in them. Either use a pen to write on the label, or just make a note of everything they go in wearing – brands, sizes and all – so you can locate their clothes in the lost property box.

If you forget non-uniform day and send your child in wearing uniform, or get mixed up and send them in non-uniform on a normal day, she will give you the hardest time imaginable. This is why you really have to keep a school calendar (see page 132).

Take your child's photo on the first and last day of school, wearing the same clothes. It's fun to see how much they have grown.

Getting Ready For School/School Mornings

Before you go to bed each evening, make sure that you have packed their backpacks with homework, reading books, signed papers, completed projects, sports or swimming gear and school supplies. It pays dividends in the morning when all you have to do is the packed lunch.

Put everything that needs to be taken to school by the front door, so that you can't miss it on the way out.

Encourage your child to put her school clothes into her gym or swim bag so that she knows where to find them afterwards.

Do your son a favour and don't give him fancy pants to wear on PE days.

Start your kids off with a multi-vitamin and mineral supplement each day. Research in the US indicates that it results in a slight IQ increase in children aged six to twelve.

If your kids wear school ties, make sure that they clean their teeth in the morning before the ties go on. White dribble down the tie does nothing for their appearance.

If your child takes a packed lunch, freeze juice or drink boxes the night before so as to keep foods cold in hot weather. By lunchtime, the juice or drink box will have thawed enough to taste like a slush puppy.

Fed up of the packed lunch coming home virtually untouched? Try asking your child to make his own sandwiches. He'll be so proud of his handiwork that he'll want to show everyone else and, you hope, eat them.

In a lunch box, put the sandwiches on top and the crisps underneath. If your child finds the crisps first, she'll go no further.

Do your child a big favour, and ban crisps containing E621 (or monosodium glutamate) from his diet generally and from his lunchbox. This chemical has been withdrawn from baby foods in the US.

Stick a little post-it note in your child's lunchbox, just to say 'Hope you're having a lovely day!'

When your kids go on school trips, make sure that you put wet wipes or a little sachet from a fast-food kids' meal in their pack so that they can clean up after lunch or cool down in hot weather.

No need to get younger children dressed when you do the school run. Just a pair of tracky bottoms and wellies, then do the job properly when you get home. Come to that, you don't have to get dressed either – just some heavy-duty pyjamas will do!

When Your Child Is Ill

As a rule of thumb for whether or not your child is well enough to go to school, take her temperature. If it's normal, try to encourage her to go to school, reassuring her that if she still feels rotten later, she can ask the school nurse or office to ring home.

When you think your reluctant child is well enough to go to school, as an extra incentive, you can promise a treat later that day, or his favourite supper that night.

Don't make staying at home on a school day too attractive. If your child is not well enough to go to school, he isn't well enough to spend the whole day sitting up playing on his Playstation. At least some of the time should be spent resting.

If your child hasn't been to school, he certainly isn't well enough to go out to a friend's in the evening or play football.

On the other hand, sometimes children are just overtired and need a day at home not doing much more than watching TV and with a lot of TLC from you. They'll return to school next day happier and with more energy.

Time Out

See page 207.

After School

Try not to worry if your child tells you that she played with no one all day. Often children only remember the final break, or the one time they were alone. If you ask what she did at lunch or about specific friends, a different picture will usually emerge.

Meet your kids from school with a little snack every day. They are often tired and frequently grumpy when they first emerge, and a quick refuelling can stop this from descending into an argument.

If you find you get no response when you ask your kids what they did at school, start by asking what they did at break, then go on from there. What did you have for lunch? Was anyone naughty? Did you do technology? (Particularly if you know it isn't the day for technology, so that they can correct you.) Ask open-ended questions that demand more than a yes or no answer.

To prompt school talk, ask what were the best and worst things that happened that day.

Don't force children to talk about their day when they don't want to. If you want to know more, invite one of your child's schoolfriends over. Make a point of driving both children home and listen quietly. It's amazing what you'll find out.

Fit in some spelling while you are driving your child from place to place. Keep the week's spelling list in the glove box (get your child to copy it out for you), and go over them as you drive along. Road signs, too, are good reading practice.

To encourage reading, make sure that your kids see you reading or hear you talk about the books you are planning to read. Without going into unsavoury detail, you can also give them a hint of why you are enjoying the book so much.

Make having a bedtime story read to her still part of your child's routine. Learning to read is exhausting and she needs a break.

In big classes your children may have precious little opportunity to read one to one with a teacher or helper. Make ten minutes' reading aloud part of your daily routine, apart from the reading books they bring home.

For older children, share the job of reading the bedtime story. When you turn over each page, let your child decide which page of the spread she will read, and read the other one yourself.

You can keep up to date with the National Curriculum through websites like www.ace-ed.org.uk, www.learn.co.uk and www.ngfl.gov.uk (the National Grid for Learning).

For homework, see page 148.

Keeping Track

Education is one area of a child's life that virtually every parent worries about at some stage. It's not surprising. School makes up a significant portion of your child's day and your only insight is what he chooses to tell you. But you don't have to worry alone and without a clear idea of what's going on.

Ways you can find out more and influence your child's school:

- Make friends with other parents – they may not hear more than you, but they may hear different things or have a different version of a particular incident.

- Talk to your child's teacher. Teachers are often around to discuss issues before the start of school or at the end of the day. If you want to talk privately, ask to make an appointment.

- Join the Friends' Association or PTA. This is often quite easy, as many parents don't want the extra responsibility.

- Offer to help at school events.

- Volunteers are often needed for playground duty, school library, extra-curricula activities including sport, music, dance and drama.

- To see your child in action with his classmates, go along as a helper on a school trip – there's no better way to get a clear idea of classroom dynamics.

Take an interest in what your child has been doing. Children have a habit of telling you everything but what you really want to know. It's important to listen.

When you read the school report, focus not on grades and marks but on effort. If you're child is getting 'Could do better' comments, you have to swing into action. Work with your child every single day, with work books, their homework or a project you invent with your child. Praise him when he gets something right and help him when he has problems understanding. Keep in constant contact with his teacher and ask for regular feedback. You can bet that the next report will show a change for the better.

Keeping track of school correspondence is a nightmare. Check your kids' backpacks and pockets every evening for school notices or newsletters. Also, ask them on the way home if there is anything special they need to remember for the next day.

Sift through all school notes and junk any you don't need. Place everything that needs keeping – permission slips, spelling lists, homework sheets – in a clipboard, one for each child.

Hang a plastic folder on your kitchen noticeboard, and put all school correspondence in there as soon as it arrives. (You can do the same with correspondence about Brownies, Beavers and sporting activities.)

Keep a separate calendar for school events, homework deadlines, projects and other important dates.

If your child is being picked on at school, always speak to her teacher even if you are satisfied with what the teacher is doing about it. It's very important to your child that you make this gesture to show how much she matters to you.

Bullying

See page 151.

Multiples At School

If your children are of differing ability, do not compare them and make sure that the teacher never does either.

Twins and supertwins sometimes feel hard done by because they rarely get your undivided attention. Remind them that they have bigger birthday parties than anyone else in their class.

As your multiples get older, unless they are identical it will probably become less obvious that that's what they are. This should help them avoid being treated as a unit in school.

Try not to refer to them as 'the twins' or 'the trips' – instead refer to them by name – and avoid making statements about them all together. Others will follow your lead.

School story books often have twins in them. Make this a source of pride for your children to help them understand how special they are.

You'll have to make a policy decision about whether you want them to be treated individually, according to their ability, or not. At school, you don't have much choice, and it can be very obvious that one is on a more advanced reading book than the other, but at swimming lessons, for example, you have more discretion. Speak to the teacher and make your preference clear. If one is better at, say, swimming, try to pick another activity for the other child which she does better. Contrived, but necessary.

SCHOOL HOLIDAYS

Marie-Laure Legroux, language teacher; Mandy Rouse; Jane Alexander, writer, www.janealexander.org

At the start of the holidays, let everyone (including the grown-ups) nominate several things they would like to do. These could be going to a particular theme park, decorating someone's room, going camping, meeting up with best friends, learning to bake a cake. Keep the list somewhere prominent, and try to do a couple of things from the list each week. Otherwise the holidays go by without anyone accomplishing their aims.

Children take time to settle in to the more relaxed routine of holidays – at school they are busy all day and the agenda is set for them. Arrange for things to do that keep them busy for the first few days until they begin to relax.

When your kids wake up in the morning, tell them what the plan is for the day. They have to accept that you have things to do as well, so try to fit in something for you alternating with something for them. For example, list the shops you have to visit, then schedule in a trip to the swimming pool.

Search through the local papers and visit the local tourist office for all the things there are to do in your home area that you have never got round to doing. If you plan ahead and take picnics, you can have as much fun at home as you can away – without the upheaval or the cost.

Collect all the competition entry forms for kids that you can find. Competitions are ideal rainy-day stuff, and they might even win.

Think of the things you don't normally get round to doing because there isn't enough time. Now you can! All the craft kits the children put away after their birthdays can now come out and get used, you can let them make bread from scratch, you can make all the Lego models up again, you can put on a puppet show and more!

The weather becomes very important during the holidays, so let your kids watch the weather forecast and plan the week out in advance. If it's going to be rainy on Thursday, make that the day you go to the cinema.

If you're trying to get your kids to do a summer diary, good luck! One way to make a diary more fun is to let them use a polaroid to take pics of the things they do. They can stick them in the diary and write about them on the same day.

Arrange to meet friends for a breakfast picnic at the park when it's cool and empty. Much better than braving it at midday.

It's tempting to pack lots into Christmas holidays and half terms, but resist. Holidays are for winding down after busy terms. Try to keep the pace slow – pyjamas till lunchtime!

FRIENDS & SOCIAL LIFE

Louise Tyrer, teacher;
Jane Larard; Sally Love

Your child brings home the rudest child you've ever met and introduces him as his best friend. Once you've got over the shock, make your ground rules clear to the friend but without embarrassing your child. Try something like, 'We never swear in the car, Oliver' or 'I can't let you watch a video if you throw food around.' Don't insist that your child stops seeing his friend. It'll make him seem far more interesting. If the friend is as bad as you think he is, your child will realise it for himself.

Make play dates as relaxed as you can, so that your child's friends feel comfortable in your house. Don't go too far away; just keep a listening ear in case you need to step in with an activity to stop them getting bored. Once your child knows his friend well, you can stop hovering.

Don't make play dates too long. It's better that the children should want more time than be itching for the occasion to end.

If the play is getting too wild, make an exception to your normal rules and let them watch a video while they eat their supper.

Try to help your kids set some rules for when they argue. No name calling or hitting, for a start, and plan some safe ways for them to deal with their anger. If they are too cross to talk to each other sensibly, tell them to run around (different parts of) the garden for a while.

If your child has had an argument with a friend, help her to understand how she feels. 'I can see how it hurts your feelings when Issy won't let you play. I would feel sad too.' If you validate her feelings, she can move on much more easily.

For more on arguments between children, see page 119.

If your child comes home and tells you his once best friend is now his worst enemy, be sympathetic but don't say anything bad about his ex-friend, beyond something like, 'Oh, perhaps Andrew was just in a mood today. I hope things go better tomorrow.' If you agree that Andrew is horrible, it can be a bit tricky when your child makes up with him and asks him round again. This applies to boy/girl friends later too.

At the end of play dates, children often want to borrow a toy to take home with them. Arrange with your child to have a special box of toys that she doesn't prize too highly for her friend to select from. It's such a shame to end a good play date with a fight.

For children's parties, see page 110.

Friends At School

See page 150.

FOOD

Anna Knight; Adèle Degremont, teacher; Melanie Byrom; Sarah Schenker, dietician; Caroline Donley, health visitor

To improve table manners at home, have restaurant training sessions. If your kids can eat properly with knife and fork without overfilling their mouths, stay seated and carry on a polite conversation with plenty of pleases and thank yous, reward them by going out to a proper restaurant (not a fast-food joint) that is child friendly where they can try their skills out on the unsuspecting world.

Induce your kids to try new things by getting them involved in selecting recipes, shopping for ingredients and cooking.

Explain the basic food groups to your child (she should be taught it at school too), so that she can select a balanced meal. That way, if she doesn't want potatoes she can choose another type of carbohydrate instead.

If your child wants to get down from the table, set a timer and ask him to stay just three minutes more. Once he goes, however, it's the end of the meal and there is no more food.

Encourage young children to clear away their plates and beakers after the meal. If the one who finishes first has to wait for the slower eater, they can do the chore together.

Hunger can have a radical effect on children's behaviour. They may even be too hungry to want to eat, and that's the start of a vicious circle. Feed them supper/tea soon after they get home from school. They may not have eaten since about midday – and if they are hungry again at bedtime they could have a sandwich/banana/apple. Adults can eat when they are hungry, but it's very easy to over-control your child's food intake.

Accept that your child may fuss about edges being burnt, foods touching each other, not liking the crusts. Teach him to push whatever he doesn't want to the side, and to explain politely what it is that is bothering him.

If your child continues to refuse a particular kind of food, don't give up on it. Just keep putting the offending item on the table without any comment and alongside other things and eventually, the theory goes, she will get used to it and start chomping.

Make water or juice as exciting as lemonade or cola by adding a couple of ice cubes and a slice of lemon or lime. Very exotic!

Give a picky eater small portions or let him serve himself. This way he won't feel overwhelmed by the amount in front of him.

While your kids are watching TV, instead of letting them eat crisps, give them carrot, cucumber and celery sticks and chopped-up apples on plates in front of them and watch their vegetable consumption soar.

Eating in front of the TV is acknowledged as a reason for overeating for some people. But if you have a kid who won't sit at the table long enough to eat, it can be an ideal way of getting some food down her. The fact that she doesn't really notice what she is eating is secondary.

Try adding a few chocolate drops to porridge to transform if from 'healthy but dull' to first choice for breakfast. Alternatively, draw a star or heart on top with maple syrup.

Sounds babyish but make a face with food on their plate or a mountain out of mashed potato. Even at this age they will love eating bits of your artistic creation.

Children's appetites fluctuate wildly, depending on the weather, if they have colds, if they are growing and probably lots of other things too. You can't make children eat – so stop getting stressed about it.

If your kids are not eating well at meal times, try cutting out snacks and cutting down on juice for a while.

Never try to make your child finish everything on her plate. Unlike most adults, children are sensible enough to know when they have eaten enough, so let her develop this sense by encouraging her to eat until she has 'a comfortable tummy'. Food is just food. Don't make it into a bargaining tool.

If your child is a picky eater, instead of concentrating on the many things she won't eat, sit down with her and ask her to help you make a list of the things she does like. It may be more than you give her credit for. Plan meals to include at least one food from her list, and keep the list so that you can update it as her tastes develop.

For optimum nutrition, give your child a rainbow to eat every day: fruit and vegetables of varied colours, including red, orange, yellow, green and blue (never mind indigo and violet) give the best blend of phytonutrients. They also look great, and the whole idea is very appealing to kids.

Don't worry if your child eats the same foods day after day. Children don't see the issue the same way adults do, and actually get a sense of comfort and security from eating the same foods. Try to get your child to take a bite of a new food, but make sure you have back-ups of some regular food available.

Don't let your child fill up on soft drinks such as juice or fizzy drinks. If your child is thirsty, offer as much water as he wants. Reserve other drinks for after he's eaten.

If your child eats sweets, pick ones without artificial colourings or flavourings. The other sort can cause hyperactivity and allergies.

See also page 103.

HEALTH

Dr Kate Crocker, GP; Caroline Donley, health visitor; Clare Baines, dentist; Melanie Byrom; Anna Knight; Marie-Laure Legroux, language teacher; Andrew Williams, paediatrician

Head Lice

Most if not all children at school will get head lice (nits) at least once. The first time it happens, you will freak out completely. But experience will make you more able to cope.

There are many medicated shampoos that you can buy over the counter, but the chemicals are very strong, the nits tend to build up resistance to them and they won't prevent your child from catching them again. If you decide to use such a shampoo, make sure that the chemist knows that it is for a child, as some preparations are not suitable.

Don't rely on scratching as a sign that you need to take action. Some children (and adults) have head lice but don't feel itchy. Check all school-aged children regularly. In the hair behind the ears and at the nape of the neck are easy places to spot the eggs, which are like tiny white or grey dots and stick to the hair shaft.

Combing with a nit comb, available from chemists, is the very best method. Apply conditioner to your child's hair; then comb it through and kill any head lice you find by cracking them between your nails. Combing damages the lice, and they won't continue their normal life cycle; thus you 'break their legs so they can't lay eggs'. Repeat the combing every three days, and make sure that you cover every part of the scalp.

For a natural remedy, try using tea tree oil mixed with conditioner combed through the hair, then use the nit comb to remove the problem completely, and repeat as before.

Check the rest of the family on the same day, and comb everyone's hair, as head lice easily pass from one head to another with close contact.

Change pillow cases and bedding, and wash the pillow to be on the safe side. Wash hats, caps, hairbrushes and combs.

Cuts, Grazes & Splinters

Clean cuts and scrapes with dark-coloured flannels so that children can't see their blood.

If a splinter is projecting above the surface of the skin, you can remove it by placing a piece of sticky tape over the splinter and then pulling it off sharply.

Give your child an apple when you have to clean a cut and tell her to bite into it at the moment you clean the wound.

When your child has an injection or other painful procedure, she might find it helpful to take a deep breath, then puff it out with short, rapid breaths.

For children who hate having plasters on, try placing a wad of lint-free bandage over a cut or blister and secure it with micropore. Much easier to take off.

Plasters with pictures are not as much of an extravagance as they may seem if they will persuade a reluctant child to have a cut treated.

Make sure you keep a stock of steri-strips, very narrow dressings, ideal for drawing the sides of a gash together.

Heat a plaster gently with a hair dryer to soften the adhesive so that it comes off painlessly.

Ease the pain of removing plasters by doing it slowly under water in the bath.

A piece of kitchen towel soaked in cold water and squeezed almost dry is the best thing for your child to apply himself on to a cut or graze.

Teeth

When teeth are wobbly, put the plug in the sink before your child brushes her teeth. Losing a tooth down the drain is a real trauma.

Very wobbly teeth are a nuisance, and can be quite painful when your child is eating. Crunching an apple can sometimes speed the tooth on its way.

The tooth fairy acknowledges swallowed teeth, and those lost at school or down the drain too.

When your child has lost a tooth, put it in a plain sealed envelope; then, in the morning when the identical plain sealed envelope containing some money is there instead – well, it must be magic.

Sometimes the tooth fairy leaves a note for a child who has lost a tooth. This is greatly appreciated by children – but once it starts, the fairy really can't give up. Every tooth must be acknowledged.

Twins losing teeth can present problems, especially if one is losing them faster than the other. Try to come to an arrangement, whereby the tooth fairy leaves some money for each child every time either of them loses a tooth.

Find out from friends what the going rate is for teeth – the tooth fairy can be very unfair, which takes some explaining.

For dentists and toothbrushing, see page 69.

Fear Of The Dentist

Don't be afraid to contact several practices before you decide which one is right for your child. Ask to speak to the practice manager, and find out if they make any special arrangements for nervous patients and/or children. If the practice doesn't sound right for you, don't make an appointment, but go on looking until you find a practice you really like the sound of. You may need to travel some distance, but it will be worth the effort when your child is no longer afraid.

There are many organisations that help people suffering from phobias. Most of them also offer help to people nervous of the dentist because it is a very common problem. Contact the British Dental Health Foundation's helpline 'Word of Mouth' on 0870 333 11 88 to discuss your child's fears and find out about other organisations to contact.

Book appointments at a time of day when your child feels at her best, and when neither you nor she has any other commitments to worry about. Allow plenty of time so that you both arrive at the practice in a relaxed frame of mind – arriving in a rush will only make her feel more nervous.

Listening to music is a good way to help a child relax. Some practices have it playing in the treatment rooms, but the best way is to take a personal stereo so that your child can have his own choice of music. By concentrating on the music – or anything else he likes to listen to – he will not hear the sounds of the treatment.

Suggest your child thinks hard about something other than the treatment. Give her a puzzle to solve in her mind, or perhaps work out a plan for each day of the school holiday. Or give her something tricky to do – like trying to wiggle each toe in turn, without moving any of the others.

Some practices offer hypnosis and relaxation techniques, which enable a child to gain control over feelings of distress or fear and can be very useful in controlling anxiety. Let the practice manager or the dentist tell you both about any that the practice offers. There are various methods available, and which you choose will depend which methods the practice is experienced with and which your child feels would help him most. He can learn relaxation techniques, either from the practice or from specialist teachers.

Hospital

Going to hospital is scary for any child, so always bring a treat – a new book or a little toy or comic – to make the experience a bit less unpleasant.

If a stay in hospital is planned, arrange to visit the ward in advance so that your child knows what to expect.

If your child needs an anaesthetic, stay with her as long as you are allowed to so that your voice is the last thing she hears before she goes under. This is important for her, but will be very, very difficult for you. Even if you are prepared for it, seeing your child slip into unconsciousness is a horrible, scary experience.

Many children are sick after an anaesthetic, so make sure that you have extra clothes with you (for both of you) in case your child pukes. Don't hurry him into eating and drinking. Let his tummy calm down first.

Tonsil operations can often result in sickness because your child may have swallowed blood and the stomach is very intolerant to it.

Hospital wards are always hot, so if you are staying in hospital with your child pack light clothes for yourself.

Make sure that you have plenty of change for phones and vending machines.

If your child has a fracture, think what he can wear to come home. He may need to borrow clothes from an older child or even you to fit over a plaster.

Make plans while you're in the hospital about the treats you're going to have when you get out. And make sure you do them!

For planned stays in hospital, ask your school to provide work sheets and books so that your child can keep up with lessons. Hospital tuition is provided for children who are admitted to hospital for longer periods. It may seem the last thing your child wants to think about, but it has been found that maintaining something close to the normal routine makes children feel better about their stay.

Play nurses will visit your child in hospital, but there may be a limit to what your child can achieve with, say, a broken arm, and it's more frustrating than fun if she makes a mess of her colouring in when she's normally quite good at it.

Reading to your child, playing board games, bringing things from home, story tapes, threading beads or Lego (if fine motor skills are unimpaired) are all diverting, as are grown-up visitors, such as uncles, aunts and grandparents. Having other kids visit can be difficult for both parties, but cards and letters are always appreciated.

SLEEP

Rachel Burn, teacher;
Lis Martin;
Harry Wentworth;
June Hume;
Jane Alexander, writer,
www.janealexander.org

After each bath, try giving your kids a back or foot massage. It should help them to drop off to sleep faster.

Negotiate a number of short stories or the length of time you will read aloud for at bedtime if you're reading through a longer book. That way, children feel they have some say and you won't be left feeling guilty that they are asking for more.

If kids waste time getting ready for bed, translate the time wasted into time taken off their story. For example, tell them you will stop reading at 7.00 p.m. (or when the big hand points straight up), and warn them that if they don't get their pyjamas on quickly, and therefore you start reading later, there will be less time for reading the story.

If your kids have bunk beds, the one sleeping on the bottom has a rather dull view. Make the underside of the upper bunk a bit more interesting by sticking velcro underneath it; then he can stick beanie babies or other cloth toys on to it.

Children need their sleep – and there is nothing sadder than a child wandering round with circles under his eyes.

If bedtime is a battle every night, give your older child a choice of times, but within a restricted band. When you offer the choice of 'Do you want to go to bed at 7.30, 7.45 or 8.00?', she really has to comply with the time she has named, particularly if you tell her that she won't be given the choice again unless she does. (By the way, she'll always choose the latest time you offer!)

Try to make your child's room as pleasant and child friendly as possible so that bed is a good place to be and it feels like it's hers.

Avoid telling your child's friends what time he goes to bed. His friends are probably fibbing about how late they are allowed to stay up, and will use the information to tease your child.

Don't wait for your child to admit to being tired. Some children never realise they are tired, and if you let them establish their own pattern of sleeping, they can get chronically overtired and unable to get back into a good routine.

Suspect your child has been reading or playing in bed after lights out? Feel the light bulb of their bedside lamp. If it's hot, they turned it off when they heard you coming upstairs.

See also Sleep & Bedtime, page 168.

Nightmares, Terrors & Fears

See page 101.

SAFETY

Lis Martin; Joy Lovett, classroom assistant and scout leader; Rachel Burn, teacher; Marie Rendall

Before you leave on a trip with your children, take a polaroid of them and keep it in your bag, so that if you lose one, you have a photograph of what he looks like and how he is dressed.

Make sure that your child knows her full name, address and phone number with area code, as well as your full name. Even four-year-olds can memorise this.

Write your mobile phone number on a piece of card and pop it in your child's pocket or backpack.

Show your children how to use a pay phone, and make sure that they have some change when they go out on trips.

Help your kids to develop their road sense by asking them to judge when it is safe to cross the road. You get the veto, or course, but let them try to assess the traffic situation.

Show your children how important it is to lock doors and windows, and enlist their help in doing a safety check, including unplugging appliances, before you go on holiday.

Take polaroids of your family members, write their phone numbers on the photos and pin them up close to the phone, so that your child will always know whose number to call in an emergency.

Tell your children to check who is at the door before they open it.

Give your kids stock answers to tell people who phone up. There is absolutely no need for any more detail than, 'Mummy/Daddy is busy. Please can you call back?' No one needs to know that you're in the shower. What you really don't want is for some undesirable to engage your child in conversation when you aren't around to prevent it.

Always listen carefully to your children's fears and feelings about people or places that scare them or make them feel uneasy. Tell them to trust their instincts.

Encourage your kids to be alert in the neighbourhood and to watch out for other people and their property too. Ask them to tell an adult – you, a teacher, a neighbour, a policeman – about anything they see that doesn't seem quite right.

Explaining 'stranger danger' to your children is an unpleasant fact of life. They don't need to know the detail; they just need to know what they have to do, which is to yell at the tops of their voices if anyone tries to pull them or any of their friends into a car, to run away but not into the road, and to tell a grown-up they know as quickly as they can.

If you're in a shop with your child, stress to him that he must not leave the shop without you, and make sure that he knows that you will never leave without him.

If children do get lost in a shop, advise them to ask a female member of staff for help or a woman with children.

For as long as you can, take your son into the Ladies with you.

When your son starts to use public loos, tell him to do what he has to do quickly, not to stare at anyone or talk to anyone even if they talk to him first, to wash his hands and to come out straight away. Tell him to yell if he needs help – and get in there straight away!

Let your child know that she can tell you anything, and that you'll be supportive.

Teach your child that his or her private parts are called that for a reason – because they are private to him or her. If you need to clean or wash your child, ask his permission first, to give him a sense that they are his and no one else can touch them without his permission.

Explain that no one, not even a teacher or close relative or friend, should touch her in a way that feels uncomfortable, and that it's OK to say no, get away and tell a trusted adult.

Don't force your kids to kiss or hug or sit on a grown-up's lap if they don't want to. This gives them control and teaches them that they have the right to refuse.

If your child is a victim of any crime or intimidation, from stolen lunch money or bullying to sexual abuse, don't blame him. Listen and offer sympathy.

TRAVEL

Jeanette Davey, Young Explorers: mail order catalogue 01789 414791, www.youngexplorers.co.uk; Janine Watson; Peter Bromwich; Peter Baker, travel consultant; Jane Alexander, writer, www.janealexander.org; Joanna Crosse; Britax, www.britax.co.uk

See also the travel advice on pages 60, 86 and 114.

If you are staying in a hotel adjacent to a large theme park for a few days, get into the park as early as possible, before day-trippers arrive, grab lunch early before the queues build up, go back to your hotel after lunch when the park is busiest for a swim and a nap, then go back to the park when everyone else is leaving.

Limit souvenirs to one or two well-chosen items. Explain this rule to your kids before you go on holiday, and stick to it. Let them buy as many postcards as they like – if you or they use them as bookmarks, you'll come across them unexpectedly from time to time and they'll bring back lovely memories.

Dress your children in brightly coloured T-shirts when you go on trips. This helps if they become separated from you. Whatever your son's wishes, don't dress him in camouflage gear – far too hard to spot.

Tell your kids to call for you by name rather than shout 'Mummy' or 'Daddy' if they become separated from you.

On a beach, buy some helium balloons and tie them to your deckchair so that your kids can find you easily.

For a long-haul flight, let each child bring a personal stereo and some story tapes.

If you are going somewhere that is cold at night, buy a sleeping bag that is about the right size for your child. This ensures that he has a tighter cocoon around his body. An adult bag with a strap at the bottom will not cocoon him so well and may leave him feeling cold.

If you are going to mountainous regions, be prepared for every kind of weather, even in midsummer. Sunglasses are essential year round, as are winter coats and thermals. It often snows in August in the European Alps and can snow every month in some resorts.

Remember that protection against the sun is even more important at high altitudes (see page 78).

By Car

SUMMARY OF THE LAW

	Front seat	Rear seat	Responsibility
Driver	Seat belt must be used if fitted		Driver
Child under 3 years of age	**Appropriate child restraint must be used**	**Appropriate child restraint must be used if available**	**Driver**
Child aged 3 to 11 and under 1.5m (approx. 5ft) in height	Appropriate child restraint must be used if available; if not, an adult seat belt must be used	Appropriate child restraint must be used if available; if not, an adult seat belt must be used if available	Driver
Child aged 12 or 13 or younger child 1.5m (approx. 5ft) or more in height	**Adult seat belt must be used if available**	**Adult seat belt must be used if available**	**Driver**
Adult passenger (from 14 years)	Seat belt must be used if available	Seat belt must be used if available	Passenger

Are we nearly there yet? Kids have no concept of what 'another seventy-five miles' or 'an hour and a half' mean. An adult passenger can show them how far you are by sticking his arm over the back of the seat and indicating with the other hand what proportion of the journey you have done, starting from the shoulder. Once you reach the elbow, you're nearly halfway.

If you have more than one child in the back of the car, try alternating their seats to avoid monotony and bickering. Place a box of treats for each child in between them.

Give yourself plenty of extra time so that you can schedule in a visit to a playground for your kids to let off some steam.

Pack a skipping rope, a ball and a frisbee so that you can play with the kids wherever you find an open space.

For travelling, dress your kids lightly in sandals, T-shirts and stretchy trousers or shorts. Pack a jacket for when they have to get out of the car.

When travelling long distances (hundreds of miles/two days or more):

- Allow about two hours' stopping time for every mealtime, for run-around time as well as eating time, and allow an hour or forty-five minutes mid-morning and mid-afternoon to let everyone stretch their legs, too.

- Crossing the channel on the ferry may take longer than Eurotunnel but it doubles up as run-around time and is exciting to look forward to.

- Dress your kids in their pyjamas after the last meal. This is when you can get some serious driving in; then just tip them into bed when you arrive.

- Put aside some of their familiar toys a few weeks before the long drive that are good to play with on the move. They will be delighted to see their old favourites again when the journey starts. Put a cardboard box or something similar between the children so that they have all the toys to hand *en route*.

- Buy a travel game or something similar as a new present for them, but don't give it to them until you are halfway through the journey.

- Story tapes are essential travel companions. Once you've suffered through the nursery rhymes, you can get on to books the whole family will enjoy: Frog and Toad stories, Roald Dahl, C. S. Lewis, Michael Morpurgo, J. K. Rowling and Richmal Crompton. Libraries lend these out, or you can buy them from a good bookshop. Get some new ones especially for the trip.

- If at all possible, invest in a 'house on your back' (motorhome, VW camper or caravan) if you think you are going to do lots of travelling in Europe. All your bulky goods can be carried so much more easily in one of these, and you will have immediate access to a toilet, food and bed at critical times.

Activity Holidays

When walking with children, encourage them with the precious gift of your undivided attention. Give them time to explore. For example, they are much closer to the ground than you, so bugs and beasties consume them with interest. If necessary, you will have to stop at each one, but you can feed your interest and theirs by taking along a guidebook so that you know what you are looking at. Ditto with flowers, but it is a good golden rule not to pick any flowers; it is illegal to do so in some countries.

Other items of interest on walks are stiles and gates – children enjoy opening them; tree trunks to jump off and walk along; bridges; streams; and, of course, patches of snow.

Things to take when walking:

- If you are in the mountains, you will inevitably find water in the form of lakes, waterfalls or streams. Pack a travel towel in your backpack, as your children will be magnetically attracted to it, of course, regardless of icy temperatures.

- Take plenty of snacks and drinks, to soothe children if they have a fall and to entice them if they get tired. Choose ones that will give them that all-important energy boost.

- A small artist's pad and pencils can give children an opportunity to take in the scenery around them.

- Give your child a backpack of her own to make her feel responsible for her belongings. Keep everything as low in weight as possible. Crisps, biscuits, teddy and the first-aid kit are good, low-weight items for a child to carry.

A trekking pole is a great incentive for walking. If it is not used directly for the purpose all the time, it can be used for poking a sibling (not condoned), investigating muddy patches and the bottom of streams, and reaching up high into trees.

If going on safari, make sure that you take binoculars for your children; otherwise they will want to borrow yours just when it matters.

Most kids can manage a trailer bike (which is like a mini-tandem attachment to your bike) when they are about five years old. Make sure that you dress your child warmly, as they will be immobile with the wind blowing at them all the way.

Exotic Holidays

Loos abroad are often unfamiliar in style and sometimes, frankly, a bit grim. Carry sachets of surface cleaner wipes with you to clean up before your kids use them.

If you are going to have to eat local food, give your kids some idea of what they are likely to encounter before you arrive. Try out a few recipes before you travel, but take fall-back supplies of pasta, cake mix, fun-size cereals and biscuits.

Drink water, and plenty of it, to help avoid both constipation and dehydration. Keep a thermos of boiled water with you all the time.

If you notice locals drinking from plastic bottles, you can bet that the tap water is unsafe to drink. Bottled water from shops is sometimes nothing more than treated tap water, and it may contain levels of minerals harmful for younger children.

Always check that bottle seals are intact before you drink from them, and in restaurants try to insist that bottles are opened at your table, within view. Most brand-name carbonated drinks, such as Coca Cola and Pepsi, are bottled under strict sanitary conditions worldwide.

Never have ice cubes in places where the water is unreliable.

Hot, freshly cooked dishes are the safest foods. Baked potatoes, boiled eggs, nuts and live yoghurt are usually a safe bet.

Don't buy ice cream and other dairy products in Africa, India or parts of the Middle East – you can't always be sure that the milk has been pasteurised or the dairy products properly refrigerated. If in doubt, choose long-life, powdered or tinned milks from a shop.

Street snack bars and market cafés often have such a rapid turnover of locals that their food rarely has a chance to go bad; their food could easily turn out to be safer than international cuisine cooked in five-star hotels.

Avoid an empty restaurant. Unless you know that the locals dine late (as in Spain, Italy and Argentina), there is usually a very good reason why nobody eats there.

Take rehydration powders with you, in case your child gets diarrhoea.

Don't, whatever you do, skimp on travel insurance. In cases of serious illness, someone in your party may have to be flown home in an air ambulance – and the cost could run into tens of thousands of pounds.

6 SEVEN TO ELEVEN YEARS

'Children begin by loving their parents; after a time they judge them; rarely, if ever, do they forgive them.'

Oscar Wilde

This is an exciting, rewarding stage. Children's individual characters are set and they have their own very definite ideas and opinions. You can hold sensible discussions with them and attempt outings that were impossible when they were smaller. Children become companions and are fun to be with. But along with being more mature, they are likely to be more judgemental, and often more challenging.

This is also a time of enormous mental and physical change. At seven your child is still an infant. By eleven, he is poised for independence, preparing to go to secondary school and almost a teenager.

BEHAVIOUR

Amanda Stevens; Cathy Johns; Ruth Williams, nanny; Sandra Wroe

Avoid making a situation into an issue. It's often easier said than done, but try to restrict battles or absolute vetoes to things that are really important.

Confrontation is rarely the best way to deal with a problem. Compromise where possible and make sure that your child feels she has a say.

Listen and try to make time for your child when he is ready to talk.

Often it is what is not said that is worrying a child. Try to encourage your child to confide in you without always asking direct questions.

Be open. Answer questions as honestly as you can. Seven-to-eleven-year-olds are quick to spot when you are being less than honest in response to their questions.

When your children are ganging up against you and being difficult, it can be useful to remember 'divide and rule'.

Learn to give one another space. Anger can build up because one little thing happens after another. Take a break.

When your child is angry, hand him a pile of newspapers or an old telephone directory and ask him to rip it up for you. It works wonders for grouchy grown-ups, too.

The role of a parent changes all the time as children grow and develop. Some stages are bound to be more difficult than others. It's worth remembering that all phases end and are quickly forgotten.

Take time to really talk to your children. Ask what they think and listen to their opinion. Don't undermine their confidence.

Try to instil in your children the idea that the family works as a team, and that you should support each other no matter what.

Boys and their fathers: research shows that boys have a very close relationship with their mothers up until the age of about seven. They will then show much more interest in a male role model. As a dad, you have a very important part to play at this stage. If you are a single mum, try to find men who can take a responsible place in your son's life at this stage: this could mean involving his natural father more, a grandfather, uncle or close male family friend.

GROWING UP

Alison Wallis;
Amanda Stevens;
Anna Knight;
Carolyn Webb,
teacher;
Dr Cathy Amin;
Deborah Woodbridge;
Dr Lisa Watts;
Liz Chowienczyk;
Sîan Annous, dental
surgeon; Tracy Martin;
William Crawford

At seven, your child is still quite young. He will have thrown off the last physical remnants of babyhood but as he moves from infants to juniors you will notice him maturing and growing up.

Don't take the fact that he no longer wants to kiss you goodbye in front of his friends as a rejection. Boys especially are often embarrassed by open signs of affection.

In private, your child may well be more affectionate than before. Ten-year-olds still want cuddles and goodnight kisses – just not when their friends are around.

Sadly, this is the beginning of the years when children discover various reasons to find their parents embarrassing. Until the age of seven, they generally view them as omnipotent and 'the best'.

Common parental embarrassments for children are: kissing them goodbye at school, your hair, your car, your house, family nicknames, open displays of affection between parents, dressing or acting too young, dressing or acting too old, liking modern music, liking 'fogey' music, your sense of humour, your choice of clothes for them – in short, just about anything. Remember, this doesn't mean that they don't still really love you.

This is the stage where you have to remember that you are the parent. Try to avoid 'yes/no' arguments and battles of will.

Don't be afraid to lead and state what's appropriate. You don't have to set rigid rules but you are the adult and not their peer.

Children of this age are starting to be aware of what's going on in the world and society around them. They quickly realise that everything is not safe and cosy.

You can't shield children from bad news and it's important that they learn from the security of home that unpleasant things can happen.

Don't stop children reading newspapers or watching the news if they are interested. Children's news programmes like *Newsround* usually deal with difficult issues sensitively.

Make sure that you are there to answer questions your children may have and to deal with worries or fears that arise from what they've learned.

Generally, try to discuss issues openly. If your child has asked a question, she has a right to an honest answer and is old enough to hear it.

Occasionally you may feel that your child isn't ready for too full an answer. Only you can judge this.

Encourage children to come to you with embarrassing questions rather than relying on misinformation or part-answers from friends.

With ten- and eleven-year-olds, it's usually best to give a straight answer to the most embarrassing questions – even the ones you would really rather not explain. Children are reaching the stage where if they don't know something they risk looking silly in front of their schoolmates.

Puberty

Expect moods. Even before there are any outward signs of puberty, hormones are beginning to surge.

Bodies will begin to change fast. It's not unheard of for girls of eight to begin to have periods and ten or eleven is quite normal.

For Periods, see page 190.

For Bras & Boobs, see page 188.

It's important to prepare children for the physical changes they will go through.

Menstruation should be explained early on – to boys and to girls. Girls because they need to be aware of what will happen to their body, and boys because they shouldn't be coy about it – it's natural and they should accept it as such. You don't want it to be a shock and the more open you are the more relaxed they will feel.

Don't hide your tampons/towels away from your children. Leave them in a fairly obvious place so that they are familiar with having these things around. Remember the first time you unwrapped and investigated one of your mother's tampons?

Find out whether school has a sex education policy and if so when specific lessons will begin. It's helpful to back these up at home.

The 1993 Education Act made it law for schools to provide sex education, but you can object if you want to. However, under the European Convention on Human Rights, your child could argue that he has the right to 'receive information'.

Tell your child what she wants to know, but don't elaborate if she seem satisfied with the information you have given. (Remember the old story about the parent who gave a long and detailed reply about reproduction to the question 'Mummy where did I come from?' only to get the response 'Oh, I thought it was Birmingham.')

Books like *Mummy Laid an Egg* and *Hair in Funny Places* by Babette Cole are good starting points – they're funny as well as informative.

Magazines aimed at girls are an excellent source of advice on menstruation, and most handle the subject sympathetically and sensibly. Buy a few copies for yourself, read what they have to say and then give them to your daughter. She may already be more informed than you think.

For more on talking about sex with your children, see page 180.

Children can suddenly become very self-conscious about their bodies. It's important to respect their need for privacy. Don't, for instance, insist that they carry on bathing with a younger sibling.

Personal hygiene becomes important. Make sure that your child is washing properly, using soap when necessary, and see page 186.

Sweaty armpits can become a problem quite early on – before any other signs of puberty. To begin with, make sure that your child washes well and uses soap. When this isn't enough, buy a mild deodorant – see page 186.

Health

Continue to visit the dentist regularly. This is all the more important when the milk teeth have been replaced by second teeth.

By now there's little chance of your doing anything more than supervising teeth brushing, but it's worth reminding children of the correct way to clean teeth and if necessary set the egg timer to show them how long to brush for.

Sugar-free chewing gum encourages the flow of saliva. Chewed after sugary food, minerals in the extra saliva produced will help neutralise bacteria in the mouth.

Opticians recommend regular eye checks. They also suggest that children wear sunglasses to protect eyes against UV and UVB damage.

Bodies are growing fast now and many children of this age suffer from growing pains, especially in their legs and joints at night.

If bedwetting is still a problem, it's time to consider asking your GP to refer you to a genito-urinary specialist. There are several approaches you could try under medical supervision.

Drugs

Make sure that your children know the basic facts and the dangers of drugs. Children of this age don't need to know all the details, but they should be aware.

At primary school, children are usually quite well protected from the issue but this changes rapidly when they begin secondary school and it's vital to prepare them.

The police are only too happy to visit schools to discuss the dangers of drugs with children – usually in years five and six. Make sure that your school is aware of this.

For more on drugs, see page 178.

Swearing

Most children will swear, just as most of us do, even if we are careful not to do so in front of the children.

Don't appear too shocked. Instead, calmly point out that there are several places where it would be completely inappropriate to swear and many people who would be very shocked.

If it's meant to be out of your earshot, ignore it. There are enough things to battle over.

Clothes & Make-up

Girls will begin to be interested in clothes and make-up. It's much better for them to experiment with make-up, nail varnish and unsuitable clothes in a safe environment at home and to feel they can be open with you.

When they try out make-up, you could join in and offer guidance with suggestions on how to be discreet.

You could also tactfully suggest that while make-up at home is fine, it's not appropriate for going out. Compromise by allowing nail varnish.

Establish certain areas where make-up and nail varnish can be used. Suggest that make-up is stored in a plastic-backed bag or Tupperware box and that it is set out on a plastic mat. That way, you will minimise the damage caused by spillages.

Everyone has their own rules and ideas of appropriate dress. Limit battles by offering a choice, but within certain boundaries.

Don't be afraid of setting guidelines and explaining why certain clothes are too mature or send the wrong signals. By the age of eleven, girls are testing their attractiveness, at least subconsciously.

Boys become very self-conscious about their hairstyles. This is serious stuff, so whatever you do don't laugh. Try to offer practical help or ask a hairdresser (preferably male) for tips on how to use products like hair gel and wax.

SCHOOL

Homework

Alison Wallis;
Amanda Stevens;
John Knight;
Beth Russell, teacher;
Carolyn Webb, teacher;
Clare Porter; Jo Caseby;
Liz Chowienczyk;
Margaret Cave;
Margaret Donovan;
Parentline Plus;
Sandra Richards,
teaching assistant;
Sandra Wroe;
Tiina Godding;
Mary Lewis, teacher;
Gail Fellows, teacher;
www.kidscape.org.uk;
www.pupiline.net;
www.bbc.co.uk/learning

Homework is never an easy issue and very few children are always keen on doing it. So don't worry that you have the only reluctant, or lazy, child.

Don't leave homework until the last minute. At this stage, homework is as much about setting good habits for the future as the work itself.

Developing good homework habits at primary school can help later at secondary school when homework is more serious.

Children often want help with their homework, and with changing teaching methods as well as the National Curriculum this is sometimes easier said than done. If you want to help with homework but find the current methods confusing, talk to your child's teacher and ask for advice. There are many useful books and it's also well worth trying www.schoolfriend.com, a website that provides exercises to help with maths, reading, spelling and vocabulary.

Encourage your child to be responsible about his work.

Help your child to plan ahead for fitting in homework. Especially at primary school children are often given several days to complete a piece of work. In deciding when to do it, it's easy for children to overlook evenings when they are busy and tempting to leave homework till the last minute.

Suggest that your child keeps a homework diary. She should write in any other activities she must take into account when planning her time.

Check that your child has her homework as she comes out of school. It's too late when you have got home. If your child gets the bus, give her a final check routine to follow before she leaves the classroom.

It's helpful to set a routine for homework that works for everyone. Children are often hungry when they come home from school, so it may work best to eat a snack and drink first, relax for a while and watch a programme on TV, and then settle down to work. Or let them have a little run around, then get them stuck in before supper. At least set a specific time that they know is homework time. Don't let your kids leave homework too late, or they'll never concentrate.

Pick a time for homework that is non-negotiable. Make sure that it doesn't clash with a favourite TV programme, or if it does, record it. Some children like to get homework over with as soon as they return from school. Others like to relax and then do it once they have eaten tea and unwound.

To help your kids concentrate, split homework into fifteen-minute intervals; then let them have a break. Let them have a timer on the table so that they can see how they are doing.

Provide your kids with a drink while they do their homework. Getting dehydrated decreases their ability to concentrate.

Or you could try making a deal with your child – homework first, after which he's free to watch TV or play on the computer.

Try to create a time and space for homework. It shouldn't be done anywhere too noisy, but children don't necessarily like being closeted away (even though they have the bedroom of their choice with a big desk and comfy chair). If they would rather lay out homework on the kitchen table, that's fine so long as the rest of the family keep well away. Alternatively provide them with good desks in their rooms, with plenty of light and comfortable chairs.

If your child likes working near you, try to facilitate this and make sure that there aren't too many distractions.

Don't allow homework in front of the TV. It's never a good idea.

Encourage children to complete their homework themselves, then help them to read it through afterwards.

Make sure that there is somewhere quiet to work away from younger siblings. Try not to let younger ones make it too obvious that they are having a lovely, free time with no homework.

If a child is particularly reluctant, offer to sit with her and point out what she is working for.

The school should tell you how much time your child should be spending on homework. When he does the homework, set a time limit – so that he can make sure he finishes within the time it should be taking him and the nightmare doesn't go on too long.

Get the pain over with. Advise your child to do the hardest piece of work first.

Offer a reward once the work is done. That TV programme you recorded, a bag of crisps, a game of football – something to look forward to.

Keep an eye on what your child is doing. Read the prep diary when she comes home, and check with her before she starts that she knows what questions have to be answered, in which book.

Stay near by, looking over your child's shoulder every now and then to ensure that he is doing the work properly.

If your child starts to doodle or daydream, pick up the book and ask her which question she is working on, then give it back when she is ready to start writing again. Try not to lose your temper …

It's very easy to look at completed work and criticise misspelt words, smudges and the like. Pick out parts your child has done well – a good diagram, a hard question answered well – then gently point out the corrections last.

Always speak to your child's teacher if you suspect that she is regularly failing to understand lessons at school.

Don't do your child's homework for her. Offer help and advice, sit with her if necessary and explain anything she doesn't understand, but it's no good for anyone if it's your work on the page.

If your child is particularly stuck with a piece of work, write a note to the teacher saying so and explaining that you have had to give a lot of support and help. This way the teacher won't wrongly assume that this is something your child understands or is competent with, and will offer extra help as needed.

Make sure that your child knows how to access information. Point him to books, reference books, libraries, computers and the internet.

If your child is not doing her homework, try to find out why. Ask for her ideas on why there's a problem – maybe she doesn't understand the work or home is too noisy, or perhaps there's another reason.

Try to motivate and encourage your child. By this age, he's probably too old for star charts but you could offer a small reward such as choosing a new story book or a sleepover with his best friend.

In independent schools, your child may be sitting end-of-year assessments for the first time. Despite your best efforts to calm your child down, schools are inclined to whip children into a frenzy. If all the work gets too much for your child, speak to her form teacher and ask for the pressure to be released a bit. This is only the start of a long academic trek. No point in peaking too early.

Websites can be useful for homework: try www.bbc.co.uk/education/revision. But beware of a child searching for information on a search engine and coming up with inaccurate answers. For more websites useful for homework, see page 239.

The old ways are often still the best. Even the *Encyclopaedia Britannica* is available online at www.britannica.com.

Parents' Meetings & Complaining

See page 203.

Time Out

See page 207.

Friends At School

You can't choose your children's friends, especially as they get older. So don't try.

Between the ages of seven and eleven, friends group and regroup several times over. It's best not to get too involved, but to offer a sympathetic ear and advice when it's wanted.

Children get upset and feel left out sometimes. Offer advice, but remember that your child has to learn to deal with this.

If your child no longer feels a part of her old group of friends, suggest that she looks for a different set to play with.

You can help your child make new friends outside school by taking up a new activity like drama or dance, or a sport.

To overcome a tricky patch with a friend, suggest that the two do something specific together rather than just playing or spending time at each other's houses.

If you suspect that there is a more serious problem with a friendship or that your child is being bullied, always talk to a teacher, and, for bullying, see page 151.

You can encourage friendships by inviting children over to your house.

Even if you don't like one of your children's friends, don't interfere. Let the friendship run its course.

At school, best friends usually don't work brilliantly together, so don't rush into school asking for your child to sit next to her chum – there's probably a good reason why they've been split up.

Working alongside different children helps to improve social skills. This works even with those who don't naturally get along.

In lessons, boys and girls work well together. They provide a balance for each other, with boys tending to reach a conclusion faster and girls better at seeing both sides of a problem.

Bullying

The European Convention on Human Rights says that no one should be subjected to degrading treatment or punishment – so your child should not have to put up with bullying and has a right in law to be educated without fear. The school should have a bullying policy.

Your child may be reluctant to admit he's being bullied. Be alert for signs.

Signs of bullying might include:

- Under-achieving, perhaps because his confidence has taken a knock.

- Negative, pessimistic emotions.

- Physical stress-related symptoms, including headaches, sickness, inability to sleep, tummy aches, nightmares, bruising or scratching and bedwetting.

- Fabricated symptoms, and a request to be allowed to stay home from school.

- Depression.

- Changes in behaviour, for example becoming withdrawn or argumentative or lacking concentration, or generally difficult behaviour.

- Changes in his routine, for example changing his route to school.

- Low self-esteem, shyness and isolation.

- Requests for money or stealing from you.

- Unhappiness during the week.

- Truancy from school.

- Bullying other children.

What to do if your child is being bullied:

- Give your child the opportunity to talk and let them know you will always listen.

- Don't take it as a rejection if your child would prefer to talk to someone else.

- Reassure your child that asking for help is the right thing to do and that she's not being weak or telling tales by talking over the problem with an adult.

- Listen carefully.

- Ensure that he does not feel that he's done wrong. Stress that no child deserves to be bullied. Some bullied children imagine it is their fault or that they've brought it upon themselves because they're unpopular.

- Make sure that your child knows that you are on his side and willing to help or listen at any time.

- Do not overreact – children need calm and rational help.

- Ensure that you believe your child and do not be fobbed off by dismissive authority figures.

- Seek experienced advice.

- Contact support groups.

- Take suicide threats seriously, seeking professional help immediately.

- Contact the school. Don't wait until parents' evening. Parentline Plus research shows that many parents feel that they will not be taken seriously if they make a complaint. Heads and teachers have a responsibility to investigate the allegation immediately, resolve the situation decisively, making it clear that bullying will not be tolerated, and give you regular feedback.

- Talk to your child's teacher about the problem and try to discuss the situation calmly with the other parents.

Bullying can build up over a period of time and changes in behaviour are often gradual rather than sudden. Watch for warning signs.

If your child is showing physical symptoms like bedwetting or regular stomach aches, it's a good idea to see your doctor.

Your child will need a lot of support and it's important to offer extra praise and approval.

Discuss practical ways to keep your child safe – for instance, taking different routes between lessons, staying with other friends at school, not taking valuables to school, walking confidently and hiding the fact that he is upset.

Try to encourage your child not to take the bullying personally and to see it as the bully's problem.

Make sure that your child knows who to speak to if there is trouble.

Young people can't really cope with tackling a bully alone. But the worst thing you can do is to hit the roof when told about an incident and threaten to storm into the school, all guns blazing: that is the fastest way to ensure that your child never tells you anything again. She will not want a fuss made, for fear it will antagonise the bully further. Be calm with your child, talk through what has happened, then work out a way of approaching the school in a discreet way she is comfortable with.

Encourage your child to keep a record of incidents of bullying, which will be ammunition once you approach the school or the situation in which the bullying is happening.

The teacher may set up a playtime book for both the bully and bullied. It's important for everyone to be honest in it.

You can't make children like one another, but you can help them to get along. All the children involved in the bullying should be asked to tackle aspects of their behaviour. It's important that everyone feels that the treatment of the problem is fair and that everyone is working to improve it.

If your child has witnessed bullying, encourage him to report it. This shouldn't be seen as tale-telling.

It's not unusual for children who are bullied to go on to bully others.

Sometimes children just have a bad day. Children can be in bad moods and say nasty things to one another. The fact that a child has been bullied in the past doesn't mean that every negative incident is a bullying one. Try to balance your view of what's really going on.

Bullying doesn't have to be exclusive to school. It could be happening amongst a group of friends who are exerting unfair peer pressure on your child. This is a harder one to deal with, because you do not have the 'protection' of school authority. See Friends, page 177.

Good websites with information for kids being bullied include
www.kidscape.org.uk, www.pupiline.net and www.bbc.co.uk/learning – search under Bullying.

When Your Child Is The Bully

It's very difficult if you find out that your child is a bully. The natural reaction is to feel guilty and want to deny that it's happening.

You must confront the problem. Monitor what's happening and look for the reason behind the behaviour.

Bullying becomes a habit of behaviour that needs tackling and changing.

Talk to your child. Tell her that her behaviour is wrong, that you know she's not a horrid person and that you believe the bullying is making her unhappy.

Look at ways to help your child manage his anger. Suggest that he walks away or does something specific like fetching a glass of water. It's important to give him something to do or say.

There are irritant bullies who irritate other children to the point where they are so angry they lash out or bully him. This is very hard for parents to recognise in their own child.

It's vital to work with your child's teacher.

Though it's difficult to be objective and not defensive, try to talk to the other parents, preferably with the teacher present. This really helps.

Fear Of School

See page 203.

Truancy

See page 203.

CHOOSING A SECONDARY SCHOOL

Alison Wallis; Amanda Stevens; Beth Russell, teacher; Carolyn Webb, teacher; Clare Porter; Emma and Jeremy Wakeling; Emily Savage; Liz Chowienczyk; Margaret Cave; Margaret Donovan; Parentline Plus; Richard and Anne Bracegirdle; Sandra Richards, teaching assistant; Sandra Wroe; Tiina Godding; Mary Lewis, teacher; Gail Fellows, teacher; www.kidscape.org.uk; www.pupiline.net; www.bbc.co.uk/learning

Start looking at schools two years before your child is due to transfer. It helps to get a perspective if you've seen schools more than once and over a period of time.

Look widely in year five (age ten) and aim to draw up a shortlist of real possibilities in year six.

As with choosing a primary school, it's helpful to talk to other parents with children at the same stage to find out what they are doing. But always make up your own mind about the right choice for your child. What one person likes may not suit another.

There's a lot of competition for places and many parents get very worked up about secondary transfer. Try to remain calm and stick to what you feel is right.

At the end of the whole process, many children end up with a choice of places and the school that is right for them.

It's worth remembering that this doesn't have to be a permanent decision. If the school proves to be the wrong choice for your child, you can move her – particularly at thirteen or sixteen.

School is not the only option. For educating at home, see page 157.

There are currently thirty-six state boarding schools. www.stabis.org.uk is the site of the State Boarding School Information Service. For independent boarding schools, see page 155.

Choosing A School

Check dates carefully for open-day visits and especially for application forms. Many popular schools are oversubscribed and operate a strict policy of not accepting late applicants.

Telephone schools to find out dates and request a prospectus.

Visit potential schools. Look at pupils' work and classroom displays. Talk to current pupils and ask for their opinion of the school.

Ask questions and find out as much as you can. Talk to other pupils and parents for an inside view.

It's useful to go along with your partner or a close friend. You're likely to notice different things.

Watch the pupils. Do they look interested? Do they look happy? What is the pupil–teacher relationship like? How lively is the teaching? Is there a positive buzz to the school?

Take a look at the classrooms. You can find out a lot from the displays and pupils' work.

Are there plenty of activities, clubs and societies on offer?

Ask about the school drugs policy. All schools should have one as they are a problem everywhere and a school that tells you otherwise is being less than open.

Make sure that you have as much information as possible. Read the prospectus carefully and check out the school website. Look at league tables, take time to look at exam results and find out the destinations of school leavers – this helps to give you an idea of the school's strengths and if there is a particular bias, say, towards science, medicine, art or music.

Make sure that you're looking at recent data. You should be checking the results for the last two years.

Ofsted reports of state schools are available for anyone to see. These are independent reports and should give you an idea of the strengths and weaknesses of a school, as well as any specialist interests and ways in which the school could improve. They will also give you basic facts like the number of pupils. To see them, look in the local library or check the internet at www.ofsted.gov.uk/reports/index.htm.

Check whether there are any criteria for acceptance at the school and what the entrance procedures are.

If the school is selective, find out what type of entrance exam is set and ask if it is possible to see past papers. Ask if prospective pupils are interviewed. Some schools interview all prospective candidates, while others only interview on the basis of exam results.

Cynical, but you can increase your child's chances of being accepted by the school of your choice by adding to their CV – interests like sport, dance, drama and language all help.

Schools can also be impressed when parents can offer a particular skill or service.

Remember that you're not choosing a school for yourself and that though you think you've found the perfect school, it may not suit your child.

Parents have very definite views about schools. Try not to be influenced by snobbery, fashion, old school tie – choose one which suits your child's needs and/or talents.

Involve your child in the whole process. Take him with you to look at schools and listen to his opinion and preferences.

It's not necessarily how far away from home a school is that's the problem, it's how easy it is to get to. A fifty-minute journey door-to-door on a school bus may be far less stressful than a shorter one involving a change of train or bus on public transport.

Independent Secondary Schools

Go along to open days but bear in mind that these are designed to show the school in the best possible light.

If you're impressed by a particular school, make an appointment for a private visit during a normal school day.

Look at newspaper reports on school league tables. Both the *Daily Telegraph* and *Sunday Times* publish regular independent school reports. It's worth remembering that there is often a very small difference between the attainment of premier league and second division schools. You should also consider whether pupils are actively discouraged from sitting exams in subjects where they are unlikely to get a high grade.

To find out exam results, you can view the Independent Schools Inspectorate report at www.isinspect.org.uk.

Another excellent reference for independent schools is *The Good Schools Guide* published by Lucas Publications: it covers tell-it-how-it-really-is reports on schools, including questions you should ask and ways of paying the fees. The publication has a website at www.goodschoolsguide.co.uk and offers an advisory service for parents on choosing the best school for their children. Call 020 7733 7861.

There's a helpful guide to boarding schools published by the DFES: *Choosing a Boarding School* (call 08700 002288, or via www.dfes.gov.uk). Also go to the Boarding School Association at www.boarding-association.org.uk (020 7798 1580 for a free booklet on schools in your area) or www.isis.org.uk, the site of the Independent Schools Information Service, which has publications including views of the parents of boarders.

The children who settle best into boarding school have secure home lives. Don't send a child to boarding school immediately following a divorce or the death of a parent.

School Fees

It's important to find out not only exactly what the school fees are but also extras like school lunches, uniforms, compulsory school trips and the cost of the school coach if your child has to travel to school.

Check whether you can pay by direct debit and any other payment schemes.

If your child is keen to board, but fees are an issue, look at www.stabis.org.uk, or consider sending her after she has done her GCSEs. Many heads find that children settle well at this age, as they are 'ready to engage in the responsibilities of community life'. Boarding school can be an excellent stepping stone to college and independence, in a controlled, safe environment.

Have a look at zero preference shares. They're low-risk tax-efficient investments which generate predictable lump sums on set dates in the future. Each has a finite life – usually four or five years – during which time no dividend is paid, so there's no income tax liability. Returns aren't guaranteed but issuers provide a 'hurdle rate' for each zero, which indicates the rate of growth required to pay investors in full. So far, no zero has ever failed to deliver its promised yield.

Private Tuition

Ideally, if you decide to tutor your child, it should be to boost their confidence and prepare them for selective exams.

Children attending a state primary school who are hoping to transfer to an independent or selective secondary school may find that they have not covered everything included in the entrance exam. Many parents, particularly those in areas where competition for places is fierce, decide that the only option is to tutor their child. Think about this issue early.

Many independent schools like children to have had some tutoring so that they know what to expect from the entrance exams.

It is never good for a child to be pushed beyond his capabilities and it is not in a child's interests to be crammed to pass an entrance exam only to find that he struggles and is constantly at the bottom of the class at secondary school.

On a more positive note, if you find the right person, children can thrive with a tutor and enjoy the one-to-one teaching and attention.

Personal recommendation is the best way to find a tutor. Talk to parents of older children in your primary school to find out who they would recommend. Make sure that the tutor is someone your child likes and feels comfortable with. The sessions should boost his confidence and help him.

Talk to a tutor about the schools you are planning to apply for. He or she should be able to set practice papers geared towards preparing for the exams.

Most people opt for a one-hour session once a week in the year leading up to school entrance exams.

Exams & Interviews

Selective and independent schools set entrance exams that primary schools do not always practise for. It's unfair to send children into exams without some preparation so that they have at least an idea of what to expect.

There are several good ranges of practice test papers for children taking 11-plus, 12-plus and independent examinations for secondary school selection. WHSmith has a wide choice. Teachers will usually give you advice on which ones to buy.

Papers covered commonly include: maths, English, verbal reasoning and non-verbal reasoning.

Prepare your child for what to expect from an interview. For most children this is a totally new experience.

To prepare for interviews, you can discuss some of the likely topics – favourite books, hobbies, after-school activities; or it may be useful to ask a friend to give your child a mock interview.

It helps if your child does a range of activities outside school and can talk about her interests.

Don't be surprised if parents are also interviewed. Be prepared and think of at least one question to ask at the end.

Appeals

If your child is not given a place at the school of your choice, you can appeal against the decision:

- Take a solicitor along with you to appeal if you feel that a solicitor could present your case better.
- If a child who has bullied your son or daughter at primary school is going to the school you have been allocated, you can use this as a valid reason to appeal for a different school.
- You can also argue that the ethos of your first-choice school would suit your son or daughter better.
- The fact that all your child's friends are going to a particular school is another reason to argue your case.

- Flatter your first-choice school. Explain what you admire about it.

- If the child who has been refused entry is the younger sibling of a child already at the school, explain the importance of keeping all your children together at the same school.

- Make sure that your face is known. If you are on a waiting list you want to be more than just another name. Attend fêtes and/or parents meetings.

Preparing For Secondary School

By the time your child leaves primary school, the chances are that he will be ready for the move and challenge secondary school will provide.

The change to secondary school can be a shock. Primary school is often quite protected. Mum can easily pop in to sort out any problems. At secondary school, your child is on his own to a much greater degree. Most schools try to ease the transfer, but it helps to prepare.

If your child is visiting a friend locally, let him go by himself. Make sure that you know exactly when he set off and let his friend's parents know what time he's due to arrive.

Children like shopping with friends. Arrange to meet up at a specific time and place.

As children attempt more by themselves, they will enjoy the extra freedom and gain in confidence.

If your child will be travelling by public transport to secondary school, make sure that she knows the route. Accompany her on the journey before letting her attempt it by herself.

If your child will be walking to secondary school, go over the best route to take with her and discuss ways of crossing difficult roads safely.

In the summer term before the September transfer, encourage your child to walk home from primary school by himself. He could start by walking with a friend until he feels more confident.

For advice on siblings at the same school, see page 281.

EDUCATING AT HOME

Choice in Education, www.choiceineducation. org.uk; Chrystia Hertogs, Education Otherwise, www.education- otherwise.org

For children of any age, schools are not the only option. Section 7 of the Education Act of 1996 expects all parents of a school-age child to ensure that she receives full-time education appropriate for her age, ability and any special needs. This education must be 'either by regular attendance at school or otherwise'. Educating at home is the 'otherwise' part and all parents have the right to take control of their children's education and school them from home.

Note, though, that the law is slightly different in Scotland and Ireland.

Educating at home is a real alternative to consider if you're not happy with what's on offer in mainstream education.

Before you decide to go ahead, it is a good idea to contact Education Otherwise (www.education-otherwise.org), a support organisation for families whose children are educated outside the school system.

Children who are home educated don't have to be isolated. There are often local groups who have banded together for support and who hold regular meetings.

Local groups organise events, visits and workshops for home schoolers and their parents. These range from pottery, music and sport through to museum, theatre and gallery visits and adventure camps. You'll be surprised just how much is on offer once you start looking. These activities have the advantage of being educational as well as social. You can find out about groups in your area through Education Otherwise and *Choice in Education* magazine (www.choiceineducation.org.uk).

To be a successful home educator, you need time, commitment and the courage to be independent. It helps to be practical, but you don't need particular qualifications or skills.

You don't need to be rich to educate at home. You don't need any special equipment and you don't have to kit out your home like a classroom.

When looking at the possibility of home education, it's important to weigh up the pros and cons.

Advantages of home education:

- Children who are home educated are usually very caring and well connected into society.

- You can mix and match courses and syllabuses to suit you and your children.

- The shared experience of educating from home strengthens the parent/child bond and gives an extra dimension to your relationship.

- Rewards for children who learn at home are immense.

- Even if they are only educated at home for the first two or three years, children have a security and inner confidence that give them a real boost if they eventually start school or go on to university or further education.

- Home-schooled children often do exceptionally well in exams.

- Home-educated children don't have the usual peer-group pressure to mix only with children of the same sex and age as themselves. They are free to mix with older and younger children as well as adults.

- Children have a real say in their own education and are therefore very committed to their chosen studies.

- They have the space to mature at their own rate and the confidence to talk to anyone.

Disadvantages of home education:

- It takes extra time and effort on parents' behalf to ensure that children meet their peers and make friends.

- It is a huge commitment and you must be prepared to put in a lot of time.

- The responsibility to make education work rests firmly with you.

- You will have to be constantly imaginative and resourceful. There are few breaks.

- It can be hard to find other people near you who have children the same age.

- You and your children are constantly together and this can lead to tensions especially as children get older.

Before you finally make a decision, find out as much as you can and talk to parents who have done it. They will be only too happy to share their experiences with you.

There are several different organisations that offer basic information on what you need and how to get started in home education. Some of these groups are more political than others or have a very definite credo. If you're looking for contacts and a social network in your area, as well as practical support and material, a good starting point is Education Otherwise (see page 157). You will find many organisations listed in *Choice in Education* magazine.

As a parent educating your children from home, you will find that you learn with your child and tackle new subjects together.

You don't have to operate like a school. You can work on what you want, when you want. If you want to follow a particular course or syllabus, there is plenty of source material on offer.

It's a good idea for home-schooled children to carry a legally drawn-up Truancy Card (available from *Choice in Education* magazine) when they are out on their own during school hours. These are not ID cards but state that the holder is being home-educated.

It's useful to sit down at the beginning of each week with your children and plan what you are going to cover that week. That way your children feel they have a say in what they learn.

Build on your strengths, and you'll be surprised how resourceful you become. But it's important to know when you have reached your limit. At that point get help: don't be afraid to ask for help when you need it.

Remember that if you find it's no longer working, you have the option to rejoin mainstream schooling at any stage.

There is no reason why home schoolers can't take exams or join in classes at adult education centres, nights schools or further education colleges. Children taught at home often do particularly well in exams because they have taken them when they are ready and followed the syllabus that suits them best.

Accept that you can't do what a school does and that you are doing things differently. Draw on the resources around you.

Provide what you can cover and find ways of adding the other subjects.

Pool skills and resources with other parents in your area – one of you may be particularly creative or arty, while another might be a linguist, a computer whizz or mathematician. Recognise each other's strengths and use them. You can also club together with other parents to employ a teacher for a particular subject.

Talk to other parents or carers who have degrees or a specialist subject and don't work. They can be a big help with project work in subjects like geography and history. All experience is valuable.

Language tapes and audio courses are a big help when you're trying to teach foreign languages.

Two hours' intense studying a day at home is probably worth a day at school.

Make an effort to join clubs and meet up with other home schoolers. It's vital that your child sees other people. Otherwise your relationship and the whole learning experience becomes too intense.

Keep in contact with old friends who are at school. It's important not to isolate your child.

Don't underestimate the value of reading a book or simple activities like gardening and looking at plants and insects.

Allow yourselves to be side-tracked when you're looking at a subject. One of the joys of home education is that you can study in as much detail as you want.

Follow where your interests lead you and make links to take you forward. Let kids' enthusiasms carry you on.

If you are educating at home as a temporary measure while waiting for a place at a particular school, go into the school and make yourself known. Ask for advice on study and curriculum notes. Make sure that you are more than a name on a list and that you are taken seriously.

HAVING FUN

Alison Wallis;
Amanda Stevens;
Anna Knight; Caroline
Dagul, music teacher;
Carolyn Webb,
teacher; Clare Porter;
Liz Chowienczyk;
Margaret Cave

Avoid the temptation to pack children's lives too full. Give them space just to be themselves.

After a hard week's learning at school, children need time to chill out and just watch TV or play computer games.

Children at this age like to have time to spend with friends. Invite classmates over after school. If you have an only child, it's a good idea to arrange an activity with a friend at weekends sometimes.

It can be difficult when parents are great friends but children aren't so keen. You need to put in a great deal of effort to make this work. It helps to take the children out to do something, like swimming. At least the children will enjoy the activity.

Children also enjoy playing by themselves and with siblings. By this stage, children are well equipped to entertain themselves and like having the time to do so. So don't pack their social lives too full.

At the same time children of this age are interested in lots of different things, which makes taking them out fun for both parents and children.

They still like many of the activities they enjoyed when younger, but now they can do them for themselves with little or no help from you.

At Home

Keep a supply of paper and paints. Kids still love painting and being creative.

Now the kids are older it's worth investing in more interesting art materials like pastels, modelling clay and water-colours.

Look out for paints suitable for china and glass. With a supply of cheap white china plates, mugs and egg cups, children can create their own designs and presents for friends and family.

There are all sorts of interesting art and craft sets with clear instructions for children to follow. Good ones to try are candle making, mosaics, metal embossing and secret diary kits.

Boys and girls find cooking fun. They can follow simple recipes and bake things themselves with your supervision.

It's a good idea to give children their own cookery books. Choose ones that

Children are now old enough to mix their own salt dough and model it into more adventurous shapes. Salt dough is great for Christmas tree decorations. Make a small hole before baking so that a ribbon can be threaded through later.

Salt dough recipe:

11oz/300g plain flour
11oz/300g salt
1 tablespoon cooking oil
7fl.oz/200ml water

Mix the flour, salt, oil and water together to form a soft dough. Sprinkle a little flour on a work surface and knead the dough until it is smooth and stretchy. Mould and shape the dough to your own design. Carefully place on a baking tray and cook for 15–20 minutes in a warm oven, gas mark 4/180°C/350°F. When cool, paint and varnish your decorations.

are not too long, well illustrated and with clear instructions – the Sainsbury's range are ideal.

Children gain a real sense of achievement from cooking for friends or a party.

For a fun supper table when children have friends over, use a paper tablecloth or make your own from lining paper. Set out a few crayons next to each place and let children decorate the table as they eat. They can draw each other, cartoons, their favourite TV character – whatever they fancy.

Don't forget gardening. Children especially enjoy growing things to eat. Potatoes, marrows, pumpkins, strawberries, tomatoes, peppers and herbs are all good choices. If they've grown something themselves they're also more likely to eat it.

Sunflowers are satisfyingly showy. Kids can collect the seeds at the end, too.

Give children their own flowerbed or corner of the garden if you can. Otherwise offer a window box or pots that children can be completely responsible for.

Try growing plants indoors on a windowsill. Hyacinth and other bulbs grow well in water and if they are placed in a clear glass jar, children can watch the roots.

Cress and herbs will yield an edible crop and grow quickly. Sprouting your own beans and pulses is easy and interesting.

Children of all ages love making dens and camps. Offer a corner of the garden where they can set up a tent or wigwam with old blankets and sheets. Keep a stock of old plates, cups and cutlery for camp picnics.

Convert an old shed into a permanent den. Let your children decorate it to their own design, and furnish it with an old rug and cushions. Look out for second-hand bargains like bead curtains, throws and chimes.

For an indoor picnic on a rainy day, cover a table with a large sheet, spread out a blanket underneath, gather lots of goodies and crawl inside.

Blackboards are still good play value – for drawing, making temporary signs, as a memo board, even to play schools.

Keep a supply of chunky chalks for games like hopscotch outside.

Don't pack away the dressing-up box. Keep adding to it. Children will raid it when they want put on their own plays or shows with friends.

Board games are always popular. Move on to the grown-up versions when children seem ready.

Keep a pack of cards handy. They're fun for all ages and really useful when travelling or staying with relatives.

At this age, children can attempt quite complex jigsaw puzzles. 3-D ones are an interesting challenge.

Read with your children. Make choosing and buying books a treat.

If your child is a reluctant reader, find him a book on something he's interested in or look out for interesting fact books.

Don't dismiss comics and comic books. For generations, reading *The Beano* has been the first step towards literacy.

Encourage reading during the school holidays by planning a trip to the bookshop in the first week. Let each child choose a few books, then agree to pay 50p for every book they read completely. The deal is that they have to explain the plot to you in some detail to prove they've really read it. (Bribery – but it works!)

Going Out

Clubs like Brownies, Guides, Cubs, Scouts and Beavers are very popular. There is a wide network of groups to join throughout the country and they provide an excellent opportunity to try lots of different sports and skills.

More than one in three eight-year-old girls in the UK is a Brownie. Guiding is the largest voluntary organisation for girls in the country and is part of an international organisation with over 10 million members worldwide.

Look out for holiday classes in your area – you can usually find ones for football, tennis, drama, art and dance.

When visiting museums or galleries, always ask at the information desk whether there are any children's packs. There are often children's quizzes or searches to make the visit more interesting.

Check for special events aimed at children. Museums, art galleries and some theatres run one-off demonstrations and workshops, or short courses aimed at children during school holidays.

Local newspapers and church newsletters are good sources of information on holiday clubs for children.

Sunday schools and youth groups for ten- and eleven-year-olds are useful meeting points for friends.

Music

Only start music lessons when your child is really keen. If she's not, it will be a constant battle to get her to practise and a waste of money and time.

There are some instruments including many brass and woodwind instruments that you can't start learning too young. Take advice from music teachers.

If possible, try to find music taster classes where children can try out several different instruments before picking a specific one to learn.

Big brass instruments or cool ones like the sax are very popular with boys and girls, and they are great to play as part of a group. Encourage an instrument your child can play with others in a band or orchestra.

Avoid saying 'do your practice' and then leaving your child alone to get on with it.

Be involved – music is a universal interest and she may be playing tunes you remember as a child. If you can, play with her.

Provide the right equipment for your child to use when practising – a music stand, good light – and try to keep it in an out-of-the-way place so that it can stay up permanently.

Fix a practice schedule, so that your child knows when he is expected to do it. Then it's non-negotiable.

Ten minutes' practice a night is better than forty minutes of agony the night before a lesson.

Exercise & Sport

Newspapers are constantly full of reports on the unfit state of the nation's children. More than a million children are classed as obese and over a third of primary school children get less than an hour's formal exercise per week. Studies show that children who exercise regularly achieve higher test results.

The years immediately before puberty are an important time to develop and build up bone strength through weight-bearing exercise. Encourage children and organise lessons or games with friends.

Walking to school is a good start. It helps children to feel fitter and more alert, and gives parents and children the opportunity to talk on the school journey. Walking is a lot less stressful than a car journey through heavy traffic.

If you live too far away to walk the whole distance, think about parking the car and walking part of the way.

Many areas are setting up walking buses with a group of children walking together, supervised by an adult. Schools often have details. Or you could try your local education authority.

Get on your bike or scooter. If you need to get somewhere quickly, it's often easier for you all to ride or scooter together.

Before booking a course of sport lessons for your child, see if he can have a taster class before signing up for a term.

It's a cliché but team sports provide good lessons for life.

Encourage your child – if she's playing in a school match, go along and support her.

You don't need masses of specialist equipment to play sport. Buy a football, bat and tennis ball, or a frisbee.

If your garden is small, go along to a nearby park. Take along friends but don't forget to sometimes play games with them yourself. Tree cricket with a bat and ball works as well with one or two children as it does with a group.

Make sure that your child can swim. Take him along to the local pool regularly or book a course of lessons during a school holiday if you think he needs extra practice. See also page 114.

At school, children often miss out on being taught basic skills like how to catch and throw a ball. As a result, they consider themselves no good at ball games and get put off sport.

Your child may not be a budding Tim Henman, but tennis lessons can be a good way to encourage hand–eye coordination and to boost your child's confidence. Many boroughs have public courts where you can set up lessons with a coach and small group of children.

For more on sport, see page 196.

Travelling

Travelling should be easier and fun at this age. Children can be more responsible for themselves and are likely to be interested in new destinations. You might even get them to try some foreign food.

Ask children to be responsible for packing their own rucksacks with things for the journey.

Make sure that your children have playing cards, a pencil case and spiral-bound notebook for games like Hangman, Join the Dots and Noughts and Crosses, a GameBoy, personal stereo, story tapes or CDs, and books.

You never need quite as many clothes as you think you will.

See also the travel advice on pages 60, 86, 114 and 140.

Parties

You can repeat many of the same ideas you had for younger children's parties – just make them a little more complex and sophisticated. (Parties for younger children are covered on page 110.)

You can even play Pass the Parcel – especially if you make it jokey and have something silly like a hot potato (in reality a little warm) going round the other way. Include chocolate coins or mini-prizes, but avoid forfeits as these can pressurise children and embarrass them.

Organise a treasure hunt with clues to solve and odd objects to find. Your own children will love thinking up tricky quizzes and puzzles.

Cut up two or three pictures into jigsaw pieces and hide them. Challenge guests to find all the pieces and complete the pictures within a time limit.

Themed parties can be fun to plan. Most kids love helping to decorate a room, making party food with a twist and getting dressed up. If it's for something like Halloween, you may also have an excuse to play traditional games like bobbing apples.

Throw a pizza party. Buy a stack of bases, set out different toppings and let the guests create their own supper.

Have a separate table with plain cakes and cookies to decorate for dessert.

It's sensible to plan large parties quite carefully. Decide when you're going to have food, how long guests will want to dance for and if you want any games.

For large numbers, team games work well. Devise fun challenges like wrapping the whole team in loo roll without tearing the tissue, picking the raisins out of flour without using hands, contorting to form the letters of various capital cities, passing a balloon between the knees without popping it and picking out baked beans with a tooth pick. Make sure that you have lots of little prizes.

Sleepover Parties

The first sleepover can be a big deal for some children. Let your child try out sleeping over with a good friend or relative before he's invited to a sleepover party. It's embarrassing to be the only one who can't hack it.

Make it very clear to a child sleeping over that he can go home any time he wants to. You'll just have to hope that he doesn't take you up on it in the early hours of the morning.

It can help children sleeping over for the first time to call their parents at bedtime. Anxieties can often be allayed by a quick chat with Mum or Dad.

When your guests arrive for a sleepover party, set them some ground rules. It's much better than having to get heavy later.

Control the children's sugar intake. If they're planning a midnight feast, stock up on plain crisps, peanuts, popcorn and juice, rather than sweets and Coke which will keep them awake and make them even more excitable.

Agree on some kind of timetable, with a fixed mealtime, then perhaps a video, another snack and then it's time for bed.

Alternatively, once the children are in their pyjamas, let them watch a video from the comfort of their sleeping bags. That usually quietens them down.

TV & Videos

Don't dismiss television. It can be a useful learning tool – there's probably not a school in the country that doesn't use TV and videos in lessons. TV's also a good way of relaxing after working or exercising hard.

Try to strike a balance so that TV is not the only extra-curricular interest your child has.

When deciding what programmes your child can watch, remember that children need cultural references to share with other children and, like it or not, many of these come from TV and film.

Make a bargain with your child. He can watch a certain programme as long as he has completed any homework.

Monitor films and programmes for scariness or horror. If your child is finding something scary or gory, emphasise that it is only a story.

It helps to discuss exactly how the film maker has achieved that particularly gruesome effect.

Watch out for sexual innuendo or gritty issues in soaps, which you might want to avoid until children are older.

Computers & PlayStations

It's not all bad – some research suggests that computer games and games consoles can improve decision making, spatial awareness and dexterity.

PlayStations can be productive – they can provide a focus for your son and his friends on a wet afternoon.

Check out games before buying. They are age-rated and many contain explicit language and scenes. They can be extremely violent and reinforce gender stereotypes.

On the other hand, they can pose tricky problems that require skill and logic to solve.

The key, as with TV, is to strike a balance. Most children, particularly boys, have a games console of one sort or another and usually a GameBoy, too. Make sure that your child doesn't spend all his spare time playing.

Boys can have a tendency to become obsessive about playing. They will need encouragement to take up other interests.

GameBoys are excellent on long journeys. A new game keeps players enthralled for hours.

For more on computers and using the internet, see page 198.

Mobile Phones

See page 199.

Pocket Money

See page 194.

PETS

Jo Caseby;
John Knight;
Sandra Richards;
Tiina Godding

Agree from the outset who does what when it comes to taking care of pets.

Accept that as a parent you will also be committed to looking after any pets and that ultimate responsibility will always fall on you.

Watch children with other people's pets first before you make a final decision about whether to have one in your family.

Check for possible allergies to pet fur before choosing a pet, by exposing your children to other people's pets.

Make sure that your children know that pets are live creatures and not cuddly toys, and that all animals need lots of love and attention, regular care and owners who will remain interested.

Think carefully about why you want a pet, what sort of animal would fit your home and lifestyle, and how long you can expect it to live.

Caring for animals can be a fun part of growing up and teaches children to take responsibility.

Especially for only children, having a pet can be a real outlet for their emotions and someone to share their thoughts with.

Dogs and cats are usually family pets, while smaller animals like guinea pigs or rabbits can be a child's own pet.

Preferably choose young animals and in the early days, handle them a lot but in small doses to get them used to you all.

Contact the RSPCA or check out its website at www.rspca.org.uk for clear, practical, unbiased information.

CHILDREN'S ROOMS

Alison Wallis; Amanda Stevens; Claire Shread, Inardec Art Décor; Gita Moore; Jennifer Hooper, JHD; Jennifer Youles; Karen Mae Birch, interior designer; Liz Chowienczyk

When decorating a child's room, remember that what seems appropriate at seven may seem too babyish at ten. It's better to paint a room than wallpaper it, and to use soft furnishings which can easily be updated to pick up a special theme.

Stick glow-in-the-dark stars and planets to the ceiling. They look effective and even children who are afraid of the dark will enjoy watching the stars go out one by one.

Memo- or noticeboards allow children to pin up pictures, notes, postcards or sketches without damaging walls. They can also be instantly changed.

Ten- and eleven-year-olds especially like having photos of their friends on display.

Stencil borders to liven plain walls. Children could design their own and help with the painting.

Paint wide vertical stripes. Paint walls with a base colour; then, when completely dry, use a plumb line with string and a weight to mark straight lines and screen with masking tape. Paint within the tape. Wait until the paint is just dry, and then carefully remove the tape. Contrasting colours or darker shades of the same colour look effective.

Use an umbrella stand for storing tennis rackets and cricket bats.

A weekend bed, with a pull-out mattress underneath, is ideal for sleepovers and weekend guests.

Self-inflating mattresses are brilliant when space is tight.

Instead of a desk for a growing child, rest hardboard on two small matching chests of drawers.

Jazz up an old table as a desk by painting it with coloured stripes. Mark out the stripes with masking tape, prime and undercoat it and use eggshell for the top colours. Cover the piece with two coats of clear acrylic varnish.

You can make your own curtain poles using broom handles or thick dowelling. Cut out interesting-shaped finials and screw them to the ends of the pole. Spray paint in the colour of choice.

Make your own curtains from calico or plain cotton. Stencil outlines with fabric paint to create your own unique design.

If space is tight, fix a triangle of MDF across the corner of a room as a desk with smaller triangles above for shelving.

Storage is always useful. Use covered cardboard boxes (see page 106) or use wicker baskets. Store trinkets and treasures in the small ones and games or even clothes in the larger boxes.

Children will enjoy using CD and tape machines in their rooms with a choice of their own story tapes and music.

Think carefully before letting children have their own TV sets. See page 200.

If children have their own computers, make sure that you have guard software so that there is no danger of them accessing inappropriate websites – see page 198.

SLEEP & BEDTIME

Alison Wallis; Amanda Stevens; Anna Knight; Mike and Judy Cooper; Margaret Cave

Children of this age never need to go to bed – or so they think! They can often be overtired without knowing it and tiredness is a common reason for grumpiness.

Like adults, not all children need the same amount of sleep and sometimes they need more than at others. There's no point in trying to force a child who is obviously not tired to go to sleep. Instead, set a bedtime that suits you all, but allow your child to read for a while or listen to a story tape before turning out the light .

Children worry about being awake when they think they should be sleeping, especially if they think everyone else is asleep. Reassure them that it doesn't matter and try to find ways to help them relax. Stay for a while, talking quietly, reading or simply just being there.

If your child can't sleep, suggest he tries relaxation strategies that work for you – like imagining he is somewhere very peaceful, watching leaves move, swinging in a shady hammock, or tensing and relaxing his muscles in turn, working up from the toes.

Moving a child who can't sleep into your bed can sometimes help, even though you're not there. Make it clear that you will move her back to her own bed later.

Make sure that you slow things down for a while prior to bedtime. Avoid going straight from lively play or homework to bed.

Even quite grown-up children still enjoy having a book read to them.

Older children might like quiet time alone, reading a book for themselves before settling down to sleep.

At this stage, story tapes can be quite grown up – it's sometimes easier for children to comprehend a complex story by listening rather than reading it for themselves.

Children in this age group often have very real fears and it's not only small children who are afraid of the dark. Make sure that you leave a light on, or keep the door open and the landing light switched on.

Nightmares, Night Terrors & Fears

Night terrors can occur at any age and when they reach junior school children have a great deal to cope with, which can sometimes act as a trigger for bad dreams and terrors.

Don't make too much of the nightmares or question your child about any fears at night. Instead settle him down again as swiftly and calmly as possible.

Try to find out whether anything is bothering him during the day. Begin by talking generally rather than asking straight out.

For more about how to deal with nightmares, night terrors and fears, see page 101.

FOOD

Amanda Stevens; Clare Porter; Deborah Woodbridge; Diana Starte; Dr Lisa Watts; Liz Chowienczyk; Margaret Cave

Avoid offering food as a reward, especially sweets. This just encourages the idea that they are a treat.

At this age children are growing a lot and often need a snack when they come home from school. Try to encourage them to eat a sandwich, cheese and fruit, or even a bowl of cereal – not just a quick-fix bag of crisps or chocolate bar.

Remember that children often behave better and enjoy mealtimes more when they sit down to a family meal at a properly set table.

Try to make family mealtimes fun. Remember that food is just food. Use mealtimes as a chance to chat about what you have all been doing.

Encourage reluctant eaters by letting them help you prepare food themselves. Fussy eaters are much more likely to eat something they have had a hand in making.

It's a good stage for eating out with your children. They haven't yet reached the point where they think it's uncool to be out with parents but they are old enough to cope with unusual food and to enjoy eating in restaurants.

For healthy ice lollies, top and tail a pineapple and cut downwards into six to eight chunky wedges, then freeze.

Most children like experimenting and will happily concoct their own fruit mixtures for smoothies and ice lollies with fruit juice and fresh fruit.

By the age of ten or eleven most children are responsible enough to follow a recipe and bake simple things by themselves. Boys and girls really enjoy cooking especially if friends are coming over or if it's for a party.

When you're cooking, take the time to explain what you're doing as well as basic principles of kitchen hygiene and safety.

Give your child some responsibility. Let him plan and cook supper one evening or a weekend lunch. He'll enjoy doing it and it will give him some idea of what it's like to cook for others (and how disappointing it is when your efforts are left uneaten).

Encourage children to help out in the kitchen and with chores like setting the table and helping to clear away after a meal.

It's a good idea to make sure that children know how to stack a dishwasher and where things go when emptying it.

Healthy Eating

Children are now old enough to understand about healthy eating, vitamins and a balanced diet. Reasoning should work now in a way it didn't when they were younger.

The Vegetarian Society estimates that one in ten children now avoid red meat. Children who do so can still maintain a healthy balanced diet but it takes planning to make sure. For more on a vegetarian diet, see page 220.

Surveys show that children as young as five are conscious of weight and body image. Even children just starting school have insecurities about the way they look. Try to encourage children to feel confident and positive about themselves.

Children in primary schools are aware of fat-free products. Make sure they know fat-free isn't always best or healthy.

Children need a certain amount of fat and sugar to grow. Low-fat and low-sugar foods are often not suitable for young growing bodies and will not give them the vitamins and minerals they need to be healthy.

Specialist clinics are treating younger patients than ever before for eating disorders and anorexia. Be aware of what your child is eating. For more on eating disorders, see page 224.

Children learn by copying you and encouraging healthy eating habits through your own example works much better than making healthy food an obsession.

Try not to label foods as good or bad. This will just heighten a child's awareness of it.

Studies suggest that children banned from eating sweets and junk food at home will eat them in private, setting up food obsessions and unhealthy attitudes.

Don't complain about your own weight in front of your children and avoid focusing on body shape and appearance. Children copy your example and are likely to follow your eating habits.

As well as making mealtimes fun, try to make food interesting and enjoyable.

If you're worried about your child's weight, talk to a qualified dietician. Don't try to put them on a calorie-restricted diet yourself. See also page 220.

For advice about diet, contact your GP's surgery. Many have qualified dieticians who visit for regular clinics.

CHILDCARE & COPING

Alison Wallis;
Clare Porter;
Deborah Woodbridge;
Eve Marshall;
Liz Chowienczyk;
Margaret Cave;
Tracy Martin

Stop feeling guilty about working or not working. All that matters is that the choice you've made works for you and your family, no matter what anyone else says or does.

You can't do everything. Sometimes some things have to go by the board. Choose what's most important to you, or what must be done and what you have to let go.

Talk to your partner about what needs to be done and share the responsibility.

Share chores with other members of the family.

If you find working full-time with a growing family simply too much, talk to your employer about the possibility of flexi-hours or working part-time. You never know unless you ask.

Childcare

Childcare at this stage creates different problems. With children at school, if you are working you usually only need someone before and after school, and some help during holidays.

Try advertising at your children's school. There may well be another mother near by who would be happy to help out.

Depending upon your hours of work, it may be possible to come to an arrangement or swap with friends.

Consider whether family or grandparents could help out. For more on childcare, see page 84.

Au Pairs

If you are working irregular hours and you have space at home, an au pair could be the answer. Au pairs help in the house, with meals and with children.

The best way to find an au pair is through personal recommendation. You can also try registered agencies. These vary in efficiency, so again ask around and find out which ones friends have used.

Before appointing an au pair, always check references very thoroughly.

Remember, when hiring an au pair, that her reason for being here is usually to learn English and travel.

If a major part of an au pair's duties is to look after children, check that she actually likes children. If possible, introduce her to your children and watch how they get along.

Give clear instructions and set out exactly what you expect from the outset, preferably in writing. This makes everything easier if there are problems later.

Make any rules about working absolutely clear – stipulate the hours and times, whether or not you allow smoking in the house and what your views are about friends visiting and staying.

You can find out the going rate of pay and the maximum number of hours of work from an agency.

You will need to provide a bedroom and somewhere to store her luggage.

You have a responsibility towards an au pair. You end up looking after them to an extent and they need support, as they are often strangers to the country.

Send a photo and details of your family to your au pair's family so that they know where their daughter is going and as reassurance.

Meet a new au pair from the airport. It's unfair not to, especially if she is new to the country.

Having a foreign au pair living in the home can be a really positive experience for children as well as introducing them to another language.

Au pairs are often young and can be great fun as childminders for children.

If you know from the beginning that things will not work out with a particular au pair, don't hesitate. Finish the arrangement as quickly and pleasantly as possible.

On a practical note, explain exactly how things like the washing machine work and what the labels on clothes and washing powders mean. Otherwise, you may come home to an array of pink clothes or your favourite jumper doll-sized after a spell in the tumble dryer.

Babysitters

Once your children are older, you can begin to use teenagers as babysitters, provided they are responsible. For entrusting your children to the care of an older child, see page 243.

Again, school and friends are good sources of recommendations for teenagers, or other people's nannies or au pairs who might babysit for you.

Older children stay up later, so increasingly the babysitter needs to be someone they like. Ten- and eleven-year-olds tend to like teenagers, especially as they're often happy to play computer or board games with them.

For more on babysitting, see page 84.

7 ELEVEN TO FOURTEEN YEARS

'Teenagers are people who express a burning desire to be different by dressing exactly alike.'

Anon.

What they can do at this age

At thirteen:

- Work part-time under certain restrictions (see page 195)
- Be convicted of rape or other offences involving sexual intercourse (from the age of ten).

At fourteen:

- Go into a pub, though not buy alcoholic drinks
- Drive an electrically powered pedal cycle
- Be convicted of a criminal offence (though the trial and sentencing will be specific to children)
- Ride a horse without protective headgear on a public highway
- Learn to fly a plane with an instructor
- Learn to fly a helicopter with an instructor
- Learn to fly a glider (depending on particular gliding centre's rules)
- Learn to scuba dive.

Legal rights

Once a young person reaches the age of ten (age of criminal responsibility), he may be detained by police.

The Police Code of Practice (PACE) determines a young person's rights if he is detained at a police station. It includes the:

- right to have somebody informed of arrest
- right to consult with a solicitor
- right to consult the code of practice.

The police officer will have to identify the person responsible for his welfare – normally you the parent – who must be informed of the arrest. The parent may act as the appropriate adult, whose role it is to ensure that the interview and the procedures are implemented correctly. You have the right to be present the whole time your child is being questioned.

Eleven sees the big move to secondary school and a leap in development. It all happens almost overnight. Your children are no longer in the relatively nurturing environment of primary school, but are surrounded by older children and all the implications and issues that come with that. They will need to be more responsible and start to motivate themselves – GCSEs are only around the corner.

This age group is still frighteningly naïve, however. Yet here they are just on the cusp of teenage, having to face the confusing emotional and physical issues of puberty. It's a steep learning curve. You'll need to help them through this tricky phase, whilst realising that they are young and impressionable.

BEHAVIOUR

Steve Chalke, Parent Talk; Parentlineplus; Sarah Kilby; Glynis Fletcher; Lynn Shone; Jane Meekin; David Raines; Samantha Davies; Jean Richmond; Linda Engles; Francis Wade

Hurrah! This is the age when children begin to learn cause and effect. Try not to say, 'Unless you put your clothes in the washing basket, you can't play on the computer.' Instead, make your child see the consequences. 'Unless you put your clothes in the washing basket, they won't be washed and you'll have no jeans/uniform/state-of-the-art sweatshirt to wear.'

Work out a series of consequences and rewards in advance for good behaviour; then you won't be tempted to think up impossible-to-achieve targets for your child.

Let your child work out for himself the advantages and disadvantages of certain behaviour. Reinforce situations – for example: 'If you finish your homework by 6.00 p.m., we'll have time for a game of football.' At this stage children are entering the age of reason and the penny will eventually drop.

Sulking? It may well be your child's way of licking her wounds alone and coming to terms with the fact that you were right all along. Let her sort it out, resisting the urge to say, 'I told you so.'

Suspect that your child has been shoplifting? Don't panic. Ask him outright where he got the suspected stolen item from without hurling accusations. He may have a legitimate explanation. If he owns up, go with him to the shop, and hand the item over to the shop owner/manager. It is highly unlikely that the shop will kick up a fuss, and more than likely that the embarrassment and shame of doing this will stop your child from ever stealing again.

As your children get older, get them to help at home, allocating a job to each child with a rota.

Discipline doesn't mean punishment, and it's OK to set rules. Rules make children feel secure. They know where they stand and where the boundaries lie. The 'anything for an easy life' approach can lead to a very hard life. Children need to know just how far you will be pushed.

Remember that it's parents who make the rules, not children, who would not necessarily make sensible ones – if you ask what time they should go to bed, they will say midnight. Set yourself rules too: 'I will only answer a request if it comes with a please in it.'

Children need to have boundaries, even if they are there to fight against. If you decide to say no, or 'only if', you must stick to what you have said and not be talked out of it. Children can develop within such boundaries, and learn to handle freedom wisely.

Children respond to deals, but strike ones that have a positive pay-off. 'Can my friend stay the night?' 'Well, your room is so messy there will be nowhere for her to sleep. Tidy it and she can stay.' 'You can go out to the cinema/have a friend over/play on the Play-Station, if you tidy your room/finish your homework/take out the dustbin.' They will learn that cooperation is more likely to get results. Works like magic!

Create a house your teenager will want to live in. Her room may look like a minefield because she doesn't like the way it is decorated, or it may not have changed since she was much younger. Work together to find a colour scheme, pictures, curtains and blinds, cushions and chairs for entertaining friends. Changes need not be expensive, and maybe they will be proud enough of it to keep it looking good.

Children are like puppies: inexperienced, disorganised, messy, totally unaware of other people's feelings and needing plenty of exercise. Work on the same principle as you would with handling a dog. Tell them off immediately for making a mess/being thoughtless etc. and then forget it. Don't bear a grudge, and be consistent.

Repeat several times a day: I must be positive, firm and consistent.

Like smaller children, kids of this age need unwinding time. Children, even at this age, have to behave so well for the seven or so hours at school that they need to come home and kick the cat (proverbially), knowing that the cat will forgive them. Let your kids let off steam when they come in from a difficult day. Making them a cup of tea when they come in from school, and not urging them to do homework straight away – even allowing time in front of the TV – will help them relax.

It's a young child's trick but it applies just as well to older ones: any attention is better than no attention, even if it is negative. Bad behaviour may be a cry for attention. If possible, arrange to spend time with one child exclusively – even if it is watching TV with him or having him help you at the supermarket. He will relish the opportunity to have your undivided attention.

The same flashpoint times apply to children of this age: early mornings, mealtimes, homework, bedtimes, car journeys, holidays. Prepare for them. Do jobs you need to do outside these times so that you are as free as possible to cope with the family.

See also Behaviour (or Living With Kevin), page 210, and Teenagers In A Group, page 214.

Mealtimes

Encourage this age group to take a leadership role by giving them responsible tasks at mealtimes, such as carving or opening the wine. They will enjoy being treated like an adult.

Let older children eat with you if you are feeding younger ones earlier. Again they will enjoy being treated as adults. Use it as a reward.

Set rules for mealtimes. Ban books or gadgets from the table, but if your teenager has finished pudding and a younger or other child is being painfully slow, let her leave the table, taking her plate to the dishwasher. Bored children who have finished eating will wind up everyone else.

Independence

Letting go is the biggest concern for most parents of teenagers. The only way children will learn is by making mistakes. They will have to get wet and cold before they realise for themselves that they need a hat and coat when it is wet and cold. Try to grit your teeth and not always do their thinking for them. Watch from a safe distance, without being blameful or making a fool of them. It is the only way they will learn. Commiserate when it all goes pear-shaped and ask, 'What can you learn from that?'

Say no to big requests – 'Can I go to the cinema with my friend?' – the first time. Next time let them with conditions. Loosen the ties slowly. This makes them think about the situation and work out for themselves in advance what things can go wrong.

Some parents find that saying no makes a teenager more determined than ever. The reason for having boundaries is to give teenagers something to push against, and they will. It's back to making compromises again, but, strange as it may seem, pushy teenagers will need to know where the boundaries lie.

Your children may have been round town with you a million times, but they may not know their way once they are on their own. Before letting them go out with friends, for example, have them direct you home in the car a few times, until you are sure they have their bearings.

Put together a wallet for them and include a £20 note. This is irreplaceable (if they spend it on irrelevancies) and should be used only in an emergency, or at worst as 'mugging' money – something to hand over if ever, heaven forbid, they were attacked.

In the wallet also include the business card of a taxi firm you know to be reputable.

Go out as a family to films, restaurants and cafés. This will help take the perceived mystery out of such places, and help them to cope with the experience once they do it for themselves. Choose things they want to do.

In the early stages of letting children do things without adults, let them go with a small group (one or two others). They are more likely to stick together and the group is less likely to fragment.

Choose a safe place for them to visit with friends – perhaps a covered shopping mall close by or one train or bus stop away – and visit it with them a couple of times first. Make sure that they know where to buy a ticket and where to get off. Give them a time limit – but be reasonable. The length of time it takes a thirteen-year-old to choose a nail varnish is much longer than you think.

Three vital questions to ask: Where are you going? Do you have enough money? Is your mobile phone battery charged up?

Self-consciousness

Boys and girls get self-conscious at this age, as their bodies start to develop. Even though as parents it's hard to forget that you once changed their nappies and had to help them dress, you need to give them privacy. Let them change in private, even if you think they are just being coy. Knocking before you go into their room is thoughtful too.

Children who feel they stand out from the crowd? All teenagers want to be like everyone else. The last thing they want is to be 'odd'. Try not to say 'You are beautiful to me' and to brush aside their concerns – or worse, deny that they are different from their peers. Listen and look at the advantages in the future. Tall children know they are tall. If you too were tall, for example, share your experiences and how you felt and dealt with them. Once they go to secondary school, and are with tall children higher up the school, they may well feel less self-conscious.

To the teenage mind average is everything. They don't want to have the smallest/biggest boobs, higher/lower voice. Try to persuade your child that body development is dictated by their genes, and that they need to see them in a positive light, and that it is their characteristics which make them special and unique.

Be aware that your children will look at your personality and physique to give them some indication of what they will be like when they grow up. Try not to transfer to them any dissatisfaction your have with your body, such as having big feet or big boobs, or being tall or being very short. They might inherit your hang-ups.

Make your child feel that you are proud of how beautiful she is becoming. Watching your child growing up can make you competitive – especially if you are the mother of daughters. Suddenly they are the dishy one and you are approaching middle age. Be confident enough in yourself not to compete with them and therefore threaten them in the glamour stakes.

Mother of boys? There's a temptation to become 'one of the lads'. Just because it helps to know who scored the winning goal in the United/Arsenal match there is no excuse to give up on your appearance. You are a feminine role model and an important one at that.

Rows

It's hard to do, but try to dispel an argument before it gets out of hand and everyone starts screaming at each other. Say that you are too angry to talk at the moment, and go to another room on your own. Let the situation simmer down and, once you have gathered your thoughts and made sure that your anger is justified, sit down together calmly to sort out the issue.

Come home from work after a hard day and flare up at the smallest problem? Have a ritual as soon as you get in: put the kettle on, change into casual clothes, give yourself time to adjust to the different pace and demands of the household. Then you can face the music.

When you are wrong, admit that you are and do it quickly. This is a good lesson in behaviour that kids will learn from you.

Children need to hear apologies too. If you have flown off the handle because your child was home later than she said she would be, explain why and that you were frightened. This is a more rational response than laying down the law and being unmovable.

When trying to settle rows, imagine that you work for the arbitration service: listen to what is being said and compromise where possible (that's a two-way situation). If the worst comes to the worst, ask someone to arbitrate – your other half, another family member, a trusted friend …

Active listening seems to be the key. Rows can easily grow to screaming pitch and things can be said that both parties will regret. You are the adult here, so try to listen to your teenager's point of view – she may have a point; then calmly explain why she can't stay out late/have her eyebrows pierced/leave school at fourteen. Your point of view is less likely to be held against you if it is delivered calmly and in a measured way.

The hardest part of growing up is grudgingly admitting that your parents may be right. Resist the urge to score points. Let your teenager realise the bitter truth in her own time and own space.

Let smaller issues go when the repercussions in terms of rows and sulks would far outweigh the crime itself. Mention later that you didn't like what your teenager did/the way he spoke to you.

Try not to have rows with your partner in front of your children. It is confusing and worrying for children – even older children – to see their parents fight.

However, if you disagree with your partner on certain issues, that is real life and your teenager needs to learn that.

Talking

Communicating is a critical part of coping with teenagers, though conversations may at times be one way. It is very important too to listen to what is not being said.

Once the 'Kevin mentality' kicks in (especially with boys), the shutters come down and it is hard to get them to talk. Try asking open questions – ones that require more than a yes or no answer. 'What happened in the maths test?' rather than 'Did you have a good day?' Remember that you do not always need to talk to them, but you do need to listen.

If your child is watching a challenging programme or reading a piece in the newspaper, discuss it with him and ask how he feels about it. He needs to talk over his reactions or fears without you saying, 'This is rubbish.' Soaps especially may deal with subjects your children have never or will never come across, but they do reflect real-life situations.

FRIENDS

Sarah Lelliott;
Shauna Smith;
Dolores Smith;
Belinda Stokes;
Rachel Greaves;
Yvonne Waites;
Lily Freeman;
Glynis Fletcher,
NCT counsellor

If you provide a welcome to all your teenagers' friends, regardless of what you may think of them, they are more likely to bring them home. And that is where you can keep an eye on them.

Be welcoming to your children's friends, providing nice meals and a welcoming home to visit. They are then more likely to bring them home.

Show a good example with your own friendships. If your children see you entertain your friends at home or are around when you chat to them on the phone, they will learn how friendships work.

Sleepover nightmares? Keep sleepovers strictly to non-school nights and when homework has been done. Give plenty of warning when you want them to stop talking, and then threaten to move the guest or your child to another room. Final threat is that they won't have any more friends to stay.

You still have a social life – hopefully – so respect your own and your partner's plans. If you have already made arrangements to go out and your child wants a friend over, stick to your plans, but make another date for the sleepover.

'But Sally's mum lets us …' There will always be (real or fictional) parents who allow their children to do more than you do. Stick to your guns and be firm.

Your child will be led by 'friends' and her peer group, and the influence will not always be good. But sure as eggs is eggs, as soon as you express a critical opinion about one of her friends, she will be more determined than ever to spend time with that friend. She will see the light eventually, but if you think she is getting involved in activities she doesn't like (bullying, smoking, stealing) or that she is being teased by friends, you could gently ask if the friend is making her do things she isn't happy about. Remind her of the old adage: someone who is making you do things you don't want to, or who is not considerate, is really not a true friend.

Friends you don't approve of? If you can, remember friends you hung around with at the same age. Didn't you eventually work out for yourself which ones were worth having and which ones weren't?

There is safety in being accepted by 'naughty' types – who are often fun to be around, let's face it – and being accepted is often easier than to stand up to them. Fill your teenager with enough self-esteem and self-confidence and he will be less likely to be influenced adversely and better able to stand up to strong personalities.

Try not to interfere in conversations with your kids' friends. Children communicate on a different level (especially boys) and there is nothing more embarrassing than an adult who keeps chipping in witticisms.

Nagging or chastising your child in front of his friends will alienate him or her. If you have something to say, take him to one side and say it out of earshot.

If your teenager is a supportive friend to a mate in trouble, make sure that you praise her for it.

PARTIES

Lynn Shone;
Sally Beecham;
Mark Davies

At this stage parties take on a whole new meaning. No more jelly and balloons. More like alcopops and music till dawn.

Before your children go to a party, find out who is having it and whether parents will be there. Parties in this age group should still be overseen by an adult. If your child cannot satisfy you with information about venue/phone number/parental presence/alcohol provision/curfew/sleeping arrangements for a sleepover, it is fair that he doesn't get to go.

Find out what time you should collect your children from the party. Better to stay up late and collect them than worry about where they are and who they are with.

Explain the potential dangers without terrifying them: see Alcohol, below and page 217, Drugs, below and page 218, and Smoking, pages 179 and 218. Children under fourteen are vulnerable and not mature enough to appreciate potentially dangerous situations or cope with getting themselves out of sticky situations.

Teenager who wants a party? They are very hard to pin down and their plans change all the time. Agree some rules before they start inviting friends. Make sure you are clear about maximum numbers, drink allowed (one alcopop per child is reasonable at this age), finishing time and exactly who is staying the night. That way you have ammunition if agreed guidelines are overstepped.

Make birthdays a rite of passage to independence. Let them go alone with friends to the movies, and collect them afterwards.

Children will still love to celebrate special occasions with you. Each year do something more grown-up – a meal out at a sophisticated restaurant, a shopping trip to the nearest city.

ALCOHOL, DRUGS & SMOKING

Alcohol

Department of Health; David Touche; Lifeline; Quitline; Peter Reynard; Bill Smith

Alcohol is part of life, so try not to make it a mystery. Let your children try alcoholic drinks, even if it is just watered-down wine at meals – and in small quantities.

If you handle drink carefully, and respect it, it is more likely that your children will as well. If you get drunk and aggressive, they will learn bad habits.

From the age of fourteen, children can go into pubs but not buy drinks or drink alcohol. It is a good idea to go there with them occasionally, to help prevent such places becoming mysterious and exciting.

Don't allow alcoholic drink at your children's parties, and make it plain that friends are not to supply drink of any kind. They may have 'doctored' it. Make sure that you supply anything to be consumed.

For more on alcohol, see page 217.

Drugs

Being well informed is the only way children are going to know to say no if they are offered drugs.

Give your children as much information about drugs as you can. Then you need to trust them to make their own informed decisions.

Learn about drugs yourself. Drugs have changed since you were growing up. Make sure that you know the names of what is available (including the slang names) and the effects they have.

Go to www.trashed.co.uk, the excellent NHS health information website. Type in the drug name or the slang name, and it comes up with information about it, effects, risks and where it is classed as a drug by law. There is also information about what to do in an emergency. Well written and easy to follow.

Think about your views and your own drug use. Did you try them when you were a teenager?

Talk and listen to your child. He may be better informed about and aware of the risks than you think.

Secondary schools often give out excellent advice and printed matter on drugs (ask if your child hasn't received anything); indeed, your children may be better informed than you are.

Make sure that you read whatever comes home, and scour the internet/books/health education pamphlets so that you know what you are talking about. You then at least have ammunition in any heated discussions about drugs and cannot be accused of being out of touch.

Drugs and their effects need to be talked about calmly without a 'Touch them and I'll kill you' attitude. If you are too dogmatic, a contrary child won't be able to resist finding out what all the fuss is about.

Recent research shows that children are less likely to become involved with drug (ab)use if they have caring mothers or come from a family with two parents. A simplistic view but the principle there is that children are less likely to be tempted if they are confident, happy and secure – whether that is achieved by a mother, father or close family network.

It may sound trite but it's a strategy that can work: explain to your children that when they were young you had to tell them what was dangerous (climbing trees, leaning out of windows) because you knew what the results could be of their actions. The same applies to taking drugs. To them it may seem fun and exciting to experiment, but your experience has shown you what the fall-out of drug taking can be. You are able to look at the issue from another (and more realistic) angle.

The Trust for the Study of Adolescence, 23 New Road, Brighton, East Sussex BN1 1WZ, tel: 01273 693311, www.tsa.uk.com, has publications and training courses throughout the country on coping with teenagers. It also produces a video called *Teenagers in the Family*.

Lifeline produces excellent publications aimed at teenagers with other titles just for parents. The subjects are handled with humour, featuring cartoon characters such as Peanut Pete, but beneath the cartoon strips is an alarmingly strong underlying message. No subject is too extreme to be talked about in a direct way written for young people. Titles include *Everything You Wanted to Know about Cannabis but were Afraid to Ask your Kids*. All the pamphlets have information on all the main drugs and information guides for parents. Lifeline Publications is at 101–103 Oldham Street, Manchester M4 1LW, tel: 0161 839 2075, www.lifeline.demon.co.uk.

There is information for parents on the Department of Health website at www.doh.gov.uk, and free drug publications for parents. Call 0800 555 777.

For more on drugs, see page 218.

Smoking

This is a vulnerable age group for starting smoking. At age eleven to fifteen, 31 per cent of boys and 41 per cent of girls describe themselves as smokers, and boys are heavier smokers, with 37 per cent of those aged fifteen smoking more than forty cigarettes a week compared to 27 per cent of girls. It will help you to be armed with these statistics, and it is well worth telling them to your children. It may be the first time that your children come across cigarettes amongst their peers, and they may well be offered them.

Your children need to have the confidence to say no. This will have to emanate from you. Tell them calmly about the dangers and how there is nothing clever about following the crowd.

Surprisingly, concerns about the risks of smoking rate very high amongst teenagers' life fears. Play on that fear.

Set an example. Don't smoke yourself and openly disapprove of others doing it. If you smoke, it will be hypocritical to tell your kids not to.

Girls especially need to learn at an age when they are conscious of their changing bodies that smoking is not a sensible means of keeping their weight down. Education from you with support from their school can help to persuade your daughter that a sensible diet and exercise is the only way to control weight and look after her health.

Keep kids occupied – bored kids will smoke more. Sport and hobbies will distract them.

Remind your teenagers of the financial cost of smoking, and what they could buy if they used the money elsewhere – two and a half packets of twenty cost the same amount as a CD.

Some parents have found that making a pact works. If their child does not smoke, they will put money to the value of a packet of cigarettes into their account each week. That's over £230 accrued in a year at current prices.

If you discover cigarettes (don't go looking for them – your children will not respect you for intruding on their privacy) or smell smoke on their clothes, try to be calm. The smoke smell may have an innocent explanation. Let them explain the presence of the cigarette packet and listen to them. Don't fly off the handle. Describe your disappointment and your fears for their health. Your calm disapproval and disappointment will be far more effective in dissuading them from smoking than hysterics.

SEX

Lynn Shone;
Beryl Chatham;
Belinda Dean

Kids can't avoid sex – it's on TV, in the papers, everywhere – and they will be exposed to normal relationships as well as lesbian/gay relationships too (have you watched the soaps recently?). But just because it's thrown in their face, it doesn't mean that they understand it all. Talk to your kids about issues raised in the media and ask them if they would like you to explain them.

Your child may think it is uncool to admit that he doesn't understand certain expressions. There's no harm in asking, 'Did you understand that?' Just make sure that you know what it means too!

There is more pressure for this age group to have sex than to take drugs. All you can do is inform your child and remind him that it is actually illegal under sixteen.

As you explain the subject, keep checking as you go along that your child understands what you are saying. He may well not stop you to clarify points out of embarrassment.

A recent study in the *Journal of Social Policy* **(2002)** says that sex education puts too much emphasis on the riskiness and danger of sex, too little on its pleasure. This leads young people, especially boys, to adopt irresponsible attitudes. They learn about sex from tabloid newspapers and porn magazines or TV, which portrays sex in torrid, risky situations. Children need to understand sex in the framework of a loving relationship. They may also find it hard to talk about the emotional issues. Children need to feel comfortable talking about sex, and to understand it. Cover the ground early enough, sensibly and in an open, unembarrassed way.

The possibility of a daughter becoming pregnant at a young age probably rates in the top three of parental worries. It is very unlikely to happen, but you can help make it even less likely.

The birth rate per 1000 girls aged 15–19 in England and Wales is still around 40, while that for Dutch girls of the same age is just over four. Sex education in Holland is more open and relaxed, without the 'Oh it's embarrassing' stigma that it seems to have over here. Go Dutch – talk frankly. Better to be embarrassed than be too coy to face the issues and the consequences.

Make the possibility of pregnancy an important part of your children's sex education. Tell them how a baby would change their lives – you can use your personal experience of raising them – and how you could not have coped without their mother/father. But reassure them that you would not 'kill them' if they became pregnant and that you would help and support them.

Education and ambition are the best contraception. Girls who most commonly opt for terminations are those with aspirations and ambitions, for whom a pregnancy is unwanted and will ruin their lives.

Include contraception and sexually transmitted diseases in your child's sex education. See page 233.

Listen to their fears: children who have read erotic literature from a book they found lying around may be frightened that they feel aroused. Don't be angry at your child's curiosity and reassure him that such a response is perfectly natural.

Teenagers will inevitably experiment with kissing and petting. They will start to learn about arousal and be confused about their sexual feelings. However, you will be the last person they want to talk to about them. A careful chosen book discreetly left by their bed may raise their eyebrows, but they won't be able to resist looking at it. There are some well-written books aimed at this age group (notably *Understanding the Facts of Life* by S. Meredith, Usborne, and *Let's Talk About Sex* by Robbie Harris, Walker Books) which cover the subject thoroughly and straightforwardly.

Don't try to be their 'girlfriend' or 'mate'. Neither girls nor boys will want to, or should be, discussing who's dating whom with you. You are there for reassurance, not a good gossip.

For more on teenagers and sex, see page 232.

Masturbation & Wet Dreams

Masturbation is an inevitable part of growing up – especially for boys. But it's unlikely to crop up in conversation. You'll have to broach the subject out of the blue. Explain that it is a natural part of growing up and a development in their feelings; then they won't feel ashamed. But stress that it is private and should be kept so.

Your son may well have been told all sorts of extraordinary stories ('It makes you go blind', 'It helps you get a bigger penis', etc.) and the subject may cause him anxiety. If you talk to him frankly and honestly, you'll be able to put his mind at rest. Don't go overboard in your descriptions – just let him know that it may be embarrassing to discuss but you'd rather he knew about it and got the facts right.

Masturbation, or at least investigating that part of their bodies, can be a good way of helping teenagers to learn about their sexuality. They shouldn't be ashamed of their genitals.

Wet dreams (or nocturnal emissions as they are so delightfully known) are perfectly normal and will happen inevitably. They may be, and usually are, completely unrelated to an arousing dream. Make sure that your son knows that they will happen and knows not to be alarmed by them.

Boys of this age seem to have a permanent erection. Don't comment on it – it will embarrass them – and if you find evidence of wet dreams, just change the sheets/pyjamas and say nothing.

Finding porn mags under the mattress is another rather inevitable fact of boys growing up. So long as they are not hard core they are harmless in themselves, except that they cheapen women. Males often need verbal or visual stimulation to come to orgasm, especially if they are masturbating, which is all very well, but your son needs to understand that this sort of stimulation has nothing to do with good sex, which happens in a loving relationship and involves give and take.

Pregnancy

See page 234.

HEALTH

Department of Health;
Acne Support Group;
The Eyecare Trust

Try to ensure that you have a good and sympathetic doctor by the time your child is a teenager, and preferably one who knows the family. You may need your doctor's support and so may your child, so it is important that he has confidence in the GP. You need to like your GP and be confident he or she will handle the sensitive issues well.

Your teenager is entitled to receive confidential information from the GP, so if you think they have something which it embarrasses them to discuss in front of you, let them see the doctor alone.

Try www.lifebytes.gov.uk, a great site dealing with health issues for eleven-to-fourteen-year-olds.

If your kids don't want to talk to you about an embarrassing problem, there's an excellent site they can visit at www.embarrassingproblems.com.

Acne & Spots

Spots can affect children once they reach puberty, but they can appear earlier in more physically mature children, and tend to be more common in boys.

The oil-producing glands that are associated with the tiny hairs which cover the face and body are the site of the primary changes seen in acne vulgaris (spots). These oil glands become active at puberty when the male hormone called testosterone acts on them. That is why acne occurs after puberty. The male hormone is a normal part of the blood of women as well as men, but is present in smaller amounts. People with acne usually have normal hormone levels in the blood. Some women with severe acne may, however, have increased male hormone levels.

Genetics play a big part in acne – if you had it as a teenager there's a good chance your children will too. Prepare them, but try not to terrify the wits out of them.

Help your child by encouraging a skincare routine (see below), and let her understand that she is not alone in being affected (as school mates may make her believe) by taking her to a chemist and showing the wide range of products available. There wouldn't be so many if it wasn't a common problem, would there? Buy products recommended for children and ask the pharmacist's advice.

Spots aren't caused by dirt. If anything, people with oily skin have cleaner skin than average because they wash it more often. But washing too much can make spots worse because it makes the skin dry and sore.

Treatments:

- A teenager should wash every day no more than twice a day, using mild soap and warm water, and after she's been exercising. Don't scrub it or rub it – this will irritate the skin more. If she has patches of dry skin, she shouldn't worry about putting moisturiser on: it won't make the spots worse. If she's still concerned, she should use an oil-free moisturiser.

- There are lots of over-the-counter creams, gels, lotions and potions. Most contain a powerful bleaching agent called benzoyl peroxide. They come in different strengths 2.5 per cent, 5 per cent and 10 per cent. The strength is written on the label. Your teenager might be tempted to go straight for the 10 per cent sort, working on the 'let's nuke 'em' principle. The likely result is that they will irritate the skin like mad. It may also go dry and scaly. Start with the 2.5 per cent. Although there may be some mild irritation at first, this usually gets better as the skin becomes more tolerant.

Stick with a treatment for a minimum of two months. By then your teenager can start to see how well that treatment is working. If there is no improvement, she should change the treatment and try something else.

For most acne sufferers, diet is irrelevant. In a small number, however, chocolate and fried food may make it worse. This is rare.

Normal cosmetics have no effect on acne, but oily make-up, particularly ethnic Indian make-up, can cause blackheads. Suggest your child opts for oil-free foundations.

Acne is often made worse in hot, humid atmospheres such as kitchens. People who work with oil often have worse acne, particularly where there is oil contact with the skin. A job at Macdonald's may not be a good idea for an acne sufferer.

When your teenager wears make-up or sunscreen, make sure that it's labelled 'oil-free', 'non-comedogenic' or 'non-acnegenic'. This means that it won't clog the pores and contribute to acne.

Stress the importance of removing make-up thoroughly with a good cleanser before going to bed.

Hair sprays or gels should be kept away from the face, as they can also clog pores, and hair that touches the face should be kept clean. Try to encourage your child not to prop her face in her hands.

Homeopaths recommend Vitamin A, Vitamin E, Vitamin C, zinc, selenium and brewer's yeast supplements to be taken every day. Visit an accredited homeopath (some doctors are now trained as homeopaths too) for advice. Give the treatments time to start working.

Treatments while they sleep: Lancôme and Synergie (amongst others) sell little 'dots' that your teenager can stick over an offending spot to treat the area overnight. They both work the same way – after the skin has been cleansed, you peel off a little sticker and place it directly over the spot. The sticker is impregnated with a strong anti-bacterial, and delivers the ingredients straight to the source. They are clear (so you can barely see them), and more importantly, they don't dry out the skin around the spot.

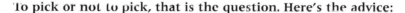

To pick or not to pick, that is the question. Here's the advice:

- If the spot is red and angry looking, don't touch it. If it is squeezed now, the contents will be forced deeper into the skin, and the result will be a redder, angrier spot than before.

- Yellow top? These can be squeezed, but there's an art to it. Wash hands thoroughly. Put a tissue over the finger, and using the thumb and the end of the finger, very gently start to squeeze. Don't use the nails, as this will damage the skin. Stop if nothing happens when pressure is applied, clear fluid appears or the spot is beginning to bleed. Afterwards dab the spot with antiseptic or an ointment containing tea tree oil. Once the yellow part of the spot is out, the spot will heal more quickly, providing it is left well alone. Wash hands again.

- If a spot looks green, see a GP. Such spots, which are rare, might be infected.

- Whiteheads and blackheads: if they are black, they can be squeezed (using the same technique as above) but if they are small, white raised lumps, they are best left alone.

Even though acne will usually disappear, it is excruciating for teenagers at a time when they are acutely aware of their appearance and appeal to the opposite sex. Acne can be severe and appear on the back as well as the face. At worst it can leave a legacy of scarring on the skin. But it doesn't have to be suffered in silence: doctors can offer a variety of treatments. If it is severe, visit the doctor together. If the doctor is dismissive, go and see a more sympathetic GP. There are mild treatments which can be very effective. Go to the doctor with your teenager if she is embarrassed – this'll also help when it comes to remembering what the doctor said.

For more information visit www.stopspots.org, the website of the Acne Support Group. Call 0870 870 2263 for free leaflets.

Eyesight

Under the NHS an eye examination is available without charge for all children up to the age of sixteen, and under nineteen if they are in full-time education. An indication of the importance of children's sight care is the fact that only a qualified practitioner – an optometrist or dispensing optician registered with the General Optical Council, or a registered medical practitioner – is permitted by law to supply children's spectacles. Following an eye examination, parents are entitled to a voucher towards the cost of any glasses or contact lenses prescribed. The value of the voucher will be determined by the prescription needed.

Reassure your children that eye examinations don't hurt!

Make sure your children are doing homework and studying with a good light source on their desk, and that they aren't straining their eyes.

Too much time in front of the computer? If they were in an office they would have to take regular breaks. They should at home too.

If you have a family history of short or long sight, astigmatism or squint, make sure that your child has regular eye checks-ups – once a year is about right.

Miserable about having to wear glasses? Point out how many cool celebs wear them, and show your child what a fantastic range of frames there are around (in your day it was NHS blue or pink – remember?). Bite the bullet and pay for some designer frames. It might be their first (and only) encounter with Armani!

Older children can wear contact lenses, though they can be lazy: make sure that they understand the importance of keeping lenses clean and well looked after.

Contact lenses and hay fever:

- *Don't* ever let your child take lenses out and clean them in their mouth to try to wash off any pollen or dust.

- *Don't* let him wear his lenses if his eyes become very sore and red. If in doubt, take them out and contact the eye care practitioner.

- *Do* ask your GP about anti-inflammatory drops, which may prevent the worst signs of irritation.

- *Do* tell him to wear prescription spectacles on days when the pollen count is particularly high, especially if you live in an urban area.

- *Do* wear lenses in the evenings. The pollen count is usually much lower then and therefore less irritating to the eyes.

- *Do* suggest he reduce the length of time he wears his lenses every day. A good benchmark is around twelve hours.

Spectacles & Lenses For Sport

Soft contact lenses are the best for most vigorous sports. Most people wear them for the duration of sporting activities even if they don't wear contact lenses for normal daily use. But remember that contact lenses provide very little eye protection. They should be worn, when necessary and appropriate, in conjunction with protective goggles.

Certain sports are best performed with the protection of special frames or goggles. Squash, for instance, requires goggles, which protect the temples and bridge of the nose as well as the eyes.

Guidelines for frames:

Should be lightweight, yet strong enough to resist strong impact.

- Can be fitted with side pieces that curl securely behind the ears.
- Should be fitted with elasticated sports band.
- Metal frames should be fitted with a padded bridge.
- Specially designed goggles are preferable.

Guidelines for lenses:

- Should be made from impact-resistant plastic or, preferably, polycarbonate.
- Glass lenses should be avoided but, if used, should be toughened or laminated.
- For indoor use, lenses should not be tinted and should be coated to reduce reflection from lights.
- Polycarbonate, tougher than other materials, must be used for squash.

Which visual aid is best for which sport?

Sport	Spectacles	Contact Lenses
Badminton	Yes, goggles are better	All, soft best
Darts	Yes	All
Fencing	Yes, or goggles	All
Scuba diving	Diving mask	Soft with mask
Snooker	Special frames	Specialised
Squash	Squash goggles only	All under goggles
Swimming	Goggles	Soft under goggles
Table tennis	Yes	All, soft best
Volleyball	Yes, or goggles	Soft

In the following sports, an ultra-violet absorber in the contact lens would be useful or, in some cases, tinted spectacle lenses.

Sport	Spectacles	Contact Lenses
Abseiling	Yes or goggles	Scleral
American football	Goggles	Soft or scleral
Athletics	Yes	All
Basketball	Yes or goggles	All
Clay shooting	High frame	All
Cricket	Yes or goggles	All
Fishing	Polarised	All polarised
Hockey	Goggles best	All
Horse riding	Yes	All, soft best
Jogging	Yes	All
Rugby	No	Soft or scleral
Skiing	Yes under mask	All under mask
Soccer	No	Soft
Target Shooting	Special frames	All
Tennis	Yes or goggles	All, soft best
Water Sports	Ventilated goggles	Scleral best
Yachting/sailing	Yes polarised	Soft

If in doubt about the best visual aid to help your child play sport, consult your practitioner for professional advice.

Growing Pains

During puberty, hormones in the body cause the breasts to grow larger. At the time of their pubertal development, boys commonly develop a small amount of breast enlargement too. This condition is called gynecomastia and is usually temporary.

Sore breasts? Breasts can hurt as they grow. Suggest that your daughter cuts down on salty foods and foods that contain caffeine, such as chocolate. Try caffeine-free tea or fizzy drinks.

Growth during puberty does not happen uniformly. Head, hands and feet show the first signs of growth, followed by arms and legs and finally trunk. Your teenage boy may look like the Neanderthal man for a while and feel gangly and uncomfortable. Reassure him if he mentions it; ignore it if he doesn't.

Breasts grow too at different rates, and for a while your daughter may be concerned that she will be permanently lopsided. Remind her to look at other adult women. How many of them are noticeably differing in breast size?

Girls' breasts can begin to develop on one side before the other. Your daughter may find that one nipple is hard and swollen. If it's inflamed or very tender, make an appointment with your GP to check that there is no infection.

Your son may not mention it, but may be concerned that his penis is growing at an alarming rate – this part of the anatomy grows to adult size in the space of two years. It's worth pre-warning him when discussing general body changes, because it's unlikely that he'll let you see him naked at this age.

The activity of hormones confuses teenagers not only emotionally but physically too. Body weight doubles during puberty and in girls muscle weight increases by about 50 per cent. At this vulnerable age when everything about their body matters, teenagers will need reassurance that they are not going to become hugely overweight, and that their smaller friends will catch up.

Plastic Surgery

See page 229.

Personal Hygiene

Whilst girls can't get hold of enough smelly products, boys in this age group seem to have an allergy to soap. Fear not. A growing interest in the opposite sex has a curious impact on their interest in bathing, and there will come a time when you won't be able to breathe for aftershave fumes.

Entice your teenagers with nice products. Shops like the Body Shop have some excellent products (with the right image) to encourage boys (and yes, sometimes girls) to bath. Offer them as a present.

Clean sweat doesn't smell. It only starts to become pongy when it is stale. If your teenager is a little too fragrant, make sure he is washing properly – and that means with soap under the armpits. Some teenagers think that standing under running water is washing. Deodorants will stop an unpleasant smell.

Even if your son won't have a full shower or bath every day, encourage him to wash everyday the areas where he sweats. Provide a flannel if necessary.

Try to avoid giving your children anti-perspirants and deodorants for as long as possible. Research has shown that their bodies can become immune to their effects and in the main, they contain quite strong chemicals. Soap and water regularly will be just as effective in getting rid of old sweat – which is what smells. Children should only start using deodorant when soap and water is no longer sufficient and when they begin to get hairy armpits.

When you do choose a deodorant, opt for one for sensitive skins – 'twenty-four-hour' deodorants can be very strong and irritate young skin. Avoid anti-perspirants, as these interfere with the body's natural need to sweat and block pores.

Check with your pharmacist which deodorants are suitable for children. Or try one of the mild, herbal varieties on sale in health stores and large chemists.

It's the hardest thing to tell your friend if they smell of BO, but it's a kindness to inform your children. Be gentle, not teasing. He may be aware of it already but too embarrassed to say anything.

Girls and boys need to be reminded that genital cleanliness needs special attention as they grow up – vaginal fluids, menstrual blood, semen and smegma are all clean, but once they leave the body bacteria can breed on them and they need to pay special attention to these areas.

They may seem normal to an adult, but your daughter may be worried by vaginal discharges. Don't forget to assure her that these are normal, especially at certain times of the month, but make sure that she knows the symptoms of abnormal discharges (these include heavy discharge, changes in colour, or discharges that smell, itch or burn).

Underpants alert: males will avoid putting on clean underpants if at all possible. Kidnap today's pair and make sure that there are clean ones ready for tomorrow.

Teeth

Teeth cleaning too seems to be missed out by this age group. Remind your kids that their adult teeth are for ever. They will be just as thrilled by quirky toothbrushes as the younger age group, so look for one as wacky as possible.

See also page 227.

Mouthguards & Gumshields For Sport

It is important for your child to wear a professionally made mouthguard whenever he or she plays sport that involves physical contact or moving objects. This includes: cricket, hockey and football – which can cause broken and damaged teeth; and American football, boxing and rugby – which can all cause broken or dislocated jaws. A mouthguard will help protect against these events.

Your dentist can make a custom-made mouthguard, which will fit your child's mouth exactly and protect teeth and gums properly. Custom-made mouthguards can prevent damage to the jaw, neck and even the brain – helping to prevent the concussion and damage caused by a heavy blow.

You cannot have mouthguards made on the NHS, so costs can vary from dentist to dentist. Ask your dentist about mouthguards and always get an estimate before starting treatment. Mouthguards are made by taking an accurate impression of the mouth and making a mouthguard to fit the teeth. The dentist will register the way the jaws bite together to make sure that the mouthguard meets properly with the teeth. There are cheaper kits available, which involve heating the product in hot water and then putting it in your child's mouth until it sets. Unfortunately these mouthguards fit badly and are uncomfortable to wear; they can fall out or even cause choking. Also the material is at its thinnest where it is needed most. When you consider the cost of expensive dental work and the risk of missing teeth, a proper mouthguard is a small price to pay for peace of mind.

Bad Breath

If your child cleans his teeth twice a day, and flosses them daily too, bad breath shouldn't be a problem. If it is, suggest he avoids spicy foods (not too many curries!) and garlic. If it persists, talk to your dentist.

Some children get bad breath when they are ill or brewing a cold.

Worried about kissing and bad breath? Suggest your teenager simply licks the inside of his wrist and leaves it to dry for a few seconds, then sniffs it. He will soon know if he has a problem. Might kill that romantic moment while he does it, though!

Diabetes

See page 223.

Jill Kenton, Rigby and Peller (www.rigbyandpeller.com – you can e-mail queries to them from the site and each question will be answered individually); Bravissimo, tel: 020 8742 8882, www.bravissimo.com

BRAS & BOOBS

For some girls starting to wear a bra is a milestone and an exciting one. For some it's the frightening reality that they are growing up. Be sensitive to both emotions.

Take your daughter to be measured for a bra as soon as breast tissue begins to appear. This could be from around ten or eleven years. For growing pains, see page 186.

Girls' shapes have changed since you were young. They are narrow around the back, but their breast size (cup size) is far bigger. This is a result of a change in diet (and in older teenagers, bust sizes increases when they go on the Pill). The average size for teenagers is 28 or 30 D.

Mothers are the key. If you influence your daughter into buying bras that have been properly fitted, that advice will stay with her for the rest of her life.

At least 75 per cent of women are wearing the wrong size of bra, so go with your daughter to have her measured properly. All independent lingerie shops offer this service – and their service is more often accurate than that offered by department stores. Bra specialists are experts – they can often tell a bra size just by looking.

It's a question of confidence: a properly fitted bra will help posture and be comfortable. It can also make the bust look smaller. Starting to wear a bra early will also help reduce the chances of stretch marks.

Tempting as it is to go for itsy-bitsy underwear, try to persuade your daughter that possibly less glamorous bras are infinitely better for their breasts (and how they look under clothes).

Keep an eye on the fit – a teenager's bust will grow quickly and she will need new bras regularly. If a bra is properly fitted, she shouldn't be aware that she's wearing it. If she can't wait to get it off, she's in the wrong size.

Some shops that offer bra fitting don't carry a large enough range of cup sizes, so they'll sell you a larger back size to compensate. It won't fit up front and will ride up at the back.

The front and back of a bra should be in one line and at the same level, and shouldn't budge. If it rides up at the back, it can't be supporting her properly and it probably means that the bra is too big. Choose one with a smaller back and a bigger cup size.

She only wants to have two breasts. If it looks as if she has four, the cup size is too small.

Underwired bras give better separation, support and lift, and give a better line under clothes. Soft cup bras are fine for sports.

If underwired bras dig in at the side of the breast or stick out, the cup size is too small. Many women complain of this, but once they've been properly fitted, they're converted.

If your daughter has marks on her shoulders from the bra straps, the bra is not giving her breasts enough support.

Pure cotton is not the best fabric for a bra, as it stretches. Aim for a maximum of 30 to 40 per cent cotton, and always have a bit of elastene.

A bra will last six months to a year, depending on how it's treated. If little bits of elastic start appearing at the back, it's high time to throw it away.

Bras hate heat, so don't wash by machine. Handwash bras and rinse well. Don't wring out underwired ones, and always drip dry. Never use a tumble dryer and never hang them over radiators.

When your daughter gets a new bra, do it up on the loosest catch, then if it stretches tighten it by moving along a catch at a time.

The adjuster straps over the shoulders need tightening with wear too. It's very hard to get them even yourself when wearing them, so help your daughter.

Big girls look smaller in a well-fitting bra. Underwires show off the shape of the breasts and separate well. If the bra gives one indistinct lump across the chest, it makes her look much bigger.

Stick to smooth bras for wearing under fitted or sheer tops.

For bigger boobs, wear fitted or streamlined shapes, as these are much more flattering than baggy clothes. Look for fitted tops with seams or darts under the bust as these will define the waist.

Round, scooped or V-necklines tend to be more flattering for bigger boobs than high necklines.

Wear plain colours to minimise a big bust – avoid busy patterns, large prints and patch pockets.

Keep tops light and bottoms dark to emphasise boobs, and wear darker tops and lighter bottoms to draw the attention away from them.

Wear jewellery away from the bust. It's more flattering to wear it around the neck than on the boobs.

For small girls, the technology has never been better. There are all kinds of little extras in bras nowadays, so a cleavage can be your daughter's, if she wants it.

Encourage your daughter to wear a good sports bra. There are no muscles in the breasts and once you stretch the ligaments and they become damaged, there is nothing to be done short of surgery.

Make sure that a sports bra is smooth so that seams and bindings will not rub. The straps should be fairly rigid to minimise bounce and be wide enough to sit comfortably without digging in. The jump test in the changing room is the best way to check out its efficacy.

Make sure that your daughter finds a good basque or strapless bra before committing herself to a strapless dress, especially if she has a big bust.

To put on a bra, do it up with the catch turned round to the front, then rotate it so that it's at the back, slip the arms through the straps, lean forward and lower the breasts into the cups (the nipple should be on the seam and in the middle), slide the straps on to the shoulders and stand up.

Front-fastening bras should be restricted for nursing bras – they just don't work for everyday use.

If your daughter's breasts enlarge before her period, get measured then too, and have a couple of larger bras so that she is comfy all month. PMT and a tight bra – definitely something to be avoided!

Every girl needs between four and eight bras. They must be washed every day, like knickers, and worn in rotation to ensure a long and supportive life.

Prevent straps from digging in and slipping by making sure they are at least 1in/2.5cm wide.

To prevent chafing around the ribcage, underarms and shoulders, get a bra with seamless cups. Make sure that seams, hooks and closures are covered.

Falling straps: first try adjusting the straps. If that doesn't help, go down a cup size, as your daughter's breasts are probably not filling out the tops of the cups. Also, look for designs where the straps are located in the middle of the cup, not at the edges. Or try a racer-back style.

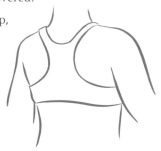

When trying on a bra, stand straight, and relax. Don't inhale and expand the rib cage as if about to blow out candles.

For corrective surgery to breasts, see page 229.

PERIODS

Sarah Kilby; Lynn Shone; Georgia Gates

Prepare your daughter by giving her pads to carry discreetly in her school bag well before her first period arrives.

It's probably so long ago since your periods started that you have forgotten the warning signs: your daughter may have a darkish discharge for a few months before the first period finally arrives, and it may be smelly – though if the smell is unpleasant it may be the sign of an infection and she should see the doctor.

Don't forget to mention the obvious side effects: sensitive breasts, period pains, bloating and, of course, pre-menstrual tension (PMT). For period problems, see page 191.

Once your daughter's first period arrives, offer her a variety of sanitary products to try out. Your choice may not suit her. Provide sanitary towels and tampons (sizes for young girls are now available) with applicator and without. Times and medical opinion have changed over the years and the (very small) risk of toxic shock syndrome from tampons has put many girls off using them; she may be happy with towels even if they would not be your choice. Leave them in a discreet place where she will know where to find them, and encourage her to read the instructions in the packet – especially as regards the regularity with which you should change tampons (at least every four to eight hours) and how to dispose of sanitary protection.

Companies like Bodyform offer free pantyliner samples over the web. Go to www.bodyform.co.uk. The site also has good advice on periods and PMS aimed at teenagers.

A non-applicator tampon smeared in a small amount of KY jelly can help insertion the first time your daughter uses one.

Give your daughter a discreet cosmetic bag to keep her sanitary protection in her school bag, and a spare pair of knickers. Some paracetomol for period pains is a good idea too. Teenagers can have severe cramps with their periods.

Be aware that starting periods can be distressing for some girls. Don't belittle her concerns, but be as understanding as you can, whilst respecting her privacy.

She may not realise obvious things like personal hygiene and the need to bath or shower often during her period – don't forget that you're an old hand at this period business.

For late periods, see page 227.

Period Problems

There are various homeopathic remedies for helping ease period problems such as PMT and pre-menstrual syndrome (PMS). Pulsatilla may help mood swings. If your daughter has a tendency to be irritable and to get a dragging feeling in the pelvis, she may benefit from Sepia. Another common remedy is Nat. Mur., particularly if she suffers from chronic tiredness around the time of her period.

Herbs commonly prescribed for period problems include valerian and passionflower, which ease anxiety and tension. Valerian is particularly helpful as it relaxes muscular tension too, helping to ease period pain.

Taking some supplements can also help – in particular, magnesium, zinc and vitamin B6. As with all complementary medicine, don't expect results overnight – a marked improvement may sometimes take two to three months.

Lots of fresh fruits and vegetables and cutting back on processed foods like chips and crackers can help. Your daughter might also want to reduce her caffeine and salt intake (salt can make you retain water and become more bloated).

A recent study indicates that increasing the amount of calcium in the diet may reduce PMS, so make sure that your daughter is drinking enough milk and eating yoghurt.

Exercise will also relieve cramps and PMT and make your daughter feel better, possibly because it releases endorphins, chemicals in the body that literally make you feel good.

Soaking in a warm bath or putting a warm compress (or hot water bottle) on the stomach won't make cramps disappear but may help the muscles relax a little.

PIERCING

Department of Health; Bodies Beauty Clinic

There are no laws governing piercing and age limits. Most salons ask for parental consent under the age of sixteen, even though strictly children can have their ears pierced when they are considered old enough to understand the implications.

If you are dead set against ear piercing, set an age date when you are happy for your child to have it done – fourteen or fifteen perhaps – but be comfortable with your choice and don't renege.

Let your child earn piercing as a treat – if she passes an exam, for example.

Once ears have been pierced (whether you wanted it done or not) make sure that your child cleanses the newly pierced holes properly. Feigning disinterest because you are angry may result in infected ears.

Go along with your child and make sure she has the piercing done at a clean and reputable place. You will have to be there to give consent under sixteen anyway. It's worth paying more to use a beauty salon than a high street shop.

Ears are just the start of it. Navels next … And once a child reaches the age of sixteen she can have piercings without your consent. Once she is eighteen she can be tattooed.

FOOD

British Nutrition Foundation; Dr Sarah Schenker SRD

A growth spurt usually begins around ten years of age in girls and twelve years of age in boys. In both sexes, an average of 9in/23cm is added to height and 44–57lb/20–26kg to weight. Before adolescence, both girls and boys have an average of 18 per cent body fat. During adolescence this increases to about 28 per cent in girls and decreases to about 15 per cent in boys. In short – they are growing fast!

Get cooking! Calorie requirements vary but broadly speaking a boy aged eleven to fourteen years needs 2220 kilocalories per day, a girl 1845 kilocalories. This is considerably more than an adult needs (about 300 respectively), so if your child is still hungry after a family meal don't be surprised. Teenagers will need more snacks between meals too.

Growing teenagers, especially boys, need a lot of fuel to keep them going. Make sure that you provide enough filling foods (pasta, potatoes, bread). They are frankly more interested in quantity not quality, so don't waste your time preparing nouvelle cuisine. It won't be appreciated.

Older children can just as easily fill up on snacks and fizzy drinks as younger children, and come to the dinner table not interested in what you have slaved over for hours. Set mealtimes well in advance ('Lunch will be at one') and discourage snacks for at least an hour before that.

Teenagers need lots of iron. After menstruation begins, girls need more iron than boys to replace menstrual losses. It is thought that about 4 per cent of adolescent boys and 17 per cent of adolescent girls are anaemic. Those who eat a poorly planned vegetarian diet or are slimming may be particularly at risk.

Foods that are high in iron include broccoli, raisins, watermelon, spinach, black-eyed peas, blackstrap molasses, chickpeas and pinto beans. To increase the amount of iron absorbed from a meal, offer food containing vitamin C as part of the meal: citrus fruits and juices (for example, orange juice), tomatoes and broccoli are all good sources. Eating breakfast cereals and/or bread that have been fortified with iron is important. If your teenager doesn't eat breakfast, encourage her to have bowl of cereal or glass of juice as a snack instead.

The rapid increase in bone mass in adolescents means that they require more calcium than adults. Boys should aim for 1000mg per day and girls for 800mg. As a guide, there are 300mg of calcium in a cup of full milk and 200mg in a slice of Cheddar cheese.

Keep an eye on your kids' vitamin intake too – see page 219.

For vegetarians, see page 220.

School Dinners

If you are concerned about what your child is eating, ask for a copy of the school weekly menu.

You can also ask to look round during a lunchtime, or invite yourself to lunch.

Since 2000, schools can spend their catering budgets as they please. Encourage your child's school to look at a catering contractor (such as Eatdot) which works by 'smart' cards. If you don't want your child eating chocolate, crisps and burgers, for example, the card system means that she will not be able to pay for them with her card. You can also request a print-out of the week's purchases so that you can see if your child isn't eating enough or is eating too much of the wrong thing, and you can set a daily limit on how much she spends.

Eating Disorders

See page 224.

MAKE-UP

James Mcmahon,
Maybelline;
Caroline Bailey

Every little girl experiments with make-up, usually from a very early age.

Try not to lay down the law. Insist on no make-up and your daughter will be desperate to try it out. Better to teach her how to use it subtly – even take her to a professional at a department store to show her how it's done. Explain that less is more. Girls' magazines can help.

Encouraging news: on the whole, girls this age ultimately tend to be quite conformist within their own parameters. In the early teens, they may experiment in the safety of their bedroom with funky make-up. So don't freak out if your daughter comes downstairs after a girlie make-up session with a friend looking like a drag queen. The make-up they tend to wear out may be comparatively subdued, though some girls will go out made up, and then plaster on more once they arrive at their destination.

Worried about how much make-up your daughter is wearing? Explain how make-up that is over the top can send signals to boys and men, attract unwanted attention in varying degrees and explain what the consequences might be.

Your daughter may be very aware of and distressed by the issues surrounding animal testing of cosmetics. Respect her views and help her find catalogues and stockists with products she feels happy to use.

Supply your daughter with a good-quality cleanser and cotton wool. Removing make-up before she goes to bed is a good habit to get into.

Knowing what's appropriate with make-up really matters. Show your daughter that there is a time and a place for a smudged black eye and it's not in a Monday morning maths class.

Young girls don't need foundation, unless it is cream or stick foundation to cover spots. Their skin is fresh and young enough to 'go bare' everywhere else.

Colours that suit teenagers are sheer ones that you can see through – pale shades in natural or soft pastel tones that look like natural washes of colour on the face. These are pretty mistake-proof too.

Creamy eye shadows look more natural than powders and go on more easily.

Help your daughter find the right colours for her skin tone. Skin tones can be roughly classified into warm or cool tones, and make-up colours that have similar undertones to those of her skin will suit her. There are also many neutral colours, which suit all skin types – these tend to be the more natural earthy shades, including bronze, copper and gold.

- Cool tones: pale skin that does not tan easily. Hair has ashen undertones: white blonde, dark blonde, brown or black. Eye colour may be blue, blue-green, grey or brown. Colours to suit her: neutrals and cool based colours – silvery pinks, cool pinks, true reds, plums, purples, blues, neutrals.

- Warm tones: golden skin, freckles or sallow skin that tans easily. Hair is golden blonde, red or strawberry blonde, brown or chestnut. Eyes may be green, hazel, golden brown or deep blue. Colours to suit her: neutrals and warm based colours – peachy pinks, peach, orange, scarlet, bronze browns.

Great tip for her (and you) when she's looking for a natural-looking lip colour: lightly bite the lower lip. Match a lipstick to the resulting flushed lip colour. Same applies to blusher: lightly pinch the apple of the cheek. Match the blusher to the resulting colour.

Tips with concealer:

- A concealer should be used to conceal spots and blemishes – it has a different formulation to foundation, specific to its purpose.

- Choose a colour similar or slightly lighter to that of foundation – and apply to the blemish using a small brush, after the application of foundation. Blend into foundation until a homogenous finish is obtained.

- Avoid use if suffering from broken skin or pustular pimples as this can aggravate the problem.

Encourage your daughter to spend little on glitter and glamour, but to use her money on good skincare products and concealer.

In the later teens, having obtained a more defined sense of identity and increased confidence, girls will become more individual and experiment with make-up. This is also due to the fact they are more willing to spend money on make-up.

SHOPPING

Dolores Smith;
Sarah Lelliott

Whilst you still control the purse strings, you still have a certain amount of control over what your children spend money on and the clothes they buy. Rather than be dogmatic about what and what is not acceptable, compromise. 'That top is too revealing – what about this one?' Ensure that your daughter understands the effect a revealing top can have on boys and the attention it may elicit.

Make shopping fun. There will still be inevitable trawls for items such as school shoes which will involve sulking, but set a deal: once we've done the shoes, let's see if we can find something for you to wear to so-and-so's party.

If you have other children, go shopping alone together with your teenager. He may be uncommunicative, but he will relish the chance to have you all to himself.

Mums: let your teenager shop with you when you are buying clothes for yourself. Accept her opinions. She won't want you looking like a tart, nor will she want you looking like a frump.

Let your teenager have time in town with a group of friends to shop – and arrange a reasonable picking-up time. Set limits on the amount of cash she takes with her, but let her have her freedom. If you don't like what she has bought, try to keep your opinions to yourself.

If you tend to come to blows in the shops, send your child shopping with a younger, trusted adult friend – who has been briefed by you.

For more on teenagers and clothes shopping, see page 236.

MONEY

Department of
Education and Skills;
NatWest; Graham
Williams; Ted Barker

Make treats just that: a treat. Children showered with every new type of Lego/Barbie accessory/newly released video will never learn the value of presents or of saving up to earn something they desire. In short they will be spoiled rotten.

Encouraging children to realise what they need to save or earn before a CD/new T-shirt/earrings can be paid for is a valuable lesson in life.

Pocket Money & Allowances

Recent figures show that annual rises in pocket money are at three times the rate of inflation! In fact Britain's nine million children (aged five to sixteen) have a total weekly spending power of £60m. Your children are bound to tell you that their friends receive more than they do, but before deciding on a figure work out between you what you are happy to foot the bill for – bus tickets, mobile phone cards (up to a certain amount), etc. – and what the cost of a reasonable treat may be, and ask friends with similar aged children how much they give their children.

For older children, a monthly allowance for some essentials as well as treats is a good idea. They will learn the hard way that they need to budget or else it will all be gone. Again you need to work out and agree what the allowance is to cover.

Earning Money

No young person under the school leaving age (sixteen) can be employed before 7.00 a.m. or after 7.00 p.m., for more than one hour before the start of the school day, for more than twelve hours a week during term time, for more than two hours on a school day or on a Sunday.

The laws on minimum wage do not apply to children under sixteen.

If your teenager is keen to work, he may have to settle for holiday jobs. But it's a good idea to restrict term-time work anyway, as it can interfere with homework and tire school-children.

There is no legal minimum age below which a young person cannot lawfully babysit. See page 243.

Children can earn money from you or friends. Be consistent about rates of pay. Perhaps a chart saying how much is to be paid for what job would be helpful.

Chores – to pay or not to pay? There is a middle way. There are some things children should do as part of helping out in the family, like putting their clothes in the washing basket, picking up towels and helping at the supermarket checkout. But you can have specials that they always earn for, like washing the car, or emptying all the wastepaper baskets in the house.

The going rate, according to a 2002 NOP Survey for Abbey National, is £2.77 for cleaning the house, £2.52 for loading and unloading the dishwasher and £2.30 for washing the car (which seems fairly unequal). Keep a diary of jobs in the kitchen: taking out the rubbish, gathering cans and bottles for recycling, tidying bedrooms, washing cars. Once these jobs have been done and ticked off, money can be handed out.

If your child has a regular chore, like caring for a pet, agree to pay weekly provided she does it every single day of that week.

Pay pocket money – or money from you – straight into a bank or building society account (see below). This way your child is less likely to fritter it away.

Bank & Building Society Accounts

This age is a good one for starting your children out with an account so that they learn how to manage money (though the average age is sixteen or seventeen for opening a bank account).

Research shows that people tend to stick with one account – even if they switch credit cards – so it is in the banks' interest to offer attractive start-up packages to children. Shop around for the best incentive deals. Look at all the banks, because although they broadly stick to the same formula (cashpoint cards from thirteen upwards, free banking, etc.) many have discount offers as incentives for young people to open accounts with them. Some banks offer phone banking for people of sixteen and over; others offer interest on current accounts. All have different names for these accounts too.

Interest rates and incentives vary, and it's worth checking when interest is paid on an account – this is usually on an annual basis.

Banks and building societies usually have three types of accounts. Those for under eights are usually in the parent's name (beware you aren't liable to tax on large balances) or with the parents as trustees. Eight-to-twelve-year-olds can make deposits and withdrawals on their own, and will have their own pass book if they use a building society. Accounts for eleven-to-eighteen-year-olds usually have cashpoint or Electron cards and chequebooks for over-sixteens.

Banks tend to be stingier in terms of interest than building societies, and the latter's pass book system is a good way of letting children actually see how much money they have and how much they are withdrawing.

If opening an account without a cashpoint card, make sure that a branch is within easy access or walking distance so they can make withdrawls.

Youngsters need access to cash, so try to open an account at a bank close to your house though, if they have a cashpoint card, they can use most ATM (Automatic Teller Machines) machines free of charge.

Supermarket and internet accounts aren't usually open to children – though if they have a high-street bank account they can use the online banking facility.

Parent-controlled debit cards for shopping online are now available (SmartCards and Splash Plastic). They work like a prepaid phone card (you 'buy' credit for your child to use shopping online), but have in-built restrictions so that you can control where your child goes virtual shopping. For instance he won't be able to buy an 18-certificate video online when under age. Go to www.smartcard.co.uk and www.splashplastic.com.

Solo cards are debit cards run by the same people who handle Switch cards. However, whereas Switch cards have a floor value – any transaction under it is accepted, over and it is checked – Solo card transactions are always checked against funds in the holder's account, so your child can shop with one yet not risk going overdrawn. For details go to www.solocard.co.uk.

There is no advantage to opening an account for your child with the bank you bank with. All accounts are treated independently – it's not like the days when branches had friendly bank managers.

Using the Post Office as a bank: it won't save money but it's often much more convenient, especially if you live in a rural area. At the time of going to press, you can make withdrawals and deposits at the Post Office if you bank with Alliance Leicester, Barclays, Cahoot, the Cooperative Bank, Lloyds TSB or Smile.

Children have the same personal tax allowances as adults and usually don't qualify to pay tax. Make sure that your child fills in a form R85 and returns it to the Inland Revenue to get any interest due on the account paid gross.

If you pay money into your child's account, you may have to pay tax on the interest if the 'gift' exceeds a certain amount.

If grandparents or other benefactors want to give your children money, ask them to give cash if the interest on the sum if placed in an account is going to be greater than the child's personal allowance.

It's never too early to learn about money. If you are opening a savings account for your child, show her that if she leaves a sum for a fixed period, it can boost the interest she earns on her savings.

HOBBIES, SPORT & MUSIC

Caroline Whaley, Nike Europe; Caroline Dagul, music teacher

A busy child is less likely to get into trouble. Find something that yours (not you) enjoys doing and go for it. Hobbies will ease him into a world of like-minded people and give him an opportunity to make new friends, in a good environment. This is a good time to lay the foundations of a pastime that might engage him for the rest of his life.

Enjoyment of hobbies is an asset laid down early in life. Encourage your children to spend time doing activities *they* enjoy and they will be more motivated to do them as they grow up. Don't belittle or dismiss any interest. Roller-blading may not be your idea of a good time, but a child who does it is getting exercise and it's a brilliant way to meet and communicate with other enthusiasts.

Give teenagers lots of hobbies and sports to try. Take them to matches/open days/exhibitions. Something of what they experience may take their fancy.

Ideas include: choirs, art and drama groups, bands and orchestras, riding, skateboarding, model building, water sports and swimming, karate and martial arts, football, rugby, cricket, gymnastics, cycling, rock climbing, mountaineering, charity work, badminton, tennis.

First stop is your local leisure centre. For information about sporting federations, try www.sportengland.org, www.sports-council-wales.co.uk and www.sportscotland.org.uk. For hobbies such as wall climbing contact the British Mountaineering Council on 0870 010 4878 or www.thebmc.co.uk who can tell you where to find your nearest climbing wall.

The Youth Sport Trust at www.youthsport.net has useful contacts for encouraging children of all ages, and especially secondary school children, to become involved in sport.

Has your daughter lost interest in sport? Research has shown that many schools offer poor sports provision for girls. Encourage your daughter's school, via the PTA, to involve girls in the planning and delivery of their lessons, to provide different games like football and aerobics, to relax policies on PE kits (if the gear's right they'll feel better), to provide positive imagery and female role models, and to encourage more community involvement. Go to www.thesportslife.com/govnikeapril.htm.

School can't provide enough sport? The National Curriculum has suffocated school sport – there simply isn't enough time in the day to fit everything in. Arrange sports activities for outside school hours and at weekends: local rugby, cricket and football clubs have youth team initiatives and training. Contact your local leisure centre too.

All the certificates for awards from swimming, school, football, music and karate make for cluttered bedroom walls. Try sticking them in date order in a photo album with plastic-covered pages.

Trouble finding trainers for big feet? Go to www.fdsports.co.uk which has trainers for sizes 12 to 20; www.sportshoes.com claims to be the world's biggest sports shoe retailer for every sport you can think of, with a Big Foot section also covering sizes 12 upwards.

Cheaper shoes can be found at www.sportsmart.co.uk, though not in large sizes. Delivery is free for orders over a certain amount.

For spectacles, lenses and mouthguards/gumshields for sport, see pages 185 and 187.

Music

Children at secondary stage may start to lose interest in instruments they began learning to play at primary school. It might be time to acknowledge that they will never be Mozart, but involving them in a band or music group might help to maintain their enthusiasm – especially if they see others of the same age (and the opposite sex) involved. Music won't be so uncool then. Speak to their music teacher or your local music shop to discover what groups exist.

Boys are particularly bad at pursuing instruments. A school that makes music lessons compulsory in year eight has revealed a hidden seam of musical talent that might have gone undiscovered. None of the boys feel geeky because they all have to play. Suggest your child's school tries the same tactic.

Find good CDs of music that features your child's instrument – classical or contemporary, jazz or pop – and ideally ones that feature music they are practising at that time. Hearing your instrument played in context with accompaniment can be very motivating.

Keep music as an important part of family life. Play music you enjoy and make an effort to listen to music they like too – painful as that might be. Don't be too enthusiastic about it, though. It will be excruciatingly embarrassing for them to have their parents sing along to their favourite Limp Bizkit CD.

TECHNOLOGY

Computers & The Internet

Sam Finch; Harry Bates; Susie Wade; Metropolitan Police; ICSTIS; Department of Health

A computer in a child's bedroom is a huge temptation when he should be doing homework. Out of sight is out of mind: connect up the computer in a place all the family have access to it, so that children can use it when they need to or want to play games, but not when they should be working.

Set certain times of day when it's OK to play on the PC. Some parents find it works banning it on school nights; some restrict it to half an hour in the evenings but longer at weekends.

It doesn't take much to stumble across porn sites on the internet. Typing in words such as 'pony' to find riding schools will reveal some eyebrow-raising options. Blocking and internet censoring programmes exist (www.cyberangels.org, for example), but there are ways to get around them and they are not foolproof. Use the internet with your kids, so that it becomes a family activity, not a babysitting alternative to the TV.

To safeguard children using the internet:

- Buy guard software to restrict access to certain sites.

- Many service providers will give you kid zones or restricted time access to specific sites, depending on content.

- Bear in mind that kids are usually smarter than you when it comes to computers and can probably hack their way round blocks if they want to.

- As a final safeguard, you can check which sites have been visited through the explorer.

Safe search engines include: yahooligans, www.lycos.com (click on Parental Controls on top of the home page and click through Search Guard, which will screen out adult, violent or pornographic sites) and www.surfmonkey.com. Try too www.cyberpatrol.co.uk.

Make sure that your child knows never to give out their full name and address over the internet – especially in chat rooms; e-mail addresses are OK, as they don't reveal where you live, but it's a good idea to have another user name.

Avoid Hotmail or AOL e-mail addresses for a child. These seem to be more vulnerable to unsolicited and unpleasant e-mails.

Set up some filtering in your web browser via the Content Advisor in internet Explorer (go via Internet Options in your tools menu, then Content).

Homework on the internet? Make sure that the sites they look at have reliable and accurate information. See page 148 for some good sites.

Want to keep them off the net? Simply don't reveal your internet access password and keep changing it regularly!

It's a good idea to keep an up-to-date anti-virus progamme on your computer as a safeguard when downloading (make enquiries when you buy your PC).

Telephoning

On your land-line home phone, have your children's best friends' phone numbers included on your Friends and Family facility.

Time they spend on the phone getting out of hand? Allow a certain number of calls per week, and then charge them a nominal amount for any over and above that.

Mobile Phones

Thinking of buying a mobile phone for your child? Try to familiarise yourself with the latest jargon, or you'll be left standing when the salesperson gets into full swing. Visit a variety of mobile phone retailers because, though the prices may be similar, the salesperson may well add accessories to the deal.

Whilst arming your child with a mobile phone offers a reassurance that she can be contacted or contact you in an emergency, needless to say 98 per cent of the time she is likely to use a mobile phone are used for fun. Have a 'pay as you go' package, whereby you can put talk time on your child's phone via your mobile. That way they and you can keep a track of how much they are spending and avoid shockingly high monthly bills. Sadly your child will learn the hard way if she uses up all the available talk time and can't ring when she's stuck. Tell her that she will have to pay you or buy vouchers herself if she wants more talk time than you allow.

More than 10,000 mobiles are stolen every month (2002 figures), with two thirds of those belonging to 13-to-16-year-olds. To lessen the chances of this happening to your child, pass on this advice:

- Keep phones out of sight in a pocket or handbag when not in use.
- Use the phone's security lock code if it has one.
- Record details of the electronic serial number (ESN) and consider separate insurance covering theft, damage and calls not made by the owner.
- Some phones have an IMEI number, which is a unique identifier for the phone. You can obtain this number by typing *#06# into the mobile and it will display a 15 digit number.
- Property mark the phone with your postcode and door number to help police identify stolen ones.
- Report a lost or stolen phone to the police immediately.
- Inform your service provider if your phone is lost or stolen.
- Don't attract attention to the phone when you are carrying or using it in the street.
- Don't park in isolated or dark areas to make a call.
- Don't leave a phone in an unattended car. If you must, lock it out of sight.

It's a good idea to see which networks your child's friends are on – cross network calls (Vodaphone to O2, Orange to Vodaphone) are expensive, but calling another mobile on the same network is often only charged at a local rate.

Dead set on a certain ringing tone? Ring tones are available everywhere but they can be very expensive. If only one tone will do, buy it direct from the network's website rather than by telephone, where you are charged at peak rate.

Avoiding text scams: some marketing organisations use computer programmes to randomly generate mobile numbers and use them for unsolicited SMS (Short Messaging Service) marketing, sending premium-rate text messages to mobile phones with spurious messages like 'Hi sexy'. Children may reply to these without knowing that instead of costing around 10p a message (usual rate), they can cost up to £1.50p. Advise your child that if she receives messages which do not include the sender's number or which do not include the cost of replying, she should ignore them and erase them from her phone. You can also contact the Independent Committee for the Supervision of Standards of Telephone Information Services (ICSTIS) on 0800 500 212.

If you are concerned about the distracting element of using mobiles, buy a phone without games. This way your child is less likely to be too absorbed in playing to notice he is about to cross the road in front of on-coming traffic.

So what are these health worries about mobiles? In May 2000 there was a report from the Independent Expert Group on Mobile Phones, chaired by Sir William Stewart. The group considered that children less than sixteen years of age should be discouraged from using mobile phones. The concern is radio waves being absorbed by the body, which can affect brain activity. Because the head and nervous system are still developing in teenagers, any unrecognised health risks from mobile phone use might make young people more vulnerable than adults. Experts and the Department of Health recommend that calls are kept to essential ones only and are kept brief …!

Good advice to give your kids if they use a mobile phone:

- Avoid speaking for long periods.
- Text rather than talk.
- Try not to talk for too long in the car as it amplifies the radio waves.
- Don't carry a mobile on your waist, as this exposes the deposits of bone marrow in the hips and the testicles to the radio waves.
- Direct the antenna away from your head, not upright in parallel with the head.

Use the internet to find out more information about phone safety. Try www.uk-mobile-phones-directory.co.uk.

Television

Living with a soap addict? There is a lot of pressure in the playground for children to be up-to-speed with the latest goings on in soaps-of-the-moment. Watch other programmes with your kids. Or suffer the soaps, but talk about the social issues they raise. Ask: 'How do you feel about that? How would you cope in that situation?' Better your children have information from you on different subjects than inaccurate information from the playground.

TVs in their bedrooms are a bad idea. Why do kids ever need to come downstairs if all their entertainment is in their rooms? TV can also be too tempting when homework should be the priority. There is a danger too that you have no control over what they are watching. You may be able to insist it goes off before the 9.00 p.m. watershed, but post-9.00 p.m. programmes are often trailed before this time. Several soaps which deal with serious and grown-up issues are on before 9.00 p.m.

SCHOOL
Years Seven & Eight

These are known in the state system as the 'dosser years'. Pupils may go over work they did at primary school, and teachers are focusing on extra tuition for older GCSE

Emma and Jeremy Wakeling; Emily Savage; Richard and Anne Bracegirdle; Ian

Hecks, head teacher;
Department of
Education and Skills;
Raj Patel; Maureen
Sage; DfES; Carolyn
Webb, teacher;
Parentline Plus; Mary
Lewis, teacher; Gail
Fellows, teacher

pupils. You may find that your child is learning little and becomes demotivated. These years also coincide with disaffected early teenage years when children want to rebel and may lose the will to learn – this is a particularly dangerous time for boys. If you are unhappy about a small amount of homework or the fact that your child is learning so little, talk to the school.

Conversely make the most of the pressure being off to interest them in hobbies and extra-curricular activities. See page 196.

Boarding School

Try to meet some children who go to or are going to the same school before your child starts there – especially ones who will paint it in a good light.

Check what sort of home clothes other children wear so that your child's are in keeping – he will want to fit in right from the start. The type of clothes suggested on the clothes list may be very out of touch, whereas in fact it may be that pupils can get away with much trendier stuff.

Pack photos, posters, teddies and drawing pins/Blu-Tack. A diary too is a good idea – especially for a girl.

Encourage friends to come home with your child for visits at weekends or in holidays. Doing so will give her a reference point with her friends outside school.

Use e-mail to contact the housemaster/tutor. It's easier to alert him to possible concerns without making things such a 'big deal' as a phone call would.

Send on post from home and write letters, even if you see and phone your child regularly – they really appreciate it. Send them off too at the beginning of term with a nice pack of writing paper and envelopes as an 'encouragement'.

Since April 2002, all 600 accredited boarding schools have been subject to the Care Standards Act, which specifies 52 requirements covering all aspects of boarding school operation. One of these is that all children should have access to a private phone. To see the Act go to www.hmso.gov.uk/acts/acts2000/00014--i.htm#107.

For your child's phone calls, pay as you go with a phone card is the best system. Establish rules as to whom he can phone if you buy the phone card. For mobile phones, see page 199.

Tell your child that you will phone so many times a week, but that he can phone you. Avoid phoning every night. Establish a regime and try to stick to it. Don't be persuaded by him to ring more frequently. Phoning too often can make him feel more homesick when he might have been fine had you not phoned.

Money: agree an allowance with your child (taking advice from other parents who have children at the same school or from the housemaster/mistress) and agree what it should be used for. Are you going to pay for toothpaste etc. or is she?

Arrange for your child to stay at school some weekends, especially at the beginning. It's at the early stages that friendships are made and it can be disruptive if children come home too often.

Some homesickness is quite normal, but take what your child says with a pinch of salt. Separation is usually worse for the parent than the child. Children can play on your worries but a child will usually be perfectly happy five minutes after having been howling on phone, while you are left a nervous wreck for the day.

Trust the school to tell you if there is a real problem. You must be committed to the idea of boarding and make sure that your child knows that you are. Don't think that acceding to the child's requests to come home will make things better. Be cruel to be kind. It may take a while for your child to settle.

If it's not working – after you have given it your best shot – be brave enough to call it a day.

Gifted Children

Gifted children are usually recognised at primary school age, but if your older child accomplishes tasks with ease and then gets bored easily, wanting more challenges, he may well be very talented or gifted. See page 287.

Holiday Homework

For termtime homework, see page 148.

Holidays blighted by holiday homework? Don't let your child rest on his laurels for too long. A little done often is a whole lot easier than trying to cram the whole lot into the last few days of the holiday. Give your children time to relax, but set aside a period of time – perhaps two nights a week – when holiday homework has to be tackled.

Holidays blighted by the 'holiday diary'? As soon as school breaks up, invest in a new diary pad or notebook, and make life easier for when the child comes to write it up by encouraging her to jot down observations, places she has been each day. Alternatively agree that the diary will be written up every other night.

Take the pressure off the diary by keeping tickets and mementos yourself and presenting them at the end of the holiday when your child comes to complete the diary. You'll be the angel of mercy.

School Holidays

Even older children find it hard to adjust from the pace of school days to home life. They will not be able to relax into holiday mode immediately, and may get bored by the sudden lack of things to occupy them. Organise activities to do for the first forty-eight hours, or arrange to leave for your holiday as soon as school finishes.

It's tempting to make the Christmas holiday a riot of activity, excitement, visits to and from friends and family, late nights, etc., but as it comes at the end of a long and exhausting term try to set aside relaxation time too, because in no time at all the kids will have to go back at school.

It is within your rights to take your child out of school (state or independent) during term time for up to ten school days in any one school year. Beware, though: such a break may seem only a few days to you, but catching up on missed work and taking in new information missed can take a child weeks; sometimes half a term can go by before a child realises that they've missed a significant development in any subject.

For holiday homework, see page 202.

Exams

See page 238.

Parents' Meetings & Complaining

Avoid parents' meetings altogether. You are allotted too short a time to really discuss your child's development. Better to pretend that you can't go at that time and make an arrangement to see the teacher(s) in question after school. Chances are that you'll have much longer to talk.

Make a list before you go to which you can refer, so that you don't forget vital points.

Involve your child: ask him if there are any issues he would like you to discuss with a specific teacher. Raising problems may come better from you as a parent.

Need to make a complaint or take a stand? Resist picking up the phone and ranting, unless it is a very urgent matter. Put your feelings in writing. This gives you time to think about what you have to say and the head teacher time to read it, think about the contents and either act on it or prepare a response.

Secondary schools allow much less contact with teachers than primary. Don't be left in the dark. If you have worries, make an appointment to see the teacher(s)/head and air your views.

Fear Of School

Some children can show an exaggerated terror of school, for no apparent reason.

If you are confident that the school your child attends is the best one for her, and that the school is not the issue, encourage her to go back to school. If she falls behind with work she will face a whole new set of problems and anxieties. If necessary, and with the full support of the school, get tough.

The problem may be related to events at home – divorce, concern about siblings, bereavement – and symptoms are a severe separation anxiety, so take a look at the overall family picture. For more on such issues, see page 262.

Eliminate any physical illness – viruses and conditions like ME may be a root cause.

Work with the school and ensure that it is sympathetic and positive, and enlist the help of friends. Children can be very supportive of each other when there is a problem.

If the problem does not get better, ask your GP for referral to an educational psychologist.

Bullying

See page 151.

Truancy

Children play truant for lots of different reasons: peer pressure to do something daring and naughty, tensions and trouble at home or problems at school – bullying, disaffection, finding schoolwork too hard or even too easy and therefore boring. Try to find out what the problem is.

Even though children may object at the time, they need to know that someone is monitoring where they are and what they are doing. This lets them know that someone cares, and helps them feel more secure.

If your teenager's behaviour seems extreme, it could be attention-seeking or a sign that she is feeling upset or disturbed about something, such as the trauma of bereavement or divorce or separation, which can have a strong effect on young people. Is there a wider issue to be dealt with?

If you suspect that your child is playing truant from school act immediately.

- Talk to your child as soon as possible.

- Try to pick a time when you're both feeling relatively calm.

- However upset or angry you feel, talk to your child rather than punishing her.

- Let your child know how the situation makes you feel: 'I'm very upset/angry/worried that you have been missing school.' Such a statement starts a discussion on an equal and open footing.

- Try to avoid making your child the 'problem'. Make it clear that the problem is your child's behaviour, not your child, and that behaviour can always be changed.

- Let her know how worried and upset you are, but try to avoid blaming or shaming. These will undermine your child's confidence when lack of it may be the key issue.

- Stress the seriousness of the situation. Make sure that your child understands this, and that you, as his parent, have a responsibility to see he attends school. Say that you want to help, and ask him how you can both work things out together.

- Listen to what your child has to say. There may be valid reasons why your child has not wanted to go to school. Try to find out if she is having problems at school such as difficulties with work or bullying. If she tells you that there is a problem, ask if she has asked for help, and if so, has help been given? If not, discuss ways of tackling the school together.

- Discuss ways of tackling the situation and solving any problems.

- Be willing to negotiate with your child. Be willing to compromise and agree a solution that works for everybody – even if it's not perfect. It might be worth finding out from the school first if there is any way it can help.

- If the school has contacted you, talk to a teacher or the head to find out exactly what's been going on.

- Make a note of everything you want to say to the school and, if you prefer, take someone along with you for support.

- Try to talk calmly and work out a strategy to tackle the problem together.

- Make sure that teachers are aware of any problems your child is having.

Always look for the reason behind the truancy and try to work with teachers to sort out the problem.

Even if things get heated, you can always return to the subject another time. The important thing is to keep on trying to talk, but this takes patience and stamina. Make sure that you are as one with your spouse or partner about how to tackle the issue, and get support from family, friends and the school.

Would your child rather talk to someone else? Don't blame yourself. Sometimes teenagers have issues that they would rather not discuss with their parents. Suggest your child talks to a close family friend or priest, or encourage her to call ChildLine 0800 1111.

Try to spend more time together, even if you are not doing anything in particular. Just being together in a room with your child demonstrates your being there for them and your support. He will eventually talk to you about his problems. It is important to remain open and accepting, in order for your child to communicate his feelings to you, even if you do not agree with what he is saying.

If you have already been contacted by the school about your child's truancy, the school will expect to hear from you and you have a responsibility to reply. Try to talk to the school as soon as possible.

If you are worried about talking to the school, or if English is not your first language, ask at your library if there are local community organisations who can help you.

Telephone or write to the school to arrange a meeting with the teacher, head of year or deputy head.

Try to stay calm when talking to the teacher. If you feel angry or upset, say so, but try to avoid being aggressive. It is understandable that you might be feeling angry. Listen to what the teacher has to say, even if you disagree, then put forward some of your own suggestions and views.

It is important to understand everything that is being said about your child. The teacher should explain things clearly. If you still don't understand, ask again. Make a note for yourself of all the main points made at the meeting. This could be useful for future meetings.

If your child has been having problems at school, or even difficulties at home, let the school know what they are and ask what can be done to help. Sometimes a teacher is not aware that there have been problems. If the problem is bullying, for example, the school has a duty of care towards its pupils. Ask to see a copy of the school's anti-bullying policy, if it has one.

If you are not satisfied with the outcome of the meeting, make an appointment to see the head teacher or a parent governor.

If the school is threatening exclusion, find out what to expect next. You can request an information pack through the Exclusion Line at the Advisory Centre for Education on 020 7704 9822.

In general, try to become more involved with your child's school. Teachers generally appreciate the involvement of parents, step-parents and carers, through attending open evenings, helping with school productions and attending PTA meetings. As well as providing you with an opportunity to meet other parents, your participation in such events can help build your child's confidence and interest.

If you are a non-resident parent, you may still want to be involved with the school. So long as there is no court order to limit this, both parents are entitled to meet or speak to teachers, attend school functions and ask for a school report to be sent home. The involvement of a child's non-resident family, organised sensitively, can be extremely valuable to him.

Even as a non-resident parent you still have a vital part to play in helping your child's education. Try to keep in regular contact – write, phone, e-mail her – and take an interest in what she is learning.

Discipline

Your child's school has a right to discipline your child as it sees fit. Detention is one of the sanctions schools can use on disciplinary grounds. All schools, except independent and non-maintained special schools, have clear legal authority to detain pupils after the end of a school session without the consent of the parent. There is no risk of a legal action for false imprisonment if a pupil is being kept at school after the session without parental consent. This covers both lunchtime and after school detentions.

Before a school introduces detention as a sanction, the head teacher must make all parents, pupils and staff aware that teachers may use detention. If the head teacher has made all reasonable efforts to make the policy known, you will not be able to challenge the lawfulness of detention because you were unaware of it.

Detentions may be imposed only by a head teacher or another teacher specifically or generally authorised to do so. Staff should take account of:

- the child's age
- any special educational needs
- any religious requirements
- whether the parent can reasonably arrange for a child to get home from school after the detention.

The school must, by law, give at least twenty-four hours' written notice of a detention to you, the parent, so allowing time for you to raise any problems. A notice to a parent should say:

- that their child has been given a detention
- why detention was given
- when, where and for how long your child will have to remain at school.

If you object to the detention, call the school and explain why. The onus is on you to show why you think the detention is unreasonable. Examples of objections would be:

- that the detention is on a day of religious observance for the family
- that you are concerned about the length and safety of the walking route between the school and home
- that you cannot collect your child that day or make reasonable alternative transport arrangements.

The head teacher, or other authorised teacher, may decide that the child should have a detention despite your objections. You can complain to the head teacher and the governing body under the school's normal complaints procedures. However, a governing body has no power to overturn a decision to detain if it considers a complaint before the detention takes place.

If after-school detention is not possible, if for instance the pupil's only means of travelling home is on a bus leaving at the end of the school day and there is no other way the pupil can get home, ask the head teacher (or other authorised teacher) to consider detention at lunchtime or another suitable sanction.

Has your child's teacher been too rough? The Education Act 1996 empowers teachers and other staff in school to use 'reasonable force' to prevent students from committing a crime, causing or receiving an injury, causing damage or causing disruption – for example to prevent a young pupil running off a pavement on to a busy road, or to prevent a pupil hitting someone or throwing something. If you think the staff have been unreasonable, contact the head teacher in writing with full details of the situation.

Be wary of 'part conversations' from your child. He may come home incensed by a telling-off or a detention, but you may be getting only half the story. Before you grab the phone to the school, sit down and talk about what happened. Ask leading questions (but you're not a lawyer and this isn't a courtroom): 'What did you say to the teacher first/What did you do to elicit the telling-off?' You may find that he roundly deserved the punishment.

Time Out

Has your child been excluded from school? If so, note that each local education authority (LEA) has to make arrangements for 'the provision of suitable education at school or otherwise than at school for those children of compulsory school age who, by reasons of illness, exclusion from school or otherwise, may not for any period receive suitable education unless such arrangements are made for them'.

If your child is excluded from school for more than five days, the head teacher has to hold a discipline meeting with the governors. Make sure that you are involved in the situation throughout.

Has your child been excluded from school on medical grounds? For conditions such as head lice, schools have the right to ask a child not to return until he has been treated. If the infestation is chronic, the LEA medical officer may ask to see the child and has the power to suspend them. If your child is ill or has been injured, and cannot attend school, ask your LEA to arrange for your child to receive as much education as his illness allows.

Is your daughter pregnant and still at school? Schools, social services and the LEA should try to keep her at school if possible and to return her as soon as possible to full-time education once the baby is born. Pregnant girls who receive education out of school during their pregnancy should remain on the school roll so that they can return to school if they want to. For pregnancy, see page 234.

Friends At School

See page 150.

TRAVEL

Louis Braithwaite;
Nick French;
Marilyn Staples

This is a tweenie age for holidays. Too old to want sand and buckets, too young to go off alone. This age group will fit in more with holidays you enjoy.

Plan together and involve everyone in the planning of the holiday. Discuss all the options and ensure that the holiday itinerary contains activities that appeal to everyone.

Say what you want from a holiday in words that you will all understand. Teenagers have very different ideas about holiday fun, curfew hours and good entertainment. By speaking your mind you are more likely to be able to find a compromise.

Try something that you have never done before. The holiday will go better if you can find common ground. If Dad is into fishing, involve the whole family; if teenage son is into water skiing have a go yourself. You never know, you might like it!

Do an activity that interests you one day, and then let the kids have their day the next. Teenagers are much more likely to join in the spirit of, say, a trip to a castle if they know that they can go shopping/go carting/surfing tomorrow.

Keep them busy: activity holidays are the answer. Find destinations that involve sports (skiing is a winner at this age), especially water sports, and can involve the whole family at varying levels of skill. For information on British holidays, go to www.baha.org.uk, the site of the British Activity Holiday Association.

Companies like Canvas Holidays or Keycamp offer activities for this age group, as well as for younger (and older) members of the family.

Grit your teeth and choose vibrant destinations that have plenty of night life and other teenagers. Forget remote villas or farm holidays. Good bets are Crete, Corfu, the Balearic Islands, which also have more civilised holidays for adults.

Plan long weekends to European cities – they could even cope with the USA – but don't go too mad with museum visits. Shorter breaks will maintain their interest and broaden their horizons and experience.

Long-haul destinations – Bali, Thailand, etc. – need cost no more than a villa on the Med for two weeks in August.

Let them take a friend with them on holiday.

If you book a self-catering holiday, make sure that it is near enough to other similar properties where there will be other families.

Beaches are still fine, so long as there are safe water sports.

Find a holiday venue with water sports courses. Have lessons the first week and let them do it for themselves the second.

Send them off alone to an adventure holiday. See page 244.

8 FOURTEEN TO EIGHTEEN YEARS

'The world is going through troubled times. Today's young people only think of themselves. They have no respect for parents and old people. They've got no time for rules and regulations. To hear them talk, you would think they knew everything. And what we think of as wise, they just see as foolish.'

Peter the Monk, AD 1274

Welcome to what many parents consider to be the trickiest part of raising a child. In fact, more parents ask for help from experts and childcare charities at this stage than at any other. Suddenly the issues at stake are less practical and more emotional. Your children are growing up – adults in the making. They are facing more adult challenges, yet do not have the maturity to cope with them. They are becoming opinionated, independent, and very aware of their rights. They will challenge your authority, but are frequently frustrated as they are not able (legally or emotionally) to be as independent as they would like.

Suddenly you are faced with issues such as drugs and alcohol, and you are forced to wake up to the realisation that they are no longer innocent babies. It's a time when you will need to dig deepest into your resources of patience and understanding, but the following might help you stay friends with your teenager and come out the other side with a happy, confident adult.

What they can do at this age

At fourteen:

See page 172.

At fifteen:

- Open a Giro account with a guarantor

- See a category 15 film.

- In the case of boys, under certain circumstances, be sent to prison

At sixteen:

- Leave school and work full-time (though not in a bar, licensed premises or a betting shop)

- Leave home with parental consent

- Change their name with parental consent or a court order, by a change of name deed

- Marry with parental or court's consent (in Scotland without parental consent)

- Decide about their own health care and choose their own doctor

- Join a trade union

- In the case of girls, consent to sexual intercourse

- Buy cigarettes, tobacco, explosives and liqueur chocolates

- Drink, wine, beer, port, cider or sherry with a meal in the dining room area of a pub or hotel

- Buy lottery tickets, scratch cards or premium bonds
- Enter a brothel
- Consent to homosexual acts
- Become a street trader
- Use a pump at a petrol station
- Drive a moped up to 50ccs, a small tractor, mowing machine or invalid car
- Join the armed forces (with parental consent)
- Be used for begging
- Fly solo in a helicopter
- Fly solo in a glider
- Apply for legal advice or assistance
- Use an air gun in restricted places.

At seventeen:

- Drive a motorcycle, car or small goods vehicle (up to 3.5 tons) or a large tractor on the highway
- Buy or hire a firearm and ammunition
- Fly a plane solo
- Get a helicopter pilot's licence
- Be tried like an adult for a criminal offence
- If a girl, join the armed forces (with parental consent).

At eighteen:

See page 247.

Legal rights

Until the age of seventeen, if a young person is detained by police his or her rights are determined by the Police Code of Practice (see page 172). After the age of seventeen, if a young person is detained by police, they have the same rights as an adult.

BEHAVIOUR (OR LIVING WITH KEVIN)

Glynis Fletcher; Sarah Lelliott; Parentline Plus; the Trust for the Study of Adolescence (produces many publications and videos to help and support parents with teenagers – see page 303); Rachel Billington, PGL Adventure Holidays

It is OK to have rules. Even teenagers feel secure knowing where the boundaries lie.

Saying to a child over 16, 'You are not to sleep with a boy/girlfriend in this house' is fine. It's your house and you can set the house rules. Under 16 and they are actually breaking the law.

Blanket ban rules may not always work. 'You are not to smoke anywhere' may be unrealistic. 'No smoking at home or in my car' may be better.

If you don't address issues (drugs, drink, smoking), they won't just go away.

It is natural for teenagers to challenge their parents' authority; as they become adults they want their own authority. But be strong on some things – sometimes children push you to the limits to find out when you will say no. Sometimes, saying no shows them that you care and makes them feel secure. It sets a boundary, so that both you and your child know where you stand.

Teenagers and respect: they have an issue with this. Teenagers feel that they are expected to respect their parents, but that their parents don't respect them and their opinions. You have been warned!

Respect teenagers' privacy. Explain that there are times when you need to go into their room (to put away clothes, open the windows, let in the environmental health officer), but always knock first.

You may think that your children treat you like a fossil – they may even think of you as a fossil – but in truth you are their rock.

You have to stand firm, but if you have never been in control, you are not going to get it suddenly.

Be consistent, but that should be an aim not a tyranny.

It is good to give teenagers privileges, such as being able to stay up later one night, going on a trip to town, having a lie in. But explain to your child that the privileges will be taken away if he breaks any of the rules in place. Teenagers soon lose respect for adults if they play up and are not punished in some way.

When a youngster does something wrong, he needs to be told what he has done wrong and also be motivated to change. Let him know what you expect from him, and come up with an 'action plan' together to help him improve. Watch his behaviour and give him feedback. Never do this in front of his peers.

Children very regularly tell you about their rights and it sometimes seems that they have the right to everything the world offers. Whenever a youngster says, 'I have the right to …', try to look for another person's right that is more important. A youngster is doing archery and you ask him not to shoot the arrow straight up into the air. He answers that it is his bow and arrow and he has the right to shoot the arrows where he wants. In reply, tell him that may be correct, but the other people around have as much right to their eyesight as you have to shoot your arrows.

'Attitude' is one of the biggest perennial problems parents come up against. Give as many positive and corrective comments on attitude as you do on performance and behaviour. Often the reason behind a youngster's misbehaviour is her attitude towards something, and if you can change that, it becomes easier to control.

Does a teenager have a full understanding of what she is expected to do? It is no good saying to a teenager, 'I want your room tidy by the end of the day.' What is tidy to a teenager will be very different to an adult and most adults have different standards. A teenager needs to know exactly what standard she is expected to achieve. Don't tell her to get up 'at a reasonable time' as that could be anything from 7.00 a.m. to midday. She needs to have clear instructions.

Youngsters love hearing their own name. When you are talking to one, use his name.

Are you being fair? Sometimes the root of a problem lies with the adult. If your sixteen-year-old son stayed out until 11.00 p.m., there should be no reason why his sister can't at the same age. Youngsters get very cross when a younger child or someone of the opposite sex is allowed something that they were not allowed at their age, or it looks as though it is being given just because the other child is a girl/boy.

Don't 'um' and 'ah'! Straight strong answers to questions and requests come across well and make the youngster feel that you are in control. If you don't know an answer, find it out and then go back and tell her.

Is your child loath to leave a party when you are collecting her? Say that you will be at the end of the road at a certain time and, if she isn't there, you will come into the party and dance!

If you are angry or worried, say so, but try to avoid losing your temper and saying or doing something that will cause your child to distance herself from you. Threats or punishment (such as not allowing them to go out) may only make her more resentful and talking more difficult. Try sitting down and discussing the matter with your teenager at a time when you and she are feeling calmer.

Give your child credit for admitting to mistakes before you hear about them from school/other people. The fact that he has told you first shows a degree of respect for you. Even though you may be angry, say thank you for owning up.

Want to avoid confrontation? When clothes, for example, are thrown on the floor, instead of being irritated, be calm and try saying, 'When you drop your clothes on the floor, I feel cross/frustrated because …' and explain the consequences: 'They will become creased/someone may trip on them, etc.' The third stage is to ask, 'What can we do about it?'

'I'm leaving home!' It is typical for teenagers to stomp off screaming that they hate you and are leaving. It's highly unlikely that they will leave for good, but they may need time to let off steam. If your child walks out, a discreet phone call to one of her friends (make sure that you have the mobile number) or to the friend's parents might locate her, or at least help you find out where she has gone.

When your child returns, do not fly off the handle, no matter how worried you have been. Let the dust settle; then sit down and talk about it. Explain that you were worried because you didn't know where she was, and face the conflict calmly.

Rather than being confrontational, talk about issues generally that pertain to a problem at home – this might involve mentioning the dangers of drugs, smoking, or the irritation of sulking. There is less likely to be a row if you are not being accusatory.

Try not to argue with teenagers. It does not matter if you are right and they are wrong; you won't be right in their eyes, and after the argument has ended they will still think you are wrong. They need to be given the opportunity for two-way communication. Listen to them, don't interrupt and take their side of a story seriously. Then you can say your bit. This way you can have an adult discussion with them and, if they do start to interrupt, you can ask them not to as you didn't with them. Get them to give their side of any trouble first: you may look silly if you say your bit and have the facts wrong.

Don't say 'don't'! Teenagers, like the rest of humanity, respond to requests better than orders.

Let things ride occasionally. Is your child's room a health hazard? Bite your tongue and be relaxed about mess. Your child will soon get fed up when her favourite jeans never made it into the laundry/earrings go missing under the debris/she can no longer open the door.

A strategy that works for some is the action replay. If your teenager swears at you when you say, for example, that a friend cannot stay over, and then flounces out, slamming the door, wait until she returns. Say calmly then that you are not happy for the sleepover, that you are happy to discuss your reasons, but first she must start the conversation again. When she finally does – after much raising of eyebrows – respond as if the bad behaviour had never happened.

Another idea is to punish a rude teenager with a withdrawal of cooperation: no lifts to friends, no washing, no meals. He will soon ask what is going on and you can then tell him that you will not tolerate rudeness.

Your teenager will recover from a row much quicker than you will.

If your teenager's done something wrong that it's too late to stop – for instance, he's got drunk – it can often make matters worse if you go in shouting and telling off. That will make a teenager defensive. If what he has done is not endangering anyone else, wait until the situation is back in control and then talk about it. Make him realise that you are unhappy with his actions. Discussing the situation then is more likely to make him feel that he has let you down and think twice about doing it again.

Communication

Keep channels open: Endeavour to have at least one meal a day together. This might be breakfast, or even a few moments over a cup of tea and a biscuit, but it's a time when talking might be possible.

Have a wipe-clean board in the kitchen where the family say where they are going to be. Include your own movements too, so that the comings and goings of the family are known to everyone.

Some families have a once-weekly meeting, chaired by a different member of the family each time. You needn't discuss things that are heavy; just keep everyone up to date with who is doing what.

For some, it works well to have an evening each week when the family meet over supper. It's a family commitment, and everyone should do their very best to be there. Make it a special event, with your children taking turns in choosing and preparing the meal (even if it's a dish you don't really approve of).

There are four key times of day to 'be there' for your teenagers: early morning, straight after school, suppertime and bedtime.

Affection should be unconditional. They also need to hear that you love them.

Confidence

Missing the cuddles? As children develop into teenagers, they lose confidence. They have this body that they are not quite sure how to cope with. Their body language says 'Don't touch me' but cuddles and physical affection can be very beneficial – loving but non-sexual. Rather than suffocate your child with physical affection, lay a hand on her back or shoulder as you talk to her at the kitchen sideboard. Comment on how nice their hair looks and touch it.

Teenagers feel immense pressure from their peers – much more so than from teachers or parents. They want to be seen to be cool, doing the right thing, behaving in a way acceptable to their age group. We all want to be liked and accepted, but the influences may be negative ones. A child with a strong sense of self and good self-esteem will be able to know when the pressure of that influence is not worth bowing to, and that kind of self-confidence comes from the adults in his or her life.

Parents are embarrassing. If you embarrass your teenager, you will never be forgiven, especially if you do so in a public place or in front of her friends, and she will pretend she has never met you before. If your penchant is for outrageous clothes, tone it down in public for her sake, and for heaven's sake don't dance in front of her.

Teenagers are work in progress. A happy and confident teenager is one who has plenty of self-esteem. As much as teenagers may drive you mad with mess/lack of communication/thoughtlessness, try to balance criticism with positive comments. If your child walks in and drop sports kit on the floor, ask how the game went and show pleasure if he did well, before you politely ask him to put the kit in the laundry basket.

If children are praised for good behaviour and you take an interest in what they are doing, they will feel good about themselves and be more able to think for themselves and express their own opinions. This is the basis of a confident teenager, who will be less likely to be dependent on her peer group for approval, and less tempted to go along with drugs/drinking/smoking in order to 'fit in'.

Descriptive praise is a great technique in building self-esteem. Be more interested than just 'That's fantastic' about a picture or good piece of work. Ask them questions about why they chose the subject/how much research they had to do. This also applies to jobs done around the house. 'Thank you for laying the table. I was in a hurry and that has helped me enormously' works better than a grunted 'About time' or worse, ignoring what they have done altogether.

Treat teenagers like adults. Show that you respect them with small details, like allowing them to sit in the front occasionally when you all go out in the car, even if you hate travelling in the back. Chances are a lanky teenage boy will need the leg room anyway.

It is easy to focus on a problem and forget to look at the good aspects of your child. Praise is very important, and you may not be giving it as much as you think.

Going Out

Curfew nightmares? For every, say, half hour your child is late back from a curfew, reduce the time he can go out next time by the same amount.

Worried about your child when she is out in the evening? You are not alone. James T. Adams wisely wrote: 'Any astronomer can predict with absolute accuracy just where every star in the universe will be at 11.30 tonight. He cannot make such a prediction about his teenage daughter.'

Before having a party at home, set some ground rules. Possible issues to talk about and agree on include:

- Is alcohol going to be provided? If so, what types?
- How will the young person/parent deal with party-goers who bring drinks that you've agreed won't be available?
- What can be done to help prevent drink-related trouble?
- Will the party be open house or by invitation only?
- Should parents be around – but in the background?
- Who will clear up and when?

Getting home safely after a night out: here you can make rules. Agree that your teenager:

- Will not drive if they have been drinking.
- Will not be a passenger if the driver has been drinking.
- Will not spend their cab fare home on other things.
- Will tell you where they are going.
- And that you will try not to interfere in their social life if these rules are kept.

Teenagers In A Group

When dealing with teenagers in groups, it is important to try to make sure that the youngsters are open and honest. It is better for you to know what is going on and for them to feel that they are being given a bit of freedom than for them to 'hide' in order to do things that they are not allowed to do. You might, for instance, decide to allow them a certain amount of alcohol, to be drunk in a designated place. This way they do not have to sneak off and the drinking can be supervised to make sure that they are not being excessive, and the teenagers are made to feel quite grown up.

Make sure that teenagers are aware that one person may ruin it for everyone else by being selfish and breaking the rules.

Get teenagers to think up the rules to live by but steer them to the rules you want. For example, ask them what time they think they should go to bed – they will always say some silly, late time. Say what time you think bedtime should be – some very early time. You can normally then, by bartering, get them to the time you want, and they will think that by bartering you up they have come out on top. The important bit of this is that the youngsters feel that they have decided on the 'rule', although really you have yourself.

As far as possible, 'punish' the group rather than the individual for minor rule breaking. This works well, as your child's friends get cross with him rather than you and his friends' disapproval may be a more powerful deterrent than yours.

As at home, adults with groups of youngsters need to set good examples and be good role models. On activity holidays, as far as possible follow the same rules as those for the kids: noise levels on site, equipment worn on activities, seatbelts on coaches.

Give youngsters choices: for example, if you say, 'If you don't stop swearing, you will be asked to leave the activity,' they can either stop or continue, but if they do continue with the swearing they will have to go. It is important to make sure the consequences are fair.

Target the leader in a group – there always is one – and then use him to get all the others to 'toe the line'. Such an individual loves feeling that you are giving him responsibility.

Don't embarrass them! It does no good at all. If you embarrass a youngster in front of his friends, he will lose respect for you. Teasing, however, can work very well – if the child can take it. In an activity holiday situation, you may have a group of boys who are persistently messy in the dining hall. Make them wash up as a group and clean the dining area. Give them aprons and then make sure that some of the other kids see them. Everyone will get a laugh out of it, including the boys, and next time they go into the dining room, you will probably see them telling the other youngsters to keep the area tidy for you.

It's easy to have a good relationship with an outgoing, popular youngster, but harder with the shyer ones. Make sure that you let shyer youngsters get involved. They may, however, be loners and quite happy sitting on their own, watching all the others. If they say no to joining in, take no to be the answer and keep an eye on them. Ensure that they are up to the activities you are trying to involve them in. It is no good trying to get an overweight youngster who has never played basketball before to join in a game of basketball with boys who play for their school. Look too at the bigger picture. If a girl with greasy hair is getting picked on, it's easy to assume that she is unhygienic, but she may be very self-conscious about communal showering. Show her where there are more private facilities.

Disagreements Over Appearance

You think he looks like something the cat dragged in? Let your child know what you consider acceptable and unacceptable. It is also important to recognise that your relationship with your teenager is changing and it may no longer be possible to tell him what to do. Your child is becoming an independent young adult and beginning to make choices of his own.

Be clear what your own values are, and be willing to listen to your teenager's views as well. This will make discussion and compromise possible. Come to an agreement about what is acceptable to you, and what she won't see as 'old-fashioned'. You may not like the top she has chosen, but will you accept the rest if she changes that?

Young people are very conscious of how they look. Let them know why you feel differently to them about the way they dress. But try not to be critical – it will only lead to more arguments. The way they dress is important to them feeling good about themselves, and helps them feel accepted by their friends.

Appear ready to go out and the clothes are ghastly? Ignore the negatives, and comment on how much you like their hair/top/make-up.

There are many other, strong influences on teenagers – such as friends, the media and the culture that they are growing up in, which may be different from your own – but remember that your teenager will still look to you for guidance – even though it may not seem that way.

Does your daughter dress like a tart? Some clothes can look stylish, but some in a similar style can look positively salacious. Explain that these sort of clothes give out the wrong sort of messages and may result in attention from boys and men that she would not welcome (or know how to deal with). Ask her which pop stars/celebrities she most admires, and point out the 'cool' ones who manage to look good without looking cheap.

See also Shopping, Clothes & Presents, page 236.

Sleep & Moods

Trouble getting them out of bed? Teenagers need at least nine hours' sleep – and something to do with a shift in their body clock (or circadian rhythm) makes them want to stay up late and get up late. Give them an alarm clock that goes off at the same time on school days.

Like anyone else, tired teenagers are horrible people. Are they getting enough sleep?

It's the hours before midnight that result in the best night's sleep – get them to bed before the witching hour and discourage late night TV viewing, which can be a stimulant.

Go into your teenager's room in the morning and open the curtains. Cruel, but it helps to reset their body clock.

Some reassuring science for parents of moody teenage girls: male and female brains are different. The female brain has 15 per cent more blood flowing into the brain than men's, which is why women process more emotional material. Women also have more oxytocin, and the level rises when they see a pet or a baby and want to hold it. Female hormones are directly linked to mood regulation, whereas testosterone is not so directly linked.

Parental Survival

Shortcomings in your child's character may remind you horribly of yourself, but try not to be racked with guilt: they may not be inherited from you. Your child is also her own person, and there is not always a logical reason for her terrible temper/shyness or whatever it may be.

A wise American once wrote: 'Teenagers who are never required to vacuum are living in one.' Get your children to help around the house. It's good training and anyway, why on earth should you do it all?

Feeling run down? Parents need to look after themselves as well as be carers. Write a list of all the things you used to enjoy doing before you had children, and before you lost your evenings (you may well be turning in for bed nowadays before they do). If you loved going to the pictures/drawing/walking/gardening, make sure that you allocate time to do those things again. You will be more relaxed and a more effective parent if you are spending time doing things you enjoy too.

Don't be afraid to ask for help. There is no shame is needing support from others in the same boat or experts in childrearing. The fact that people become 'qualified' shows that parenting's a difficult job!

Keep a sense of humour: this is the single most important element of parenting. If you find a situation ridiculous – you've been rowing for forty-five minutes about what colour socks your child can wear – then laugh. It will defuse the situation. One mother, driven mad by her teenager's mess, wrote little poems about the washing up and her son's trainers begging to be allowed back into his room.

ALCOHOL, DRUGS & SMOKING

Alcohol

Glynis Fletcher;
Alan Weaver; Lifeline,
Department of Health;
Quitline; Peter
Reynard; Bill Smith

Some pubs and clubs do not rigorously enforce minimum age limits for drinking. This is especially true with girls who often look older then they are, and bars actively want to encourage girls to frequent them. Remind your children that it is an offence to drink alcohol under the age of eighteen.

Spiking drinks: drinks served in glasses are more vulnerable to being spiked. Suggest to your children that they drink bottled drinks and keep drinks with them all the time. Keeping a finger over the spout of a bottle will discourage people from tampering with drinks.

Be reasonable. Teenagers will want to stay until closing time, so it's better to try and stay awake and offer to collect them at eleven than to embarrass and anger them by collecting them earlier.

Conversations about alcohol can all too easily turn into lectures, accusations or rows. Try to stay calm. Show that your main concern is your child's health, safety and well-being. Discuss how you feel about your child's safety, the possible effects of alcohol, the pressure she may feel from friends, or any strong beliefs you have about alcohol.

Try to explain clearly how you feel but listen to your child's point of view. Talk to each other, not at each other, and compromise. If he says he will be sensible, you have to trust him until he breaks that trust.

Think about how your child may view alcohol: she may be curious about it; not want to be left out; want to drink alcohol because her friends say that their parents let them; want to do something that adults do.

Be realistic and give your kids some sound advice on how to drink without getting drunk (eating first to line the stomach, drinking plenty of water) and how to cope with hangovers.

We all had to get very drunk once to realise how terrible it can feel. If your teenager is very drunk, stay with him to make sure he doesn't vomit – and to be with him when he does – but try not to be too judgemental when he wakes up next morning feeling like hell. It's part of life's rich tapestry …

Remember to explain to your kids that after a binge the night before they may still have a dangerous amount of alcohol in their blood the morning after – too much to drive, operate machinery or concentrate.

Worried your child's drinking has got out of hand? Get further information and advice from:

- Alcohol Concern – 0207 928 7377 – for general information about alcohol.

- National Alcohol Helpline – 0800 917 8282 – all calls are free. For confidential information, help and advice if you are worried about a young person's drinking, the drinking of someone else in the family, or your own drinking.

- Al-Anon Family Groups – 0207 403 0888 – for the families of people with drinking problems.

- Alateen Groups – 0207 403 0888 – for teenagers in families where someone has a drinking problem.

The Health Education Authority produces a range of leaflets about alcohol. To order copies, phone Marston Book Services: 01235 465 565. Your local health promotion unit (in the phone book under Health Promotion Unit or Health Education Unit) may also have copies.

For alcohol and parties and going out, see page 214.

See also page 178.

Drugs

Fifty-nine per cent of young people will have tried cannabis by the time they are eighteen (*Key Data on Adolescence 2001*). You can help teenagers resist temptation, though, by making sure they know about drugs (see page 178) and are understanding the information they receive at school, and have thought carefully about it.

Make sure that your kids know the law. The main law is the Misuse of Drugs Act, which divides drugs into three classes:

Class A: cannabis oil, cocaine and crack, ecstasy, heroin, methadone, processed magic mushrooms, LSD and amphetamine if it is injected

Class B: amphetamine, cannabis resin and herb

Class C: some tranquillisers.

Explain to your kids how disastrous it is to have a criminal record, and how easily they could end up with one.

If your kids feel under pressure to buy drugs, suggest that they reply to anyone who offers them something, 'No thanks, I'm sorted.' It's a much more face-saving reply than 'My mum/dad said I mustn't.'

Remind your kids that 'supplying drugs' does not have to be on the scale of South American drug barons who illegally import kilos of the stuff. It can mean one person from a group, which has pooled its money, going off to buy a small amount of drugs for the group.

The law affects you too. It is illegal for you to allow your house to be used by a child to smoke cannabis, but it is not illegal for you to destroy it if you find it – that is, flush it down the loo – and you do not have to tell the police.

Know where and how to get help if you or your kids need it.

If your children tell you that they have used drugs, the worst thing you can do is fly off the handle. The only thing you will ensure is that they never tell you again. Try to stay calm and talk it through.

Keep it all in perspective: even if children try out drugs, very few of them get into serious problems. Talk to other parents and share concerns. They may have more experience and strategies they have used which have been effective.

If your child is caught with illegal drugs, get some advice from a solicitor, or ask at the police station to speak to the duty solicitor. See also Legal Rights, page 210.

The National Drugs Helpline number is 0800 776 600.

Smoking

For advice on preventing your children from smoking, see page 179.

If your teenager is smoking, try helping him to quit. He has to want to give up – you cannot force him. If he wants to, try the following:

- If he needs to put something in his mouth, suggest he tries sugar-free chewing gum, or something healthy and non-fattening.
- If he needs to do something with his hands, suggest he finds something to fiddle with – a pencil, a coin or anything but a cigarette.

- Suggest that he tries drinking juice or eating fruit when he feels like having a cigarette.

- One day at a time: congratulate him and remind him to congratulate himself each day he hasn't had a cigarette. Inspire him to make it his goal to get through each day.

- There will be times when he feels tempted to give in. Remind him why he is stopping and be positive.

- Reward him after one week and again after one month.

- Keep him busy. Boredom will present temptations.

- Suggest that he keeps away from friends who smoke until he feels that his resolve is strong enough. Friends who still smoke may be jealous of his success and pressurise him to have 'just one'.

- Remind him that alcohol will lessen his resolve.

- Give him the number of Quitline: 0800 002 200 – for help, guidance and counselling and a free info pack for those who want to stop.

If you smoke, and discover that your child is too, give up together and set yourselves a big treat to do together (a holiday perhaps) when you have quit.

FRIENDS

See page 177.

FOOD

British Nutrition Foundation; Dr Sarah Schenker SRD

Fuel them up. Calorie needs vary but broadly speaking a boy of fifteen to eighteen years needs 2755 kilocalories per day, a girl 2110 kilocalories.

Teenagers have the same blood-sugar-level lows as young kids. If they are grumpy, they may well just be hungry. A bowl of cereal or a banana is a good boost.

A recent survey amongst the fifteen-to-eighteen-years age group showed that intakes of a number of essential minerals like zinc, iron and calcium are low, partly because children are not eating enough milk and red meat. Teenagers are also eating high amounts of saturated fatty acids, non-milk extrinsic sugars and salt, and not eating enough fibre. On average, British children are eating less than half the recommended five portions of fruit and vegetables per day. Though you can't keep an eye on everything they eat, whilst you are still providing meals it's worth over-compensating with the right foods.

Teenagers not eating enough fruit and veg? Try making up a fruit milk shake with semi-skimmed milk, bananas, strawberries, raspberries. They can drink it and still have the benefit of calcium and fruit.

Growing children need iron (see page 192), B vitamins (folate, riboflavin, thiamin) and vitamin D, particularly during the winter months. Recent research showed that teenagers were lacking in the right vitamins too, often because they skip breakfast – cereals have a high vitamin content. Adequate levels of vitamin D are required for the absorption of calcium, which in turn is required for the development and maintenance of strong bones. If you can't persuade your kids to eat cereals, you may need to encourage them to take a vitamin supplement.

Lead by example. If your diet includes lots of fruit and veg, your children are more likely to accept the message. If you skip breakfast, it gives a bad message to your children, and they are likely to copy your habits.

Concerned about under-eating? Girls especially will skip meals and chew gum to suppress their appetite. Try to be present at meals with them, especially breakfast, and offer a variety of interesting but nourishing choices.

'I feel fat' can be a cry for help: 'I feel sad, overwhelmed, lonely.' If your daughter is dieting for no apparent reason, try to ask gently what her reasons are for doing it.

If you are not in the habit of doing so already, let your children contribute to ideas for and the preparation of food. It's good practice and fun too. Hand over one meal a week to them to prepare. Any Jamie Oliver recipe will be cool enough.

Remember not to mention your own unhappiness at your weight. Your teenager will think it is OK to be obsessed with her body.

For eating disorders, see page 224.

Overweight Children

Children grow at an alarming rate – about 10in/25cm during puberty before reaching their full adult height – but they can also put on weight. It's quite a modern phenomenon and comes as a result of a diet of fast food like chips and hamburgers, and too little exercise.

Avoid buying sweets and snacks – we all know the temptations of a full biscuit tin. Make sure that the fruit bowl is overflowing.

Encourage exercise as well as healthy eating:

- Instead of taking short trips in the car to buy things from the local shop, encourage your children to walk or cycle there themselves.

- Exchange pocket money for physical jobs around the house and garden.

- Again, lead by example. If you aren't exercising, why should your children?

- Avoid nagging. Make exercise fun. Go bike riding with your children. Go swimming with them. Drop them at the pool with friends. Children do not want to be route marched because 'it's good for them'.

If your child is overweight, provide rewards when weight is lost. A new pair of jeans, a new pair of trainers …

Try not to go on about weight all the time or discuss your child's weight in front of other people. It's humiliating for her.

Is your child comfort eating? He may have anxieties which run deep. Talk to him about problems he might have at school or with friends. Eating can be a way of burying problems.

Check out what your child is eating at school by asking to see the menus. If the food is stodgy and high in fats and calories, see if there is an alternative option or the option of a packed lunch.

Vegetarians

Vegetarianism is very popular with teenagers, particularly young girls. Don't dismiss their choice if your child decides to go that route. It may be a life choice or a passing phase, but it is part of striking out as an individual. Your role is still to see that he eats well, so try to work out recipes together, resisting the urge to throw down the wooden spoon and say, 'Well, you'll have to fend for yourself.'

The key to a healthy vegetarian diet (that is, a diet without meat or fish) is variety.

A healthy, varied vegetarian diet includes fruits, vegetables, plenty of leafy greens, whole grain products, nuts, seeds and pulses, dairy products and eggs. If your teenager is vegetarian, make sure that she is eating plenty of protein and calcium (see below), iron (see page 192) and vitamin B12.

Vegetarian teens eating varied diets rarely have any difficulty getting enough pro-

tein as long as their diet contains enough energy (calories) to support growth. Cow's milk and cheese are protein sources; beans, breads, cereals, nuts, peanut butter, tofu and soya milk are also some foods that are especially good sources of protein.

You don't need to plan particular combinations of foods to obtain enough protein or amino acids (components of protein). A mixture of plant proteins eaten throughout the day will provide enough essential amino acids.

Include three or more good sources of calcium in your child's diet every day. Cow's milk and dairy products contain calcium, as do tofu processed with calcium sulphate, green leafy vegetables including greens, mustard greens and kale, and calcium-fortified soya milk and orange juice.

A vegetarian teenager needs to eat a varied diet to meet the body's iron needs. For foods that are high in iron, see page 192.

Vegans (vegetarians eating no dairy products, eggs, meat or fish) need to add vitamin B12 to their diet. Some cereals and fortified soya milk have vitamin B12 (check the label).

HEALTH

www.kidshealth.org; Dr Helen Gunton; Diabetes UK; National Centre for Eating Disorders; Eating Disorders Association; the Eyecare Trust; British Dental Health Foundation www.dentalhealth.org.uk); Miriam Fitch, dentist

Children under sixteen are entitled to confidential advice from their GP and the Family Planning Association. They may be advised to talk over issues with you, but for their own protection, their privacy will be respected. From sixteen your child has control over her own healthcare and can change to a GP she prefers.

Depression

Your child spends lots of time in his room, with the curtains shut. He may sleep a lot, laugh rarely and be uncommunicative. It could be normal teenage behaviour, but there may be something more seriously wrong. It's possible that your child is depressed.

As many as 1 in every 33 children may have depression; in adolescents, that number may be as high as 1 in 8. A depressive state, or mood, can linger for a long time – weeks, months, or even longer – and if it limits a child's ability to function normally, it can be diagnosed as depression.

Two types of depression, major depression and dysthymia, can affect children. Major depression is characterised by a number of symptoms (see below), including a persistent sad mood and the inability to feel pleasure or happiness. A child with major depression feels depressed for most of the day, almost every day. If the sadness is not as severe but continues for a year or longer, the condition may be dysthymia (see below). Bipolar disorder is another type of mood disturbance and is characterised by episodes of low-energy depression (sadness and hopelessness) and high-energy mania (irritability and explosive temper).

Depressed children have described themselves as feeling hopeless about everything or feeling that nothing is worth the effort. They honestly believe that they are 'no good' and that they're helpless to do anything about it. If your child is depressed, she may blame herself, so push away your approaches to help. Persist without nagging.

If you think your child is depressed, you will both need the support of your GP, who may diagnose depression if your child has had five or more of the following symptoms for more than two weeks:

- a feeling of being down or really sad for no reason
- a lack of energy, and a feeling of inability to do the simplest task
- an inability to enjoy the things that used to bring pleasure
- a lack of desire to be with friends or family members
- feelings of irritability, anger or anxiety
- an inability to concentrate or care about appearance
- a marked weight gain or loss (or failure to gain weight as expected), and little or too much interest in eating
- a significant change in sleep habits, such as trouble falling asleep or getting up
- feelings of guilt or worthlessness
- aches and pains even though nothing is physically wrong
- a lack of caring about what happens in the future
- frequent thoughts about death or suicide.

A child will be diagnosed as having dysthymia if she has experienced two or more of the following symptoms almost all the time for at least a year:

- feelings of hopelessness
- low self-esteem
- sleeping too much or being unable to sleep
- extreme fatigue
- difficulty concentrating
- lack of appetite or overeating.

Depressed children and teens are more likely to use alcohol and drugs than those who aren't depressed, because they provide a momentary escape from the symptoms of depression. They can make a depressed child feel even worse.

Don't dismiss your concerns or think that the symptoms will go away by themselves. If your child is showing these symptoms you need to take them seriously. They won't go away and they may get worse.

Don't think that you're responsible for your child's depression – even if something you did (such as a divorce) triggered it. It's not your fault. It's nobody's fault. Depression is an illness and should be treated as such.

Your GP may refer your child to the local child and adolescent mental health service. Sorting out stresses may be enough to solve the problem, or the service may recommend a psychological approach such as cognitive therapy. Medication may also be advised, but this is rarely a first-line treatment for teenagers.

Let your child know that you are there for her, whenever she needs you and wherever you may be. Remind your child of this over and over again – she may need to hear it a lot because she feels unworthy of love and attention.

If your child shuts you out, don't walk away – remain there for her. Once she begins to talk to you, let her talk about whatever she wants to talk about and don't criticise. The important thing is that she's talking and communicating her feelings. This will help her begin to realise that her feelings and thoughts really do matter, that you truly care about her and that you never stopped caring even when she became depressed.

Do something regularly together, even something as simple as washing the dishes or going for a drive. It might give you a chance to talk and discover what is making her so miserable.

For more information go to www.rcpsych.ac.uk, the website of the Royal College of Psychiatrists, which has free fact sheets on child and adolescent mental health issues (020 7235 2351). Or www.youngminds.org.uk. Young Minds offers advice and support on mental health problems affecting children and young people (020 7336 8445).

Diabetes

There are two types of diabetes, but the one most likely to affect children is Type I, when the body produces no insulin at all. It can appear at any time, but it is most common for early symptoms to appear in the late teens and early twenties.

Symptoms to look out for include:

- increased thirst
- visits to the loo all the time – especially at night
- extreme tiredness
- weight loss
- genital itching or regular episodes of thrush
- blurred vision.

If you are concerned about your child or have a family history of the disease, take your child to see your doctor.

The charity Diabetes UK has a Teen Zone which is useful for teenagers who have the disease: go to www.diabetes.org.uk/teenzone/index.html. There is also a Parent Zone at www.diabetes.org.uk/manage/parents.htm. The charity also runs a Careline on 020 7424 1030, open Monday to Friday, 9.00 a.m.–5.00 p.m.

Eating Disorders

Anorexia nervosa is a psychological illness and sufferers have an obsessive desire to lose weight by refusing to eat. Many may exercise vigorously or use slimming pills to keep their weight as low as possible. Female anorexics often stop menstruating. The grave danger is the effect lack of the right nutrients can have on a growing body.

There are lots of warning signs, which include:

- rapid weight loss

- eating much less than usual or making excuses for eating somewhere else

- refusing certain types of food, or making a fuss about dressings, butter on vegetables, etc.

- refusing to eat with you

- excessive exercising

- refusing to acknowledge that anything is wrong – to the point of becoming aggressive about it.

Bulimia nervosa sufferers are also obsessed with the fear of gaining weight, though they may not actually lose weight. There is a recurring pattern of binge eating followed by self-induced vomiting. The foods eaten tend to be high in carbohydrate and fat. Sufferers may also use large quantities of laxatives, slimming pills or strenuous exercise to control their weight. Many bulimics have poor teeth because of regular vomiting – vomit is acidic and can erode teeth.

Warning signs of bulimia include:

- disappearance to the bathroom after meals

- running water or turning the radio on loud to disguise the sound of vomiting

- spraying a lot of air freshener

- food disappearing in large amounts and wrappers being hidden behind cushions or under pillows

- stashing food or laxatives.

Anorexics and bulimics are often very secretive about their eating habits. Before the sufferer can be treated for her disorder it must be recognised, not only by a doctor, friend or family member, but also by herself. If an anorexic is very underweight it is obviously important to persuade her to eat and seek medical advice as soon as possible. Both anorexics and bulimics will need some kind of psychiatric treatment.

If you suspect that your child has an eating disorder, look at the whole picture. Are her studies suffering at school? Is she withdrawn or avoiding a normal social life? Is she being secretive or lying to you? Is she suffering mood swings above and beyond those one would expect from a teenager?

Trust your instincts. If you suspect there is something wrong, there probably is.

What to do:

- Let your child know that you are concerned, without being hostile.

- Try to discuss your worries in a calm way, rehearsing what you are gong to say beforehand. Confrontation will not achieve anything.

- Choose a time when you are both relaxed – meal times are the worst time to talk about it.

- Let your child respond so that she doesn't feel she is being lectured.

- Don't give in to your child's denial.

You may need to talk to medical experts and/or the school to work with you, and to find out how to approach the problem in the best possible way.

It may help to go with your child to a therapy group.

Joining slimming groups may sound like a good idea – because it is a safe way of controlling weight – but such groups are not designed to cope with people with a very distorted relationship with food.

Over-exercising? You are within your rights not to let them become involved in too much exercise – though your child may bully you into letting him. Explain that it is detrimental to his health. Let him know that you are aware that he is over-exercising, but try not to be critical.

Learn about eating disorders and their treatment. Treatment is more than talking or force feeding someone refusing to eat.

Don't give up on being involved, even if your child is having treatment.

The disorder is not your fault.

Hard as it may be, try not to be judgemental. Try to accept your child for what they are at the present moment.

Make your home a place for a supportive recovery, and be sensitive about the kinds of food you keep around. A large chocolate cake in the cupboard 'for the rest of the family' is not helpful to a bulimic; nor is it good to banish all forbidden 'tempting' foods on which they may binge from the home. You will need to consider the rest of the family and strike the right balance.

Don't make comments about your own weight or that of anyone else – particularly critical ones. Or ironically say, 'You are looking better now that you have put on weight.'

Don't discuss the issue in front of other people.

Make mealtimes as fun and relaxed as possible, without policing what people eat. It may help to remind your anorexic what she has agreed to do in therapy.

Recovery from an eating disorder is a slow process and may involve setbacks. Remind your child of any changes you see as positive.

Don't forget the person behind the illness, and maintain a constant love and support for her. She is in a lot of pain and dealing with a multitude of emotions.

There comes a time when the constant battle to find a solution to the problem actually works to support the problem. The person with the eating disorder has to work out the solution for themselves and you may need to adopt a 'tough love' approach. This involves offering your complete support and love whilst setting boundaries of tolerance. Get advice from an expert on how to follow this through.

You will need a lot of support yourself. An eating disorder can and will affect the whole family and you will need to work together with your partner to maintain a strong resolve. Make sure that everyone in the family has a chance to talk about their feelings and their own lives – try not to let them feel they are less important than the person with the eating disorder. You might consider fixing a time when all discussion about the eating disorder is banned.

Make time for yourself to alleviate the stress.

The Eating Disorders Association operates a helpline on 01603 621414 (open 9.00 a.m.–6.30 p.m.) and a Youthline for people under eighteen on 01603 765050 (open 4.00 p.m.–6.30 p.m.). There is also an excellent carers guide, aimed at parents, available from: Eating Disorders Association, First Floor Wensum House, 103 Prince of Wales Road, Norwich NR1 1DW.

The National Centre for Eating Disorders at 54 New Road, Esher, Surrey KT10 9NU runs counselling programmes. E-mail: ncfed@globalnet.co.uk or call 01372 469493 for more information.

Eyecare

For general eyecare and visual aids for sport, see page 184.

It is vital that your child has a check-up before he learns to drive. As a minimum legal requirement, motorists must be able to read a number plate from a distance of 67ft/20.5m and have a 120°-wide field of view.

Some spectacles are better than others for driving, those with rimless designs or with thin rims being particularly suitable, as they allow greater all-round vision than those with heavy frames. Spectacles with plastic lenses are lighter and safer than glass ones. Anti-reflection coatings, which help the wearer to see more clearly and cut down on glare, especially when driving at night, can be applied to any lenses at a reasonable cost.

It's sensible to keep a spare pair of glasses in the car in case your child forgets his. This is also important if he normally wears contact lenses because on long journeys when the eyes get tired it is often more comfortable to switch to a pair of glasses. It's also a useful safeguard if he suffers from hay fever.

Use the free prescription sunglasses offer available at some opticians so that your child isn't a danger or in danger wearing normal sunglasses instead of glasses when driving.

Glandular Fever

Glandular fever is caused by a member of the herpes family of viruses, the Epstein-Barr virus. It is called the kissing disease because that is how it is spread, but there are no tips to stop teenagers kissing that are not downright cruel!

Symptoms of glandular fever might include

- feeling sick
- fever
- headache
- a sore throat and general enlargement of the lymph nodes – these may be felt as rubbery swellings in the neck, armpits, elbows and groins and behind the knees
- enlargement of the spleen, which can in severe cases rupture if struck or too vigorously felt.

Some of these may be the symptoms of other illnesses, so see your GP, who will take a blood test.

Glandular fever can take time to recover from and leave affected teenagers feeling tired, depressed and lacking in energy. A healthy nutritious diet can help, as can a course of vitamin and mineral supplements recommended for that age group. See a qualified practitioner.

Older teenagers recovering from glandular fever should avoid alcohol.

Periods

For general advice on periods, see page 190.

Teenagers all want to be the same – perfection for them would be a national period day when all girls started simultaneously. If your daughter is concerned about her lack of periods, don't laugh it off saying, 'It'll happen.' Listen to her worries and be reassuring.

Late periods can be genetic, so tell your daughter if you started when you were older.

Girls who indulge in very vigorous exercise may find that their periods are late appearing. If your daughter is concerned, suggest that she lessens the level of activity.

Weight too can be a factor. Overweight or underweight girls may have delayed menstruation.

Your daughter may feel a freak at school. Although it won't help ease the embarrassment of not being like her peers whose periods have started, it will help her to know that the late appearance of periods is normal.

Skincare

Boys are very cavalier about using sun cream – it's just not macho – and will avoid it rather than risk looking like an idiot. Encourage them to use a 'designer' brand – Piz Buin rather than Boots for Children – and they are more likely to slap it on.

A baseball cap with the latest logo is more likely to stay on too.

Acne & Spots

See page 182.

Teeth

Children's dental treatment is free up to the age of nineteen whilst they are in full-time education. Beyond that (or if they leave school at sixteen) they may be able to get help by completing an HC1 form available from the local health authority.

Your teenagers should have adopted good dental health practices by the time they are this age – you've been telling them for long enough! – but some children (especially boys) get lazy about cleaning their teeth. Nagging may be the only answer – or maybe their girl/boyfriends will drop a hint!

Adults can have a maximum of thirty-two teeth. The wisdom teeth are the last to come through, right at the back. They usually appear between the ages of seventeen and twenty-five, although sometimes they appear many years later. Nowadays people often have jaws that are too small for thirty-two teeth – twenty-eight is often the most we have room for. So if all the other teeth are present and healthy there may not be enough space for the wisdom teeth to come through properly.

If part of the wisdom tooth has appeared through the gum and part of it is still covered, the gum may become sore and perhaps swollen. Food particles and bacteria can collect under the gum edge, and it will be difficult to clean effectively. This is a temporary problem that can be dealt with by using mouthwashes and special cleaning methods. If the problem persists, advise your child to visit the dentist, who may prescribe antibiotics or decide that it is better to remove the tooth.

A mouthwash of medium-hot water with a teaspoonful of salt will help to reduce gum soreness and inflammation. Check that it is not too hot before using it. Swish the solution around the tooth, trying to get it into the areas the toothbrush cannot reach. An antibacterial mouthwash such as Corsodyl can also be very useful to reduce the inflammation (Corsodyl should only be used for short periods as it can cause discoloration of the teeth). Pain-relieving tablets such as paracetamol or aspirin can also be useful for short-term use, but consult your dentist if your child's pain continues.

Why might wisdom teeth be removed? When it is clear that the wisdom teeth will not be able to come through into a useful position because there is not enough room (see above), and when they are also causing some pain or discomfort. Or if they have only partially come through and are decayed – such teeth will often be susceptible to decay as it can be difficult to clean them as thoroughly as other teeth; if a wisdom tooth is causing a cleaning problem and has no real use; or if a wisdom tooth starts to 'over-grow'. Always consult your dentist, if you are in any doubt about a wisdom tooth.

Bad Breath

See page 188.

Braces & Orthodontics

If orthodontic treatment is to work, it's important for a teenager to have the support of parents. It is important to attend visits to the orthodontist regularly with your child, and ensure that he carries out any instructions given. The success of the treatment also depends on the commitment of the patient: it is very important that your child is as keen as you are.

Caring for braces:

- Clean the teeth carefully every day, including between the teeth where possible. Your dentist or hygienist will be able to show your child the special techniques to use depending on the appliance he or she is wearing.

- Keep sugary foods and drinks to a minimum. Avoid 'snacking' with foods or drinks containing sugars, especially fizzy drinks. Also, sticky and hard foods may damage the delicate orthodontic appliances.

- Always use a fluoride toothpaste and mouthwash. The dentist or hygienist may recommend a fluoride toothpaste or application for your child to use. Look for a product carrying the British Dental Health Foundation accreditation logo. This shows that the product has been checked by a panel of experts and does what it says on the packet.

Mouthguards

See page 187.

Fear Of The Dentist

If a real fear of the dentist persists at this age, or if your child needs a lot of dental treatment, talk to friends who might be able to recommend a dentist who is good at treating children. A dentist who is personally recommended by another nervous person is usually a very good choice. It can also be a good idea to look in the Yellow Pages for practices that mention treatment for nervous patients.

Counselling is one way of dealing with persistent feelings of anxiety. This is usually carried out by a member of the practice team, in a room away from the surgery. Your teenager would be encouraged to discuss their fears so as to deal with and overcome them.

For more on fear of the Dentist, see page 137.

Personal Hygiene

See page 186.

PLASTIC SURGERY

Nick Percival, consultant plastic surgeon; Simon Harries MS, FRCS; British Association of Aesthetic Plastic Surgeons (www.baaps.org.uk); NHS Direct; Rosemary Blakesley; Priscilla Chase; Susanna Wadeson

An offhand reassurance that sticking-out ears, big boobs or a large nose 'are part of your character' will not pacify an excruciatingly self-conscious teenager. Teenagers want to be normal and to be attractive, and unhappiness with a part of their body can have a deep impact on how they feel about themselves. It can even affect they way they behave, consciously or subconsciously. Short legs or a big bottom she may have to live with, but if her unhappiness is with an area of her body that can be corrected, take it seriously and look into corrective surgery.

Be very careful how you approach the subject. Your comments may confirm a problem or may highlight something your child didn't think was an issue. (A recent study showed that children with bat ears said that teasing had come not from friends or siblings, but from fathers.) Take your lead from the child. Wait until he mentions it, then say that something can be done if he wants.

Let the idea sink in. Give the child time to digest it and think about it, and leave the decision up to her. It may take weeks for her to come to the conclusion to proceed.

Teasing usually starts about the age of eight or nine – younger children are far less likely to comment. A child who has to wait for surgery will need understanding from you and self-confidence to be able to cope with tactless remarks.

Avoid private clinics that advertise in the backs of magazines. If your child really is intent upon having plastic surgery, go through the conventional route: see your GP for a referral to a consultant surgeon, private or NHS.

Reduction rhinoplasty – or a nose job – is a very common procedure. The shape of the nose develops during adolescence but it stops growing at about sixteen. Before this age it's unwise to have an operation.

Make sure that your child is clear about what it is about his nose he does not like, so that the surgeon has an idea of what changes he would like. Some changes may not be possible surgically – completely correcting a broken nose, or reducing the size of the nostrils without leaving scars – so prepare him for disappointment.

Schedule the operation for a time when your child can be at home for a while and won't have to see friends – the beginning of the holidays for example. After rhinoplasty, the face can be bruised and swollen for some time and can take up to three weeks to settle.

It will take your child time to get used to his new nose. If he is concerned about friends' reactions (he may think he will be criticised for being vain), a change of hairstyle is a good idea. He can use that as an excuse when people say, 'You look different.'

Pinnaplasty is the correction of prominent ears. It should not be done under five years old, as the cartilage is too floppy to hold stitches. Sticking-out ears can cause terrible teasing, but plastic surgeons recommend that you wait until your child recognises the problem and wants it corrected. Children are generally more cooperative and happy with the outcome when they fully understand why the surgery is taking place.

Breasts

Large boobs are usually inherited and aside from the psychological issues (they can make girls feel very self-conscious, make flattering clothes hard to find and elicit unwanted comments from boys and men), they can also cause backache, neck pain and grooves in the shoulders from bra straps. Surgery can often be carried out on the NHS if your daughter can prove that having a big bust is causing her psychological and physiological problems, but most surgeons will not carry out a reduction on a girl under eighteen (boobs stop growing at about seventeen or eighteen), though it is not unheard of.

Could your daughter's bust size be as a result of being overweight? Weight loss can often change bust size. She is unlikely to be allowed the operation if she is very overweight anyway, as being overweight can cause complications in recovery.

Does she want a bigger bust? Augmentation is a less clear-cut issue, and most surgeons prefer a girl to have a consultation with a psychologist before agreeing to carry out the operation. They will want to know that she is psychologically mature enough to understand the implications of what she is agreeing to. Also, implants may only last around fifteen years and further surgery may be necessary when she is older. Augmentation is unusual even at eighteen.

Birthmarks

A strawberry mark (superficial angioma) is a small, bright red, raised tumour that appears during the first few weeks of life, grows quickly to its full size during the first six months or a year and then usually starts to become paler and flatter. Often it has disappeared altogether by the age of five. Although they affect the appearance and, at first, grow with the child, these birthmarks should not be treated surgically until it is certain that they are not going to disappear further by themselves, spontaneously.

The port-wine stain (capillary haemangioma) is a pale pink to deep red, stain-like flat tumour of the smallest blood vessels (capillaries). It is present at birth and is permanent. It usually occurs on one side of the face and is often a conspicuous blemish. Such stains can be treated by laser at any age, though younger kids might need a general anaesthetic, whereas older children could have topical anaesthetic creams. Extensive port-wine stains are treated by a surgeon with dermatological lasers, with reasonable success. A small port-wine stain can be treated by full-thickness skin removal.

One type of port-wine stain, called a 'stork bite', appears on the nape of the neck and disappears spontaneously early in life. No treatment is needed.

Pigmented birthmarks are usually brown in appearance and are present at birth. If they cover larger than a 1 per cent area of the body there is an increased chance of malignant change. In the early days of a child's life such a mark is near the skin surface and can be curated off, so have the mark looked at quickly. If a birthmark covers less than 1 per cent of the body area in size, there is less risk of the birthmark developing into a malignant melanoma, but your child may want it removed for cosmetic reasons. Under twelve he will need a general anaesthetic, and younger children can suffer worse scarring so it's better to wait until they are older for treatment, when the birthmark can be cut out with a local anaesthetic. Lighter brown (café au lait) marks can be removed, though not always completely, by laser.

Your child needs to be happy about any birthmark removal procedure. Cooperation makes the removal a more positive experience for her and easier for the doctor treating her. Try not to force the issue.

SHAVING

Geo. F. Trumper Barbers (www.trumper.com/shaving_tips.htm. They

Shaving is a rite of passage for boys, and there's a lot of pressure when someone in their peer group announces that they are shaving to rush home and have a go themselves. They will nick Dad's (or Mum's) razor, cut themselves and be disillusioned. Shaving is an art – though a simple one – that should be taught properly.

also run a shaving school at their branches in London)

A nice touch would be for you to buy your son a decent razor and a supply of blades.

Electric razors are not kind to sensitive teenage skin. Wet shaving, with a razor and a creamy, moisturising shaving soap will exfoliate and cleanse the skin, which at this age is inclined to be greasy.

Most boys start shaving at about sixteen – though very few will shave daily until they are about eighteen or nineteen. Early 'bum fluff' can be taken off with water and a bit of soap – even with a dry razor. Your son should start shaving when it becomes uncomfortable to leave on, then when he begins to look scruffy and when it is obviously growing actively. Even when he starts to shave every day, suggest he gives his skin a rest at weekends.

To start, teach your son to feel how the hair grows on his face. Encourage him to wet his fingers with a bit of soap and to feel around his face, especially that awkward bit under the chin where the hair is inclined to grow out in several directions. If it feels smooth, he is going with the grain – and it will pull if he is working against the hair growth. He should never shave against the grain of the beard growth. That's how shaving rashes result.

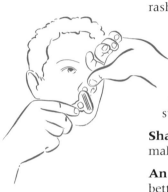

> **Those tricky bits under the nose:** use the thumb to pull up the tip of the nose and the hair becomes accessible. Above the lip he should shave sideways, never directly away from the lip in case he catches it with the blade.

> **Cut himself? Don't stick on loo paper!** Rinse the skin with cold water, which will close up the pore. A styptic pencil (available from chemists) dipped in water will also stop bleeding.

Shaving after a shower will make facial hair soft and easier to remove. Failing that, make sure that he rinses his face in hot water first to soften the hairs.

An oily shaving soap will irritate the skin. When choosing between a foam or gel, it's better to go for a gel that needs water to make it foam up. It should be applied in a circular motion on to the skin, which makes the hair stand proud. Once your son has finished shaving he should rinse his face with cold water.

Holding the razor in a fist means that the movements come from the elbow and can be awkward. Suggest your son holds the razor as Groucho Marx held a cigar – in the tips of his fingers. The movement then comes from the wrist and is much gentler.

Shaving and acne: wet shaving keeps grease under control and cleanses the skin, but make sure that your son shaves using very gentle movements, applying no pressure.

The best shave is not the closest shave – it's the one that leaves him feeling most comfortable.

Blades should be changed after every six shaves, not every six months.

Until your son's an expert, it's a good idea not to shave just before he goes out to a club or party but instead to shave in the morning. Teenagers will have negligible hair growth by the evening anyway.

After shaving: the best thing to apply is a non-greasy moisturiser (non-oil-based) but not one designed for girls, who have very different skin. Something like E45 is ideal.

It is not a good idea for your son to 'slap on' fragrance after he has shaved. Traditional aftershaves were used to sterilise the skin after men had been shaved by the penny barber and had shared a razor – they are too astringent for young skin and will hurt. Suggest he puts the fragrance on the hot spots – back and side of the neck, chest, behind the ears. When he sweats from all that dancing the fragrance will rise.

Hair Removal For Girls

Once, shaving legs, bikini line and armpits was the only option. There are now a mass of products – creams, waxes, foams – on the market. Select one that is gentle to young skin. If she chooses to shave, the basics above – wet skin, good-quality razor, sharp blades – apply to girls as much as boys.

Depilatory products are very strong. Most beauticians recommend waxing as the most effective hair removal method. Waxing is not recommended for diabetics because of the danger of infection.

If your daughter is determined to use depilatory products, ensure that she follows the following advice:

- Hair that is dark and coarse appears to be more resistant to chemical depilatories than hair that is light and fine.

- A depilatory is best used after a warm bath or shower, when the hair is softer and the pores of the skin are open.

- Never use a depilatory where there are wounds on the skin such as cuts or abrasions or on skin sensitive from sunburn.

- Apply the depilatory in a generous, smooth thick layer. Do not rub it in.

- Always test a small area of skin first. A small patch on the inner arm below the elbow is a good place. Keep the application on the skin for the time recommended in the instructions and remove. Wait for twenty-four hours. If there are no signs of irritation or allergic reaction such as redness or broken skin, proceed over a larger area.

- Follow the timing instructions very closely by setting a timer and removing the chemical immediately the timer signal goes off. Do not exceed the time recommended, to avoid burning or damaging the skin.

- If the skin becomes itchy or irritated, discontinue use of the depilatory and apply a soothing gel such as aloe vera or an anti-inflammatory skin cream.

- To minimise irritation, try not to exfoliate (through scrubbing, or using a mask or cleansing agent) beforehand and be sure to follow up with a thorough rinsing and moisture-rich cream.

- After using a depilatory, apply sunscreen to areas that will be exposed to the sun.

- To avoid damaging underlying layers of skin, some recommend not using a depilatory more than every twenty-eight days. Generally, a new outer layer of skin is formed every twenty-eight days.

MAKE-UP

See page 193.

SEX

Steve Chalke,
ParentTalk; Glynis
Fletcher; FPA; BPAS;
Joanna Brian, Brooks,
www.brook.org.uk;

One in three teenagers has sex before the age of sixteen. Sixteen is now the average age a teenager has sex for the first time. This is a quantum leap in parenting: no longer is it an issue of 'if' but 'when'.

By the time your child is sixteen plus, his sex life is his own affair and you must accept that it is none of your business. You must hope that you have armed him with the

British Pregnancy
Advisory Service
(0845 7 30 40 30
www.bpas.org)

emotional equipment and factual information to make the right choices. Resist the urge to make the choices for him.

It's not enough just to tell your child that 'under sixteen' is too young to have sex. It's important to explain to her why there is an age of consent. She needs to know the difference between good and bad choices, as well as how to resist the various pressures to have sex before she is really ready to – before it is genuinely her choice.

Discuss reputations as well as the technicalities and/or legal implications of sex under the age of consent. Teenagers may suffer from peer pressure, but they are very aware of girls with a reputation for being easy. Ask your child if she wants people to think of her in the same way.

Is your child frightened of going too far? It all comes down to having the confidence in herself to be able to say 'enough is enough'. It helps to give her a framework of your own values to think about so that she sets herself limits before she gets caught up in the heat of passion. Your child needs to know not only the emotional and physical consequences of all stages of intimacy, but also that sex is exciting and that in the heat of passion her sensible attitude may go out of the window. Most of all, your child needs to have the confidence to be able to come to you to talk about it.

But your child probably won't come to talk to you about sex (God, how embarrassing!). If you feel that your child is concerned about sexual issues but won't discuss them with you, leave her a book to read that will provide information – see page 180.

Control needs to be invisible. Teenagers hate it when their parents are nosey.

Even when your child is above the age of consent, don't flaunt your own sex life. Their parents' sexuality is (and will always be) something teenagers would rather not think about.

He wants his girlfriend to stay the night whilst you are away? They are both over the age of consent but it is still your home. Make yourself feel better by making up a spare bed, but console yourself that (1) he has respected you enough to ask and (2) it is better that they are at home than having to sneak off to have sex somewhere else.

Sex and your son: there is a nasty possibility that a girl might think your son has forced sex on her against her will. Tell your son, as part of a chat about sex and relationships, that he should stop if he thinks a girl has suddenly become unwilling or that her keenness for sex has suddenly changed.

Don't take it for granted that your child will start dating a member of the opposite sex. In establishing his sexual identity, your teenager may explore different types of relationships, or feel confused about whether he is straight or gay. This is normal, and it's important for your child to feel that he can talk to you about what he is doing and who he is seeing. If he doesn't feel ready for a relationship yet, that's perfectly normal too.

Contraception & Sexually Transmitted Diseases

Research has shown that only 50 per cent of young people under sixteen use contraception at first intercourse and one in three girls and one in four boys don't know where to get free contraception. You will need to tell them.

Children under sixteen can get confidential contraceptive advice from their GP or the Family Planning Association (FPA). They can also go to websites such as www.brook.org.uk, the site of the Brook Advisory Centres.

Be open about the subject of contraception. Leave condoms somewhere discreet if necessary – better that they 'disappear' without comment than your children are too shy to buy them for themselves.

If your child is over the legal age of consent (sixteen), and you know that she is using contraceptives, tell her you are proud that she is being responsible. Remind her, however, that pregnancy can occur however careful anyone is, and that she needs to consider the consequences should that happen.

Boys need to know that the buck does not stop with the girl. Condoms are ideal contraception because not only, if used properly, are they effective in protecting girls against unwanted pregnancy, but also they protect against sexually transmitted diseases. Explain to your son that he can take responsibility for contraception too, and that contraception is free from the Family Planning Service (address in the phone book).

Part of your child's sex education must be discussions about sexually transmitted diseases (STDs). She must be aware of the risks of HIV, and also STDs such as genital warts, urethritis and chlamydia (which men get as well as women and pass on). These are the most common. Chlamydia can lead to pelvic inflammatory disease. The symptoms can be pain in the penis or vagina when weeing or having sex. If it is not treated, chlamydia can damage the fallopian tubes and lead to infertility. It can also cause ectopic pregnancies. Stress to your child the importance of using condoms, even with the Pill, and of the increased chances of catching an STD if she has several sexual partners.

Unprotected sex? The emergency pill (or morning-after pill) comes in two sets. The first pill needs to be taken within seventy-two hours (three days) of the unprotected sex. The second pill has to be taken twelve hours later. Emergency contraception can be obtained from your GP, any Family Planning Clinic (FPA), or the Brook Advisory Centre, most genitourinary medicine/sexual health clinics, and some hospital Accident and Emergency departments.

Early in 2001, an 'over-the-counter' version of the morning-after pill was introduced in the UK. This can be bought from any chemist – unless the pharmacist has any moral objections. However, it can only be sold as an over-the-counter product to women who are sixteen years of age and older. The pharmacy is obliged to offer brief counselling and advise on its possible side effects before handing it over. The cost is currently about £20. Don't pretend that you are buying it for yourself when it is for your daughter: there are important health issues involved. If she is under sixteen, she needs to talk to her GP or Family Planning Clinic, whose advice will be confidential.

If you or your child would like to know more about emergency contraception or any other method of contraception, you can ring the Family Planning Association's contraceptive education service helpline on 0845 310 1334. FPA is at 2–12 Pentonville Road, London N1 9FP.

Teenage Pregnancy

If you have said that you would support your child if she ever became pregnant, stick to your promise. It is no good promising but, when something happens, flying into a rage.

Your daughter may well be terrified of your reaction to her pregnancy. Children know what parents will feel, are frightened of losing parental love and affection, and will expect their news to be very damaging. Try not to hit the roof and hurl accusations of stupidity at her. She will already be feeling the stigma of having become pregnant; she has been brave enough to come to you and she needs your help.

Listen to what your daughter says and avoid making assumptions. Don't assume that she became pregnant because she forgot to use a condom or take the Pill. It could happen to any of us – pregnancy happens even when contraception is used and her pregnancy may be the result of a contraceptive failure or even abuse.

If your daughter becomes pregnant, you may be convinced that a termination is the best option. Try not to push your opinion on her. Look at all the options and let her come to her own conclusions. She may opt for a termination anyway, but she needs to come to that conclusion herself.

Were you pregnant as a teenager? It may help to talk about your experiences with your daughter – even if she was not the result of that pregnancy. However, you need to feel comfortable about this, and an important role for a parent is not to burden your children with problems from your past.

Don't forget boys in the equation. If a pregnancy happens, they have a strong responsibility.

If your son's girlfriend becomes pregnant, avoid being judgemental – your son will be frightened and confused, and will need your support. Everyone will be panicking, and someone has to remain calm. It has to be you.

Your son might feel helpless and left out of decisions. Discussions about pregnancy and/or terminations happen between the girl and her doctor. Your son may feel marginalised, but may also be expected (and want to) support his girlfriend. You can in turn support him.

Your daughter wants to have an abortion? She needs to see her GP as soon as possible or someone at one of the charitable clinics such as Brooks (two doctors need to approve the termination). The earlier the abortion happens the safer it is physically and emotionally for your daughter. Legally an abortion can be carried out on children over the age of sixteen without your consent, so long as it is with your daughter's consent and if the doctors feel she understands the issues. However, medics will strongly encourage your daughter to discuss her pregnancy with you.

If you visit a clinic with your daughter, you may well be asked to leave the room while the counsellors talk to her alone. Do as you are asked. They need to make sure that she understands all the issues about her pregnancy and/or a termination. You will be given the opportunity for confidential advice and support, and to talk about your anger and/or confusion too.

Parents can help with the emotional fall-out of a termination. If your daughter wanted the termination she may well feel relief, but she may also feel regret for having got into the situation of needing one in the first place. Adolescents often feel a strong sense of guilt. Your daughter may feel that by having an abortion she has committed murder. Let her talk if she wants to, and try not to be judgemental.

Don't be hurt if your daughter feels that you are not the right person to talk to. A counsellor may be better qualified, especially if she felt that she wasn't allowed to talk the issues through properly before her abortion.

Good advice for both you and your teenagers can be found at www.brook.org.uk, the British Pregnancy Advisory Service (01564 793225) and www.teenagepregnancyunit.gov.uk.

Masturbation

See page 181.

RELATIONSHIPS

Grace Kirby; Sarah Kilby; Samantha Kirkpatrick

Your teenager brings home a boyfriend/girlfriend for the first time. It's a painful moment as a parent – especially for fathers with their daughters. Firstly be grateful that your child has brought this new person home to meet you. Secondly be as welcoming as possible. You may think that he/she is the spawn of the devil/not good enough for your little girl, but bite your tongue. It is highly unlikely this is a relationship for life. Let them find that out for themselves.

There is no love as deep as teenage love – or at least that's what they think. Don't patronise them or belittle their feelings. Falling in love and losing love are part of growing up.

See also Sex, page 232.

Break-ups

Don't belittle your child's emotions after a relationship is over. Teenagers are very sensitive, and the pain of love at that age is enormously powerful. You can help by telling your child that the relationship was mismatched, but whatever you do don't mention fish and the large amount of them in the sea. It's patronising, and will do nothing to lessen the pain of having just been given the heave ho. To a teenager there is simply no one else and life as she knows it has effectively ended.

If your child is recovering from a broken heart, offer a shoulder to cry on, a box of tissues and a good listening ear. Take her out to do something she enjoys: a film, a pizza, shopping. Make sure she is looking after herself, with plenty of sleep and delicious food. Let her indulge herself in her misery – up to a point!

Remind your child what is good about her. After a relationship has finished, a teenager might easily blame herself for what has happened and pick faults in her looks or personality. She will need a confidence boost. Even if it sounds as though she isn't listening or believing you, the message will get through. Knowing that you still care and love her will matter hugely.

Keep lovesick teenagers busy. Plunge into a project together, suggest he tries a new activity or hobby, redecorating his room, send him to stay with friends for the weekend – anything that will shift the focus for a while.

Broken hearts take time to heal – remember? Give teenagers time and they will bounce back. Make sure that they make time to see their friends and concentrate on their school work. Beyond that it's a waiting game.

If your teenager admits to a sexual mistake, take comfort in the fact that she felt sufficiently at ease with you to tell you about it. Don't make judgements and tell her that she was stupid. If she knows that she has your unconditional love, and that it's not the end of the world, even if the effects are world-changing (pregnancy for example), she won't have to be a prisoner to the past. For pregnancy, see page 234.

HOBBIES, SPORT & MUSIC

See page 196.

TECHNOLOGY

See page 198.

SHOPPING, CLOTHES & PRESENTS

Lynn Moran; Sarah Lelliott; Faith Bridges

Teenagers are very picky when it comes to presents they like to receive. Money is always a safe and popular option – especially if they are saving up for something – but vouchers, though not exactly awe-inspiring, let the child choose their own gift. Vouchers for music shops or WHSmith (where their spending options are wider) will hit the mark. Consider too vouchers for cinema tickets, offered by all the bigger cinema chains.

Girls love to browse make-up and beauty product shops. Vouchers for these sort of places will be a wow. What about a make-up lesson or beauty treatment?

Let teenagers know that you consider them grown-up when thinking about gifts. Try and be a bit ahead of their age group. Coffee-making machines, money for travelling … will show that you are taking them seriously.

What about contributing to driving lessons for a seventeen-year-old?

Not seeing eye to eye when buying clothes? Teenagers and their parents rarely do, but try to remember the sort of things you wore then and how much your parents disapproved. Peer pressure amongst teenagers is immense, and they will not want to look foolish (nor will you want them to). Be flexible about what they want to buy and wear. There aren't many of us still wearing the same sort of things we did at seventeen.

Look at magazines together (boys' and girls'), making sure they include *Vogue* **as well as teenage ones.** Talk about looks you like and the ones you don't. Doing this might help your children to see your point of view if they see certain clothes on different people.

Reverse psychology: at the end of the day teenagers will wear what they want to, but if you strongly disapprove of what your child likes to wear, show great enthusiasm for terrible clothes whilst out shopping. Or if she tries on an outfit you loathe, say, 'It looks so wonderful, I might buy one too.' It'll be back on the hanger before you can say Kylie Minogue!

Falling out in shops? If you are providing the money for clothes/shoes/trainers and they have their beady eye on the latest (expensive) fashion, say how much you are prepared to spend and that, if their mind is made up, they must find the balance of the cost of the item.

Compromise on what you buy. Offer to pay for the jeans your child needs, but suggest that she pays for the top that goes with it.

Encourage your child to earn his own money for clothes (see page 243). But it is reasonable for you to still pay for the essentials like uniform, shoes, shampoo, soap, socks and sanitary protection.

Clothes are a great reward for teenagers. If you know that your child has her eye on a particular top/pair of earrings/T-shirt, buying them as a gift will show her how much you care or appreciate good work or good behaviour.

See also Disagreements Over Appearance, page 215.

MONEY

Wall's 27th Annual Pocket Money Monitor (2001); NatWest

For allowances, earning money, and opening bank and building society accounts, see page 194.

Overdrafts aren't given to under-eighteens, so even with a cashpoint card teenagers under this age cannot go into the red as the cashpoint machine will not issue cash if there are insufficient funds. However, banks such as NatWest offer CardPlus accounts to over sixteens. Such an account is a normal current account but with a slight margin for overspending – say around £50 – but it is discretionary 'depending on the account behaviour'. In other words if your child is permanently in the red, the facility will be withdrawn.

SCHOOL

Ian Hecks, head-teacher; DfES; Laura Fortune

There is a lot of useful information about your involvement in your child's education at www.dfes.gov.uk/parents.

See also School, page 200.

Homework

For general advice on homework, see page 148.

By this stage teenagers are expected by the school to motivate themselves. That doesn't mean that you can't enquire what your child is expected to do tonight. If you don't ask, you may find later that she is not doing enough.

You can make a real difference to your child's results by being on hand when he is doing homework. Coursework sometimes provides a substantial chunk of the overall mark (30 per cent of the marks in English Literature and 20 per cent in English Language are derived from coursework, and art courses can be 100 per cent on coursework).

Find out what percentage of the final grade a particular piece of coursework represents. This will help to get a perspective on how much time and effort a project/essay should merit.

Just when it matters the most, as major exams loom, some teenagers lose interest in doing schoolwork. Computer games are more appealing, and the more you nag the less inclined they are to listen. Move the computer into a family room, so that you can monitor how much time they are spending on it, or let them work in a quiet place close to where the rest of the family are (and away from the PC).

You will have less access to the work your child is doing at this stage, so ask to see essays – not because you want to check the standard – and praise good work.

Poring over a set English text? Read the novel/play, if you haven't already, and discuss it with your child – it could be a point of contact between you.

Websites can help with homework and revision: try: www.bbc.co.uk/education/revision, www.bbc.co.uk/education/gcsebitesize/index.html, www.gcse.com (an approved provider for the National Grid for Learning), www.learnfree.co.uk and www.revise.it (with free revision guides written by teachers). Try too www.channel4.com/amazinggrades – an online index of good-quality sites chosen by teachers.

For homework advice try www.standards.dfee.gov.uk/homework/, www.eduweb.co.uk/ and www.freecampus.co.uk (see also page 148).

Dropping Out

'I'm fed up with school and want to leave'? This is a common cry from fifteen- and sixteen-year-olds who have had enough and can't face the sixth form. College is an option, particularly if your child has a very strong vocation. However sixth-form departments in schools consistently return better A-level results than colleges. Ask why she wants to throw away the chance of better qualifications.

Some children would rather drop out than face failure. If your child's school results have suddenly taken a nosedive, talk to him and to the teachers. Concentrate on getting to the root of his concerns. Reassure him that you are not expecting the moon – just the best *he* can do.

Your child doesn't want to learn? With the school you may be able to work out a curriculum that takes into account your child's strengths and weaknesses. See if the school offers an alternative to the National Curriculum – perhaps the opportunity for your child to spend a day a week on a vocational course.

Tutorial colleges often have a more relaxed approach to education (no uniform, less restricted timetables) and would suit some children who are bored of school, are being disruptive or need a more laid-back routine.

Child with special non-academic talents? Be flexible. Some children who may be very sporty would do better in an independent college (crammer) which will leave them time outside the main curriculum to pursue other passions, whilst still enabling them to take GCSEs, AS- and A2-levels.

Exams

Need a bit of extra help before A2-levels (or Curriculum 2000)? Consider an Easter cramming course at one of the revision courses run by Conference for Independent Further Education (CIFE). Contact CIFE on 020 8969 0324 or visit the website at www.cife.org.uk. For more information, see the websites of two colleges: www.mpw.co.uk and www.dld.org.uk. Check that they cover your child's syllabus, though. Questions to ask the college: does the course cover the board and exam your child is studying? How big is each group size and is there a maximum? How many hours a day tuition is there? Does the tutor have A2- and AS-level teaching experience?

Many schools do revision and retake courses in the holidays. Go to www.isbi.com, the Independent Schools of the British Isles website, and click on their revision and summer schools section. Other places to look at include:

Oxford Science Studies (covering most subjects). Call 0800 013 1006 or e-mail info@oxss.co.uk www.abbeycolleges.co.uk

www.did.org

www.easterrevisioncourses.com

www.harrowschool.org.uk/revision

www.mpw.co.uk.

Don't laugh. Some children – especially girls – can overwork for exams. The pressure to be the best is so huge that a conscientious teenager may develop into a workaholic.

Boys cope better with exam stress than girls: it is uncool to been seen to work too hard, and they can externalise feelings of pressure – by getting angry, for instance, or getting plastered. Girls tend to internalise stress, and their conscientiousness can cause problems.

Be aware that some children feel exam pressure acutely because they want to do well for you, their parents. Help them by saying you only want them to be happy and relaxed, and that how they do will not in any way change how much you love them.

Be a good role model. Don't work too late yourself.

More is not necessarily better. Encourage your child to rely on his abilities.

Don't be too pushy. Your child's panic may actually be emanating from your panic.

If your child becomes tearful, bad-tempered, listless and unenthusiastic, and is finding it hard to sleep or laugh, ensure that her UCAS application is not unrealistic and that she has a safety net if she fails to achieve the grades required. Remind her that exams can be retaken, and that education is not a race but an opportunity to get as far as you want to go at your own pace.

Agree an achievable timetable for revision, incorporating plenty of breaks, and leaving time for exercise and a change of scene. This allows the rest of the family to make a noise too. This is especially important during the Easter holidays when your child needs to relax after a tough term. Three hours of concentrated revision from 10.00 a.m. until 1.00 p.m. can be as productive as a whole day at it.

Avoid the word revision – it sounds dull and repetitive. Some teachers suggest that the word 'preparation' is more motivating.

Reduce the number of outside activities, which will only tire your child and distract him. It may even increase his sense of panic.

Don't nag! It won't work. Neither will bribery, comparisons to more conscientious siblings or friends, or threats. Children need to realise that learning brings its own rewards.

Children who don't feel pressured but whose parents provide a supportive home environment usually take responsibility for their own work.

Provide plenty of refreshing drinks and delicious food – even things your child can take from the fridge and eat on the hoof – but make sure that she is eating properly by arranging that she stops work and joins you for meals in the evening. Revision and an empty stomach don't go together.

Find your child a quiet, comfortable place conducive to work – see page 148.

Panicky friends calling at all hours can be a pain – they will only add to your child's sense of panic and be a distraction. Suggest that you look after her mobile phone while she works.

Getting your child to work out what knowledge he is expected to have – facts and figures concerning a geography case study, for example – and the kind of understanding he is meant to demonstrate with this knowledge will help him to structure his revision.

Find out what revision programmes are being screened in the wee small hours – especially on the BBC – and tape them.

Experienced examiners urge children not to score own goals by throwing away marks on silly errors. Encourage your child to make sure that her handwriting is readable, that she uses proper nouns and punctuation properly, that she doesn't mix up those old chestnuts it's/its, they're/their/there and that her spelling is correct.

Put up an exam timetable so that you know what time which exams start. It will help relieve your child's panic if he knows you have the information too.

Be firm about bedtime. Teenagers need plenty of sleep, though they are probably convinced that 3.00 a.m. is their most productive time. Research proves it isn't.

Making sure that there are no gaps in your child's lesson notes and that there's nothing missing will make revision much easier.

Help your child to organise his lesson notes into bite-sized form or cue card reminders – even diagrams. These will make the subject less of a mouthful to memorise.

Remind your child that she can ask for help. You may not be the best person (what do parents know?), but you might know a man (or woman) who is.

Offer to test your child, or arrange for his friends to come over one evening for a testing session.

Your child's being lazy about studying? Perhaps he needs motivating – in which case create positive images about what will be in the envelope/on the college notice board when the results arrive: say, 'When your get your results, you will be thrilled to get the ones you've worked for.' Or perhaps he doesn't know how to go about revising or is frightened of the consequences of failure – in which case you can help (see above).

When the exams are over, let your kids let off steam and agree to collect them at a pre-arranged time.

Fill up the time after the exam season is finished by organising plenty of activities, trips to stay with friends, even a part-time job if they are old enough. The devil makes work …

Summer Schools

Many schools run residential holiday courses in a wide variety of subjects that both children and adults can enjoy. For a copy of *Guide to Spring and Summer Schools* (programmes offered by independent schools), call 020 7798 1500. See also Active Training and Education at www.ate.org.uk, Music Courses at Dartington International Summer School www.dartingtonsummerschool.co.uk, Cricket and Tennis Coaching at Repton School (01283 559322) and Visual and Applied Arts at West Dean College, Chichester www.west-dean.org.uk.

CAREERS & FURTHER EDUCATION

Gail Smith;
Tom Finch, careers
advisor; Brian Harper;
Caroline Syndenham

There is so much wisdom gained from hindsight. Your children need to make their own decisions, not have you make them for them. Help them to explore all the options if a career path isn't obvious, but if you sit them down for a 'let's discuss your future' chat, they may well run a mile.

Your teenager may think that because you are an accountant it is obviously the most boring job on earth. She needs to work out for herself that what she perceives as boring career choices may in fact be good and sensible ones in the end.

Is university or college the best option? Too often children are encouraged to pick a career for life. There is no such thing any more. Be open-minded about the fact that your child may not want to be accountant, but have a passion for horses/design/dress making/ceramics/fashion/writing …

Remember that many excellent careers do not require further education. This might apply especially to a child whose interests and skills revolve around arts, craftsmanship, sport or riding, for example.

Your child may have a vocation that would be better served with a Modern Apprenticeship, An 'apprenticeship' may be a good route, especially one where you can take qualifications 'on the job'. Contact your local college of further education or Local Education Authority for advice.

Unsure on what career to pursue? Vocational guidance – expert analysis of psychometric testing – can open unexpected career ideas. Try Career Psychology (www.career-psychology.com or 020 7976 1010) or Career Analysts (www.careeranalysts.co.uk or 020 7935 5452).

Unsure about what a particular career involves? There are very few companies who wouldn't welcome a student who wishes to work-shadow. This involves shadowing someone in their job for a few days. It's usually unpaid but it can be a great way to learn about a particular type of work and get a foot in the door of a company. Pull all the strings of contacts you have, and encourage your child to be bold and approach the company/professional of interest with a polite, well-written letter. Again most careers advisory centres will be able to help with names of welcoming companies.

Poor results? Put your child through a tutorial college or crammer. These colleges teach GCSE, A-level and AS-level courses on a full-time basis. Courses can be expensive (up to £3000 a year), but because they are geared towards an intensive programme of work, they can be very effective. Contact the Council for Independent Further Education (0208 767 8666 or www.getthegrade.co.uk).

See also Careers and Getting a Job, page 259.

College Or University

The choice of college or university should be your child's. You can offer help and advice, but try not to impose your prejudices on your child.

For children to make the right choices regarding further education, they need to exploit the careers advice given in schools. Most should have plenty of information about colleges and universities. If your child's school doesn't, he will have to investigate himself, using bookshops, the library and the internet – sites such as the Further Education Funding Council's website at www.fefc.ac.uk. Most colleges and universities have their own web sites too.

To help find the right course to suit your child's chosen career, visit www.education.independent.co.uk/careers-advice (the education section of the *Independent* newspaper), which has an excellent database of careers information and articles.

A child who wants to study abroad? www.allaboutcollege.com lists every university in each country, and takes you directly to each website. Study in Europe and the fees are the same as for native students.

Some US independent universities offer 'need-based grants and merit scholarships' to their first-year students – more than half might receive over £11,000. Contact the university in question's Office of Financial Assistance when you decide to apply.

University and college places are dependent on exam results. Check out how well classed your child's prospective degree is by looking at the Quality Assurance Agency's website at www.qaa.ac.uk. University and Higher Education League Tables are published annually and can be seen on www.universityoptions.co.uk.

Let your child attend open days, so he can visit a variety of similar departments at different universities. The content of courses will vary enormously and he will need to find strands and approaches which suits him.

Your child should treat a university visit as you would a school – are the students looking lively and interested, and are there lots of activities advertised on notice boards? Are the bars, library and canteens well attended and lively?

Your child should find out how much the universities or colleges on her shortlist expect self-directed study. If she is not self-motivated, a looser regime may not suit her.

It might be worth considering a college near home. It's certainly cheaper for students to live at home and attend college or university close by, and research has shown that students at home report a greater satisfaction, security, sleep, privacy and ability to study. They also consistently score higher than students who have left home.

What home-based students lack, though, is social support. They can feel left out and that they're missing out on hall of residence life, and they may find it harder to settle. Living away from home in the controlled environment of college is good for your teenager's development, and can help your relationship with them.

In 2001, over 100,000 children between the ages of eighteen and twenty-one were in higher education and the government plans to increase that figure. That's great news, in that it creates a more qualified workforce, but it means that there is stiff competition to get into the course you want at the university or college you fancy. Your child needs to be quick off the mark in applying (entries must be in by mid-December the year prior to entry), which can be done online through www.ucas.com, the website of the University and Colleges Admissions Service (UCAS).

Popular course at a popular university? Your child could apply for a more unusual course (Chinese for example) and then swap courses once he has entered the college or university, although this is becoming harder to do.

Don't be led too much by the league tables (published annually in many national newspapers). Some lower-league universities excel in certain departments, even if they are not winners overall, and examination of the figures shows that the percentage differences in the tables can be point one of a per cent.

With GCSEs, AS-levels and then A-levels, children have three years of tough exams. Let your child take a gap year if he wants to (see page 248), but help him plan it out so that it is rewarding.

If your child fails to be selected for her chosen course – particularly if it is for a popular one such as media studies – suggest she takes a year out to gain as much work experience as possible or takes a gap year (see page 248) and reapplies again the following year.

For funding for college or university, see page 257.

Gap Year

See page 248.

WORK

Department of Health

Young people under the minimum school leaving age (sixteen) are protected by the terms of the European Directive on the Protection of Young People at Work. No child may work:

- if under the age of fourteen years, though they may be licensed to work at thirteen – this might include doing a paper round or light farm work

- during school hours

- Before 7.00 a.m. and after 7.00 p.m.

- for more than two hours on any day in which a 14-to-16-year-old is expected to attend school

- for more than two hours on a Sunday for a 14-to-16-year-old

- in any industrial undertaking

- where they are likely to suffer injury from any lifting, carrying or moving heavy items.

These restrictions can be further amended by local authority by-laws.

From sixteen to seventeen there are a few restrictions. Children of this age cannot normally work in a bar, unless it's a restaurant serving meals or they are being trained in the business.

Your child's rights as a part-time worker are the same as those for a full-time worker. For example, children are protected by the disability, race and sex discrimination laws and unfair dismissal laws, and have the right to be given notice if they have worked for one month.

No longer at school? Sixteen- and seventeen-year-olds are guaranteed a place on a Youth Training Scheme. It can be full or part-time, and a Foundation or an Advanced Modern Apprenticeship.

If your teenager is earning, no longer in full-time education and living at home, let him contribute to the family budget. It will give him a sense of responsibility and a greater respect for the costs of running a house.

Encourage your teenagers to make the most of the long summer vacation. *Summer Jobs*, published annually by Vacation Work (www.vacationwork.co.uk), and available from bookshops, tells children where to start and the pitfalls of jobs both here and abroad.

See also Money, page 237.

Babysitting

There is no legal restriction to the minimum age at which a child can babysit, paid or unpaid. However, if the child being babysat is thought to be at risk because he or she is being inadequately supervised, criminal proceedings could be taken against the child's parents or care proceedings taken against the child. So it is at your discretion whether you think your child is too young to cope with looking after a young child and it is the parents of the child being babysat who are taking the risk. If your child is over sixteen and something happens to the child they are caring for, she may be prosecuted for negligence.

Don't know the parents? Ask who recommended your child as a babysitter and check out the parents before letting him babysit for them.

Discourage your child from advertising babysitting services in supermarkets,

village shops or bulletin boards. Who knows who will be looking at her name and phone number? Call friends with young children and offer your child's services, or ask if they know anyone who might be interested.

Make sure that your child knows the ages of the children to be sat, how he will be escorted to and from the job and the hours he is expected to work.

If you think that your child will have to be babysitting late, suggest she asks if she can stay the night or take a friend with her. Some parents seem to think that 2.00 a.m. is a reasonable time to return, even for a fifteen-year-old babysitter.

Not sure that the people your child is babysitting for are fit to drive your child home? Arrange for her to stay overnight or set the alarm and collect her yourself. Better to be safe.

Just because your teenager is legally allowed to babysit, it doesn't follow that she has childcare abilities. If the child she is to babysit for is very young, help her cope by giving her advice – or suggests she reads the first few chapters of this book!

Ensure that your child is safe when babysitting by reminding him to ask the parents:

- what time they are coming home
- where they can be contacted
- who to contact in an emergency
- how unfamiliar doors and windows and alarms operate
- where first aid, cleaning supplies and fire extinguishers are kept
- any routines they have which will help make babysitting easier
- rules about bedtimes, TV watching, snacks, etc.
- whether there are animals to look after
- how the TV works
- whether he should answer the phone
- whether he can use the phone for emergencies/calling home
- if he can have the heating on longer – especially if he is in for a long night.

Unsure about charges? Check with friends and other teenage babysitters and see what the going rate is. Your child can state a rate and is under no obligation to accept less than friends receive.

TRAVEL

Caroline George;
Martin Waddell

For family holidays, see page 207.

See also Gap Year, pages 248, and Travel, page 251.

Holidaying On Their Own

Find a pen pal (school should be able to help) who would be prepared to do an exchange, or link up with friends abroad who would be happy to have your child for a short time during the holidays. At least you can be reassured that she will be with someone *in loco parentis*.

Let your child travel without you but with a group of friends. Hostel holidays at youth hostels are an independent experience (in a safe environment). Let her start with weekends away in the UK before loosening the reins further and for longer. Go to www.yha.org.uk.

Activity holiday companies specialise in safe holidays for children of all ages, with many holidays abroad for older kids. CampBeaumont is for children up to fifteen years (www.campbeaumont.com) and PGL Holidays is for those up to eighteen (www.pgl.co.uk). They are an excellent way of giving your children freedom (PGL is known to some kids as Parents Get Lost) within a secure, controlled environment.

DRIVING

Philip Lelliott;
David Bridges

Learning to drive is a teenager's passport to freedom. But with the skill comes a host of responsibilities. Your child needs to learn good road sense and about driving sensibly from you.

From the age of sixteen teenagers can ride a moped up to 50cc's, as a learner (with L plates) but they will need a valid Compulsory Basic Training certificate (valid for two years) and are not allowed to carry passengers or ride on a motorway. For information on CBT courses, contact your local motorcycle dealer, your local authority road safety officer or the Motorcycle Rider Training Association. Go to www.motorcycle.co.uk/#Training to find out where your nearest training school is.

Once your child decides to learn to drive a car, which she will be allowed to do on the road at seventeen, she will need a provisional licence. D1 and D750 (photocard) application forms are available from the Post Office. It cost £29 in 2002. Applications need to be sent to DVLA, Swansea, SA99 1AD, or you may be able to use the Post Office checking service. Expect to wait fifteen working days before the licence arrives. Your child cannot drive until he or she receives the licence. Go to www.dvla.gov.uk/drivers/applydl.htm#how_to.

Your child doesn't need to wait until he is seventeen to learn – try an off-road course. There are also residential 'crash' courses for people keen to cram in learning to drive quickly. For details go to www.learners.co.uk.

Teaching your children to drive takes the patience of a saint and nerves of steel. If you can't cope, ask a relative to teach them, or arrange for professional lessons. A few professional lessons to start with are a good idea anyway. Long-time drivers get into sloppy habits which they might pass on to their children. When you are with them, try very hard to resist contradicting what their instructor has told them.

The 'instructor', who must travel in the front passenger seat with the learner, must be over twenty-one and have held a full EU driver's licence for three years at least. Don't let a friend who has just passed her test sit in with your child who is learning.

The driving test comes in two parts: a practical test and a theory test. The theory test takes forty minutes and is made up of thirty-five multiple-choice questions answered on a computer. The results come back in half an hour. Make sure that your learner is up-to-speed with the Highway Code, especially areas such as driver awareness, the meaning of road signs, stopping distances and the effects of alcohol and drugs.

Your child can apply to take a test in any Driving Test Centre. Pass rates for the 335 permanent Driving Test Centres in the UK vary widely. In recent years, the centre with the highest overall pass rate has been Carmarthen in South Wales. It may be worth taking the test in a different location to give your child a better chance of passing.

Girls lack confidence and have a higher failure rate than boys in the practical test, but a better pass rate in the theory test. Make sure that your daughter has plenty of time to practice, and that you are relaxed and encouraging when she is out driving with you.

Warn your child about the ten most common reasons for failing a driving test:

- failure to act properly at road junctions

- reversing round a corner incorrectly

- failure to make proper use of steering

- problems with parking

- failure to make proper use of gears

- failure to make effective use of the mirrors

- driving too slowly

- failure to act properly when turning right

- causing delay by not pulling out promptly at junctions

- failure to move away correctly from stationary positions.

Children's activity company, PGL Holidays, do six-day driving courses (off road) for twelve–to-sixteen-year-olds, giving basic driving skills tuition, with Department of Transport approved driving instructors. The course also gives instruction on basic car maintenance and everything necessary to pass the theory test. Telephone booking number 01989 767767 or visit www.pgl.co.uk.

Remind your child that he is no better a driver five minutes after he has passed his test than he was five minutes before it.

If your child is driving you, resist the temptation to be a backseat driver. And credit him for being sensible. He will realise that he will lose his license if he drinks and drives or drives dangerously … you hope.

Once your child has passed, you may never see your car again. You will need to arrange times when she can borrow it.

Failing that, you could buy her a runabout, but on the understanding that she is responsible for paying for petrol.

If you buy do buy a runabout for your child, the following tips might be useful:

- Make a deal: you will pay for servicing and insurance. Your child must pay for the road tax.

- Insurance is very expensive for teenagers and adults in their early twenties. Look at fully comprehensive policies, covering any driver/any age, or put the insurance in your name with your teenager as a named driver.

- Insurance is cheaper if you wait until your child has driven for two years before starting him with his own policy. Then he can start accruing a no-claims bonus.

Once your son or daughter is learning to drive or has passed their test, check your insurance policy on your car. If it is comprehensive, named drivers only, you will have to add their name. Their age may affect your premium.

Your child has had an accident. Once you know that she's not hurt, don't fly off the handle. It takes an accident to teach a child to respect a car and she may well be very shocked.

9 EIGHTEEN YEARS AND BEYOND

'A child becomes an adult when he realises that he has a right not only to be right, but also to be wrong.'

Thomas Szasz

Hurrah! Your son or daughter has come of age and in law he or she is no longer your responsibility. He can take on the world and all those irksome adult responsibilities that involves. Whether or not he decides to go on to further education, start a career, get married or leave the country is his decision and you can sleep at night knowing that your job is over.

Oh, if only that were true! That rookie adult is still your child; and he still needs your emotional support as he finds his way in life. He'll make mistakes and need you to be there to pick up the pieces. Unfortunately he will probably need your financial help too until he is earning enough to support himself, and if he goes on to further education, you may even have to find funds to help educate him.

The plus side of coming of age, however, is that, with a bit of luck, your child will have emerged into a beautiful adult who, on finding out more about how the world works, will begin to realise what a remarkable thing you have done in raising him. He will be your friend and meet you on equal terms.

WHAT THEY CAN DO AT THIS AGE:
vote
marry
serve on a jury
make a will
buy alcohol
buy fireworks
drive a van or lorry up to 7.5 tons
work in a bar
be tattooed
own land or property
donate blood and body to science
go into a betting shop, licensed casino or bingo club, or go into a sex shop
enter into binding contracts
change their names
not be made a ward of court
see a category 18 film.

What they cannot do until they are 21:

stand in a local or general election

apply for a liquor licence

drive a lorry or bus

hire a car.

LEAVING HOME

Sylvia Kirkpatrick; Gloria Davies; Louise Jones; Val and Frank Ogden; Sarah Vince

At eighteen your children are considered adults in the eyes of the law – but your influence is still with them (and you have a washing machine).

Time to spread his wings? If he has not already done so, or does not have plans to do so, encourage your child to leave home at around eighteen. This doesn't mean for ever, but living with friends or going to college far enough away that they need to live in is good for helping them to find their independence, and good for you as a parent.

Make sure that your children know how to fend for themselves. They may have swanned through their teenage years blissfully unaware of how to wash/clean/mend things (if they have – shame on you!). Arm them with a cookery book – either a basic learn-to-cook version (no prizes for guessing who has written one of those) or compile one yourself of their favourite recipes from home, writing them in a nice notebook.

The amount of dust detected in a student home is more than fifty times that detected on the floor of a shop, according to research published recently by the vacuum cleaner manufacturers VAX. Don't panic – wait until they have their own place which they will want to care for – hopefully.

Offer to make a contribution to phone costs – land line or mobile. It will help to ensure that your child keeps in touch.

Try not to interfere. She will make mistakes, but she needs to learn the consequences and she will ask when she needs to know.

Your child will use your house like a hotel when he comes home for college vacations (well, hasn't he for years?). The fact that he is older, though, doesn't mean that you can't still lay down the law. Don't allow yourself to be a doormat – if he is earning during the holidays, let him provide some treats for the family, and a refresher course on the controls of the washing machine wouldn't go amiss either. But show him that you are glad he is home – it's a tough old world out there!

Empty Nest Syndrome

Might be for days, might be for weeks, but for a while the silence left by your child's absence will be deafening. Try to prepare for it by arranging things to do with yourself(ves) to bridge the gap. Book a holiday, take a few days away, enrol on a course which starts the same time as the term, plan a spring clean – something to help you avoid having hours of unplanned time on your hands to mope.

Do things for yourself that you haven't had a chance to do for years. Play your Barry Manilow records full volume (no one to tell you that you are sad), repaint the bathroom, take the papers back to bed on a Sunday, listen to Radio 4, watch *Panorama* …

But avoid going mad with your freedom. If your child can never get you on the phone or feels that you are too busy to talk, he will feel insecure and find it harder to settle. He is in a new environment and needs to know that the other half of his life is still the same.

Try not to be too hasty cleaning and sorting your child's room. She will still come home, and may feel rejected if suddenly it looks as though she has been eradicated from the house.

GAP YEAR

Tom Griffiths, the Gapyear Company Ltd; Foreign Office; STA Travel, tel: 020 7361 6129, www.statravel.co.uk; Phil Martin; Stephen Russel; Daniella Graziani

A well-spent gap year can be a fulfilling and rewarding experience and an opportunity to gain life skills that will look impressive on a CV to potential employers.

In a recent Gap Year Report, all those involved with young people – including university admissions tutors, careers advisers and employers – showed that they were unanimously in favour of a gap year because of the opportunities afforded to students of:

- Gaining independence and a broader outlook on life.
- Having the opportunity to learn essential 'soft skills' such as communication, decision-making, organisation, setting and meeting personal deadlines, how to focus on and develop specific tasks, tolerance, team work, gathering and using resources.
- Coping with their own finances and learning how to budget.
- Stepping back, meeting a wide variety of people and having new experiences, thus better

equipping students to think, focus and choose a university course or career that they are really interested in.

- Taking a much-needed break from the academic 'hamster wheel' that starts at GCSEs and has no let-up through the sixth form or university years.

- Increasing the chance of retention on a course or in a career.

A gap year is a good way to earn money to fund university living costs.

The overwhelming benefit of a gap year is the growth in maturity that the experience of such opportunities effects.

University admissions departments like to see gap-year intentions on admissions applications. They show ambition and initiative.

The year doesn't have to involve backpacking through the outback (a frightening prospect for some eighteen-year-olds and almost all parents), but could involve a fulfilling few months spent gaining experience closer to home.

If your child's stuck on what to do with the year, do a weekend challenge. Encourage her to spend Saturday writing down all the things she would like to do: train to be an astronaut or a chef, join a circus or the Foreign Legion, write a website, write a book – it doesn't matter how wild and wacky it is. Next day advise she crosses out all the things she couldn't or wouldn't do. She will then be left with realistic options, which might be local or involve travel. This approach will open up her mind. Leave the list for a week and then come back to it and action whatever options seem most appealing.

Read the *Gap-Year Guide Book* **by Rosamund McDougall** (Peridot Press), which includes reports of student's experiences. It can be ordered online from www.schoolsearch.co.uk/bookshop or look at the Gap-Year site at www.peridot.co.uk.

Other Gap Year sites include:

www.gapyearjobs.co.uk

www.projecttrust.org.uk

www.teaching-abroad.co.uk

www.worldwidevolunteering.org.uk

www.yearoutgroup.org.

Other good reads, for those who are travelling in a gap year (see page 250), are *Before you Go* and the *Virgin Travellers' Handbook*, both by Tom Griffiths, available from www.gapyear.com and *The Backpacker's Bible* by Elaine Robertson (Robson Books, 1999).

Gap Year At Home

If you can support your child, or she can earn money in the evenings or a few days a week, consider voluntary work. Charities are crying out for helpers. Voluntary work can be very useful for students wanting to pursue careers in caring professions: nursing, occupational therapy, physiotherapy, for example.

Dead keen on pursuing a specific career? Suggest that your child shadows a professional – a physiotherapist, a hairdresser, a vet. Many experts are happy for enthusiastic young people to gain experience by working voluntarily.

Does your child have an interest for which there is not an obvious career? Look at ways to earn a living from non-mainstream career choices. Mad keen to be a footballer? Look at avenues where they can follow this interest. Suggest, for example, that he offers to coach young children at a local football club whilst earning money as a waiter/selling hamburgers. There are opportunities to gain coaching qualifications, which could open up job prospects at a leisure centre as a sports coach specialising in football.

Gap Year Away From Home

Gap year programme companies organise programmes here and abroad covering a broad range of projects. Gappers often stay with a host family. If you decide to go to a gap year programme company, chat to friends whose children have participated in good programmes and try to find one that's right for your child. Ask any company you are considering the following questions:

- How long has the organisation existed?
- Is it a partnership, limited company, public company, charity, sole trader?
- How has the particular programme they are offering been chosen?
- Has a representative of the company checked the programme over thoroughly?
- Are the host organisations paid to take the student?
- Is a host family paid or are they volunteers?
- Will your child be paid?
- What exactly will he be doing?
- Who will your child be placed with or will he be working alone?
- What is expected of your child and what will be his responsibilities?
- Will there be a written agreement?
- What do the costs include?
- Is there a recommended budget for 'extras'?
- What about the deposit? Is it refundable?
- How should one pay and what happens if you cancel?
- Can you get advice on raising funds?
- What arrangements are there if there is an emergency?
- Does the organisation have enough funds to deal with one?
- Who deals with travel arrangements, visas, etc.?
- Insurance: what cover is there, what is included and do you need to provide cover yourself?
- Vaccinations: what is necessary?
- Is there a pre-departure briefing?
- Is there any training?
- Who is responsible ultimately when your child is on a programme?

Many youngsters decide to go travelling in their gap year. The options are to go with an organised group, travel with an address book full of contacts in the country of your destination (and *en route*) or travel with friends. These need to be chosen with care. Three can be a crowd, and even a great mate can become an arch-enemy after a few weeks in each other's company. One in three students travel alone.

When to go? The usual gap year begins when exams finish in June. If your child is planning to travel, she would get a job right away, after a week or two of parties and general chilling out. She would then work the full summer and the run-up to Christmas, for as many hours as possible, and save like mad. Christmas is always a great time to work with the extra hours and bonuses available – gappers volunteer to do all the lucrative shifts others do not want to do; it is also a time for the last push, and to ask for kit for the gap year as presents. The vast majority of gappers leave the country from January to March when the ticket prices fall, the weather is fine for the bulk of the standard round-the-world route and the majority of the structured placements start.

How much will it cost? People are often put off by the idea that round-the-world tickets cost the earth. On average people estimate tickets cost £3317. The actual price is nearer £850.

Funding

Raising money for travel or a structured placement is quite daunting and your child may have to be inventive with money raising ideas. This can take courage, but your child is not alone.

Help your child to get organized. Start planning early. Divide the total amount needed into smaller amounts and decide what he will do to achieve each target – for example, £500 from a raffle, £300 from a sponsored event, £1000 from secured donations and grant applications. Then all he has to do is achieve each target in isolation – which is easier than achieving the total amount.

Tips for funding a gap year:

- Ask local clubs: Rotary, Lions, Round Table, etc., many of whom are extremely happy to support enthusiastic locals.
- Apply to local funds and charities: see Directories of Grant Making Trusts (in libraries). Millions of pounds are untouched by gappers each year.
- Set up a company: for example a car-washing business. These can rake in the cash – but do it properly. Tax to pay and all that …
- Organise an event: spend twelve months organising one event that will raise over £5000.
- Get sponsorship: people do sponsored walks or sponsored silence, others get sponsored for shaving heads, sitting in a bath of baked beans …
- Hold raffles with donated prizes.
- Unusual ideas: get friends to be auctioned off as 'slaves'/helpers at local events, dress up as a human fruit machine, write an interview technique booklet.

TRAVEL

Tom Griffiths, the Gapyear Company Ltd; Foreign Office; STA Travel (020 7361 6129 www.statravel.co.uk); Phil Martin; Stephen Russel; Daniella Graziani

It is up to your child – whether travelling in a gap year or during university or college vacations – to plan his trips abroad and look after himself while travelling. As a parent you can encourage him, though, to read or take the following advice.

Excellent advice can be gained from the Foreign Office website at www.fco.gov.uk/travel/tips, where you will find information on travelling in every country in the world. There is also advice on what to do before you go, and if it all goes wrong. Well written and easy to follow. There is also a travel advice line on 020 7008 0232.

Before Setting Off

These tips may help your child:

Get information on each country you plan to visit using guidebooks (the Rough Guides are excellent), the internet, the local library or the Foreign Office website (see above). Find out about local laws, customs and culture.

When planning an itinerary, check weather cycles and miss the rainy or hurricane seasons.

If you're a first-time traveller, you may find it less of a culture shock to travel in developed countries first. Leave the harrowing stuff until last if you're a bit shockable.

Circumstances can change quickly and without warning in some countries. Find out about possible risks and avoid troublespots. Ask friends who have visited the area. Check the news for reports of problems in the places that you plan to visit. Just before you leave and when travelling to a new country consult the Foreign Office advice line (see above) – it is regularly updated.

Get adequate travel insurance to cover illness, injury, loss of money, baggage and tickets, and emergency evacuation. Check that it covers all the activities you are likely to do.

You can arrange extra cover by telephone or e-mail if for instance you want to extend your stay. You must have your policy number to do this. Avoid activities for which you are not insured. If you have any doubts about your cover, check with your insurer. Of the 200,000 kids who leave the country each year to travel, 25 per cent are uninsured or under-insured. Try www.insureyourgap.com for quotes or speak to your insurance company.

Complete a form E111 if travelling within the European Economic Area. The E111, which offers free or reduced-cost emergency medical treatment, can be obtained from any post office. Make sure that you fill out the E111 and have it stamped by the post office before you go.

Three months before you intend to travel, ask your doctor or a specialist travel clinic about the vaccinations you need and any other health needs (such as malaria tablets). Take any documentation with you as proof of vaccination. For free vaccination advice, call the Nomads Travel Health Information Line: 0906 863 3414.

If you need to carry medicine, check that it is legal in the country you are visiting. Take a prescription and a GP's letter in case you are stopped by customs or lose your medicine and need to replace it. Make sure that your doctor knows the conditions in which you will be travelling. The medication may not survive extremes of heat or humidity. Order extra prescriptions to cover the entire period of your journey.

If you have any allergies or special medical requirements, make sure you and your travelling companions know about them, and carry some documentation about your person in case of an accident.

Pack your medication in your hand luggage.

Check that your passport is valid for a minimum of six months at return date. Make sure that you write the full details of your next of kin in the back of your passport.

Check entry requirements for British nationals with the embassy/High Commission of the country/ies that you are visiting. Get all necessary visas and permits before you go.

If you plan to work abroad, obtain a valid work permit before you leave. Check requirements with the embassy/High Commission of the country that you are visiting. You may be deported if you work illegally. For long-term stays, consider getting an internet bank account.

If you plan to drive abroad, find out about the laws and driving licence requirements of the country to be visited. Get an international driving permit (valid for one year) before you leave, as you can only obtain this in the UK. An IDP is an extra form of photo-identification.

Take enough money for your trip. Check the validity, expiry dates and cash available on your credit/debit cards. Make a note of your card numbers and the 24-hour emergency numbers and keep them separately. Make sure that you have back-up funds such as US dollars (accepted virtually everywhere), sterling or traveller's cheques. Have a return ticket, or enough money to buy one.

Plan to stay in touch. Consider taking a mobile phone and/or getting a free web-based e-mail account – set up an e-mail address with Yahoo or Hotmail before you go – and put friends' and family's contact details into the e-address book. There are internet cafés in most places. Leave details of your journey with your family and friends; tell them of any change of plan. You can make use of the International Poste Restante service for receiving letters and packages abroad (brightly coloured envelopes are easier to pick out).

Take photocopies of important documents (such as back page of passport, visas, tickets, medical certificates, UK driving licence and IDP) and keep them separately. If you are travelling with a friend, carry a copy of each other's passport and travel documents.

Send important information (such as insurance policy number and 24-hour emergency number; passport, visa and ticket details; and 24-hour emergency numbers for lost and/or stolen credit cards) in an e-mail to your web-based account, in case you lose all your travel documents and hard copies.

Get a list of British consular offices in the countries you plan to visit. Find out the office telephone numbers and working hours beforehand. Leave at home copies of the phone numbers and addresses of the British consulates in all the countries you are visiting.

Your first night … Plan ahead! Be aware that you will be at your most vulnerable when you arrive, so before you go book accommodation if at all possible. If you don't like it when you get there, you can always go elsewhere the next day. If you are going to arrive late, be aware that it may be difficult to find accommodation at night.

What To Take

Take with you all the documents, money, information and medicines mentioned in Before Setting Off above, plus:

- a good guidebook and a phrase book that you can use in emergencies
- your insurance policy number and 24-hour emergency number
- a first-aid pack. Consider buying a comprehensive first-aid pack
- a second form of photo-identification with you for visas, permits and so on.

Pack light but include a padlock with a combination to keep belongings safe at airports, railway stations, on buses, etc.

If you are backpacking:

- Small plastic bags with a seal come in handy for lots of things.
- Pack a bulldog clip so that you can hang anything wet (towel, socks, T-shirt) safely from the backpack as you walk along.
- A drawstring bag made of synthetic fabric (like a gym bag) is useful for stashing dirty or wet clothes, and for day trips.

Before buying a sleeping bag, find out what the temperature is like at night. Even very hot climates it can turn chilly once the sun goes down.

If your wear contact lenses, make sure that you have enough cleaning solution for the trip, but pack specs as well, just in case.

It can be difficult to get good-quality condoms abroad, and impossible in some places. Take your own – they don't take up much space in a rucksack. Apart from the obvious use, they can make sterile wound dressings and can be used for carrying water.

Buy an AIDS kit. You can buy them at pharmacies or at some health centres. They contain sterile equipment that could save your life in an emergency.

Tampons are hard to find in many countries. Pack plenty. Even if you don't usually use the applicator type, they can be more practical if you can't get to wash your hands very often.

A tubular bandage is useful in case of a sprain, but is also good for tucking cash inside when worn at the top of your arm or leg.

When buying shoes, forget quality. Leather will rot in humid conditions. Get some cheap pumps and replace frequently. If desperate, wear flip-flops, which are very useful in grubby shower blocks.

Lots of travellers lose weight for one reason or another. Drawstring waists will shrink with you.

While Abroad

Your first night ... Phone home! Tell your family that you have arrived safely.

When you first arrive, you won't be used to the currency, so try not to use big notes outside familiar places like hotels when you won't have time to check your change. Nor is it a good idea to stand in an unfamiliar place holding large quantities of money.

Carry your valuable documents and money in a secure money belt worn under clothing. Carry loose change and money for day-to-day spending in a wallet. Be extra vigilant in areas where you could be pickpocketed or have your bag snatched – in busy streets or crowded bars.

Do not let documents out of your sight, even if authority figures ask for them. Sometimes money will be demanded for their return.

Obey the local laws. You can be imprisoned, fined or deported for offences that incur only a caution in the UK. British consular staff cannot get you out of prison abroad.

Do not get involved with drugs. It is possible that you may be offered drugs at some point during your trip; obey local drug laws. Penalties are severe and include massive fines and long prison sentences in grim conditions. You can receive the death penalty in some countries. The Foreign Office cannot get you out.

Never carry packages through customs for other people. Do not sit in anyone else's vehicle when going through customs or crossing a border; always get out and walk. If driving, do not lend your vehicle to anyone else. Always pack your own baggage and never leave it unattended.

Do not drink and drive. Be aware of the local laws and attitudes to alcohol. Do not try to import alcohol into a country where it is prohibited – penalties can be severe.

Do not work illegally. You can be deported, fined and imprisoned if you do. You may also be prevented from entering the country again in the future.

If you work abroad, make sure you comply with all the relevant employment regulations – you may have to pay tax.

Do not overstay your visa. You can extend your visa in most places; if you do not, you can be imprisoned or fined.

If in doubt, don't buy wildlife souvenirs. If you do, make sure that they can be legally taken out of the country and legally imported into the UK. Don't be fooled by statements like 'Believe me, it's OK.' Some wildlife souvenirs are banned from international trade; many more require special permits for the UK, the country of export and any countries visited in between. Customs throughout the world confiscate illegal souvenirs and in the UK you could face a criminal prosecution and unlimited fines.

Stay healthy. If you need to take medication, make sure that you continue to do so. Don't give medicines prescribed for you by a doctor to people you meet on your travels.

If you get diarrhoea, drink flat Coke which will help to rehydrate you. No ice cubes, and make sure you open the can yourself.

Respect local customs and dress codes. Think about what you wear and how you fit in. Be discreet about your views on cultural differences and behave and dress appropriately, particularly when visiting religious sites, markets and rural communities. Look at what the local people are wearing if you feel you need guidance. Don't wear expensive jewellery. Wearing dark glasses can boost your confidence and reduce harassment, but remember to remove them when talking to people.

Advice for girls:

- Girls should pack a sarong. There are lots of places where shorts will get unwanted attention.

- Blondes need to be prepared for unwanted attention in many parts of Africa, India, South East Asia and the Middle East.

- Consider wearing a wedding ring, even if you aren't married. It can help you to avoid harassment.

- Tight clothes are hot and uncomfortable and will attract unwanted attention. Go baggy.

- In some cultures, making eye contact with a man is seen as a direct invitation. Try to get out of the habit.

- If you are groped, shout and make a fuss, making it clear that this is unacceptable – you may be doing a favour to the next woman to come along.

Stay in touch: e-mail, telephone and write home regularly.

If there is a natural disaster or if trouble flares up in the country you're travelling in, contact your family and friends to let them know that you are safe and healthy. Do this even if you are not that close to the problem – remember that family and friends will not know exactly where you are, but they will worry if they think that you are in potential danger.

Change money in banks or with legal foreign exchange dealers. It is often illegal to change with unauthorised persons, and if you do so you run the risk of receiving fake currency and arrest. Keep all receipts, as you may have to prove that you obtained your local currency legally.

Ensure that you pay your credit card bills whilst travelling.

Be security conscious. Avoid unlit streets at night. Carry only the minimum amount of cash when sightseeing and leave your valuables in the hostel or guesthouse safe. Never resist violent theft.

Watch out for scams. Check your guidebook for warnings on scams and keep your wits about you at all times.

Be very cautious about hitchhiking, especially at night. Ask the local guesthouse to recommend a taxi firm and, when possible, try to double up with someone you know when travelling by taxi. If you must hitchhike, always travel in pairs and be aware that drivers may expect payment.

Be wary of newfound 'friends'. Don't tell strangers where you are staying or give out too many details about your travel plans.

If you are travelling alone, you may attract unwelcome attention and you may receive unwelcome propositions or remarks. It is usually best to ignore them.

Act confidently. Plan your daily itinerary. Know where you are going and what you are doing. Leave details of your plans with your hotel or guesthouse. Make sure that when you go out you know how to get back. Some guesthouses can give you cards that show you how to get back.

Avoid unfolding a map at night – you will look lost and vulnerable.

At hotels and guesthouses:

- Use only a first initial when checking in. Don't put 'Ms', 'Miss' or 'Mrs'.
- Never leave your key where someone can note your room number.
- When inside your room, do not leave your window open if your room is on the ground floor. Use a door wedge on the inside of your door for extra security.
- Never open your door to anyone – maintenance, flower delivery or whoever – without checking with reception to verify the service.

Avoid risky situations such as travelling or walking alone at night or drinking by yourself in a bar. Drug-assisted rape is a real and growing risk, so never leave your drink unattended.

Alcohol can affect your judgement and your ability to react. Be aware of your environment and stay in control.

Returning From Abroad

If your child falls ill in the weeks following her return, make sure you tell your doctor where she's been. The information could help with a correct diagnosis and protect those she comes into contact with at home.

Your child will need time to settle. He may return a more mature, wiser person. Things that have previously been worries become trivial: teenage anxieties, materialism, schoolyard 'posturing' and childish peer pressure become irrelevant compared to third world poverty, learning to look after yourself in unknown circumstances, learning to understand what the world is really about and what really matters in life. But he may take time to return to normality of life. Give him three weeks to get used to it.

COLLEGE & UNIVERSITY

National Union of Students; UCAS, www.ucas.ac.uk; DfES; StudentUK.com; Universities UK; Eileen Tracy, study skills counsellor; Sherry Ashworth, teacher; Tom Griffiths; Gail Smith

Even the most assured child can find university daunting, especially if it is the first time she has lived away from home. She may have to motivate herself for the first time. When you call, your new student offspring may make it sound as though she's having a ball, but even if you don't sense concern, remind her that she can seek advice from personal tutors. She may well be trying not to burden you with worry, especially if you are stretching yourselves to pay for her studies.

If your child becomes despondent and withdrawn, and is struggling, don't rely too much on the university for support. Call on the help of your GP, who can refer him to relevant sources. If things have become very serious, approach your child's faculty to look into suspending his studies.

He's got a fat cheque in his hand: this may be the first time that your child has had so much money at his disposal and he may well go mad with the freedom. Remind him that this sum has to see him through the year, and resist the urge to rush to the rescue if things go wrong or he runs out of money. Your children need to learn to bail themselves out of problems, so remain supportive and forgiving but not Mr Moneybags.

Bear in mind that 5 per cent of students swap courses or even institutions, and 16 per cent drop out of college or university altogether. Neither of these is a failing – see such a move as the result of the wrong educational choice.

Student Mobiles (www.studentmobiles.com) caters specifically for students, providing a range of deals on pre-pay and contract terms, with special offers in association with NUS (National Union of Students). You can connect to all the UK networks and on the latest handsets whilst benefiting from the incentives offered on numerous packages. Special offers are updated regularly and are designed to suit the needs of students.

Funding

If you went to university or college, forget how it worked then. Funding has changed dramatically since the days of minimum and maximum grants, and you may well have to contribute substantially to your child's further education. At time of going to press, FE funding is under review.

Use your children's personal tax allowance once they are at university: look into the possibility of buying them a house or flat in their university town in their name so that rent received from housemates can go towards their personal allowance.

The income that a student can get is a maximum £4815 loan annually (38 weeks) for students in London, £3905 for those studying outside London, of which about £1800 goes on hall of residence rent, and £1000 on tuition fees. That leaves £1000 to live off, and buy books (2002–2003 figures). The 2001 shortfall between loans and living/tuition fee costs for students was around £4500 per year. These figures mean that your child will have to fund himself with holiday and evening jobs or else you will need to find funds for him.

Paying rent can swallow up all a student's funds. You could offer to go halves on rent costs, or offer to make a contribution.

Contact the student union of the university or college your child is attending for advice on local costs, level of rents, etc. It is more qualified to help you than the National Union of Students.

A good site for student and funding information is www.studentuk.com.

Students whose family income is over £20,480 a year are required to make a contribution. However, most students get help with their fees, which does not have to be repaid.

Help towards living costs comes mainly from student loans from the local education authority (LEA). These are not commercial loans that are offered by high street banks. Your child will not have to start repaying a loan until after he has left university or college and his income has reached a certain level (currently £10,000 a year). Repayments take account of inflation, but do not have the same interest rate that banks and other lenders charge. The rate at which your child will repay the loan is directly linked to his income once he has graduated.

Seventy-five per cent of the maximum loan is available to all eligible students regardless of any other income they have. Whether your child can get any or all of the remaining 25 per cent depends on her income and yours as a parent.

How to apply for a student loan:

- Apply to your local education authority (LEA). You can get an application form, called an HE1, from your LEA or www.dfes.gov.uk/studentsupport/formsandguides.cfm. If your child is still studying for A-levels, he might be able to get the form directly from his school or college.

- Complete the application form and return it to the LEA by the deadline. If your child is eligible for help, the authority will send a financial form, called an HE2, to complete. The HE2 form will ask you to submit details of your family income, so that the LEA can assess how much support your child will be entitled to. Although your LEA should send you an HE2, you can also download a copy of it from the Forms and Guides page on the website above. Go to the section headed Forms for the Academic Year 2002/03 (or whatever year is relevant).

- Complete the HE2 financial form and return it to the LEA by the deadline. Your LEA will then tell you whether fees need to be paid and the size of a loan your child is eligible for. As a general guide, if your child does not pay fees, she will be able to get the maximum loan. Your LEA will also send a loan request form.

- Complete the loan request form and send it to the Student Loans Company (SLC). (The SLC issue student loans on behalf of the government.) Note: the SLC will usually pay the loan in three instalments. The first instalment is likely to be in the form of a cheque, which your child can collect from college at the start of term. Further instalments will be paid directly into his bank or building society account.

- Do not worry if you have missed these deadlines set by the LEA. It will still accept applications made after these dates. However, if you apply late it cannot guarantee that your child's loan will be ready for him when he gets to college.

Check out all the options on offer. Further details on how to get financial support are given in the DfES guide: *Financial Support for Higher Education Students in 2002/2003*, which is available from the website (see above), your LEA, or by calling free on 0800 731 9133.

Funding In Scotland

It's worth being educated in Scotland. If your child is starting a full-time degree, HND or HNC course in Scotland, she will not pay any course tuition fees and may be eligible for a non-repayable bursary as well as a partly means-tested loan to help with living costs. Some diploma courses also come into this category.

To qualify for this support your child must have lived in the UK and Islands for three years immediately before the first day of the start of the course. He must also be ordinarily resident in Scotland on the first day of the course – in other words, not just in Scotland to start the course. If you are not sure if your child qualifies, contact www.student-support-saas.gov.uk, the Student Awards Agency for Scotland that assesses eligibility for tuition fees and loans.

The above only applies if your child is starting a suitable full-time course in Scotland. If she is going to a university or college elsewhere, she will be expected to contribute to her tuition fees if it is judged that she can afford to do so.

Although your child studying in Scotland will not have to pay any tuition fees, he will need money to support himself while he learns. There are student loans available for this (see above). These are partly means-tested – that is, the size of the loan depends on your family's income. The maximum loan a student can get currently if he is living away from home while studying is £3815, of which £750 is not means-tested. If he is living at home with you, the maximum loan is £3020, of which £500 is not means-tested. The money is borrowed at a rate of interest linked to inflation. This means that what he will end up paying back is broadly equal in real terms to what he borrowed.

If your child is starting a higher education course in Scotland, she may be able to get a non-repayable grant. This is paid instead of part of the loan, so it means that she will not have to borrow so much. It is available whether your child lives with you or away from home while she studies. The maximum bursary of £2000 a year will be paid if your income is under £10,000 a year. If your income is greater than that but no higher than around £25,800 a year, your child will receive a reduced amount. These bursaries are administered by SAAS and you can get more information from them or their website (see above).

Exams

If your child is taking exams at college or university away from home, it will be harder to give your support, but you can still help by keeping in contact, sending treats or visiting him. Some of the advice on page 238 may be useful.

Read a very useful book by Eileen Tracy, a study skills counsellor, called *The Student's Guide to Exam Success*, published by Open University Press at £9.99.

For more on exams see page 238.

CAREERS & GETTING A JOB

Tom Finch, careers advisor; Brian Harper; Caroline Syndenham; Mark Ashworth, Crown Castle International and Young Enterprise

Most colleges and universities have a careers advisory centre which offers interview advice and careers directories. You can find information about the service from the college website.

For more on choosing a career, see page 241.

A Good CV

A good CV is a passport to a job. It will get noticed by employers inundated with job applications. It may be the first time your child has written about herself, and you can influence how she puts the information together so that it has the maximum impact, by giving her the following advice.

Put the name at the top, not 'Curriculum Vitae', so that the name will stick. The content will be obvious.

Be relevant: a CV should avoid including Grade 1 piano, but mention experiences that will have a bearing on the job being applied for. Music can be put as a hobby.

Personal statements are the rage: include a few lines at the top summing up strengths, relevant skills, experience and characteristics.

Include contact details: home and term time. An e-mail address is a good idea too, but remind your child that including phone numbers means that she needs to remember to answer the phone in the right manner!

Keep it simple. Avoid the temptation to italicise, underline and use funky fonts everywhere.

Keep it to two pages at the most. If a potential employer has to hunt for details, he will lose interest.

Explain responsibilities held in other jobs (even holiday jobs), but keep them as bullet points under company title and dates of employment.

Put the most recent college/university and qualifications first and work backwards. But if you've had some amazing job placement, start with that.

Don't be shy about including details of menial holiday work alongside more meaty (and relevant) work experience. Such work shows that you are trustworthy, have grafted and have a broad experience.

Remember to include sporting achievements and school positions held, and don't underestimate the power of hobbies and interests. Were you in the school debating society? Did you excel on the stage? May seem irrelevant, but such information could set you apart from the competition.

Employers want to know what distinguishes the applicant from the crowd. They will also want to find something on the CV to use to put an interviewee at ease. Make sure that your CV includes Duke of Edinburgh Award, gap year activities or something that will show tremendous initiative, as well as providing a conversation point.

Use 'action' words: negotiated, evaluated, delivered …

References: state 'available on request' and line up a character reference and an academic reference for when they are requested. Teachers and people in authority are very used to providing these, so don't worry about asking.

Never, ever lie or be economical with the truth.

Always, always include with a CV a covering letter stating why you are applying for a job and the strengths you have which make you believe you are ideal for it.

Check and recheck CV and letter for spelling and punctuation mistakes.

Looking For Jobs

Use friends and contacts. There is no harm in using influential friends to give your child a job or to get her on the employment ladder.

Permanent job hard to find? There is no shame in using employment agencies.

Nor is there any shame in doing the odd week or two here and there. A temporary job will help your child learn about workplaces, and indeed he may find that he changes his plans about a chosen career as a result; and a good temp that the company knows is often in an ideal position to be offered a permanent job.

Job Interviews

The more practice you have at interviews the better you get at them! Job interviews are really hairy, but it might be a good idea for your child to attend a couple for jobs he's not really interested in, just to get some experience.

It's worth remembering that most interviewers gain their first impression within thirty seconds of the interview starting and will have decided on the outcome within the first four minutes. Remind your jobseeker to look alert, interested, interesting and friendly right from the word go.

All the obvious 'attention to detail' points apply – looking neat, being on time, finding out about the job beforehand, having a list of questions ready to ask – but your jobseeker will need to stand out from the crowd too. If she feels confident in herself, she'll be better armed to sell her skills.

An employer is not looking for barrels of experience at this stage; he will be on the lookout for enthusiasm, initiative and communication skills. When he asks 'What can you offer us?' the answer needs to show these.

It's always useful for an applicant to have a few (truthful!) stories to illustrate a point she is trying to get over. Even if an applicant hasn't got direct experience of a job (and she is unlikely to), she can often use something similar to show her suitability. For instance, setting up a family party or an event at school would show that you can organise people.

Be truthful. Remind your child not to make up a past experience. Most interviewers are trained to probe and are likely to rumble a fibber.

Is your child likely to be nervous when under stress? He can help himself by doing lots of preparation (see below), having an early night beforehand and having a good look at his CV again to remind him what he wrote in it – he'll be asked to elaborate.

It's not what you know but who you know. It can help to mention a friend or acquaintance who works for the company in the interview, and also to use that person's inside knowledge to find out about the company. Someone who has bothered to do some research will stand out from the crowd.

Most companies now have a website. Make sure that your interviewee has read it thoroughly.

WORK & MONEY

Department of Work and Pensions

The minimum wage level is currently £3.60 per hour for workers aged 18 to 21. In calculating the hourly rate of pay, your child should include her gross basic pay, any bonuses, incentives, tips or gratuities which were paid to him or through the employer's payroll, and the value of any free living accommodation she gets. The minimum wage level does not take into account overtime pay, shift premiums and most 'benefits in kind' (such as lunch vouchers). Exactly how your child works out her hourly rate depends on the type of contract she has. The Minimum Wage Helpline number is 0845 6000 678 and the Low Pay Unit is available on 020 7431 7385.

But the minimum wage doesn't apply to au pairs and nannies, apprentices and undergraduates on sandwich courses, volunteers or the self-employed.

An employee cannot agree orally or in writing with his/her employer to be paid less than the minimum wage: even if he does, the employer will still be committing an offence.

Check that your child knows his rights. These apply to part- or full-time workers. The Department of Education and Skills will supply you with the information at www.dfes.gsi.gov.uk.

If they haven't already got one, your son or daughter will need a bank account or building society account to stash all that lovely money they are now earning. See page 194.

Once your child is eighteen and earning money, he or she may be liable to pay tax. The Inland Revenue can advise you. Go to www.inlandrevenue.gov.uk. Welcome to the adult world!

DIVORCE & SEPARATION

With one in three marriages in the UK ending in divorce, children whose parents are no longer together are less likely to feel as isolated or different from friends as they might have done a few years ago. Today, in an average classroom, there is usually at least one other child in the same situation. This doesn't mean that there aren't still potential problems for children following separation. Conflict and parental distress, the loss of contact with one parent and the general disruption to their everyday lives are all hard for children to understand and cope with. The following may help you and your child through this difficult time.

Alison Wallis; Gingerbread, www.gingerbread.org. uk; Tracy Martin

New research is constantly being published showing the effects of divorce on children. None of it is conclusive. Invariably new studies contradict previous ones. Ignore it! It's not helpful and if you're in the middle of a break-up, you need to focus on finding a way through and looking after yourself and your children.

Choose your moment carefully and sit down with your children to explain exactly what is going on.

Encourage your children to ask questions and try to remain calm, whatever you're really feeling.

It's important that children feel you can cope and are still in control, even if you're upset.

Keep on talking to children. Help them to feel free to ask more questions whenever they want to. If you're finding it difficult, try to find someone else to discuss everything with them.

Grandparents and other close relatives are often better at talking to your children if you're finding it hard. They know everyone involved and care about your children.

When children are still young at the time of the break-up, they often accept separate households as completely normal. It can be years before they start to ask questions or want to know reasons why parents are no longer together.

Reassure your children that you still love them, tell them they're special and repeat reassurances often. Children's confidence and self-esteem can be dented as a result of family break-up.

Children frequently worry that they will be abandoned or will lose contact with the parent who is moving out of the family home. They need reassurance that both parents still care for them.

Try not to make children feel guilty about enjoying their time with their other parent. You don't want them to start hiding what they feel from you.

Talk about the parent who has moved away and avoid being negative as much as possible.

Try to talk to children as openly as possible without burdening them. Even young children are more aware of what's going on than parents suspect and what they're not told they may well make up.

Children can often feel guilty and worry that they're to blame for the break-up. Stress that the fact that Mummy and Daddy are no longer together is nothing to do with anything they have done, and that though you may no longer love each other, your children are just as special and loved as ever.

Children commonly feel angry and frightened. This is especially true if they were aware of conflicts and overheard parents arguing. Try to get them to talk about how they feel. If necessary, find someone outside the family for them to talk to.

Allow children their own emotions. Don't try to force them to put on a brave or happy face if that's not the way they feel. They have a right to feel cross, hurt or upset just as much as adults.

Teenagers can find it particularly hard to come to terms with parental break-up. They are at a stage when they are struggling to find their own identity and this process is often tied up with their family and parents, so when a relationship breaks down they can feel doubly knocked.

Some children are able to discuss their feelings but this isn't always the case. Don't try to force children to talk before they are ready. Children often don't communicate easily. It may take a lot of patience on your part, but all the messages will be heeded even if they don't respond or ask questions.

If they are feeling cross or depressed, children may act out these feelings through play or in their friendships rather than talking openly about them.

If you or your children are suffering from stress, depression or anxiety, or just need support, ask for help. Speak to your GP or contact the Health Information Service freephone, 0800 66 55 44, who will give you advice on finding a counsellor or local support groups. The British Association for Counselling and Psychotherapy is another useful organisation – 0870 443 5252, www.bacp.co.uk – as well as Gingerbread, an organisation set up to help lone-parent families – 0800 018 4318, www.gingerbread.org.uk.

It's helpful for children to meet up with children in a similar situation or a support group. It can be comforting for children to know that they're not alone.

Children learn from other children in similar circumstances and it's useful for them to hear what others say.

It is not unusual for concentration to lapse at school and for work standards to drop. They may take less of an interest in friends or hobbies.

Compensatory presents are best avoided, especially if they are used as a form of competition between parents.

A pet can be wonderful as an emotional outlet for a child, but always check with your ex-partner first. Adults usually bear the brunt of the day-to-day care of pets and you don't want to introduce another point of conflict between you.

Children are unlikely to welcome a new partner, with or without the partner's own children. It's not unusual for them to be openly hostile. Give them time to get used to your new partner. When they see that you are happy and that the other person doesn't change your relationship with them, they will get used to the idea and may even welcome having another adult around.

Expect initial difficulties with a new partner and try to help them adjust gradually. Support groups and counselling can help.

Dealing With Your Ex-partner

Try not to involve the children in your own negative feelings. However appallingly your partner has behaved, don't try to poison the children against him or her.

Avoid bad-mouthing your ex and try not to apportion blame, whatever's happened.

Don't use children as go-betweens or messengers and avoid burdening them with accusations about the other parent.

Children are desperate to love and be loved by both Mum and Dad. However you feel about each other, try to do everything to make the children's relationship with both parents work.

When your ex-partner is being malicious towards you and trying to blame you for any problems, don't retaliate. Children are not stupid; they make their own minds up from what they see.

If visits are set by court, arrange everything through official channels – your welfare officer or solicitor. Ex-partners can and do twist things to their own advantage.

Try to keep all channels of communication open with your ex-partner. It's very difficult at first, but as the years go by it gets easier and it's worth it for your child's sake.

Sometimes visiting arrangements are settled in court. If not, decide an amicable arrangement that works for everyone. There will be occasions when you need to be flexible. As children get older, give them some say over plans.

However much emotional blackmail your ex-partner tries to apply, stick to the rules set by the legal system. In the long run it makes things simpler and safeguards your own position.

Be honest with your children, especially as they get older. You have a problem with your ex-partner, but your children don't need to. It's right that your child should still love their other parent and want to spend time with them.

If your divorced partner has a habit of not turning up for planned visits, just don't tell children about the proposed visit in advance. Children get so upset and invariably blame themselves for the failure.

Talk directly to the other parent about anything relating to the children, whenever possible.

If you have custody, allow the other parent to be involved in your children's day-to-day lives – don't exclude them from parents' evenings at school, sport events or problems.

Encourage openness and easy everyday contact between children and both parents (assuming there is no abuse).

Especially if you're the parent who is not living with your children, try to develop and build on a shared interest.

Children need a space that is theirs in both homes, even if they can't have a whole room to themselves. It's practical as well as comforting for children to keep basic clothes, toiletries and possessions in both homes, too.

After seeing the parent they don't live with, children can seem keyed up and disruptive. Their behaviour may be more difficult than usual. This is to be expected for a while until children adjust to the separation.

Try to discuss such behaviour with your ex-partner without sounding as if you think it's their fault or something they're doing wrong. Try to develop strategies for dealing with awkward behaviour.

A quiet chat with children during the week about the changed family relationships may also help.

Keep an organised diary. If you thought planning holidays and events was difficult before, it was nothing compared with now.

It can be very hard to organise visits, especially as children get older and have their own social lives. Make arrangements as far ahead as possible in order to keep everyone happy. Avoid leaving plans to the last minute.

Plan holidays well in advance and let your ex-partner know before arrangements are fixed.

Make an effort to stay in touch with your ex-partner's immediate family – your child is their grandchild, niece or nephew, too.

Older children, in particular, can sometimes bail out of their current living arrangements and choose to move to the other parent rather than face up to the normal tensions that arise as teenagers grow up. This doesn't always help to solve problems, although it can help to give both sides a breathing space.

Encourage a positive relationship with both parents and try to make sure your children have fun with both. This is the best way to make sure children adapt and move on.

Grandparenting & Marriage Break-up

See page 275.

STEP-PARENTING

Orla Reilly;
Steve Douglas;
Geraldine Staines

You may feel unsure of where your authority lies as a step-parent, and so will your partner, who has to walk the tightrope between you and a demanding child, who will probably feel resentful and hurt by the changes in his life. Whilst it may be a relief for your partner to share the burden of parenting, it is his or her final responsibility to set rules and boundaries.

Work together with your partner to set out how you will work together as parents. You can disagree without the family falling apart. If you are all living together as a family you have a right to a say in discussions about what is acceptable and what is not.

If you have no children of your own, respect your partner's experience, but don't be afraid to acknowledge that there is some behaviour which you will not tolerate: rudeness, swearing, etc.

Give the relationship time. Your new stepchildren may be unwelcoming at first, but you will find a role as time goes on.

COPING ALONE

Sarah Brown;
Tracy Martin; Gingerbread,
www.gingerbread.org.uk

The major problem for children in single-parent families is low income and poor housing. The crucial factor in determining how well children fare is not whether they have one or two parents, but poverty. Look at your financial situation and try to plan ahead.

Many people are frightened of being alone. You shouldn't be: it's not all bad. Life alone can be much simpler and freer. There are many positive aspects to being a single parent:

- More energy for a start. Bad relationships are very draining emotionally.

- You know that it's up to you now and consequently you are more inclined to focus and get on with things – from decorating to a career.

- Children are happier if you are. They can be upset by seeing their parents arguing and feeling torn between you both.

- Bad relationships leave no room for your own development and creativity.

- One good side effect of being on your own can be a closer relationship with your children. You are no longer torn between keeping your partner happy and your children.

- As a single parent, you often do more with your children.

- Financial worries – yes, you do have less money but you are freed from the emotional pressures of a relationship that's going wrong and are more likely to do something to help yourself.

If you are working or self-employed, take out life assurance or accident cover.

If you are a single mother, contact the Child Support Agency (CSA). This can be a lengthy process but it's worth the wait. It may be simpler, and make dealings with your child's father easier, if you receive any payments through the CSA rather than directly from your ex-partner.

Make a will specifying guardianship of your child. This is especially important if you were not married to your ex-partner and would like him to take over guardianship, as this might not be automatic on your death.

Think about how you are going to support yourself and your child in the long term. Consider all the options, including retraining for a job that would tie in with being a parent. It's often easier to go back to college when children are little, before they start nursery or school. Most colleges run subsidised crèches, which make childcare easier while you're studying.

Lone parents can feel isolated and excluded. They can also feel the burden of taking on all the responsibilities of the family.

Make sure that you are fully aware of your rights and any benefits due; also where to find information and get help when you need it. There are several organisations to contact, including: Gingerbread, the National Council for One-Parent Families, the National Council for the Divorced and Separated, Families Need Fathers and the Shared Parenting Information Group (SPIG) UK. Addresses and contact numbers can be found on pages 291. See also the box opposite.

Especially when your family doesn't live near by, friends become very important and it's vital to build up a support network.

If your child is still a baby or toddler, become involved with groups like the NCT and church or community centre parent and toddler groups. These are all good places to meet people. When children are older, get involved with their schools – PTAs and Friends' Associations are always on the look-out for extra helpers. Find out about other parents' and toddlers' activities in your area that you would both enjoy.

You'll be surprised how many other people you meet who are in the same situation as you.

It's not always easy to conduct any kind of social life when children are small, but try to organise a babysitter occasionally and see friends.

At least make sure that you go out somewhere during the day with your baby or toddler. It's important to make contact with other people and to keep busy; otherwise the demands of a small child can make you feel very alone.

It's good for children to see you getting on and doing things. They realise that anything is possible.

It is empowering to see women coping alone and achieving. This can be a valid lesson especially for girls.

For coping alone after a bereavement, see page 271.

Don't suffer alone: there are many organisations set up to help. Here are just some of them:

- Gingerbread, the organisation for lone-parent families, national advice line and membership 0800 018 4318, www.gingerbread.org.uk.

Organisations providing counselling for children whose parents are splitting up:

- Relate 01788 573241, counselling line 08451 30 40 10
- Young Minds – parents' information service 0800 018 2138, www.youngminds.org.uk
- Parentline Plus offers advice on bringing up children 0808 800 2222.

For counselling and local support groups:

- British Association for Counselling and Psychotherapy 0870 443 5252, www.bacp.co.uk
- Health Information Service 0800 66 55 44.

For financial or legal help:

- The Child Support Agency enquiry line 08457 133 133
- Children's Legal Centre 01206 873820
- Solicitors' Family Law Association 08457 585 671
- Citizens Advice Bureaux 020 8733 2181 (for details of your local branch).

For step-parents and lone parents beginning new relationships:

- Contact the National Stepfamily Association through the Parentline Plus helpline on 0808 800 2222.

If you're in debt:

- Contact your local Citizen's Advice Bureau or the National Debtline 0808 808 4000 for free, confidential advice.

For housing advice:

- Contact your nearest Housing Advice Centre or Citizen's Advice Bureau.

BEREAVEMENT

The death of someone you love is probably the most painful experience anyone can suffer. Every year thousands of families are bereaved and while everyone's circumstances are different, they share feelings of grief and a sense of overwhelming loss.

The Child Bereavement Trust estimates that around 200,000 children face the death of one of their parents each year and over 3000 children and teenagers between the ages of 1 and 19 die through illness or accident. Each day, 18 babies die before, during or soon after birth and another 1000 will die before their first birthday. 5000 families are bereaved anually through suicide.

The Child Bereavement Trust, www.childbereavement. org.uk; Anne Worth;

Be honest with children about death. If it is discussed, it becomes less frightening.

Don't be morbid, but if someone is very ill, whether a parent, grandparent or friend, don't feel that you should shield children from the truth. Be as gentle as possible, but also as honest as you can about the fact that the person may be too ill to get better.

Cruse Bereavement
Care; Janet Wheeler
and Richard Davison

Younger children, especially, will not really understand what death means and you must judge how prepared they need to be.

It's useful to realise that children will be aware that something is going on and what they are not told they often make up.

Even young children need honest information geared to their age and need to feel included.

It is important to explain to young children that the person who has died has gone to heaven to be with God. Children need this reassurance, even if this doesn't match your own beliefs.

Children's first experience of bereavement is often the death of a grandparent. As well as missing the person, they can be jolted into realising that people close to them can die. They are likely to worry about losing their parents or siblings, and it's worth emphasising that their grandparent was old or had been ill for some time.

Tell your child's teachers that she has lost someone close. Teachers need to know to be a caring eye during the day.

Saying Goodbye

Saying goodbye is an important part of the grieving process. From about the age of seven, children should be given the option of attending the funeral. Some children won't want to go and it's vital that they are not forced.

The farewell element of a funeral is very therapeutic.

It may be a good idea for a child to go along to the funeral service but not to the burial or cremation.

When a grandparent dies, the surviving partner sometimes has very strong feelings that it's inappropriate for children to attend the funeral. It's important to respect their wishes, but try to find some other way for your children to say goodbye, such as planting a tree, or making a memorial plaque.

If a child doesn't want to go to the funeral or to a specific part of it, try to find a friend or relation he can stay with who can share and understand his feelings.

Your child may find comfort in prayer even if you don't.

Older children may also benefit from saying goodbye to the person's dead body in a chapel of rest or in bed at home. Again it's vital that this is the child's choice. Dead people can look very peaceful and saying goodbye may be a help in coping with grief and coming to terms with loss.

Grieving

Death is always a shock, even when it's expected. Confusion and panic are very normal reactions.

When someone close to them dies, such as a parent or sibling, children commonly react in one of two ways: they may cry and scream, or they can be so shocked that they don't want to believe what's happened and withdraw emotionally. Both reactions are completely normal, but they shouldn't go on for too long.

Children may not want to discuss what's happened or how they feel. They may want to appear to get on with their normal lives. The fact that they are not showing any outward signs of being upset does not mean they are not grieving.

After a death, people can go into an 'automatic' mode. This can be a result of shock and is the body's way of coping. If your children seem to be unaffected by a death, let them behave that way, without forcing them to talk about and acknowledge it – they will react and grieve in their own time.

If a parent dies, children need reassurance that they are going to be cared for and looked after – that their world will continue. Fears for the future become frighteningly real.

Children feel the same emotions and sense of loss as adults, but they don't know how to express these feelings. They need grown-ups to support them and share their grief.

Don't feel that you have to protect children from their emotions.

Allow children to be children. In some ways they are more resilient than adults and will seem to carry on with their lives and play as if nothing has happened. They are affected but need to act their age and protect themselves. Don't expect them to react and behave like adults.

It's often impossible to explain why someone has died. It's just important to show that you care and are there whenever your child needs your support.

It's normal to feel anger and resentment. Older children in particular may feel very angry with the person who has died for leaving them. These feelings will pass but might need to be discussed. Such feelings can lead to insecurities and feelings of isolation.

If a parent or sibling has been ill for some time, especially if they were often away in hospital, at first nothing may seem very different after their death. It's often only later that grief really hits – at Christmas, birthdays or another special occasion.

Birthdays and other significant dates bring back memories. At first these will be very painful but over time your children learn to cope with the changes and enjoy remembering. If they forget milestone anniversaries, don't make them feel guilty. Grief can happen any day for any reason, and 'forcing' them to remember at a particular time can be unwise.

It's often hard to find the right words. If you can't, physical comfort will help.

You don't have to hide the fact that you are upset. In fact, it often helps if children see you cry – they then feel free to express their own grief and know they're not alone.

Resist the temptation to clear away the clothes and possessions of the dead person immediately. This will be a very sudden and final shock for children. Try to make it a gradual and gentle process.

Give children mementoes to keep, explaining, 'Mum [or Dad] would have wanted you to have this.'

Children who have lost a sibling often feel guilty that they are still alive. They may feel an extra burden that they must make up for their missing sibling. Try to make it clear that you love them for being them – they don't have to be someone else as well.

Especially when their sibling had been ill for a long time, children may have resented the attention the sibling received or even felt jealous. When their sibling dies, they feel guilt as well as grief. Children can feel angry at being left but will also feel guilty about this. Try to discuss their feelings and reassure them.

Children need to be reminded that the person who has died loved them very much and didn't want to leave them. These affirmations need to continue for years, with reminders such as saying that Mum or Dad would have been so proud of you for passing your exams or behaving like that.

Talking about grief and the dead person may be too difficult for a child with close family who are too personally involved. A grandparent or teacher the child is close to might be better.

It's important that the person your child talks to knows them well and also knew the person who died.

It's helpful to remember that more damage is done by not discussing bereavement than is ever done by talking.

Watch out for signs of depression in children (see page 221). Buried grief can manifest itself that way.

Children who hide their grief when someone close to them dies can struggle emotionally later in life.

Sometimes grief only manifests itself much later in life – after a life-changing event like the birth of a child. This can act as a trigger and all the emotions that have been suppressed for years erupt to the surface. Be prepared as their parent.

With support, children will recover from bereavement and there is evidence that it can be less damaging emotionally than divorce as they feel less rejection.

Talk about the person the children have lost as much as possible. Remember funny moments and happy times, and tell them often how like their mum/dad/grandmother they are.

There is comfort in memory and if a child has lost a parent, it is important to talk about the parent or else a vital link in their lives will be lost. This is especially true when a child is too young to have clear personal memories of her own to draw upon.

Keep photos, letters and other mementoes. In the early days, they may be painful reminders, but in later years they will be very important, a source of comfort and a vital connection with the person who has died.

Warn your children that some people will be too embarrassed to talk to them about what's happened or not know what to say. This is particularly important for teenagers. Reassure them that this means not that their friends don't care but that they are not mature enough to know what to say.

Reassure them that it's OK to laugh or mess around with friends. They don't have to be sad all the time.

If you meet another partner, or remarry, don't expect your children to welcome them with open arms. They may well feel rejected and betrayed. Be honest that this new person in your life makes you happy, but that no one will replace their father or mother.

Seek professional help when you need it. For organisations that offer advice and counselling, see the box opposite and page 291 onwards.

Teenagers & Grief

Teenagers can find grief extremely difficult to cope with. They are going through a time of change and insecurity anyway.

The death of a parent will mean that family life is completely altered and the one constant in their life has gone. Teenagers will be very aware of the loss of security and need extra reassurance that life does continue, and that they are still safe and cared for.

Try to help them not to cut themselves off from others and offer support or help them to find someone they are happy to talk to. This could be a friend, a teacher, doctor or trained counsellor.

Teenagers need reassurance that it's natural to want to cry and feel depressed, to feel angry, embarrassed and unable to talk.

If a teenager has lost a sibling he may feel guilty that he's still here. He may also try to take on some of his sibling's interests. This is fine, but it's important to encourage him to hold on to his individuality.

Teenagers in particular may feel guilty about arguments they had or nasty things they said to the person who died. They need help to forgive themselves and to realise that the dead person knew how they really felt.

Teenagers may irrationally blame themselves in some way for the death. Talk as much as possible and try to rationalise these feelings.

Grief can have physical effects, making if difficult to eat and sleep properly. It can make a teenager irritable and have trouble concentrating at school. Be prepared for this.

Watch out for destructive behaviour – risk-taking, dropping friends, turning to drugs or alcohol. Always seek professional help if you're worried.

If needed, let your child take time away from school. Everyone's different and a break may be helpful to give time and space.

Coping As A Bereaved Parent

Try not to become too dependent upon your children.

If you feel unable to cope with your own grief, talk to your GP about counselling. This will help you to deal with your children's feelings, too.

For practical advice on coping as a single parent, see page 265.

The Death Of A Child

Many couples who lose a child find themselves feeling isolated in their grief and unable to support each other. Grief is solitary and can push couples apart.

It can help to realise that men and women face grief differently. Women tend to focus on their loss and frequently need to recall the person they've lost and share memories. Men tend to look for solutions – to want to repair the hurt and return to a semblance of normality. This does not mean that both do not feel the loss acutely – it's just that their reactions are different.

These differences can cause resentment and place unbearable strains on the closest relationships. Try to share and explore feelings.

For the long process of recovery to begin, couples need to acknowledge their loss and grieve for the dead person. Sharing emotions is part of this process.

Grief is very tiring.

There will be good and bad days, and at first the bad will outnumber the good. With time, the days where you feel you can cope and go on will increase. Don't feel guilty about feeling better.

It's not a sign of failure to need counselling and couples may find it helpful to talk to someone for whom the grief is not so raw.

Don't suffer alone: many organisations offer advice and counselling, and can put you in touch with support agencies and groups in your area.

- The Child Bereavement Trust provides trained support for families following the death of someone close to them, both in the immediate crisis and the following months: 01494 446648, www.childbereavement.org.uk

- Cruse Bereavement Care offers advice and counselling 0870 167 1677

- British Association for Counselling and Psychotherapy, 0870 443 5252, Health Information Service 0800 66 55 44, www.bacp.co.uk

- Many GPs also offer counselling services at their surgeries

- See also Useful Addresses & Websites, page 291.

GRANDPARENTS

There is one other moment as wonderful as giving birth to your own children, and that is when your children give birth to theirs. You only have to listen to new grandparents bursting with pride as they extol the virtues of their new grandchildren to realise what a special time in life this can be. As a grandparent you have all the joys of young children and all the reflected glory, without the responsibility of having to raise them.

But the nature of grandparenthood has changed. As more and more women have to pursue their careers to make ends meet, and as there is less and less support around to help them do it, you may find that you are asked to take on some responsibility in child-rearing. Whether you accept or not is a decision that only you can make.

The most satisfying part of grandparenthood is that it is not until your own children reproduce that they fully realise the magnitude of the job you have done in raising them. Only now will they appreciate how much you love them, and how much you have sacrificed. You can give yourself a slap on the back as you watch them instil in their children the values you worked so hard to instil in them. (The downside is that they'll recognise where you went wrong too!)

ParentlinePlus;
Barbara Stileman;
Marjorie Tombs; Sally
Shone; Sally Wright;
Elizabeth Clare;
Grandparents
Federation, Helpline:
01279 444 964

Grandparents fall into two categories: those who live close by and/or are very involved in the raising of their grandchildren, and those who feel they have 'done their bit' as far as child-rearing is concerned. The former will be an enormous help to their children and emotionally close to their grandchildren, though need to be wary of being too involved and becoming a pain. If you fall into the latter category, make as much contact as you feel able to, but don't be surprised if you find your children resent what appears to be a lack of interest.

Parenting has changed – this generation has a more liberal view of the way they bring up their children. That doesn't mean it is wrong, so listen before offering advice that may not be appreciated.

Some areas of babycare have changed too – lying babies on their backs instead of on their fronts has greatly reduced the incidence of cot death, for example. Babies are weaned later, and adding cereal to bottles is now considered dangerous. Your methods may have worked when you brought up your family, but let your children as parents be led by the experts.

Hard as it may be, try not to interfere with the upbringing of your grandchildren. Just offer love and support unconditionally. Hold your advice until you are asked for it. Your best intentions can sometimes be interpreted as interference. Accept the fact that your children will raise your grandchildren in the manner that they think is best.

Today's parents generally have far less help (practical and emotional) in raising their children than the previous generation did. When thinking about what role you can play as a grandparent, remind yourself how much support you received.

Pressures are different for parents these days. Many more women go out to work and have their children in childcare. Respect that, even if you don't agree with it. Your daughter or daughter-in-law may not want to be working but may have no choice, in which case the last thing she needs is your disapproval adding to her guilt.

Keep your values strong. Children are much more affected these days by their peer group, and parents find it harder to keep control. Your values are still important.

Avoid comparing one grandchild with another at all costs. 'Oh, cousin Freddie was out of nappies by eighteen months' will not go down well with a fraught daughter-in-law potty-training her first child.

Grandchildren live a long way away? Because of the changing nature of jobs, most grandparents are now far away from their family. This makes grandparenting harder work and relationships harder to sustain. Your role is still critical as a mainstay, though. Get online so that you can e-mail your family wherever they are. E-mail is quick and talks the right language for teenagers especially.

Ask to have your grandchildren to stay. Don't wait to be asked. It will be very encouraging for your children (and less guilt-inducing) if they think you want your grandchildren over. Try not to make it seem that you are 'doing them a favour' all the time.

Be a good guest – just because you are family you can still outstay your welcome. Be sensitive especially to daughters-in-law: they may love you for a short time, but you will cramp their style after a while.

Live close to your grandchildren? Tempting as it might be to drop in unannounced all the time, ring first. Your children may find your continual presence an imposition.

Try not to be too well meaning. You may have time on your hands to share responsibility and help out, but even if your intentions are entirely honourable, your children may read it as interfering.

When appropriate, compliment your children on their parenting of your grandchild. Take their good parenting as a compliment to yourself – because it shows that you have set a good example.

You can be a source of wisdom and stability, but being a grandparent is much the same as parenting a teenager. Your children will make mistakes, as you did in child-rearing, but they need to realise these for themselves.

Grandchildren are fun – much more fun, in many ways, than you found your own children. That's because you have more time to spend with them and less of the responsibility – you can hand them back at the end of the visit. But let their parents know that you understand that the real work begins when you walk away.

People learn best by hearing ideas and then being supported in trying them for themselves. As parents, your children need your approval and your help. But they may feel judged and not good enough if you seem to be interfering or taking over.

Offer a listening ear. Your children may want to tell you about their triumphs and joys, so welcome them when they do – after all, you are about the only people they can boast to. But parenting is a tough job and there are times when they may need a good moan. Be prepared to hear about anger, sadness, jealousy and uncertainty as well as pride and love.

Feel you are being relied upon too much? Offer to help when you can, but gently remind your children that you have a life beyond your grandchildren. Offer specific dates when you can babysit or be around as an extra pair of hands.

Encourage your children to write a will, appointing a guardian in the event of their deaths. You can offer yourself as guardian, but be realistic about how long you would be able to care for your grandchildren.

Grandparenting Young Children

Having them to stay? Make a set of 'Grandparent rules' so that from their first visit the grandchildren learn what behaviour is acceptable in your home. These rules may not be the same as those the children have at home, but the children should respect them. There is security in discipline and it's much easier to enforce discipline on grandchildren than on children. But don't criticise their parents' rules in front of them – in fact, be very careful about criticising their parents at all.

Act your age! Having your grandchildren around will remind you how exhausting children can be. Go easy on yourself. You are not as young as you were, added to which it is an extra pressure to look after someone else's child, even if it is your grandchild. You'll find that you don't take the shortcuts you might have as a parent. In a way it is a far more onerous task.

Be aware of safety. If you haven't had young children around for a while, look at your house from a toddler's point of view. Remember the danger of stairs, medicine cabinets, glass and china where it can be reached … For more on safety, see page 66.

Have a good selection of toys – ask friends who have older children who have grown out of them to give you hand-me-downs, or invest in a few games and toys for your home. Make these special to your house to give your grandchildren something to look forward to playing with. If possible dig out toys that their parents played with – with a bit of luck you will have had the foresight to have kept the Lego!

Ensure that old or second-hand toys are still safe to use. Broken toys can be dangerous, especially older soft toys, which may contain wires not permitted in toy manufacture these days. Some older wooden toys may also contain lead in their paint. Newer toys now carry a Lion Mark, developed in 1988 by the British Toy & Hobby Association as a symbol of toy safety and quality.

Young children love the old-fashioned games such as Hunt the Thimble and Happy Families. Play imagination games with them too, making up stories, playing charades. Keep a box of old clothes for dressing up. They will love discovering old clothes, hats, shoes and coats.

Children still enjoy the games and outings your children did. As a grandparent you have time to read to them, take them for walks, and can provide respite from videos and TV which many parents have to resort to as babysitter at some time.

Be prepared. It's worth having some equipment at your house, especially the unwieldy things that your grandchildren's parents won't want to lug around – high chairs, car seats and playpen. If these are only going to be used occasionally, good second-hand will do. For naps, a travel cot is fine and can double up as a playpen. Later on, you might want to keep the second-best bike, skateboard and a helmet at your house, along with a stack of videos.

Ask the children's parents to supply a change of clothes, especially pants, that you can keep at your house for emergencies. Find out too what stage nappies younger children are in so that you can have a ready supply.

When looking after your grandchildren, respect the routines your children have created. You may think that some of them are strange (or even ill-advised) but ignoring them will confuse the children and following them will make life a whole lot easier.

Create a 'sameness' about your home. Children love the security of knowing that life has a constancy. Have, for instance, a mug which is for their use exclusively, a drawer for sweets, a basket with toys that is always in the same place, even their own room.

Children are far fussier now than they used to be about what they will eat. It's not worth fighting it. Go with the flow.

Try not to spoil them – tempting though it may be. It creates a sense of competition with their parents, and is unfair because parents cannot (nor should they want to) sustain that level of indulgence.

Children love to hear about their parents when they were young, especially their misdemeanours, so make sure that you share past experiences, stories and memories about yourself and your family. Children will also enjoy hearing about how they are like their parents and/or cousins.

Keep family heritage and tradition, but don't foist it on unreceptive children. They will want to hear it when they are ready.

Never tell your grandchildren that they are not as clever, athletic, good-looking, etc. as their parents (in any case, you have probably conveniently forgotten their bad points!).

Grandparenting Teenagers

As grandparents you can provide an extra layer of love and care on top of that your grandchildren receive from their parents. This love is a security net for children. If your teenage grandchildren want to have a gripe about their parents, let them – it is a compliment that they are confiding in you and you can provide a valuable buffer – but help and advise them. Don't abuse this special friendship by using it as a bargaining tool against the children's parents – especially if the confidences concern a marriage break-up.

Affirm what their parents tell them. This is not only true for rules: remind them also how much their parents love them. In the hurly-burly of raising a teenager, the parents may have forgotten to tell them for a while.

You are neutral ground in teenage/parent rows. Teenagers are not as emotionally bound to you as they are to their parents, so you can be an emotional sanctuary. However, avoid interfering between parents and their children when they are arguing – unless the situation gets very out of hand. And don't take a child's side in an argument. If you disapprove of something the parents are doing which you feel is an important issue, speak to the parents about it, but never in front of the children.

Beware of teenagers playing grandparents and parents off against each other.

Let teenagers involve you. Ask your teenage grandchildren to teach you about mobile phones/the internet/e-mail or tell you about *Pop Idol* or *Big Brother* – even try to sit through one of their favourite programmes. They won't appreciate you using the jargon – heaven forbid – but it will help you to relate to them and to understand where they are coming from.

If you have a mobile phone, ask your teenage grandchildren to show you how to text – it's a great way to keep in touch with them, even if it's just to say hello.

You have an important role to play in explaining the past and your childhood. Teenagers can be riveted by times gone by and even though stories about your youth or when your children were young won't feel like history to you, it is to them and worth explaining fully – when they ask!

Don't be afraid to invite teenagers over to stay. Remind yourself how exhausting it is raising that age group – you will be providing a respite for their parents.

If you live near where a teenage grandchild plans to study, offer a teenager a room in your house if you can. You can keep an eye on her and her parents will know that she is safe and in loving hands. It will be exhausting, but the experience will keep you young.

Teenagers need feeding … copiously!

You may have regrets about your own children, or about your relationship with them. You may be hoping to get parenting right with your grandchildren and feel upset if this is not happening. As a result, you may be tempted to criticise or impose your views. Try not to: rather, take an interest, listen to your grandchildren, talk about your values and help them to build their confidence as young adults.

Praise your grandchildren (whatever their age). Praise builds self-esteem and confidence. They are your grandchildren, so they are bound to be brilliant, witty and beautiful and it is the privilege of grandparenthood to be able to tell them so.

Grandparenting & Marriage Break-up

When family break-up occurs, you will be a mainstay for the grandchildren. Try not to be partisan, though your child may well turn to you for support.

Keep out of arguments. Tell both parents that you don't want to be involved in arguments although you're happy to help them talk things through.

Don't take sides. It may seem that your child needs you to defend him or her and attack the other parent, but this only hurts your grandchildren. Don't forget that the ex-partner is still their parent.

It is not your place to criticise the other partner.

Your grandchildren will look to you as a constant. You can provide a valuable stable influence during the trauma of break-up and divorce.

However you feel about the family change or the people involved, and even if your child isn't talking to the other parent, it may be important for you to keep in touch, while staying out of the argument. Whatever has happened and whoever you feel is to blame, your grandchildren need and deserve you.

Keep in contact with your grandchildren. You can do this by phone, letter or e-mail as well as face-to-face.

Lost access to your grandchildren? This could be because they now live with your son- or daughter-in-law. You have no legal rights of access, but you can apply to the courts for leave to apply for a contact order, or for indirect contact (when you can receive letters and photographs). Do this via your solicitor, or get a form from a magistrates court (it costs about £30). The whole process can cost money and there is no guarantee of success.

Grandparenting Step-grandchildren

Try to accept step-grandchildren as part of the new family unconditionally. Though it will be hard not to favour natural grandchildren, you have a big role to play in helping the whole family accept one another.

Be welcoming. Making a new family is a difficult and stressful task. They all need as much support and confidence-boosting as they can get.

Be fair. This means that if you're giving presents, time and attention, share it out equally. Ignoring a child you see as 'not yours' hurts not only the child, but also your own child and the other children involved too.

Give them a chance. You may well find you that enjoy spending time with the step-grandchildren more than you anticipated.

Give yourself time. Don't be surprised if you don't like the step-grandchildren at first, but be open to the fact that relationships change, given a chance.

Grandparent Turned Parent

Should your children die without appointing a guardian or making provision for their children, you can apply for a residence order via the courts, which gives you parental responsibility. Consult a solicitor on the Children Panel.

You can apply for a residence order even if both or one parent is still alive, especially if your grandchild is in the care of the local authority. You may have most but not all parental responsibility, and it will not affect your grandchild's legal relationship with its parents.

If you have put aside money for your retirement, you may not be eligible for financial help if you successfully get a residence order. Ask your local benefits office or go to www.legalservices.gov.uk for information on legal aid.

If you are called upon to raise your grandchildren, the contents of this book will help to remind you of your parenting skills, but remember that the basics of parenting (love, support, encouragement) have not changed.

The following will help you with grandparenting support, legal and emotional:

- Grandparents' Federation, www.grandparents-federation.org.uk

- Family Mediators Association – offers independent mediators in cases of family dispute throughout the UK: 46 Grosvenor Gardens, London SW1W OEB, tel. 020 7881 9400, fmassoc@globalnet.co.uk

- Childrens Legal Centre – provides free advice and information to parents involved in education and contact disputes: University of Essex, Wivenhoe Park, Colchester, Essex CO4 3SQ, adviceline 01206 873820, clc@essex.ac.uk

- National Association of Citizens Advice Bureaux (NACAB) – provides free, impartial and confidential advice and help through local bureaux to anybody on any subject, including legal and financial matters; look in the phone book for details of your local Bureau.

Websites for grandparents:

www.bbc.co.uk/england/grandparents/contact.shtml

www.grandparents-federation.org.uk

www.parentlineplus.org.uk

www.seehowtheygrow.com.

SIBLINGS

Where you fall in the sibling line-up can have a profound effect on the type of person you become. 'Oh, he's typical eldest/middle/youngest child,' you hear people say, but that is simplistic: though there are very definite patterns, how children relate to the rest of the family and the dynamics of family life are complex subjects.

Relations between siblings are deeply complex, too. Sibling love can be a love so deep that it is unfathomable and unexplainable. Your relationship with a brother or sister can be the strongest of life, and it's worth parents encouraging that level of closeness. Siblings understand each other better than anyone because they both grew from the same foundation.

However, dislike and even hatred between siblings can run just as deep as love. Sibling fights are terrifying to behold – probably because they know it is safe to vent their aggression in a relatively safe environment when more than likely they will be forgiven. 'How can two people I love so much hate each other so much?' you may ask despairingly. It's not your fault as a parent – it is simply a clash of personalities (personalities which may be frighteningly similar). All you can do is share your love fairly and hope that your children learn to live with each other.

Rebecca Stileman; Jill Summers; Mark Nicholls; Trevor Yates; Hector Wills; Louisa Hope; Ian Hecks, headteacher

No matter what anyone may say, there is no perfect number of children, and no perfect interval between them. Unless you are brilliant or just plain lucky, the interval is not possible to plan anyway.

They are all different: the fact that number one child was an angel, slept through the night at six weeks and hasn't given you a moment's problems doesn't mean that you have cracked parenthood. Number two will show you that no two children are the same. The approach you used for one child may not work for the other. Be flexible.

However well siblings get along, there will always be rivalries.

Try to give each child some time to themselves and some time with you alone.

Let your children show you their differences. It's very convenient to shoehorn them into a mould – even dressing them the same way – but they need to express their personalities right from the start.

Try not to give your children first names beginning with the same letter (Sam and Susie Jones, for example). It will become very confusing when post arrives in the future addressed to S. Jones – especially bank statements.

Look at where you fall in the pecking order amongst your own siblings and try to remember how that felt as you deal with your own children.

Let your children fight and only interfere when things get really heated. If they never settle their own arguments and you do so for them, they will never learn to compromise. Family feuding can be a good idea – it's learning how to compromise within a safe, forgiving environment. Stay out of it, unless there is a danger that they will hurt each other.

If one sibling has a friend to play, either arrange for the others to have one too, or make sure you spend time with the one left playing alone.

Staggering bedtimes is a good idea. Write out a chart outlining what time each child must be in bed, which gives older children time to finish homework, and you time to read to each one and discover what they did with their day.

Be fair: if you buy a present or treat for one child and not the other, the one who missed out is fully entitled to be miffed – wouldn't you be? But if the gift is a reward for a school prize/excellent report/skill learnt, make it exclusive to the deserving child. It detracts from the importance of the treat if an undeserving sibling gets one too.

Save money on name tapes: have one set of name tapes printed with one child's initial at the beginning and the other child's at the end (for instance, T Smith L). You can then fold over the irrelevant end on each respective child's clothes as you sew them on.

As you put clothes away as each child grows out of them, mark them clearly with the age range on the outside of the bag or case and pack them away in small batches. Doing this will save time later – you won't have to trawl through to find a particular item for the younger sibling.

Children love routine and familiarity. Let them sit at a particular place at the table, which they can then call their own …

… But to make them feel special, let each one sit at the head of the table in turn, for a special meal each week.

Whose turn is it in the front? Keep a rota in your head so that each child gets a turn in the front of the car in strict rotation and stick to it.

'He's better at everything than I am.' One clever or able child can easily overshadow his sibling and steal the limelight. This is especially painful if the clever sibling is younger. How galling to have a squirt of a younger brother able to play football better/tie his shoelaces/get better grades. Be sensitive to the child who finds it harder to achieve. Make sure that praise is given and meant as often as possible, and avoid comparisons.

There is nothing a child likes more than to rile a sibling. Children seem to know just where to find the Achilles heel and go for it. Have a warning word that you agree you will say when you see the situation arising. It should nip it in the bud.

Be aware of your children being protective about their particular interests and talents. An eldest daughter who has found a niche at drama classes, for example, may be very put out by a younger sibling wanting to become involved too. She will be possessive – and rightly so. Younger children pursuing an elder sibling's hobby have a chance to see what they need to achieve to measure up or be better – it's not unlike being the last act in a singing competition. Try to vary your children's interests, even if they are broadly in the same field – suggest each plays a different brass instrument/sings in a different choral group/play a different position on the football field.

Youngsters know exactly who their parents favour (which inevitably parents do, though this should vary through the family at different times). Be aware that children are merciless in exploiting and manipulating their parents' favour to get what they want.

Leaving the eldest alone to babysit younger brothers and sisters? This can be a tricky one, as younger siblings may resent being told what to do by an elder one. Legally it is your decision at what age you feel the eldest is responsible enough to care for younger siblings and it's your responsibility if anything goes wrong.

- Make your children feel that this is a very grown-up thing to do: that you now trust them to get on together and be cooperative. Your eldest will be grateful for your respect; the younger ones will feel you have confidence in them. Get the children together and lay down the ground rules: 'Your bedtime is at eight, yours is at nine' and so on, so that they all hear and there can be no misunderstandings.

- Make your first foray out a brief one, so that everyone gets used to the idea and you are not leaving them all alone together for too long. Make sure that they know where you have gone and come home when you say you will.

You want your children to get on, love each other and be supportive friends for ever. They may not. In fact, they may hate each other. Whilst your children still live with you, you will have to find a middle ground where life is tolerable. Once they leave home, it's best not to force them into 'happy family' situations if the atmosphere will be unbearable. Let them go their own way.

For the arrival of a new sibling, see page 93.

The Eldest Child

Being the eldest is a tough role to play. She may be the eldest but she is still a child.

Avoid saying 'Act your age' or 'You are the eldest, so be responsible'. Why should he? Let your eldest do grown-up things, which will make him feel special ('Could you help me lay the table because I know you are good at it'), but give him the time, space and confidence to behave as he will and should for his age.

He wants to watch a favourite TV programme which is on late? Respect his need for a special time by allowing him to watch it without his brothers and sisters around. That way it's a treat.

If only we had a dress rehearsal. Eldest children have to put up with their parents learning to be parents, and they often get the blame for everything. Try not to be too tough.

Middle Children

Not easy being second or third in the pecking order. Family surveys show that middle children are often the naughtiest, possibly in an attempt to win adult attention away from an older child – any attention is OK, even if it's bad attention. They may need lots of positive and quality time with both parents.

'Why don't I ever get anything new?' Clothes and toys are usually in good-enough condition to hand down to number two – it's number three child who gets new things when their siblings' trousers and Brio train set are too worn out or broken to hand on again. Remember that number two deserves new toys and clothes occasionally too.

What was right for your eldest may not be right for your second or third. That could mean anything from routine as a baby to schooling. All children have different talents; a second child may, for example, like or dislike a teacher the eldest one had in the past. Be flexible and try not to force round pegs into square holes.

Oldest and youngest children can be very demanding on their parents, and the middle one(s) are often left to their own devices. Playing on their own can be fun (and is to be encouraged) but it can mean loneliness. Make time for middle children between their siblings' demands on your time.

It's not fair! Younger children are always the baby (until they are middle-aged) and may get away with things the middle children never do. Meanwhile the eldest is being allowed the treats that come with being the eldest. It's a tough call on middle siblings and you may have to be fairer than fair.

Try to remember what age your eldest child learned certain skills/read certain books. It is tempting to encourage a second child with the same skills too quickly when he may not be ready to learn, and he will become dispirited if he fails.

The plus side of being piggy in the middle: you have other siblings to play with either side of you.

Youngest Children

Being the youngest is a double-edged sword. As parents you are now more experienced and as a result will be more relaxed in handling your youngest child. This can often mean that youngest ones settle quickly into happy, contented children. However, youngest children get carted around as you take older ones to parties, the park, school events. All babies and toddlers thrive on routine and need the same basic care that you gave their older siblings.

Don't be offended when a youngest baby beams enthusiastically at their interesting older siblings and ignores you. Just enjoy it!

'He hit me!' Younger children are experts at blaming older ones, to get them into trouble. Don't always believe what you hear …

Youngest children can be quite offended as they grow older and realise that there are precious few photos of them about when their older siblings have albums full of every first smile and step. Hard as it is, be conscientious in making photographic/camcorder coverage fair for each child.

The big advantage of being the youngest: everything she does has probably been done before by her siblings; she can get away with murder and may be allowed to do things younger (disadvantage: nothing she does is new). As a parent, be aware that older children at any age may get fed up when their little brother or sister is allowed to go to bed later than they ever were/have a glass of wine at an earlier age.

You may find that you are more on the ball educationally with the youngest than you were with the others. You know what to expect at each stage of development, and feel it is irrelevant how they compare to other children (when you were neurotic first time around). Rather than speed her up, you may find that you are actually trying to slow her down.

Children – especially teenagers – need to feel that they are individuals. Saying 'That's what we did with your sister' will not wash with the younger one.

You may have given up on Tumble Tots, extra-curricular activities and pursuing hobbies by the time you have your third or fourth child. You've simply run out of steam, when first time round you probably jumped on the 'I must let her try everything and be stimulated' bandwagon. The compensation for your youngest is that he will have your undivided attention whilst his older siblings are at school. What playgroup isn't there to provide you can make up for with home-based activities.

Only Children

Whether having one child was a choice or an accident of nature, the hardest thing for any parent of an only child is to not invest all your expectations in that child. Children's weaknesses/shortcomings are easier to handle if the family 'pot' is diluted somewhat by other siblings. Take your child at face value and let him be himself, not what you want him to be.

Does your child share none of your interests? It can be very disappointing if you were mad keen on football and your son's idea of hell is watching the Arsenal game while you have a beer. Try to find some common ground and celebrate his individuality.

Only children tend to grow up very fast. They spend much more time with adults and often have a very precocious attitude. This is wonderful from the point of view of their maturity, but can make them lonely amongst their peer group. Right from the word go they need to spend time with children their own age.

Be aware that as a growing teenager your child may feel a huge responsibility for you as her parents. Who else is there to share the burden with when you are in your dotage? She might need reassurance that you are not going to expect her to look after you as you get old.

Having only one child does not ensure that yours will be the perfect parent/child relationship. In fact, an only child can feel stifled by the enormous waves of love coming from two devoted parents. Avoid being over-protective and unrealistic about your expectations. At worst you will sour the relationship.

Only children are used to receiving all the attention, even as they get older. They may need reminding that you have other interests and demands on their time. A tough lesson, but one that will help them settle into the real world.

Siblings At The Same School

If you already have a child attending a state school and you live in the catchment area, the chances are very high that younger brothers or sisters will be accepted too. Make sure, though, that you get your application in on time.

But there is no guarantee that younger siblings will get into the same school as their older brother or sister. Inclusion may be the mantra of comprehensive schools, but these days they are performance-motivated and the trend is towards selection. If your younger child isn't accepted (into the private or the state system), it may be because the school does not consider it's the right school for her or that she is not as able as her older sibling. Ask yourself if you have made the right choice or want your children at the same school for your own convenience.

Younger siblings joining older brother or sisters will be familiar with the school, and some of the other children – also the teachers. This may result in over-confidence or cockiness, which peers (and older pupils) may not like. Talk to the younger sibling before he starts – reminding him that there will be things that he won't know and that he must listen and learn.

Older siblings need to be supportive, but know when to encourage younger brothers and sisters to play in the playground with their own friends.

Teachers will inevitably compare siblings to each other – especially if they have been class teacher to both. Try not to fall into the same trap, but take each one at face value.

Even if you are familiar with a school because your eldest attends it, make sure that as the next child joins it is a special experience for her. Beginning your first day in hand-me-down uniform and a 'You'll be fine' farewell can be a crushing disappointment for a nervous newcomer. She won't care that you already know her new teacher: the teacher is new to her. Attend all the new pupil events, try to kit her out in as much new equipment and uniform as you can afford, and be as enthusiastic and interested as you were the first time round.

11 SPECIAL NEEDS AND GIFTED CHILDREN

If your child is different in some way, you can feel very isolated, and suffer your child's isolation too. It's so easy to focus on the ways in which your child is not fitting in and to view the whole situation as a set of problems that you have to solve. This has been aptly described as looking at the hole, rather than at the doughnut. You know that you love your little doughnut, however frustrating the situation you're coping with may be, but it's easy to get bogged down in the negative stuff, whether it's coping with school, behaviour or the way your family functions as a unit. You can find yourself missing the point that your child is an individual with her own strengths and weaknesses, and trying to develop her own way of coping with her situation. Also, your child may be in the minority, but your problems are far from unique. And parents who have been through the same dilemmas are very generous in sharing their information.

This chapter covers some common problems and conditions. For organisations that can help with other conditions and disabilities, see page 301.

ALLERGIES

Justine Jordan;
Libby Tillotson

Signs to look out for: permanently stuffy nose, itchy skin, diarrhoea, failure to thrive could all be signs of allergy and should alert you to be careful and to arrange to see your GP. Symptoms like severe skin reactions, swelling up of lips or face, hives or reddening, vomiting or breathing difficulties are danger signs and could indicate severe allergy. Don't hesitate to call a doctor or an ambulance if your child has a severe reaction.

Zinc and castor oil cream can cause a problem for some babies. If so, use petroleum jelly instead.

Steer clear of grapeseed and nut oils for baby massage. They may trigger allergic reactions.

Asthma

Your child may have asthma if he has a persistent cough that wakes him regularly in the early hours of the morning. You may also notice him wheezing. See page 95 for information on asthma.

Eczema

For information on eczema see page 97.

Food Allergies

Make sure that everyone knows what your child can and can't eat. Often people don't realise that, say, dairy products or soya can be found in unexpected places. Most people do not understand how serious food allergies can be, and may think it is all right to give just a small amount of a food that your child is allergic to.

Teach your child about her allergy from the earliest stage, so that she can learn to avoid foods that she is allergic to and explain the situation to others.

If your child's allergy is serious, get him a medical alert bracelet to notify others of his condition, and make sure that there is an epipen for him at school and on every school trip, and that the staff know how to use it. When he gets older, he should carry an epipen himself.

Read all food labels, and if in doubt don't give your child the food. Call manufacturers to check on ingredients, and suggest they label their product more clearly.

Labelling legislation means that 25 per cent of what is in food does not have to be described or broken down into its constitutents. Always check with the manufacturer first.

Supermarkets are waking up! If you call their customer care lines and explain your child's allergy, they can usually provide lists of products you can use.

Beware of 'new improved' formulas. Even if your child has eaten the product before with no problems, the manufacturer could have introduced something that will cause a problem.

Food that is safe for your child may come from unexpected sources. One fast-food chain fries its chips separately from the fish, so they can provide a quick snack for an allergic child out with friends.

Pack a quick snack if your child is out and about. You don't want hunger to tempt him into taking risks.

Resign yourself to having to provide food for your child at parties. You can't expect parents of other kids to handle that as well as everything else. Ask them not to put sweets into your child's party bag, though.

Health food shops are a good source of snack foods and sweets that don't contain nuts or dairy products.

If your child has lactose intolerance:

- Some over-the-counter medicines are based on lactose. Check with the pharmacist.
- Homeopathic remedies are sometimes supplied on lactose tablets. Select the little round translucent pills, based on sucrose.
- Some preserved meats and bouillons contain lactose.

Get creative with Christmas and Easter treats if your child has an intolerance to milk/colourings. Make your own Advent calendar or Easter treat hunt using mini raisin boxes or boxes of a similar size filled with hair bands, sweets, magnets, rubbers.

For a child on a gluten-free diet, you can make damn fine breakfast pancakes, biscuits and muffins using a blend of rice, potato and soya or gram flour. Some ground almonds make a richer blend.

Stick to simple breakfast cereals. Many are gluten-free, including puffed rice and cornflake products.

Pasta in restaurants can be tricky if your child is allergic to egg, so ask the chef what it includes.

If you want to go to a restaurant with your child, call ahead and explain the situation. Some places will go out of their way to accommodate you. If they won't, ask if you can bring special food for your child.

Teenage to twenty-five years old is the period when most deaths occur through anaphylaxis as non-compliance and peer pressure kick in.

Travelling With An Allergic Child

Get a translation of your child's needs before you go abroad. Embassies will sometimes help with this, or you can advertise in a foreign language school. Also get a translation of the words you should look out for when buying food.

When passing through customs, always declare your medical kit. You can't risk having it confiscated. This is another time when a translation or a doctor's letter will help.

If your child has a food allergy, when planning holidays resign yourself to self-catering. It's simply not worth the stress of wondering if each meal in a hotel is all right.

Don't even bother trying with airline food. Take your own, but alert the airline and make sure they acknowledge in writing.

When you go on holiday, take a cold bag of the very basics your child can eat. That way, if you're delayed or you can't get to the shops, you'll still be OK.

ATTENTION DEFICIT HYPERACTIVITY DISORDER (ADHD)

Sabine Noel;
Patrick Bresnahan;
Dr Andrew Williams,
paediatrician

If you or your child's teacher thinks he may have ADHD, get expert help in diagnosing it. It has become such a buzzword that everyone thinks they know what it is. An educational psychologist's report is a very useful document that will help define your child's strengths as well as weaknesses.

Try thinking of ADHD as not so much an inability to pay attention as an ability to pay attention to lots of things at once. Unlike most other children, your little fidget is aware of everything going on around her, and has trouble blocking it out. In prehistoric times, she would probably have been very successful as a hunter/gatherer!

There is a great deal of support on the Web, particularly on US sites, for parents with ADHD children.

Keep an open mind about the options for treatment, and read other people's opinions. Some people find that drug therapy works a treat, others don't.

Life at school can be very difficult for an ADHD child. The fidgety, restless behaviour that is absolutely natural for him can lead to a lot of telling-off from teachers. Make sure that all the teachers know what the problem is, and that they are not giving him a hard time for simply being who he is.

Sitting at the front of the class can help an ADHD child avoid being distracted by what is going on around her.

Practise increasing your child's attention span by giving him a sequence of tasks to perform, increasing the number of tasks as he gets better at it. Make it a game and involve other children so that he doesn't feel got at. For example, 'Hop to the door, put on a pair of gloves, turn round three times, pick up the biscuit tin and bring it back to me, hopping on the other foot.'

You'll need to tell your child to do things again and again before they get done. Getting ready to go out can be a nightmare. Prepare as much as you can in advance, and make sure that all her clothes are laid out where she can see them.

Learning a musical instrument can help your child develop his concentration, and as there are so many things to think about at once when you play music, he might find it easier than a child who is used to thinking only about one thing at a time.

Some parents find that yoga and meditation can help a hyperactive child to calm down.

Diet may play a part in hyperactivity, but it is rarely the whole story. By all means, limit fizzy drinks and food colourings, but don't feel that it's your fault your child has ADHD, and don't embark on any weird exclusion diets without the advice of a dietician.

School can be exhausting for your child, especially as ADHD can be associated with other problems, such as dyslexia or dyspraxia. Don't take on too many after-school activities. He needs a chance to relax too.

Try to keep a calm atmosphere at home, so that your child doesn't get too hyped up. Limiting television and computer games to a minimum is a very good idea; try not to shout; and give your child plenty of warning about what the day has in store for her. Many ADHD children get much worse if they are put under stress.

Hyperactive children need to burn off energy somewhere. Going out for a run is a far better option than having them go wild in the house.

There are many positive sides to ADHD, although it is sometimes hard to remember that. Some of the greatest and most successful people in history are thought to have had ADHD, including Edison, Churchill and Einstein.

Children with ADHD may find team sports difficult, but more individual pursuits such as athletics, rock climbing, canoeing, martial arts and tennis may suit them down to the ground. Help them to find something they excel at, and watch their confidence grow.

LIVING WITH A SPECIAL NEEDS CHILD

Joelle Marchant; Eleanor Brown; Miles Edwards

Many parents wait too long to start controlling behaviour. It's much harder to redirect an eighty-pound child than a thirty-pounder.

Don't compare. Your child is special. Comparing your child to others of the same age is not fair.

Change your standards and learn to live in the present. The milestones of a special needs child's life are less defined and the future less predictable – though your child may surprise you!

Different doesn't mean fragile. While it is true that you have to change your expectations of a special needs child, you don't have to lower your standards of discipline. It's tempting to let a special needs child get away with behaviour you wouldn't tolerate in other children, but remember that he needs to fit in with other people too. Let him know, early on, what behaviour you expect.

Make sure that your child knows what is expected of her, and when. A developmentally appropriate structure to every day and, as far as possible, every week makes life easier for everyone.

Get down to your child's level when reprimanding him, and ask for eye contact before you start talking.

View behaviour as signals of what your child needs. Jumping up and down in front of other children, pulling clothes or even pinching can come from a need to be acknowledged. Try to divert the behaviour into something more likely to get the desired result – like doing a double thumbs up instead of pinching.

Give your child choices, but be sure you like all the alternatives. Present the choices in the child's language, which may mean using pictures, pointing or reinforcing your verbal instructions with visual ones. Choices make your child feel great and more empowered, and teach you about your child's abilities and preferences.

Help your child to learn self-control. So instead of saying, 'Stop kicking your sister,' say, 'Please control your feet.'

DYSLEXIA

DDAT Centre,
www.ddat.org;
the Dyslexia Institute,
www.dyslexia–inst.org.uk;
Diana Cockerton, teacher;
the Sunflower Trust,
www.sunflowertrust.org.uk.

Encourage fine motor skills with activities like:

- rolling a marble between the thumb and forefinger, then thumb and middle finger, thumb and ring finger, thumb and little finger; passing the marble along without using the other hand

- bead threading, making patterns on a peg board, games using counters and dice, etc.

- using a teaspoon to transfer rice or sand from one container to another

- transferring pegs attached round the sides of a paper plate or sheet of card to another plate or card

- sewing cards, dot-to-dot books, colouring books.

Improve eye-tracking by throwing a ball or bean bag hand to hand and following it with your eyes.

Practise remembering lists of instructions, but make it a game. Start with two, then build up to as many as your child can manage. For example: 'Go to the kitchen, bring an apple back, give it to your sister and hop round the table.' This is very good for encouraging the kind of sequencing that dyslexics and other special needs children find so hard.

If eye-slip is a problem, help when your child is reading by putting your finger at the start of each line to help her keep track of where she is.

When checking work over, tick the lines where all spellings are correct, and put a dot next to the ones that need correction – much more positive than marking only what's wrong.

Remember to praise what your child does really well. Many dyslexics are creative, imaginative lateral thinkers with great practical abilities.

Make maths problems practical with props like coins, counters or clocks to help with calculations.

When a child is learning to form letters, it helps to draw them in the air using the whole arm at first then gradually getting smaller before transferring the shape to paper.

Story books with tapes are ideal for relaxing bedtime reading.

Choose books of short stories rather than long-chapter books.

When reading with your child, agree to read a page each, but give him the choice of which page he reads (it'll be the one with the picture!).

Remember that school is very hard work for your child, and she'll often be grumpy when she comes out. Bring a snack.

Cartoon magazines, like *The Beano* and *Dandy*, can encourage a reluctant reader to follow a story using the pictures as cues. The spelling can be a bit wild, though!

DYSPRAXIA

Dyspraxia Foundation,
www.dyspraxiafoundation.
org.uk; Alex Gardner,
psychologist;
Dr Andrew Williams,
paediatrician

Sports and activities that call for balance and coordination, but not in a team setting, can be very helpful. Horse riding, golf, circus skills, swimming and martial arts can give a dyspraxic child the opportunity to do really well.

Once Velcro do-ups look too babyish, use round black elastic, done up permanently in a double knot. Then your child can just slip his shoes on and off.

Use packed lunch cups with screw-on lids to carry drinks around the house.

If your child has a tendency to throw covers off and can't get them back on again, use a sleeping bag at night.

Lay clothes out in the order your child has to put them on. So pants go on top and jumpers at the bottom. Lay them out in the shape of the body too, if you have room.

Have a special place for homework sheets and make sure that your child empties his bag as soon as he gets home.

Use a bendy straw so that your child won't tip his drink over so easily.

Make lists of what your child needs for each day, and display them somewhere she can find them easily. Colour-coding works well.

Put labels in all school clothes, and try to sew them in a consistent place, so that your child knows which way round each garment goes.

If you can choose, select a peg or locker at the end of a row so that your child can find it easily.

Choose pencil sharpeners with a reservoir to catch the shavings.

Discourage your daughter from wearing high heels, or choose chunky ones that are easy to balance on.

Don't allow your child to stuff her pencil case full of things she doesn't need. It's just more to lose or drop.

Attach keys or wallets to belt loops or backpacks using a chain or springy plastic key ring. Luckily this is very fashionable.

Choose a calculator with big buttons.

Try to make your child's school bags, lunch box and sport bags stand out from the rest to make them easier to find.

Packed lunch is the right choice for children who may be unconfident about their ability with a knife and fork.

GIFTED CHILDREN

Rachael Barber;
Gifted Monthly,
www.giftedmonthly.com

To help your gifted child develop his ability, but without hothousing, try getting him to learn a musical instrument – or two.

Learning a language can help a gifted child expand her horizons and avoid boredom. Consider Latin as well as the more obvious choices.

Other activities to help a child develop but without setting him apart at school are chess, bridge or other strategy games, including computer games.

Your child may be gifted in one area but somewhat behind in others. This is quite common, so try not to get impatient if, for example, your child has a reading age of thirteen but can't do her shoelaces up.

Some gifted children have terrible handwriting and this can lead to problems at school, where such matters are given a great deal of importance. In the real world, people don't write much any more, so let your child use a computer to write stories at home and ask if she can do the same at school.

Asking for more challenging work at school for a gifted child doesn't always yield results and some teachers positively resent it. If your child's teacher insists he ploughs through the reading scheme, accept this, but get it done as fast as possible to give plenty of time for books he enjoys.

Talk to your child using adult language and teach her about the subtleties of words. Games of opposites, making up limericks and rhymes and finding alternative adjectives all appeal to children who love language.

Many gifted children get on better with adults than their peers. Try to help your child find some common ground with his classmates. He may not be genuinely interested in football or Pokémon, but his fabulous memory can help build up the kind of encyclopedic knowledge that goes down well in the playground.

Parents of gifted children often end up home educating which, as there is no legal obligation to follow the National Curriculum, can allow your child to work to her own pace. You may, however, have to provide evidence to your LEA that you are providing a suitable education. For more on home educating, see page 157.

Gifted children usually show their skills in mathematics and sciences. The arts subjects need more emotional maturity, but a child who has passed exams in the former at a young age may become bored as he completes his other GCSE, AS- and A-level subjects. Consider an Open University Degree, to be done at home at his own pace during these interim years. See www.open.ac.uk.

Check out the website for the National Association for Gifted Children at www.nagcbritain.org.uk, which offers advice. NAGC has a helpline on 0870 7703217 which is open Mon, Wed–Fri, 9.30 a.m.–2.30 p.m.

Mensa produces a publication for gifted children under sixteen called *Bright Sparks.* Go to www.mensa.org.uk/mensa/junior.html.

LEFT-HANDED CHILDREN

Mark Stewart, Anything Left-Handed, for pens, equipment, and the 'Writewell' writing mat (for both left and right handers), tel: 01905 25798, www.lefthandeducation. co.uk

Don't underestimate how demoralising it can be for a left-hander to struggle with right-handed implements. If everyone else in the class has managed to cut out a shape neatly, and your child just can't manage, he'll blame himself, not the scissors.

It is a fallacy to think that some scissors are ambidextrous, because scissor blades are set for either right or left-handed use, not both.

All components of handwriting are critical for left-handers. As right-handers write, they are always going away from the writing but the left-hander is coming from behind the writing; this often leads to smudging when using ink pens, and that is why left-handers need to have a different technique. Even though the letter formation may be fine when the child is young, encouraging good habits from a young age will minimize problems later.

Don't sit a right-hander to the left of a left-hander, as they will knock elbows with each other. Not helpful for either!

When helping your child to write:

- Make sure that she is sitting comfortably; sitting at the wrong height makes for a bad posture and may encourage the 'hook' style of writing.

- Ensure that she holds the pen properly; the tripod grip is the best to use (it can be used for both right- and left-handers), where the middle finger goes under the pencil/pen and thumb and forefinger on either side.

- Put the pencil/pen in the correct part of the hand: sit the pencil/pen in the 'V' shape between thumb and forefinger, parallel with the thumb.

- Place the paper/book to the left of the body mid-line and turn the top of the page clockwise to no more than 45 degrees.

- Straighten the wrist so that there is a straight line running up the forearm and wrist.
- Line the edge of the paper/book up with the edge of the arm. As she writes, she should move the whole of the arm from one word to the next; she should not turn the wrist as she will probably smudge the writing.

Use lined paper to show the child the angle at which he should be writing.

When buying a fountain/cartridge pen, seek advice and try it out if possible as what pen is best depends on the style of writing.

If all else fails to stop smudging, as a last resort buy a non-smudging pen (there is now such a thing).

STAMMERING & SPEECH IMPEDIMENTS

The Michael Palin Centre for Stammering Children, national centre providing free specialist assessment service for stammerers ged two to eighteen from any part of the UK, tel: 020 7530 4238, ww.stammeringcentre.org

Speech problems such as lisping or pronouncing 'r's as 'w's, are very common, particularly in children under the age of seven. Most children grow out of their speech impediments without extra help, but a health visitor or school nurse can give you advice on whether to consult a speech therapist; school hearing tests may reveal an underlying hearing problem; and dentists will be able to tell if teeth are causing the problem.

At least one in twenty children stammers for a while when learning to talk. It's often a case of the mind working far faster than the mouth. Don't draw attention to it – it may go away on its own.

Stammering

It may be unhelpful to tell your child to slow down. Adults find it hard enough to change their rate of talking and we shouldn't ask a child to do something that we can't do. Your child may be able to go more slowly for a moment or two, but it is unlikely that it will last and then you will both end up feeling frustrated.

While your child will probably be more fluent if you ask him to say the problem word again, this is unlikely to help him the next time he tries to say the same word.

Telling your child to think first before she speaks has a short-term effect. It can also add to the frustration.

Try to arrange some time during the day – perhaps five minutes – when the child can have your undivided attention in a calm and relaxed atmosphere.

Listen carefully to your child, concentrating on what he is saying, not how he is saying it. Try not to look away from him when he is having difficulty talking.

Use normal eye contact. This doesn't mean fixed staring! We all glance around when we are talking to each other.

Slow down your own rate of talking, as this helps to create a calm and relaxed atmosphere for speaking.

If you are a fast speaker, this adds pressure and speeds up conversations. Monitor your own rate of talking and 'change gear'.

Don't ask lots of questions, one after another. Reduce the number of questions you ask, and make sure that you give your child time to answer one question before asking another.

Allow time for your child to finish what she has to say, rather than finishing it for her.

Pay attention to the number of times the child who stammers is interrupted or interrupts others. Explain to all the family the importance of taking turns when talking.

Avoid guessing the word or finishing sentences – it is very tempting, but you may get it wrong or it may just make your child feel cross.

It can be uncomfortable listening to a person whose speech is disrupted by a stammer, but try to show that you are at ease and are ready to listen.

A sense of urgency builds tension. Try to show that you are not in a hurry and that you have time and will listen. If you don't, say: 'I really want to hear what you have to say, but I have to make this phone call now – can we talk later?' Make sure that you remember your promise.

Don't tell the child to 'take a deep breath' as this can become part of the problem.

If the child is aware of the problem, it may be OK to mention it thoughtfully; for example: 'That was a hard word to say, but well done – you tried your best.'

Often children who stammer do so more on long, difficult sentences. Be a good model and keep your sentences uncomplicated.

Children find ways of helping themselves, often using distraction or avoidance techniques, but in the long term these may not help. These could include:

- changing words
- avoiding certain speaking situations
- taking a deep breath before talking
- not looking at people
- tapping a hand or foot
- nodding the head or moving the body
- adding in extra sounds or words.

Make your child aware of these ploys – he may be doing it without realising – and enourage him to drop them.

Urge your child to notice other people's communication skills – no one is perfect!

Suggest that your child try to notice the colour of people's eyes when she talks to them – this will help her to maintain eye contact.

Your child can stop people asking her questions by asking them something first (such as 'Where do you live/work/go to school?').

Praise your child for the things he does well (not related to talking), as this can help build confidence.

Treat your stammering child in exactly the same way as you would any other child regarding their behaviour – discipline needs to be appropriate and consistent.

Stammering and a fast pace of life don't always go well together. Some routine and structure in daily life can be helpful.

As with all children, enough sleep and a healthy diet are important to mental and physical development.

USEFUL ADDRESSES & WEBSITES

Bereavement & Pregnancy Loss

British Organ Donor Society (BODY)
Balsham
Cambridge CB1 6DL
Tel: 01223 893636
Website: www.argonet.co.uk/body
E-mail: body@argonet.co.uk
Run by parents of a donor, for advice and counselling.

The Child Bereavement Trust (CBT)
Aston House
West Wycombe
High Wycombe
Buckinghamshire HP14 3AG
Tel: 01494 446648
Website: www.childbereavement.org.uk
E-mail: enquiries@childbereavement.org.uk
The CBT produces resources and information for bereaved children and families.

The Compassionate Friends (TCF)
Helpline: 0117 9539639, 7 days a week, 10.00 a.m.–4.00 p.m. and 6.30–10.30 p.m.
Website: www.tcf.org.uk
E-mail: info@tcf.org.uk
Self-help group of bereaved parents which offers support and friendship to others who have lost children, including parents, siblings and grand-parents.

Foundation for the Study of Infant Deaths (FSID)
(England, Wales and Northern Ireland)
Artillery House
11–19 Artillery Row
London SW1P 1RT
Tel: 020 7222 8001
Fax: 020 7222 8002
Helpline: 0870 7870554, 24 hours
Website: www.sids.org.uk/fsid/
E-mail: fsid@sids.org.uk
Works to reduce the risk of cot death and offers support for bereaved families.

The Miscarriage Association
c/o Clayton Hospital
Northgate
Wakefield
West Yorkshire WF1 3JS
Helpline: 01924 200799, Mon–Fri 9.00 a.m.–4.00 p.m.
Scottish Helpline: 0131 334 8883 (answerphone with names of local contacts)
Admin: 01924 200795, Mon–Fri 9.00 a.m.–4.00 p.m.
Website: www.miscarriageassociation.org.uk
Provides support and information on all aspects of pregnancy loss. Over 50 support groups across the UK. Leaflets and factsheets are available online.

Scottish Cot Death Trust
Royal Hospital for Sick Children
Yorkhill
Glasgow G3 8SJ
Tel: 0141 357 3946, Mon–Fri 9.00 a.m.–5.00 p.m.
Fax: 0141 334 1376
Website: www.gla.ac.uk/departments/child-health/SCDT/
E-mail: hb1w@clinmed.gla.ac.uk
Provides information about cot death, as well as carrying out research and extending support available to bereaved families.

Stillbirth and Neonatal Death Society (SANDS)
28 Portland Place
London W1B 1LY
Tel: 020 7436 7940
Helpline: 020 7436 5881, Mon–Thurs 10.00 a.m.–3.30 p.m. and Fri 10–1p.m.
Website: www.uk-sands.org
E-mail: support@uk-sands.org
Support, advice, local support groups, leaflets and books for parents whose babies have died before, during or shortly after birth.

Tommy's Campaign
Head Office
1 Kennington Road
London SE1 7RR
Tel: 020 7620 0188, Mon–Fri 9.00 a.m.–5.30 p.m.
Website: www.tommys.org
E-mail: mailbox@tommys.org
Provides information on toxoplasmosis and support for families affected by the condition. Also has information on miscarriage, stillbirth and premature birth.

Fathers

Families Need Fathers
134 Curtain Road

London EC2A 3AR
Tel: 0207 613 5060
Helpline: 01920 462825
Website: www.fnf.org.uk
E-mail: fnf@fnf.org.uk
Aims to give information and support to parents, including unmarried parents, of either sex, chiefly concerned with the problems of maintaining a child's relationship with both parents during and after family breakdown.

Fathers Direct
Herald House
Lamb's Passage
Bunhill Row
London EC1Y 8TQ
Tel: 020 7920 9491
Fax: 020 7374 2966
Website: www.fathersdirect.com
E-mail: mail@fathersdirect.com
Information and online magazine for expectant, new, solo and unmarried dads, with news, articles, chat and support.

Feeding Babies

Association of Breastfeeding Mothers (ABM)
PO Box 207
Bridgwater
Somerset TA6 7YT
Helpline: 020 7813 1481, 24 hours
Website: http://home.clara.net/abm/
E-mail: abm@clara.net
Offers 24-hour voluntary mother-to-mother support, counselling and information for breastfeeding women.

Baby Milk Action
23 St Andrew's Street
Cambridge CB2 3AX
Tel: 01223 464420
Website: www.babymilkaction.org
E-mail: info@babymilkaction.org
Campaigns for the ethical marketing of breast-milk substitutes.

The Breastfeeding Network
Helpline: 0870 900 8787, 9.30 a.m.–9.30 p.m.
Website: www.breastfeeding.co.uk/bfn
E-mail: bfn@btinternet.com
Offers free confidential telephone information on breastfeeding and one-to-one local support.

La Leche League
Helpline: 020 7242 1278, 24 hours
Website: www.laleche.org.uk
Helpline offering advice and information on breastfeeding, plus local group meetings.

NCT Breastfeeding Helpline
Helpline: 0870 444 8708

The National Childbirth Trust has trained breast-feeding counsellors who can offer individual advice and support.

UNICEF UK Baby Friendly Initiative
Website: www.babyfriendly.org.uk
E-mail: bfi@unicef.org.uk
The Baby Friendly Initiative works with the health services so that parents are enabled and supported to make informed choices about how they feed and care for their babies, and the site also includes information and advice for parents and research into the benefits of breastfeeding.

Fertility

CHILD – The National Infertility Support Network
Charter House
43 St Leonards Road
Bexhill on Sea
East Sussex TN40 1JA
Helpline: 01424 732361
Fax: 01424 731858
Website: www.child.org.uk
E-mail: office@e-mail2.child.org.uk
Information and support, with medical advisers, local groups, factsheets and articles.

Childlessness Overcome Through Surrogacy (COTS)
Helpline: 01549 402401
Website: www.surrogacy.org.uk
E-mail: cotsuk@enterprise.net
Aims to help and support surrogates and couples. There is a recorded COTS information line on 0906 680 0088, calls are charged at 25p per minute.

Ectopic Pregnancy Trust
Maternity Unit
Hillingdon Hospital
Pield Heath Road
Uxbridge
Middlesex UB8 3NN
Helpline: 01895 238025
Website: www.ectopic.org
Concerned with raising awareness and providing information and support for those affected by ectopic pregnancy.

Foresight
28 The Paddock
Godalming
Surrey GU7 1XD
Tel: 01483 427839
Fax: 01483 427668
Website: www.foresight-preconception.org.uk
Advice on preconceptual care for parents and healthcare professionals.

Gestational Trophoblastic Tumour Screening Unit Department of Medical Oncology
Charing Cross Hospital
Fulham Palace Road
London W6 8RF
Website: www.hmole-chorio.org.uk
Information and support service on hydatidiform mole (molar pregnancy).

Human Fertilisation and Embryology Authority
Tel: 020 7377 5077
Website: www.hfea.gov.uk
The statutory body which regulates, licenses and collects data on fertility treatments has a great deal of information available on its website. The 'Patient Information' pages will help people who are considering IVF, Donor Insemination, ICSI or GIFT with donated sperm or eggs to decide which treatment would be the best for them and to give advice on how to choose a clinic. The 'Choosing a Clinic' section can be downloaded and gives you ideas for questions you may want to ask prospective treatment centres. There is also a section entitled 'Sperm and Egg Donation' for anyone considering becoming a donor or receiving treatment with donated sperm or eggs.

ISSUE – National Fertility Association
114 Lichfield Street
Walsall
West Midlands WS1 1SZ
Tel: 01922 722888
Fax: 01922 640070
Website: www.issue.co.uk
E-mail: info@issue.co.uk
Provides a totally confidential comprehensive service, which includes factsheets, information, support, counselling and literature on infertility and reproductive health.

Food & Eating

Anaphylaxis Campaign
Tel: 01252 542029
Website: www.anaphylaxis.org.uk
E-mail: info@anaphylaxis.org.uk
Aims to raise awareness of potentially fatal allergies (including peanut allergy) and to provide information and guidance to sufferers.

British Allergy Foundation
Allergy UK
Deepdene House
30 Bellegrove Road
Welling
Kent DA16 3PY
Helpline: 020 8303 8583, Mon–Fri 9 a.m.–9 p.m., Sat–Sun 10 a.m. to 1 p.m.

Website: www.allergyfoundation.com
E-mail: info@allergyuk.org
Provides information and support for people who have allergies.

Eating Disorders Association
Helpline: 01603 621414, Mon–Fri 9.00 a.m.–6.30 p.m.
Youthline: 01603 765050, Mon–Fri 4.00 p.m.–6.30 p.m.
Website: http://www.edauk.com
E-mail: info@edauk.com
Offers support and advice if there is any aspect of your eating which causes you concern, including anorexia nervosa, bulimia nervosa, binge eating disorder and related eating disorders.

Eating for Pregnancy Helpline
Tel: 0114 2424084, Mon–Fri 10.00 a.m.–4.00 p.m.
E-mail:
pregnancy.nutrition@sheffield.ac.uk
Based at the University of Sheffield, the helpline can answer your questions on all aspects of nutrition and food safety in pregnancy for women who are trying to get pregnant or those who are pregnant.

Sainsbury's/Wellbeing Eating for Pregnancy Helpline
Helpline: 0845 1303646, Mon–Fri 10.00 a.m.–4.00 p.m.
Advice from qualified nutritionists on all aspects of diet, nutrition and food safety for women planning a pregnancy, pregnant women and women who are breastfeeding.

The Vegan Society
Donald Watson House
7 Battle Road
St Leonards-on-Sea
East Sussex TN37 7AA
Tel: 01424 427393, Mon–Fri 9.30 a.m.–5.00 p.m.
Website: www.vegansociety.com
E-mail: info@vegansociety.com
Practical guides to diet during pregnancy and childhood, booklets and leaflets on vegan nutrition, vegan products, animal welfare, a travel guide, a shopping guide, for people wishing to avoid the use of all animal products.

The Vegetarian Society
Parkdale
Dunham Road
Altrincham
Cheshire WA14 4QG
Tel: 0161 925 2000, Mon–Fri 8.30 a.m.–5.00 p.m.
Website: www.vegsoc.org
E-mail: info@vegsoc.org
Information and advice on vegetarian diets and cooking.

Health

AIDS

National AIDS Helpline
Tel: 0800 567123, 24 hours, 7 days a week
Ethnic Language Helpline: 0800 917 2227, 7 days a week, 6.00 p.m.–10.00 p.m.
A free service for advice and support.

Positively Women
Tel: 020 7713 0222, Mon–Fri 10.00 a.m.– 4.00 p.m.
Helpline for HIV-positive women.

CHILD HEALTH

Action for Sick Children
Helpline: 0800 074 4519
Website: www.actionforsickchildren.org.uk
Support for parents of sick children, and for parents who have problems with the health service.

Association for Children with Life-Threatening or Terminal Conditions and their Families (ACT)
Tel: 0117 922 1556
Website: www.act.org.uk
Coordinating body for services; working to improve care and services for all children in the UK with life-threatening or terminal conditions and their families.

Association for Spina Bifida and Hydrocephalus (ASBAH)
Tel: 01733 555988
Website: http://www.asbah.org
E-mail: postmaster@asbah.org
Advice and practical support for people with spina bifida and hydrocephalus and their carers.

Baby Life Support Systems (BLISS)
Helpline: 0870 7700 337
E-mail: information@bliss.org.uk
Provides equipment for neonatal units, sponsors specialist nurse training, funds research and offers support and information to parents and families of 'special care babies'.

Birth Defects Foundation
Helpline: 08700 70 70 20, Mon–Fri 9.30 a.m.–6.00 p.m. and Sat 9.30 a.m.–12.30 p.m.
Website: www.birthdefects.co.uk
E-mail: help@birthdefects.co.uk
Information and support for parents whose child has a birth defect.

British Epilepsy Association
Helpline: 0808 800 5050
Website: www.epilepsy.org.uk
Information and counselling on all aspects of epilepsy.

British Heart Foundation
Tel: 0870 600 6566
Website: www.bhf.org.uk
Information on types of heart disease, prevention and treatment and free information packs.

British Institute for Brain-Injured Children (BIBIC)
Tel: 01278 684060
Website: www.bibic.org.uk
Help to overcome disabilities and help children reach their full potential and live a fulfilling and more rewarding life.

British Lung Foundation
Tel: 020 7831 5831
Website: www.lunguk.org
Information and support for people with lung illness and breathing difficulties.

Changing Faces
Tel: 020 7706 4232
Website: www.changingfaces.co.uk
Offers advice, information and support to carers of young children with conditions that affect their appearance, including burns, birthmarks and cranio-facial conditions, such as cleft lip.

Children's Heart Federation
Helpline: 0808 808 5000
Website: www.childrens-heart-fed.org.uk
Provides a range of information about all aspects of bringing up children with heart conditions, from coping with siblings to understanding heart conditions and their treatments.

Children's Liver Disease Foundation
Tel: 0121 212 3839
Website: www.childliverdisease.org
E-mail: info@childliverdisease.org
Cares for all families and children affected by liver disease.

Cleft Lip and Palate Association (CLAPA)
Tel: 020 7431 0033
Website: www.clapa.cwc.net
E-mail: clapa@cwcom.net
Information and support for children and families affected by cleft lip and/or cleft palate. Bottles and teats for children with clefts are available by mail order.

Cancer and Leukaemia In Children (CLIC)
Tel: 0117 311 2600
Website: www.clic.uk.com
E-mail: clic@clic-charity.demon.co.uk
CLIC offers care and support to children with cancer and leukaemia and their families.

Coeliac Society
Tel: 01494 437278
Website: www.coeliac.co.uk

Promotes the welfare of people who have coeliac disease, dermatitis herpetiformis or related conditions.

Cystic Fibrosis Trust
Tel: 020 8464 7211
Website: www.cftrust.org.uk
Practical information for families with advice about nutrition and physiotherapy, with detailed research information about CF, and chat and support.

Down's Heart Group
Tel: 0152 522 0379
Website: www.downs-heart.downsnet.org
About 40 per cent of babies born with Down's Syndrome will also have a heart defect. The Down's Heart Group offers support and information and can put you in contact with other families in similar circumstances, by location, heart defect or other criteria.

Down's Syndrome Association
155 Mitcham Road
London SW17 9PG
Tel: 020 8682 4001
Website: www.downs-syndrome.org.uk
Offers support, information and advice for parents and carers of people with Down's Syndrome and works to improve the lives of those with the condition. Call for information on local branches, information booklets and newsletter.

Down's Syndrome Scotland
Helpline: 0131 313 4225, 24 hours

Encephalitis Support Group
Helpline: 01653 699599
Website: www.glaxocentre.merseyside.org/enceph.html
Advice, information and a listening ear for families. Can also provide some direct support for families who need an advocate.

General Osteopathic Council
Tel: 020 7357 6655
Website: www.osteopathy.org.uk
Can provide details of registered osteopaths plus general information about cranial osteopathy.

Genetic Interest Group
Tel: 020 7704 3141, Mon–Fri 9.00 a.m.–5 p.m.
Website: www.gig.org.uk
Information about any aspect of genetics; this is a national alliance of organisations which support children, families and individuals affected by genetic disorders.

Group B Strep Support (GBSS)
Tel: 01444 416176
Website: www.gbss.org.uk
E-mail: info@gbss.org.uk
Provides information and support to pregnant women affected by Group B streptococcus (GBS) and families whose babies have been affected by GBS.

Herpes Viruses Association
Helpline: 020 7609 9061
Website: www.herpes.org.uk
Provides advice and information on cold sores, genital herpes, chicken pox and shingles.

Left Heart Matters
Website: www.lhm.org.uk
A support group for families whose children have the congenital heart defect known as Hypoplastic Left Heart Syndrome.

Mencap
See Special Needs, Disabled & Gifted Children, page 301.

Meningitis Research Foundation
Website: www.meningitis.org
Helpline: 080 8800 3344, 24 hour (freephone) o-call in the Republic of Ireland 1890 41 33 44
The helpline provides information on meningitis and septicaemia to the general public to help prevent death and disability resulting from these infections; works with health professionals, schools and employers who are managing cases of meningitis and septicaemia to ensure that people get the information they need without causing unnecessary fears; offers information, befriending and support to families affected by meningitis and septicaemia.

National Association for the Education of Sick Children
Website: www.sickchildren.org.uk
Online guide to news, publications and events from the charity set up to improve educational opportunity across the UK for children whose education is disrupted by illness.

National Asthma Campaign
Helpline: 0845 70 10 203, Mon–Fri 9.00 a.m.–7.00 p.m.
Website: www.asthma.org.uk
Information and advice on all aspects of childhood asthma.

National Autistic Society
See Page 301.

National Eczema Society
Helpline: 020 7388 3444
Website: www.eczema.org
Aims to improve quality of life for people with eczema and their carers.

National Meningitis Trust

Helpline: 0845 600 0800, 24 hour
Website: www.meningitis-trust.org.uk
The helpline is for those who are in any way concerned, anxious, or distressed about meningitis and meningococcal disease.

Scope

Freephone helpline: 0800 800 3333
Website: www.scope.org.uk
E-mail: cphelpline@scope.org.uk
The disability organisation in England and Wales whose focus is people with cerebral palsy. Friendly and confidential.

Scottish Spina Bifida Association

Tel: 0131 332 5510

The Sickle Cell Society

54 Station Road
Harlesden
London NW10 4UA
Helpline: 020 8961 7795
Website: www.sicklecellsociety.org
E-mail: sickleinfo.line@btinternet.com
Provides support for anyone with sickle cell disease and their families.

SOFT (UK) – Support Organisation For Trisomy 13/18 and related disorders

Helpline: 0121 351 3122
Website: www.soft.org.uk
E-mail: enquiries@soft.org.uk
Provides support, information and assistance for families affected by these genetic disorders.

SPACE

Tel: 01908 676313
For all children with cerebral palsy.

GENERAL HEALTH

British Dental Health Foundation

Helpline: 0870 333 1188
Website: www.dentalhealth.org.uk
Advice and information on all aspects of dental health and hygiene.

Ruralwellbeing

Website: www.ruralwellbeing.org.uk
Ruralwellbeing is a health information service especially designed for the people of rural Wales.

See also Special Needs, Disabled & Gifted Children, page 301.

Legal Advice & Information

Advisory, Conciliation and Arbitration Service (ACAS)

Tel: 020 7396 5100
Website: www.acas.org.uk
For information on maternity rights and benefits.

Baby Naming Society

Tel: 01905 371070
Offers an alternative ceremony.

The British Humanist Association

Tel: 020 7430 0908
Website: www.humanism.org.uk/baby.asp
The British Humanist Association conduct Naming Ceremonies, so that all families and friends can relate to what is said – whether they are religious or not.

Citizens Advice Bureaux

Website: www.nacab.org.uk
Free and confidential advice on a wide range of issues.

Consumers' Association

Tel: 0800 252100
Website: www.which.net
Campaigns on consumer issues and tests equipment.

Department of Trade and Industry

Enquiry line: 020 7215 5000
Websites: www.dti.gov.uk; www.tiger.gov.uk
The website's interactive guide to Maternity Rights will help you to work out what you might be entitled to when it comes to maternity pay and leave.

Family Rights Group

Tel: 020 7923 2628, Mon–Fri 1.30–3.00 p.m.
Website: www.frg.org.uk
E-mail: office@frg.org.uk
Advice and support for families whose children are involved with social services.

General Register Office

Tel: 0870 243 7788
E-mail: general.section@ons.gov.uk
England and Wales:
www.familyrecords.gov.uk
Scotland: www.gro-scotland.gov.uk
Northern Ireland: www.groni.gov.uk
Provides information about how to register a birth.

Health and Safety Executive

Tel: 08701 545501
Website: www.hse.gov.uk
Information about health and safety at work. A Health and Safety Executive booklet, *Working with VDUs*, is available free online.

Inland Revenue

Helpline: 0800 597 5976 / 0845 609 5000
Website: www.inlandrevenue.gov.uk
Can provide information on the Working Families Tax Credit system and child tax issues.

Maternity Alliance

45 Beech Street
London EC2P 2LX
Information line: 020 7588 8582
Website: www.maternityalliance.org.uk
E-mail: info@maternityalliance.org.uk
Expert advice and information on antenatal care, health and safety at work, maternity leave and pay, changes to the law and returning to work.

For more on working parents and parental leave, see Working Parents & Childcare on page 303.

Multiple Births

The Multiple Births Foundation
Hammersmith House Level 4
Queen Charlotte's & Chelsea Hospital
Du Cane Road
London W12 0HS
Tel: 020 8383 3519
Fax: 020 8383 3041
Website: www.multiplebirths.org.uk
E-mail: mbf@ic.ac.uk
Runs educational programmes for health professionals and offers help to parents and children in multiple birth families. The website has a useful section on how to find help.

TAMBA (Twins and Multiple Births Association)
1a Gardner Road
Guildford
Surrey GU1 4PG
Helpline: 01732 868000, Mon–Fri 7.00 p.m –11.00 p.m., weekends 10.00 a.m.–11.00 p.m.
Tel: 0870 770 3305 (for information packs)
Fax: 0870 121 4001
Website: www.tamba.org.uk
E-mail: enquiries@tamba.org.uk
Runs a helpline where volunteer listeners are all parents of twins or triplets.

Nappies

National Association of Nappy Services
Tel: 0121 693 4949
Website: www.changeanappy.co.uk
E-mail: info@changeanappy.co.uk
Can provide a list of nappy laundering services by area postcode.

The Real Nappy Association
PO Box 3704
London SE26 4RX
Tel: 020 8299 4519
Website: www.realnappy.com
E-mail: contact@realnappy.com
Information and advice on all nappy-related issues.

The Women's Environmental Network
Website: www.wen.org.uk/nappies/nappies.htm
E-mail: nappies@wen.org.uk

Parenting

Children in Wales/Plant Yng
Tel: 01222 342534
Website: www.childreninwales.org.uk
Information provided on all services for children and their families in Wales.

Disabled Parents Network
Helpline: 0870 241 0450
Website: www.disabledparentsnetwork.com
E-mail: info@disabledparentsnetwork.com
A national organisation of disabled parents which offers peer support and works for changes in attitudes and policy.

Grandparents' Federation
Advice line: 01279 444964, Mon–Fri 10.30 a.m.–3.00 p.m.
Website: www.grandparents-federation.org.uk
E-mail: info@grandparents-federation.org.uk
Advice, information and publications for grandparents.

Home-Start UK
Tel: 0800 686368
Website: www.home-start.org.uk
Supports parents in stressful situations by providing practical support ranging from domestic help to a listening ear for worries.

National Family and Parenting Institute
430 Highgate Studios
53–79 Highgate Road
Kentish Town
London NW5 1TL
Tel: 020 7424 3460
Website: www.nfpi.org
A campaigning charity, working towards a more family-friendly society. Unable to offer telephone advice, but the website has lots of useful information for parents.

National NEWPIN
Tel: 020 7358 5900
Website: www.newpin.org.uk
E-mail: info@newpin.org.uk
NEWPIN works with parents and other carers of children who are in need of support in their role as parents. Individuals may refer themselves or be referred by social workers, health visitors, GPs, courts and so on.

NSPCC
Free confidential helpline: 0808 800 5000
Website: www.nspcc.org.uk

Parentline Plus

520 Highgate Studios
53–79 Highgate Road
Kentish Town
London NW5 1TL
Helpline: 0808 800 2222, Mon–Fri 8.00
a.m.–10.00 p.m., Sat 9.30 a.m.–5p.m., Sun 10.00
a.m.–3.00 p.m.
Website: www.parentlineplus.org.uk
Provides courses and publications on parenting issues.

Parentline Scotland
Helpline: 0808 800 2222, Mon, Wed and Fri 10.00
a.m.–1.00 p.m., Tues and Thurs 6.00 p.m.– 9.00
p.m., weekends 2.00 p.m.–5.00 p.m.

Parentalk
PO Box 23142
London SE1 0ZT
Tel: 020 7450 9072
Website: www.parentalk.co.uk
E-mail: info@parentalk.co.uk
Designed to provide help, advice, books and booklets to help parents.

Sure Start
Tel: 020 7273 4830
Website: www.surestart.gov.uk
E-mail: sure.start@dfee.gov.uk
Government Sure Start Unit. New sponsored scheme of local programmes for children under four years and their families.

WATCh? (What about the children?)
Tel: 01386 561635
Website: www.jbaassoc.demon.co.uk/watch
E-mail: enquiries@whataboutthechildren.org.uk
Voluntary organisation aiming to raise awareness of young children's emotional needs.

Pre- & Postnatal Support

Antenatal Results and Choices (ARC)
73 Charlotte Street
London W1T 4PN
Tel: 020 7631 0285
Website: www.arc-uk.org
E-mail: arcsatfa@aol.com
ARC provides information and support for parents who are having antenatal tests, especially those who are told that there is a risk of an abnormality.

Association for Postnatal Illness
145 Dawes Road
Fulham
London SW6 7EB
Tel: 020 7386 0868
Website: www.apni.org
Call for telephone advice and an information pack. Mothers with the illness can be matched with a volunteer who has recovered from post-natal depression and can give one-to-one telephone support.

Birth Defects Foundation
Helpline: 08700 70 70 20, Mon–Fri 9.30 a.m.–6.00
p.m., Sat 9.30 a.m.–12.30p.m.
Website: www.birthdefects.co.uk
E-mail: help@birthdefects.co.uk
Information and support for parents whose child has a birth defect or are concerned about having a child with a birth defect.

British SPD Support Group
Helpline: 01843 587356
Website: www.spd-uk.org
Provides information, support and advice on pelvic pain, SPD and DSP.

Continence Foundation
Helpline: 020 7831 9831
Website: www.continence-foundation.org.uk
Offers advice and information to those whose lives are affected by incontinence. Can put people in touch with a local continence advisory service.

Contraceptive Education Service Helpline
Helpline: 020 7837 4044
Website: www.fpa.org.uk
Help and advice on contraception and sexual health.

Meet-a-Mum Association (MAMA)
77 Westbury View
Peasedown St John
Bath BA2 8TZ
Tel: 020 8768 0123, Mon–Fri 7.00 p.m.–10.00
p.m.
Website: www.mama.org.uk
Aims to provide friendship and support to all mothers and mothers-to-be, especially those feeling lonely or isolated after the birth of a baby or moving to a new area.

National Childbirth Trust
Alexandra House
Oldham Terrace
Acton
London W3 6NH
Enquiry line: 0870 4448 707, Mon–Thurs 9.00
a.m.–5.00 p.m., Fri 9.00 a.m.–4.00 p.m.
Breastfeeding support line: 0870 444 8708
Website: www.nctpregnancyandbabycare.com
Runs antenatal classes and postnatal support groups. Ring enquiry line for details of local services.

Parents In Partnership-Parent Infant Network (PIPPIN)
Tel: 020 8989 9056
Website: www.pippin.org.uk
E-mail: martin@pippin.org.uk

Offers a new approach to parenthood through NHS antenatal and post-natal classes and support. Promotes early family and parent-infant relationships.

Relate
Tel: 01788 573241
Website: www.relate.org.uk
Relationship counselling for couples.

Serene (formerly Cry-sis)
Tel: 020 7404 5011, 7 days a week 8.00 a.m.–11.00 p.m.
Website: www.our-space.co.uk/serene.htm
Will put you in touch with a local supporter, for advice about excessively crying, sleepless and demanding babies and young children.

Pregnancy & Birth

Action on Pre-eclampsia (APEC)
84–88 Pinner Road
Harrow
Middlesex HA1 4HZ
Helpline: 020 8427 4217, Mon–Fri 10 a.m.–1 p.m.
Website: www.apec.org.uk
Support for women at risk of or affected by pre-eclampsia.

Active Birth Centre
Tel: 020 7482 5554
Website: www.activebirthcentre.com
Antenatal workshops and yoga-based exercise classes, baby relaxation classes, information and advice, as well as water birth pool hire.

Alcohol Concern
Waterbridge House
32– 36 Loman Street
London SE1 0EE
Information line: 020 7922 8667, 7 days a week, 1.00–5.00 p.m.
Website: www.alcoholconcern.org.uk
Advice on alcohol and pregnancy.

ARC – Antenatal Results and Choices
See Pre- & Post-Natal Support, page 298.

Association of Chartered Physiotherapists in Women's Health
Website: www.womensphysio.com
E-mail: webmaster@womensphysio.com
To find a physiotherapist specialising in pregnancy or women's health near you.

Association for Improvements in the Maternity Services (AIMS)
Tel: 01753 652781
Website: www.aims.org.uk
Support and advice on maternity care including rights, choices and complaints.

Association of Radical Midwives (ARM)
Tel: 01695 572776
Website: www.midwifery.org.uk
Supports those with difficulty getting maternity care.

Back Care
16 Elmtree Road
Teddington
Middlesex TW11 8ST
Tel: 020 8977 5474
Fax: 020 8943 5318
Website: www.backpain.org
E-mail: website@backcare.org.uk
Information and tips to help keep your back healthy during pregnancy.

British Doula Association
Helpline: 020 7565 2640
Website: www.topnotchnannies.com
E-mail: theteam@topnotchnannies.com
Provides details of doulas who live in your area and works in association with Top Notch Doulas to set standards of practice.

British Pregnancy Advisory Service
Austy Manor
Wooten Wawen
Solihull B95 6BX
Tel: 01564 793 225
Helpline: 08457 30 40 30
Website: www.bpas.org
Advice for teenagers and parents.

Brooks Advisory Service
Helpline: 020 7617 8000, 24 hours
Advice helpline: 0800 018 5023, Mon 9.00 a.m.–5.00 a.m., Wed and Fri 9.00 a.m.–4.00 a.m.
Website: www.brook.org.uk
Advice for pregnant teenagers and parents on sex, contraception and pregnancy, with listings of centres near you.

Herpes Viruses Association
See Health, page 295.

Independent Midwives Association
Tel: 01483 821104
Website: www.independentmidwives.org.uk
Provides a list of independent midwives and lobbies for the traditional role of the midwife.

Vasa Previa Foundation
Website: www.vasaprevia.com
E-mail: info@vasaprevia.com
The International Vasa Previa Foundation gives information about this pregnancy complication.

Safety

British Red Cross Society (BRCS)
Tel: 020 7235 5454 (England)
Tel: 028 902 46400 (Northern Ireland and Isle of Man)
Tel: 0141 332 9591 (Scotland)
Tel: 029 2048 0289 (Wales)
Website: www.redcross.org.uk
Runs first-aid courses through its local branches. Publications include *First Aid for Children Fast* and *The Babysitter's Handbook*.

Child Accident Prevention Trust
Tel: 020 7608 3828
Fax: 020 7608 3674
Website: www.capt.org.uk
E-mail: safe@capt.org.co.uk
Books and free information leaflets on child safety and accident prevention at home, on the road and in the car.

Foundation for the Study of Infant Deaths
See Bereavement & Pregnancy Loss, page 291.

Health and Safety Executive
Tel: 08701 545501
Website: www.hse.gov.uk
Information about health and safety at work. A Health and Safety Executive booklet, *Working with VDUs*, is available free online.

Save A Baby's Life training programme
Tel: 01789 773994
Promotion of life-saving in water.

St Andrew's Ambulance Association (Scotland)
Tel: 0131 229 5419
Website: www.firstaid.org.uk
First-aid training.

St John Ambulance
Tel: 0870 235 5231
Website: www.sja.org.uk
First-aid training.

Single Parents

Gingerbread
7 Sovereign Close
Sovereign Court
London E1W 3HW
Helpline: 0800 018 4318, Mon–Fri 10.00 a.m.–4.00 p.m.
Website: www.gingerbread.org.uk
Local and national support for single-parent families.

Gingerbread Scotland
1014 Argyle Street
Glasgow G3 8LX
Tel: 0141 576 5085/7976

Gingerbread Ireland
29–30 Dame Street
Dublin 2
Ireland
Tel: 00 353 16710 291

Gingerbread Northern Ireland
169 University Street
Belfast BT7 1HR
Northern Ireland
Tel: 028 90 231 568

National Council for the Divorced and Separated
168 Loxley Road
Malin Bridge
Sheffield S6 4TE
Tel: 07041 478 120
Website: www.ncds.org.uk
Organises local groups to provide support and entertainment for the divorced and separated.

National Council for One-Parent Families
255 Kentish Town Road
London NW5 2LX
Tel: 020 7428 5400
Helpline: 0800 018 5026 (freephone)
Website: www.oneparentfamilies.org.uk

Parentline Plus
See Parenting, page 297.

Relate
Herbert Gray College
Little Church Street
Rugby
Warwickshire CV21 3AP
Tel: 01788 573241
Counselling service: 0870 6012121
Website: www.relate.org.uk
Couple counselling, relationship and family education.

E-quality-women
Website: www.e-quality-women.co.uk
E-mail: info@e-quality-women.co.uk

Families Need Fathers
See Fathers, page 291.

Shared Parenting Information Group (SPIG) UK
28 Garraways
Wooten Bassett SN4 8LL
Tel/Fax: 01793 851544
Website: http://spig.info
Promoting responsible shared parenting after divorce and separation. Provides information, research and resources.

Single Parent Action Network (SPAN) UK
Tel: 0117 951 4231
Website: www.spanuk.org.uk

Provides information and support for single-parent families.

Special Needs, Disabled & Gifted Children

AUTISM

Autism UK
Website: www.autismuk.com
Information and links for those working with or affected by autism, including key facts, latest research on treatments and a guide to learning aids.

National Autistic Society
393 City Road
London EC1V 1NG
Helpline: 0870 600 85 85, Mon–Fri 10.00 a.m.–4 p.m.
Website: www.nas.org.uk
E-mail: autismhelpline@nas.org.uk
Includes information and advice about autism and Asperger syndrome, and about the support and services available in the UK for people with autism, the family and professionals.

BLINDNESS & VISUAL IMPAIRMENT

Royal National Institute for the Blind (RNIB)
Tel: 0845 766 9999
Website: www.rnib.org.uk
Detailed information on the services, products and publications provided by the RNIB for people with sight problems. Includes information on training and on how to make your own service accessible to the visually impaired.

SENSE (National Deaf, Blind and Rubella Association)
Tel: 020 7272 7774
Minicom: 020 7272 9648
Website: www.sense.org.uk
E-mail: enquiries@sense.org.uk
Information and support from the UK's leading organisation working for people with deafness, blindness and associated disabilities.

DEAFNESS AND HEARING DISABILITIES

British Deaf Association
Tel: 0870 770 3300 (voice phone)/0800 6522 965 (text phone)
Website: www.britishdeafassociation.org.uk
E-mail: helpline@bda.org.uk
Information and advice on all aspects of deafness.

Defeating Deafness
Helpline: 0808 808 2222, Mon–Fri 9.30 a.m.–5.30 p.m.
Website: www.defeatingdeafness.org
Advice on deafness and hearing tests for babies and young children.

Deaf World Web
Website: www.deafworldweb.org
Leading deaf website, providing a comprehensive deaf-related resource on the Internet. Features international links plus a question and answer section for all deafness related queries.

National Deaf Children's Society
Tel: 020 7250 0123 Mon–Fri 10.00 a.m.–5.00 p.m., voice and text
Website: www.ndcs.org.uk
Supporting all deaf children, young deaf people and their families in overcoming the challenges of childhood deafness.

SENSE (National Deaf, Blind and Rubella Association)
See above.

GIFTED CHILDREN

National Association for Gifted Children
Website: www.rmplc.co.uk/orgs/nagc
Site giving advice and support to gifted children and their families. Includes a special section for schools wanting to develop their own policies for highly able and gifted children.

LEARNING DIFFICULTIES & SPECIAL EDUCATIONAL NEEDS

British Dyslexia Association
Website: www.bda-dyslexia.org.uk
Site offering practical advice, information and help to families, professionals and dyslexic individuals, and raising awareness and understanding of dyslexia. The 'practical help' section provides a comprehensive one-stop resource for teachers.

Centre for Special Educational Needs
Website: www.dfee.gov.uk/sen
A special SEN section of the DfEE site offering advice and materials for teachers, parents and others interested in or working with children with special educational needs.

Mencap
(England) Learning Disability Helpline: 0808 808 1111, Mon–Fri 10.00 a.m.–4.00 p.m.
(Wales) 0808 8000 300.
Website: www.mencap.org.uk
E-mail: information@mencap.org.uk
Support for children and adults with learning disabilities; free, confidential and independent

information and advice on virtually any subject to do with learning disability.

In Northern Ireland, people with a learning disability, their families and carers can receive support and advice by contacting a Mencap Family Adviser on 0845 763 6227.

Mencap's sister organisation, Enable, works in Scotland.
Tel: 0141 226 4541
E-mail: enable@enable.org.uk

NGfL Inclusion Site
Website: www.inclusion.ngfl.gov.uk
A site developed by the DfEE and BECTA to provide a free searchable catalogue of online resources to support individual learning needs. Teachers can search for key documents, or nominate their own resources for addition to the site.

The Sunflower Trust
1 High Street
Godalming
Surrey GU7 1AZ
Tel: 014830 428141
Website: www.sunflowertrust.org.uk
Provides a multi-discipline, holistic approach to improving the health, performance and self-esteem of children with learning difficulties.

DISABILITY & SPECIAL NEEDS

Contact a Family
Helpline: 0808 808 3555
Website: www.cafamily.org.uk
E-mail: info@cafamily.org.uk
Support and advice for families caring for children with disabilities and special needs.

Disability Net
Website: www.disabilitynet.co.uk
internet resource for disabled people with news, services and soon to be developed kids' pages with links and downloads.

Disability Pregnancy & Parenthood International
Information line: 0800 018 4730
Website: http://freespace.virgin.net/disabled.parents/
E-mail: dppi@eotw.co.uk
Helps disabled parents work out their own solutions for practical everyday parenting with information about baby and childcare equipment. Information officers will answer queries.

Family Welfare Association
Tel: 020 7254 6251
The Association offers a range of services for disabled parents including information provision, counselling services and some financial support.

STAMMERING

The Michael Palin Centre for Stammering Children
Finsbury Health Centre
Pine Street
London EC1R OLP
Tel: 020 7530 4238, Mon–Fri 9.00 a.m.–5.00 p.m.
Fax: 020 7833 3842
E-mail:info@sta.m.meringcentre.org
National centre provides free specialist assessment service for stammerers aged two to eighteen from any part of the UK.

Teenagers & Help For Children

Adfam National
Waterbridge House
32–36 Loman Street
London SE1 0EE
Helpline: 0207 928 8900
Website: www.adfam.org.uk
Information and condidential support for families of drug users.

Anti-Bullying Campaign
185 Tower Bridge Road
London SE1 2UF
Helpline: 0207 378 1446, Mon–Fri 9.30 a.m.–5.00 p.m.
Step-by-step guidelines on working with schools to combat bullying.

British Association for Counselling and Psychotherapy
Tel: 0870 443 5252
Website: www.bacp.co.uk
E-mail: bacp@bacp.co.uk
Phone or visit the website to get a list of registered counsellors in your area.

Childline
Freepost 1111
London N1 0BR
Tel: 0800 1111
Website: www.childline.org.uk
National helpline for children and young people.

Eating Disorders
See Food, page 293.

Families Anonymous
Helpline: 020 7498 4680
Website: www.childline.org.uk
E-mail: office@famanon.org.uk
Support groups and helpline for relatives and friends concerned about the use of drugs or related behavioural problems.

Family Planning Association (FPA)
2–12 Pentonville Road
London N1 9FP
Tel: 0845 310 1334, 9.00 a.m.–7.00 p.m.
Website: www.fpa.org.uk
Advice on sex, sexual health, contraception and pregnancy.

FPA Northern Ireland
113 University Street
Belfast BT7 1HP
Tel: 028 90 325 488 (Belfast) or 028 71 260 016 (Derry), Mon–Thur 9.00 a.m.–5.00 p.m., Fri 9.00 a.m.–4.30 p.m.

FPA Scotland
Unit 10
Firhill Business Centre
76 Firhill Road
Glasgow G20 7BA
Tel: 0141 576 5088, Mon–Thur 9.00 a.m.–5.00 p.m., Fri 9.00 a.m.–4.30p.m.

Kidscape
Tel: 020 7730 3300, Mon–Fri 10.00–4.00 p.m.
Website: www.kidscape.org.uk
Charity to prevent child abuse and bullying.

Lesbian and Gay Switchboard
Tel: 020 7837 7324

National AIDS Helpline
See Health, page 294.

Trust for The Study of Adolescence
23 New Road
Brighton BN1 1WX
Tel: 01273 693311
Website: www.tsa.uk.com
Promotes the study of adolescence with research.

Young Minds
102–108 Clerkenwell Road
London EC1M 5SA
Tel: 020 7336 8445
Fax: 020 7336 8446
Parents' Information Service: 0800 018 2138
E-mail: enquiries@youngminds.org.uk
Support for children with mental health problems.

YouthNet UK
Website: www.thesite.org.uk
Gives young people access via the internet to the most comprehensive information available for them.

Vaccination

Association of Parents of Vaccine Damaged Children
78 Campden Road
Shipston-on-Stour
Warwickshire CV36 4DH
Tel: 01608 661595
Acts as a campaign group for children who have been damaged by vaccines and advises parents in claiming vaccine damage payments.

Department of Health
Website: www.doh.gov.uk
Information on the lastest research findings and recommendations.

Health Promotion England
Website: www.immunisation.org.uk
A vaccination timetable, frequently asked questions about immunisation, and information about the diseases they protect against.

Informed Parent
Tel: 020 8861 1022
Offers information about the possible risks associated with childhood immunisations.

JABS (Justice, Awareness and Basic Support)
1 Gawsworth Road
Golborne
Near Warrington
Cheshire WA3 3RF
Tel: 01942 713565
Website: www.argonet.co.uk/users/jabs
E-mail: jabs@argonet.co.uk
Self-help group providing basic support for parents whose children have had a health problem following an immunisation.

Working Parents & Childcare

Childcare Link
Tel: 0800 096 0296
Website: www.childcarelink.gov.uk
Government body providing information about childcare and early education services throughout England, Wales and Scotland. The website can search for childcare in your area, and factsheets are also available.

Daycare Trust
21 St George's Road
London SE1 6ES
Tel: 020 7840 3350, Mon–Fri 10.00 a.m.–5.00 p.m.
Website: www.daycaretrust.org.uk
E-mail: info@daycaretrust.org.uk
Information about childcare issues for parents, employers, policymakers and providers. Publishes *Check Out Childcare*, a guide to choosing childcare and coordinates annual National Childcare Week.

Department for Education and Skills
Website: www.dfes.gov.uk
Need a Nanny? A Guide for Parents: for copies, telephone the DfES helpline: 0845 6022260, or download it from their website.

Department for Work and Pensions
Tel: 020 8682 8000
Website: www.dss.gov.uk
The former Department for Education and Employment, it provides information on child benefit and social security benefits.

Home Office
Tel: 020 8760 1666 (recorded information)
Website: www.homeoffice.gov.uk
For information on regulations about au pairs.

Kids & Co
Tel: 020 8981 3131
Website: www.childcare-info.co.uk
Advice on how to choose childcare.

National Childminding Association
Tel: 0800 169 4486, Mon–Fri 10.00 a.m.– 4.00 p.m. (freephone information line)
Website: www.ncma.org.uk
National charity promoting registered childminding and providing information for parents, registered childminders and local authority workers. NCMA cannot supply a contact list of childminders in your area. This information is available from your local Children's Information Service. Call Childcare Link, freephone 0800 096 0296.

Parental Leave Helpline
Tel: 020 7215 6207
Information on rights and parental leave entitlement.
Leaflet orderline: 0870 1502500 for leaflets on 'Maternity rights', 'Parental leave' and 'Time off for dependants'.

Parents at Work
45 Beech Street
London EC2Y 8AD
Tel: 020 7628 3565
Information line: 020 7628 3578
Helpline: 020 7628 2128 (for advice on working rights and benefits), Wed and Fri 11.00–2.00 p.m., Thurs 6.00–9.00 p.m.
Website: www.parentsatwork.org.uk
E-mail: info@parentsatwork.org.uk
Helps parents balance work and home by providing information and advice on working family-friendly hours, parental leave and childcare.

Working Families Tax Credit Helpline
Helpline: 0845 609 5000
Website: www.dss.gov.uk
Includes Childcare Tax Credit information.

For more on working parents and parental leave, see Legal Advice & Information on page 296.

Appendix

IMMUNISATION

What Is Immunisation?

Immunisation is a way of protecting ourselves against serious disease. Once we have been immunised, our bodies are more able to fight those diseases if we come into contact with them. An immunisation programme vaccinates people against a specific disease or diseases. This is to reduce the number of people contracting the disease in a population, and to prevent the disease being passed on. In some cases, when the disease, such as smallpox or polio, exists only in people, it is possible to eliminate the disease completely.

What Is A Vaccine?

Vaccines stimulate our immune system to produce antibodies to a specific disease without us having to become infected with the wild disease.

A dose of vaccine may contain:
• a suspending fluid to carry the vaccine into the body
• preservatives and stabilisers so the vaccine can be stored safely, and
• an adjuvant to improve the body's immune response.

How Do Vaccines Work?

Vaccines work by generating one of the two types of immunity: active or passive.

Active Immunity

Vaccines generate active immunity. This means they trigger the immune system to produce antibodies against the disease as though the body had been infected with the disease. This also teaches the body's immune system how to rapidly produce appropriate antibodies. If the vaccinated person then comes into contact with the disease itself, the immune system will recognise the bacterium or virus and immediately produce the specific antibodies needed to combat it.

Passive Immunity

This is provided when the body is given antibodies rather than producing them itself. In vaccines this is in the form of an immunoglobulin injection. A newborn baby has passive immunity to several diseases such as measles, mumps and rubella, from antibodies passed from its mother via the placenta. Passive immunity only lasts for a few weeks or months. In the case of measles, mumps and rubella it may last up to one year – this is why MMR is given just after the first birthday.

The Mother's Immunity

Newborn babies have some immunity to disease passed on to them from their mothers. In the last three months of pregnancy, some antibodies pass through the placenta from the mother to the unborn baby. The amount and types of antibodies depends on what immunity the mother has. The protection given to the baby by these antibodies varies. For example, a mother's antibodies to measles usually protect her baby against the disease for 6-12 months, but those against other diseases, such as whooping cough and Hib, only last a few weeks. This is why the immunisation schedule starts at 2 months of age.

Premature Babies

Babies who were born early are at even greater risk from infections than babies born on time. This is because their immune systems are less mature, and also they do not have as many antibodies passed on to them from their mothers. So it is important that premature babies receive their vaccines according to the recommended schedule. Many scientific studies have shown that giving premature babies vaccines according to the recommended schedule is safe and effective.

The Recommended National Schedule

There is a recommended schedule for childhood immunisations. It gives children the best chance of developing immunity against these diseases in a safe and effective way and minimises their risk of catching the diseases.

When to immunise	What is given	How it is given
Two, three and four months old	Polio	By mouth
	Diphtheria, Tetanus Pertussis and Hib (DTP-Hib)	One Injection
	MenC	One injection
Around 13 months	Measles, Mumps and Rubella (MMR)	One injection
Three to five years (pre-school)	Polio	By mouth
	Diphtheria, Tetanus and acellular Pertussis (DTaP)	One injection
	Measles, Mumps and Rubella (MMR)	One injection
10 to 14 years old (and sometimes shortly after birth)	BCG (against tuberculosis)	Skin test then, if needed, one injection
13 to 18 years old	Tetanus and low dose diphtheria (Td)	One injection
	Polio	By mouth

The Importance Of Timing

If a vaccine is given when the baby still has antibodies to the disease it protects against, the antibodies can stop the vaccine working. This is why routine childhood immunisations do not start until a baby is 2 months old when the mother's antibodies have gone. It is important to stick to the schedule as delaying immunisation can leave a baby unprotected. It also increases adverse reactions to some vaccines, such as pertussis.

Missed An Appointment?

If you miss a vaccination appointment, you do not have to start the course of vaccines again. The recommended gap between vaccines is an ideal. Just make a new appointment as soon as you can.

Giving Different Doses

Some vaccines are given more than once. The gap between these different doses of vaccines is there to ensure that each dose has time to work. However, the recommended gap is only a minimum.

For answers to frequently asked questions about immunisation, go to www.immunisation.org.uk/faqgen.html.

Information courtesy of the Department of Health www.immunisation.org.uk.

Index